THE MYSTIC OF
FRIENDSHIP

CLASS 200 NEW STUDIES IN RELIGION

A SERIES EDITED BY Kathryn Lofton and John Lardas Modern

THE MYSTIC OF FRIENDSHIP

Divining the Present in
Settler Amazonia

ASHLEY LEBNER

The University of Chicago Press
Chicago and London

The University of Chicago Press, Chicago 60637

The University of Chicago Press, Ltd., London

© 2025 by The University of Chicago

Published 2025

34 33 32 31 30 29 28 27 26 25   1 2 3 4 5

ISBN-13: 978-0-226-84575-3 (cloth)
ISBN-13: 978-0-226-84577-7 (paper)
ISBN-13: 978-0-226-84576-0 (ebook)
DOI: https://doi.org/10.7208/chicago/9780226845760.001.0001

Library of Congress Cataloging-in-Publication Data

Names: Lebner, Ashley, author.
Title: The mystic of friendship : divining the present in settler Amazonia / Ashley
    Lebner.
Description: Chicago : The University of Chicago Press, 2025. | Series: Class 200:
    new studies in religion | Includes bibliographical references and index.
Identifiers: LCCN 2025020917 | ISBN 9780226845753 (cloth) | ISBN 9780226845777
    (paperback) | ISBN 9780226845760 (ebook)
Subjects: LCSH: Amazon River Region—Colonization. | Amazon River Region—
    Religion.
Classification: LCC F2546 .L 2025 | DDC 981/.15—dc23/eng20250429
LC record available at https://lccn.loc.gov/2025020917

Authorized Representative for EU General Product Safety Regulation (GPSR)
queries: **Easy Access System Europe**—Mustamäe tee 50, 10621 Tallinn, Estonia,
gpsr.requests@easproject.com
Any other queries: https://press.uchicago.edu/press/contact.html

CONTENTS

ACKNOWLEDGMENTS

I have accumulated many debts in the years this book has been in the making. The first people I must thank are my interlocutors and hosts along the highway that this book follows, the PA-150 in Southeast Pará, Brazil. I am especially grateful to the people I call the Solanha family, though I am most indebted to "Ina Solanha," who was a safe harbor for me in Marabá and who remains a good friend. Similarly important are the other people who figure prominently in these chapters (with pseudonyms): Aurora, Cleusa, Mona, and Osias. And then behind the scenes were also supporters from the Pastoral Land Commission and allied entities, especially Geuza, Batista, Leidiane, and Airton. I was lucky to meet all of them during my fieldwork; they were all keen to explain things carefully to me and to make space for me to learn more. I always look forward to their company and stories when I return to the region. *Estou sempre com saudades.*

This book also benefited from the input and support of many people and institutions beyond Pará.

I have been fortunate to receive generous funding from the Social Sciences and Humanities Research Council of Canada, the Cambridge Commonwealth Trust, the Quebec Fund for Research on Society and Culture, Darwin College, the William Wyse Fund, the São Paulo Research Foundation, and Wilfrid Laurier University. Chapters 2 and 3 and parts of chapter 6 appeared as articles, and I am grateful for the permission to reprint them here. The citations, in their respective order, are as follows:

Lebner, Ashley. 2021. "The Work of Impossibility in Brazil: Friendship, Kinship, Secularity." *Current Anthropology* 62 (4): 452–83. By permission of The Wenner Gren Foundation for Anthropological Research/University of Chicago Press. Copyright by the Wenner-Gren Foundation

Lebner, Ashley. 2021 [2022]. "After the Medium: Rereading Stories on a String
    and the War at Canudos." *Journal of the American Academy of Religion* 89
    (4): 1290–333. By permission of the American Academy of Religion/Oxford
    University Press.
Lebner, Ashley. 2019. "On Secularity: Marxism, Reality, and the Messiah in Brazil."
    Journal of the Royal Anthropological Institute 25 (1): 123–47. By permission of
    the Royal Anthropological Institute/Wiley.

I am grateful to the Brazilian anthropologists who helped me see how
I could move on from my original research plans. I arrived in Pará with a
project located squarely within a conventional political anthropology. Soon
enough, however, I noticed that my interlocutors consistently lamented
that "no one has friends, only acquaintances . . . except for God." This disposition resonated with recent anthropological work on Northeast Brazil,
notably work by Laura Rebhun (1999), who found people lamenting "love."
Yet Rebhun argued that political-economic conditions determined emotions (see also N. Scheper-Hughes 1992), and she said nothing about God.
Confounded by this missing piece—this was before the "anthropology of
Christianity"—I decided to go find some anthropologists to talk to.

Conversations with two senior anthropologists in Rio especially inspired
me. The first worked in Brazil's Northeast, and when I told her about the
refrain "no one has friends" and about my sense that this seemed vital, she
bluntly replied, "That isn't interesting at all—everyone says that." Chastened
but also encouraged (if everyone says that, isn't it interesting?), I went to see
Otávio Velho, one of the few anthropologists to have worked with settlers in
Southeast Pará. To my relief, he was encouraging, and he gave me an article
of his, "The Peasant and the Beast" (1995 [1991]). I was embarrassed not to
have read it already, but it offered welcome confirmation that my nascent
insights were neither uninteresting nor unhinged. Velho too had encountered a resilient Christianity, a concern with pervasive evil, and what he
called an "ontological mistrust."

Although my discussion of the mystic of friendship can be read as
speaking to questions of trust and mistrust, I did not ultimately turn to
this analytical language for a number of reasons, first because my interlocutors' discussions of trust were usually embedded in concerns with named
relationships (friend, colleague, acquaintance, kinsperson, enemy). Second
and most importantly, rather than finding a static or ontological state of
trust or mistrust, I had encountered a dynamic ambivalence, an oscillation,
a perennially renewed longing, *saudade*, for social support operating along-

side a sense of fallibility, which could not be reduced to politics, economy, or "secular" sociality, yet which influenced them all.

My hope is that this book captures this relational dynamism and its effects. It wasn't easy to get at an adequate description of it, and while all failings are my own, I am grateful to many teachers, friends, and colleagues who helped along the way. At Cambridge, where the seeds of this book were sown, I owe special thanks to Stephen Hugh-Jones, who let me find my own way after I had to abandon a project in Northwest Amazonia. My radical change of project from Indigenous to non-Indigenous Amazonian issues may not have been the easiest choice, yet it allowed me to follow roads less (anthropologically) traveled. Thank you, Stephen, for your patience and willingness to guide.

Friends around Cambridge were crucial intellectual and moral supports during the initial pre- and post-fieldwork period. Simone Frangella, who was then a visiting scholar between Cambridge and London, provided a vital early link to Lady Selma Albernaz, who helped me all the way to Pará. *Obrigada, queridas.* I was also lucky to enjoy the friendship of Youngho Nam, Patrice Ladwig, Bernhard Krieger, Hugo Reinert, Emilia Sanabria, Matthew Carey, Irene Peano, Ricardo Roque, Kim Wagner, Jacob Copeman, Olivier Allard, Ann Kelly, and Sabine Deiringer. Though I saw the following people less, I am grateful for the times they lit up a day or a thought, or set me back on the right path: Olga Ulturgasheva, Madeleine Reeves, Maja Petrović-Šteger, Jon Mair, Vera Skvirskaja, Signe Gunderson, and Janne Flora. Jonathan Oppenheim deserves special thanks for offering great physics stories to take my mind off the hard times and a safe place to land even after I had left the UK (and thanks to George Danezis, who sometimes cohosted too). Annabel Pinker, whom I met at the end of those Cambridge years, remains a cherished interlocutor on all matters. *O, my friends, thank you again.*

I am also grateful to the many senior and other colleagues who provided feedback and advice on my writing, teaching, or on navigating academia as I left Cambridge and went on to the Universities of Liverpool, São Paulo, Toronto, and then Laurier. All of your contributions have been of real value to me. My sincere thanks to Maria José de Abreu, Talal Asad, Andreas Bandak, Barbara Bodenhorn, Lindsay Bell, Janice Boddy, Nils Bubandt, Jon Bialecki, Katherine Blouin, Simon Coleman, John F. Collins, Alberto Corsín-Jiménez, Brent Crosson, Girish Daswani, Matthew Engelke, Terre Fisher, Khaled Furani, Alex Ungprateeb Flynn, Charles Forsdick, Caroline Humphreys, Aaron Kappeler, Hillary Kaell, Webb Keane, Michael Lambek, Sian Lazar, Tania Li, Mohamed Amer Meziane, João de Pinal-Cabral,

Anne Meneley, Yael Navaro, Joel Robbins, Elizabeth Roberts, Eve Rosenhaft, Steven Rubenstein, Robert Sauté, Anthony Shenoda, Jackie Solway, Alice Street, Yunus Telliel, Piers Vitebsky, Zoë Wool, and Umut Yildirim. Marilyn Strathern has offered special inspiration from my early days as a graduate student until today. I am also indebted to the anthropologists who welcomed and supported me as academics and friends in Brazil: in the early years Neidi Esterci and Deborah Lima, and later Ana Claudia Marques (who luckily believed in me and invited me to apply for a FAPESP postdoc), Miguel Palmeira, Jorge Villela, John Comerford, Uirá Garcia, and Graziele Dainese (with whom I share warm memories as a roommate and later transcriber of some of my interviews). Ana Claudia deserves my special gratitude for her advice and support over the years and into the present, *minha gratidão imensa*. I was also lucky to have had some solid years (2011–18) debating Critical Catholic Studies with Valentina Napolitano, Carlota McAllister, and Andrea Muehlebach: thank you, ladies, for this fruitful period of reflection. I also often recall another wonderful experience of debate and learning with Ajay Singh Chaudhary and classmates at the Brooklyn Institute for Social Research online in 2023—thank you for a wonderful course about Walter Benjamin's Arcades Project.

I owe special gratitude to Stephan Palmié for his recent support and encouragement, especially his introduction to Dylan Montanari at the University of Chicago Press. And really what luck it has been to work with the wonderful editorial team for the Class 200 series at Chicago. In addition to Dylan, I am very fortunate to have had the support of Kathryn Lofton, John Lardas Modern, Kyle Wagner, and Fabiola Enríquez Flores. I must also thank my superb copy editor, Catherine Osborne, whose close reading improved more than just my sentences!

My collegial and supportive colleagues at Laurier and the University of Waterloo have also been a blessing. Thank you for your intellectual engagement and for making faculty governance so much more fun: Abderrahman Beggar, Gavin Brockett, Kevin Burrell, Doug Cowan, Michel Desjardins, Carol Duncan, John Ejobowah, Mavis Fenn, Erich Fox Tree, Paul Freston, Doris Jakobsh, Janet McLellan, Jason Neelis, Edmund Pries, Kirsten Pries, David Seljak, Meena Sharify-Funk, Chris Ross, Jeff Wilson, Ali Zaidi, and Jasmine Zine. I thank my local anthros, whom I have been fortunate to have as friends, interlocutors, and readers of early versions of different chapters: dear Alicia Sliwinski and Tanya Richardson. And then there is Seçil Dağtaş, whose insight and moral support I have especially treasured. Laurier and Waterloo students have also been wonderful—those who participated in my seminars on secularism were sounding boards for some of the ideas mentioned in this book. John Wrublewskyj made especially generous comments on parts of the book's introduction.

I have also benefited greatly from discussions with colleagues and students when I have presented versions of these chapters (or ideas) at invited talks or workshops at Laurier; Arizona State University; Clark University–Luxembourg; Columbia University; McMaster University; the Glasgow Anthropology Network; the Political Anthropology Network of the Federal University of Rio de Janeiro (National Museum) and the Fluminense Federal University; Rice University; the Research Group on Conflict at the University of São Paulo and the Federal University of São Carlos; the University of California, Berkeley; the University of Cambridge; the University of Copenhagen; the University of Freiburg; the University of Michigan; and the University of Toronto.

I am so lucky that my family has been unstintingly supportive of me in all my endeavors over the years, even when they didn't quite understand what I was doing. To my parents, Iris Nowa and Gilbert Lebner—though especially to my mother—and to my grandmothers Betty Nowa and Sylvia Lebner, my deep gratitude for keeping me close, for freeing me to wander, and for facilitating my returns. Thank you for trusting me and for eventually getting it. I am sorry, Grandma B., that you are not here to see this book.

Finally, to Erik Mueggler, my most valued reader, interlocutor, and partner in life, who read this whole manuscript at least twice. I have often thought (okay, half in jest) that it would be enough if he were my only reader. I am so grateful that we have created a space of peace, felicity, and creativity amid the tumult all around. And though Max Mueggler might still be boyishly embarrassed to hear that he is a part of that space too, I thank him for all he has taught me about making it. And finally, there's Kitty, who barely has a real name but nevertheless deserves his cuddly due.

INTRODUCTION

I'll tell you a dream I had, it left me in awe. I went and forgot about it for some time until now.

I arrived in a house. There were only men, and the men distanced themselves. It was a big patio-like space, and I was in the center of it, in a house, the house was in the middle. It was a big ranch, *uma fazendona*, and *clean-clean-clean*, I mean clean that it only had grass all around—*capim* [short grass for cattle]. But then I looked at the grass; I saw fat coming, fat beginning to run over it. The old people say that when the world is going to end, it will end in oil. . . .

And the oil comes. It comes frying—sssssssssssss; frying, frying, frying; it comes down, down; it comes burning, burning; it comes with fire. *All black.* It keeps coming; it starts cracking, cracking, breaking, surrounding. And then there was this woman, and the woman ran, she stayed right at the edge of the fire. At the time I didn't think, she wasn't with me. Oh my God. And then there comes [a cold draft] a kind of air conditioning on me, and the fire is now burning high but just perfectly surrounding the space of the house. I see the woman go closer to the fire, and I call out: come over here—the name of the woman was Erínea[1]—"Here it is nice and cool, Erínea, come on, come on!" And she said, "No, no, I won't go." And then I remembered. My God. It is the world ending. The world ending in oil. And all my people already all burned, I was alone, they were not with me. And after I said, "Lord, if it is for my people to die and I am to be saved, kill me too. I can't stand staying without my people. If it is for me to stay alone, I don't want to, Lord. I want to be saved along with my people."

But my people were already burned; there was no world left for them, there was no world left. There was only this darkness all around. I was in the middle, in a house and a bit of green grass. And after I woke up, I said,

I have now seen my heart, and how I am going to be saved and people will not be saved. This is how Jesus does it. . . . The people say, though, that there is no hell, hell is *here*, you have to pay [for your guilt] here, and there are many paying.[2]

Olina Rocha related this dream to me late one morning as we rested in our hammocks on her porch in Goianésia do Pará, the northernmost town on Brazil's PA-150 highway in the Amazonian state of Pará. I had gone to participate in Goianésia's Pilgrimage of Liberation, the Romaria da Libertação, held yearly on September 17. This year—2006—I had stayed longer to rest and talk to various residents. Olina, a Catholic woman in her late sixties who could not walk, was an eager and animated interlocutor who sat upright in her hammock as she talked and looked out over a space much like the one she had described in her dream: a covered patio next to a wood-plank house, all surrounded by a porch. But here, there was no grass to be seen. We were on a dusty, unpaved, and especially red Amazonian town road. And instead of the darkness of Olina's dream, I could see the white-hot morning sun streaming onto the road in the distance.

Just before Olina described her apocalyptic vision, we had been talking about the recent untimely death of Florencia, whose funeral had brought a throng of people to her house. Olina had never seen a house so full, she said, and people were throwing themselves on the casket to cry—throwing themselves with such force that eventually the casket fell to the ground. "*Caiu?*" I asked, incredulous. It fell? "*Caiu*," Olina repeated, matter-of-fact. Florencia had been very poor, Olina said, her house was bad, *ruim!* But she took people in, she *helped* people, she was a friend to all and was dearly loved. Here Olina's rapid speech halted; she began thinking, changing gears. "I am not Evangelical," she said, "but my heart is quiet-quiet. Only my body isn't, my mouth speaks things, but my heart is pure." She drew on her cigarette, smiling, thinking, exhaling through darkened teeth. Then she told me her fiery dream.

"Why was hell on earth?" I asked after she finished. She replied emphatically, with a laugh in her voice:

There was never no hell, woman! God never let anyone into no hell!
    It's here! So many people burning here, and this is how Jesus does it. *Menina* (girl), here, one day when my husband was a candidate in the local elections, our opponents would drive by blaring their little jingles right at our house. At the time, my leg was bad, and I was staying in bed,

and they kept passing by my house *the whole day*. And there I was, laying there, dying of anger, and I said to myself, "No one is going to die still owing me. One day you will see!" And when the election ended, that candidate got sick, sick, but *so sick* that he ended up asking my husband for charity. And I said in my heart, "Yes, *agora deu* (there it is); now you see how no one will die without paying me their debt?!" That's how God makes people pay. The mayor [and my husband's party] won, and no one even knew that the man had ever existed, he was forgotten.

Olina's dream and related images, despite their spectacular quality, reflect the everyday concerns that have animated settlers on the PA-150 highway since it opened in stages through the 1970s.[3] My task in this book is to describe the PA-150's colonization, especially as it has continued into the present, and Olina helps me begin an ethnography that will not take a traditional linear, historical, or state-centric form. First, Olina helps evoke our location: a region of relatively small towns, farmsteads, government-made settlements, and larger (often appropriated) estates where, for most people, everything from everyday relationships to politics is an allegorical affair. This is to say that here, if you look closely, certain events, or constellations of relations, offer messages from the Christian divine. Second, Olina's images suggest that while Christian millenarian apocalypticism might not always be a *conscious* everyday orientation, it is at least a resource for local reflection. Finally, Olina's images of mass destruction alongside Florencia's distraught mourners show that, while the region can be allegorically seen as morally compromised—evil appears to be everywhere—its residents also hope for that unique and elusive good, that rare person who "helps," who (almost) like God is a true, a constant, friend.

Allegorical accounts of relations like Olina's were common in the region, and are what inspired me to seriously shift my research during my first extended period of formal fieldwork in 2004–05.[4]

I had originally been drawn to the legacies of the Southeast Amazon's recolonization by Brazil's military dictatorship as part of its Plan for National Integration, launched in 1970. Many factors influenced this need to recolonize and "integrate": geopolitical anxieties, the 1967 discovery of iron ore in the Carajás Mountains, and the catastrophic droughts and subsequent mass migrations from Brazil's Northeast Region through the 1960s and into 1970 (Hall 1989; Nys et al., 2016). The construction of the Trans-Amazon Highway came first: a 4,000-kilometer road crossing six states and running from João Pessoa, among the easternmost cities of Brazil, to the Amazon.

FIGURE 1. Map of Brazil. Detail: General area of research in Southeast Pará.

The Trans-Amazon was inaugurated in 1972, and soon a network of roads branched out from it. The PA-150, which intersects the Trans-Amazon near the city of Marabá, eventually incorporated a highway built through Eldorado do Carajás all the way to Redenção and came to be considered Pará state's central artery.

All of this construction attracted thousands of poor, mostly Northeastern migrants of mixed heritage—African, Indigenous, and white. They were heeding the military's propaganda: "A land without men, for men without land" (Souza 2020, 134). It is true that the Indigenous people of the region, namely the Gavião and Guarani groups,[5] had already lost most of their population by the 1970s, but the promise of easy settlement was misleading (Laraia and DaMatta 1967; Ferraz 2000). The influx of migrants led to intense land conflicts among rich land-grabbers and poor farmsteaders, which continued through a major gold rush in 1980 and the transition to democracy in 1985. Finally, these conflicts erupted in 1996, leading to one of the most consequential acts of state violence in post-authoritarian Brazil: the Eldorado Massacre. Nineteen people were killed instantly, seventy-nine were injured, and two more died later due to complications from their wounds. Southeast Pará continues to be one of the fastest-growing and most volatile regions in contemporary Brazil.[6]

Initially I went to study the current politics of settlement, focusing on the most hotly contested stretch of the highway, which is between the towns of Marabá and Eldorado do Carajás. But in the course of my fieldwork, my interlocutors brought me further north along the highway. I also began listening to settlers like Olina, who drew my attention to their powerful concerns beyond politics. Namely, people across the region conveyed their profound hope and will to unity, support, and *friendship* with others, coupled with a sense of friendship's elusiveness, even impossibility in the face of immanent evil. I have come to call all of this—the worry, intention, and longing-saudade[7]—*the mystic of friendship*,[8] without which, this book shows, the region's colonization cannot be fully described.[9]

"No one has friends, only acquaintances," people told me, "except for God." I have heard this regularly since 2004, through more than two cumulative years of fieldwork and over two decades of thinking about the region. The people who first explained this popular saying to me, the people at the center of this ethnography, are relatively poor workers of mixed ancestry (like Olina) who have migrated and settled along the PA-150 or are descended from these settlers. Many were struggling for land during my research, often together with political agrarian movements like the Landless Rural Workers' Movement (Movimento dos Trabalhadores Rurais Sem Terra, or MST), the largest organization in Brazil that mobilizes workers for land rights. Yet it was the refrain "No one has friends, only acquaintances (except for God)" that first turned my attention from agrarian politics to questions of friendship and what I call *common Catholicism*, a fluid repertoire of "official" and "heterodox" theologies that variously coincide and inspire everyday, generally allegorical, thought, practice, and relationships.[10] Eventually, thinking about the dynamics of friendship also made me aware of my interlocutors' general ambivalence toward the secular "reality" of politics, a theme that recurs across the chapters of this book.[11]

In other words, it wasn't only millenarian visions that compelled me to seek other ways to understand this colonial context; I heard them rarely. Still, millenarianism resonates in the common Catholicism of the region.

And Olina was not even the only one to offer me an elaborate vision of fundamental evil leading to the apocalypse. In 2004, some 270 kilometers south along the PA-150, Osias Martins, a survivor of the Eldorado Massacre, shared with me another startling and complete millenarian vision with similar relational significance. I will reflect on the massacre and Osias's vision in chapter 6. However, before we can fully understand such visions, we must travel the highway and explore the effects of the mystic of friendship, this common Catholic longing and will to find unity in others and with God, amid a sense of the precarity, even impossibility of this quest.[12] We will find that this mystic of friendship echoes with centuries of Catholic reflections on the divine—from allegorical and mystical-body theologies to more contemporary liberation theology. We will see that it resonates in Afro-Brazilian and even Evangelical forms (which is why I sometimes move between Catholicism and Christianity in what follows).[13] In short, we will find that it has shaped religion, politics, and the dynamics of settlement along this colonial highway. We will discover that the mystic of friendship remains the key to grasping and transforming the struggles for land and life on the Amazonian frontier.

BRAZILIAN AMAZONIA AND COLONIALISM

The Southeast Amazon is rarely studied in terms of the "colonial" or even the "postcolonial." A central reason is that Brazil threw off its status as a colony more than two hundred years ago. In 1815, the Portuguese royals who had resettled in Rio to escape Napoleon rechristened Brazil a kingdom, a coequal member of the "United Kingdom of Portugal, Brazil, and the Algarves" (Klooster 2013, 554). Brazil became an autonomous empire in 1822 when King Dom Pedro IV declared independence, becoming Emperor Dom Pedro I, after his father, King João VI, was forced to return to Portugal. By 1889, when the Brazilian Republic was formed, Brazil had left its former colonial status far behind, identifying itself as an independent and modernizing nation. While the republic acknowledged Indigenous groups as original populations, they were rarely celebrated, and from the 1930s forward Brazilian national identity was crafted around the idea of mixture, or *mestiçagem*. The notion of "racial democracy" associated with *mestiçagem* discourses has been roundly criticized in recent years—rightly shown to have covered up ongoing, especially anti-Black and anti-Indigenous, racism. Moreover, ideas of the national uniqueness of an "independent" Brazil contributed to occluding Brazil's ongoing internal colonial projects, especially in the Amazon.

Although some notable studies critiqued the military's colonization policies and described the "spontaneous colonization" that subsequently occurred along Amazonia's new highways, interest soon turned to other themes (Hébette and Marin 1977; see also Ianni 1979; Velho 1972, 1976).[14] Then, during the boom in postcolonial studies in the 1990s, many scholars across Latin America distanced themselves from these debates. They argued that conceptualizations of the postcolonial were largely inapplicable in the Latin American context, citing various historical, contemporary, and ethnic-racial reasons (see especially Adorno 1993; Alva 1992, 1994).[15] They even underscored the threats of academic colonialism (Mignolo 1993). Despite the fact that Latin American–born conversations about "coloniality" have since gained ground, scholars of contemporary Brazil still only occasionally discuss contemporary colonization and allied conceptual practices (though see Marques 2013b; Reinhardt and Cesarino 2017; Segato 2022 [2013]).[16] Meanwhile, along the PA-150 in particular, smallholders who used to be called colonists (*colonos*) and smallholder squatter claimants (*posseiros*) are today generally referred to as landless people (*povo sem terra*), while their land struggles are discussed in terms of agrarian reform (see also Costa 1999; Faulhaber 1999). This change in language is partly a reflection of the early 1990s arrival of the Landless Rural Workers' Movement in the region (the MST), which has rightly connected struggles in Pará to its nationwide call for agrarian reform, a generalized land redistribution (see chapters 2, 5, and 6).[17] Certainly, smallholder struggles counter the original state aim to colonize with large estates (and proletarianize the poor). Still, understanding the waves of settlement along the PA-150 as part of the ongoing dynamics of colonization reminds us of the oft-forgotten Indigenous peoples of the region and helps us think in new ways about colonization past and present.

Ann Stoler, a leading anthropological historian, has noted that occlusions of colonialism are common in many regions. They are fueled, Stoler says, by the languages of empires, nations, and scholars alike. On the one hand, contemporary empires and nations no longer want to see themselves as colonizers. On the other, scholars of colonialism tend not to study the "internal" Latin American variety because it is deemed less authentic than the dominant version of colonialism (Stoler 2016, 191). Stoler's resulting call is useful to think with: we should focus less, she says, on perfecting typologies ("internal" versus "settler" colonialism, "colonial" versus "postcolonial") and instead "train our senses beyond the more easily identifiable forms that some colonial scholarship schools us to recognize and see" (6). Stoler's earlier work already began to do that. She went beyond the traditional concerns of colonial studies to examine how Dutch colonial formations in Indonesia shaped understandings and practices of race, intimacy, sexual desire, and affect (Stoler 1995, 2010 [2002]). Stoler was not merely trying to understand these intimate practices on their own terms. Like others inspired by the work of Michel Foucault, she hoped to offer a "history of the present," insofar as the "racial and sexual politics of empire . . . [had] reverberating postcolonial effects" (Stoler 2010 [2002], 9; see also Stoler 2016, 63). Her 2016 book invites scholars to further expand notions of the colonial by deploying a "recursive analytic" that brings into view the "partial reinscriptions, modified displacements, and amplified recuperations" of colonial practices in spaces not traditionally recognizable as "colonial" (27).

In approaching settler Amazonia, I accept Stoler's invitation to expand what counts as colonial without focusing on typologies. I am also inspired by her interest in recursions. However, when I consider the masses of poor settlers who came to the PA-150, it becomes clear that their religiously infused interpersonal relations, which shape the dynamics of settlement—of colonizing—would be of relatively negligible interest even in Stoler's more open approach.[18] Indeed for Stoler, as for most scholars in her field, studying colonialism/colonization means studying governance.[19]

There are two analytical effects produced when governance is treated as the sine qua non of colonialism. First, relationships become merely the effect of governance, rather than a force of their own. Second, secular analytics are unduly privileged, a tendency that has persisted in colonial studies despite a number of influential critiques and scholarly movements—from *Provincializing Europe* and the post-9/11 "return of religion" to the anthropology of Christianity.[20] In Stoler's case, for example, though she is not the only one, anything that looks like "religion" falls out of the frame, despite the fact that in many colonial instances, including in the colonies that Stoler has studied, Christian relations were vital forces of colonization on the ground and were entwined with experiences of intimacy, desire, and affect—that is, relationships. In other words, Stoler's focus on (secular) colonial governance has its own occlusions. By blinding us to the more everyday, relational, and religious forces animating colonization, her approach, if applied wholesale to the settlement of the PA-150, would also eclipse important ways in which the present is shaped by the past and hide the futures being cultivated in the present.

The colonization of the Americas is unthinkable without Catholicism. Some might consider such a statement only applicable to times gone by, or to the role of missionaries. Yet I show in this book that Catholic concerns animate and even drive colonization in contemporary Brazil because they are entwined with everyday understandings—from kinship and friendship to senses of hope, will, and longing—even as these concerns gain new religious and nonreligious inflections within a growing pluralism.

COMMON CATHOLICISM

Scholars have often suggested that the expansion of Evangelical Protestantism is changing the face of Christianity in Brazil (Freston 1995; Mariz 1994; Montero 1999). While this might be true, the majority of Brazilians remain Catholic (56.75 percent, with 83.6 percent overall identifying as Christian).[21] This means that conversions to, and deconversions from, Protestant forms of Christianity still generally occur from a base of what I am calling common Catholicism.[22]

More significantly, Catholicism in Brazil has never just been about the institutional church. As the popular saying goes, Brazilian Catholicism is a tradition with "much praying and few priests, many saints and few sacraments, many feasts (*festas*) and little penance, many promises and few Masses" (e.g. Hoornaert 1992, 191; Bingemer 1998, 15). Riolando Azzi, for his part, has described Brazilian Catholicism as "[more] medieval, lay, social and familiar" (1978, 9). This does not disregard the major changes that Christianity underwent with the Reformation and in the encounter with the New World. Rather, Azzi refers to how, in Brazil, the more rationalized, individualized, and clergy-centric Tridentine reforms only really began to be implemented in the twentieth century—some four hundred years late. More traditional Christian social interests prevailed instead, particularly what John Bossy (1985) famously identified as the cultivation of community and friendship to protect against enemies in a violent world.[23] In the Brazilian context, this more socially concerned Catholic worship was fused with Indigenous and African traditions, ultimately shaping how Brazilians rely on more personal, spontaneous, and heterodox devotions. We will have a chance to explore Afro-Brazilian forms *as part* of common Catholicism in chapter 2; my point for now is that, since the early colony, Catholic relations have constituted one of the central contexts through which settlers past and present have lived.

Along the highway it has been no different. The everyday process of occupying and settling the PA-150 was carried out predominantly by Catholics who never just looked upon what they were doing as a process led by the state. Certainly, the state construction of roads made colonization possible. Similarly, as many poor colonists would learn, the poor suffered more violence because of the tacit alliances that state agents made with their preferred colonizers: rich land-grabbers. I discuss this in chapter 4. But this ethnography shows that the state was not the biggest concern of the poor who sought their fortunes along the PA-150. Instead, the key context for their thoughts and reflections was an originally Catholic hope to create friendship and unity both within and beyond families, despite the dangers and evils around them.

The vitality of this Catholic relational context is one reason why a conventional "history of the [colonial] present," as pursued by scholars like Stoler, is overly circumscribed for my purposes in this book. Note that I use the phrase "history of the present" to refer to Marxist as well as Foucauldian approaches, even if Foucault coined the phrase. While Foucault's work has become second nature in the social sciences and humanities, scholars have since fused Marxist and Foucauldian insights into a broader critical theory. Useful though this has been, such theory has produced largely secular, governance- and politics-focused scholarship, and often still quite linear accounts of (post)colonial spaces.[24] With the present ethnography, although questions of politics appear often, I hope to offer another kind of description along with different analytical and even political possibilities.

Of course, not all scholarship inspired by Foucault is unselfconsciously secular. One of the first bodies of work to systematically unpick naturalized, transhistorical understandings of religion and the secular is that of Talal Asad, who drew liberally on Foucault.[25] But scholars who have mobilized Asad's work have tended to reinscribe a Marxist-Foucauldian, and ultimately secularist, truism: that secular power, lodged in sites of governance, is what most determines religion—indeed, life—and is therefore the most worthy of study (Lebner 2015, 2019). I discuss this at more length later, including my distinct approach to the issue of secularity. First, however, let me set out how this book offers a *divining of the present*, an alternative to the predominant colonial histories of the present that I described above.

DIVINING ALLEGORICAL IMAGES

To say that *The Mystic of Friendship* offers a divining of the present refers to its ethnographic content as much as its form. While at one level form and content are indistinguishable, one can only start conceiving of form after making some basic decisions about description. In my case this took some time: my ethnography here has been marked by much post-field reflection on friendship among Amazonian settlers and on what I now consider friendship's mystic quality.

As I tacked between what my interlocutors taught me and the fields of scholarship that I thought spoke to their concerns, I realized that the mystic of friendship was a product of an allegorical way of *divining*—their way of deciphering divine presences and messages in the world through constellations of interpersonal relations. We have already seen an example of such divining with Olina's account, above, where I also referred to her "images": the sets of relations she described and interpreted from her dream and waking lives. "Image" is a relatively colloquial term that helped convey the basic message I wanted to start with, namely how a vivid description was offered to tell a complex story. Conjuring up a specifically Christian allegory, Olina's images helped communicate how good and evil animate persons and relations, leaving few true friends and connecting people to either salvation or damnation. While it is not so common for settlers to reflect on salvation, they often consider how good and evil, or the agency of God and spirits, work through their relationships. And they also think about how this should inform their future actions.

Yet there is also more to this allegorical divining, this decomposing of images to reveal relations. While Strathern has always been an influence, I began expanding my thinking in this regard by rereading Walter Benjamin (1999, 2019), whose work may have been a source of inspiration for Strathern's thinking on images, too.[26] Benjamin's writings on baroque allegory and its recurrence in the nineteenth century[27] reminded me that allegorical practice was not unique to the settler frontier.[28] I came to see that contemporary allegory in Amazonia resonates with past theologies developed between Europe and its colonies, including theologies not necessarily promoted by contemporary Catholic clerics—such as the millenarian theology reflected in Olina's dream. Other theologies abounded, as we will see. Benjamin does not elaborate on any formal theologies in his main work on allegory, *The Origin of German Tragic Drama (Trauerspiel)*,[29] nor does he speak about relationships, the Americas, or even "divining." Still, what he says—and what he neglects—has helped catalyze my thinking on modern allegorical divining and has encouraged me to connect it to Brazilian colonial contexts and questions of friendship.

Oddly, contemporary social scientists of Christianity and religion rarely address allegory, even as they engage theology and imagery (though see Port 2011; Callahan et al. 2010; Menezes 2022).[30] In fact, as I discuss in chapters 1 and 3, predominant assumptions about "material religion" have recently impeded our understanding of common Catholic interpersonal relations, particularly how these relations are vitally shaped by allegory. Yet the contemporary aversion to allegory has deeper roots. When I first began reflecting on this issue, I imagined that allegory had simply been dispensed with alongside the symbolic approaches that were critiqued in the 1980s—a critique that opened the door to various new approaches to the study of religion and, most recently, to the material turn.[31] However, the rejection of allegory can be traced even further back: to the Romantics who, as Benjamin shows, elevated the symbol at allegory's expense. Benjamin maintains that Romantics failed to grasp the post-Reformation transformation of allegory and imagery, whose production of a new uncertainty of meaning was the condition of the Romantics' desire for the symbol in the first place.[32]

Famously cryptic, *Origin* has long been relatively marginalized in Benjamin studies.[33] Today, if it is read at all, it is often engaged as a source of theory. I will come back to Benjamin's critical "theoretical" insights regarding the writing of history generally, but first I draw on *Origin*'s description of allegory's past, which sheds considerable light on the present ethnography. Benjamin's simple affirmation has been key: baroque allegory was not just a literary, artistic, or even just a German phenomenon. Rather, it was a practice and experience that touched all of Europe and reflected the religious and existential crisis of the Reformation and early modernity. Indeed, the rupturing of the one church had shaken European cosmology; divine will had become more opaque, and the world suddenly appeared more riven with evil, even in the more stably Catholic regions.[34] And thus a new, more restless allegorical way of seeing began coursing through Europe.

This brings me to the second inspiring point from Benjamin's account: this new allegorical concern was quite literally indexed by an "eruption of imagery" (2019, 182), most notably in "emblems," a sort of picture puzzle with figures and writing that swept the continent in books and other forms from the sixteenth to the eighteenth centuries.[35] Emblems elaborated on

Renaissance forms, but whereas earlier pictorial inscriptions were used for more decorative purposes, the emblem built on the baroque's "passionate Christian emphasis on the fallenness of nature and humanity" and was geared toward interpretation and learning how to live in this fallen context (McCole 1993, 134).

What Benjamin doesn't engage, however, is that this transformation of allegorical thought and practice was entwined with new ways of conceptualizing—and worrying about—interpersonal relations, and that these anxieties were exported into Europe's conquests overseas, including those in Portuguese America. Specifically, the Reformation had essentially shattered the "mystical body," the *corpus mysticum* of the church, which is one of the oldest ways to describe, and evoke the unity of, Christian community (Lubac 2006 [1944]; Rust 2014).[36] This fragmentation of the community was deadly serious. Even in the most modern of theologies, communal disunity remains the essence of sin and evil (for example, see the discussion of liberation theology in chapter 4). Thus, post-Reformation disunity and evil became a problem for all of the Christian world, and Catholicism had its own response: the Catholic Church sought to fend off enemies who would divide it and aimed to reconsolidate and even expand its unity. Specifically, it could expand unity by supporting empire-building, that is, by incorporating the new lands and peoples it had "discovered" (and enslaved) in the Americas into the mystical bodies of church and empire (J. Scheper-Hughes 2021; Luz 2013).[37]

Crucially for our purposes, this hope to unify the *corpus mysticum* was referred to colloquially as a search for friendship, especially in Portuguese America. It is true that in both theology and secular scholarship, the *corpus mysticum*, whether of empire or otherwise, is rarely described in terms of friendship or love. Yet a little digging reveals that since early modern colonial days, friendship, unity, and *corpus mysticum* could be synonyms, in addition to being allegories of each other. In Portuguese America, as Guilherme Luz (2013, 557) explains, maintaining "the health of the mystical body of the empire" entailed the use of a "vast repertoire" of theological-political practice to produce "concord," which was synonymous with a hierarchical "order founded on love" and friendship, as Pedro Cardim (1999) might add. To say that there was a "vast repertoire" is not an exaggeration: Cardim notes that friendship and love were the theme of a "truly crushing" number of Portuguese publications in the early modern period (1999, 32).[38] And Luz takes it farther, stating that the will to promote concord within the mystical body spanned discursive as well as "imagetic, ritual, and performative practices" (2013, 553–4).[39]

Significantly for my account, the interest in unity in and with the mystical body has transcended the early modern period.[40] As the Brazilian church turned its eyes back to Europe in the early twentieth century, it met with a new mystical body "craze" in global Catholic theology, which despite overt differences retained essential similarities to its baroque forerunner.[41] As such, this new theology enabled mystic longings for unity and friendship to intensify and recur throughout the twentieth century, even as mystical-body theology faded into the background after the Second Vatican Council opted for a new image of the church: the people of God. Avery Dulles (2002 [1974]) would remind us that, in any case, images of the church do not fully disappear; some of the meanings they convey live on. And certainly, the will to unity did not disappear. Unity remained a key concern of liberation theology (Comerford 2003; and see note 42), which I explore in chapter 4.

Despite the relations that he misses, rereading Benjamin alongside these mystical-body itineraries has helped me articulate why I pursue a "divining of the present" rather than merely a "history." Benjamin's later work, which is more informed by *Origin* than is usually acknowledged, rejects conventional history at least in part due to the recurring allegorical practices it ignores. Specifically, Benjamin suggests that scholars should seize on an "image that flashes up" rather than describe events in a sequence, as if they were "beads of a rosary" (2003a, 390, 397). But Benjamin is not looking for just any kind of image; he is most interested in the political potentials of allegorical images, images entwined with the possibilities of redemption, the Messiah, and salvation from adverse conditions (389–90, 396–97). Benjamin inspired me to try to write through a form, a method, that makes visible what animates my interlocutors' experience of events, namely recurring allegorical images, worries, and practical readings of friendship, unity, and the evils that could rupture them. In short, I have attended to images that are *divined*—whose resonances, in all their uncertainty, are at once interpreted and made transtemporal. And this is why I do not structure my descriptions in a strict chronology, either within each chapter or in the book as a whole. Instead, I use each chapter to describe a distinct moment of settlement along the highway and view that moment as an allegorical image and event containing past and present.

THE MYSTIC OF FRIENDSHIP

My decision to call settlers' insatiable longing "the mystic of friendship" was similarly inspired by encountering the recurrences of the past in the present—especially wishes for, and conceptual extensions of, mystical unity.[42]

On the one hand, I was specifically encouraged by my reading of *The Mystic Fable* by Michel de Certeau, who considered his study of the changing field of sixteenth and seventeenth century *mystics*—denoting an emergent science of the divine developed beyond traditional theologies—to be a sequel to (and subtle critique of) one of the most important theological works of the twentieth century, Henri de Lubac's *Corpus Mysticum* (2006 [1944]).[43] On the other hand, there was what sixteenth-century Jesuits in Portuguese America called *mística*, "the apparently sporadic and disconnected religious . . . path[s] taken [to] restor[e] direct and free communication with the sacred" (Hoornaert 1997, 129). According to Eduardo Hoornaert, this *mística* included the precise kind of personalized devotions and spiritual animus that I encountered during my fieldwork and discuss in the chapters of this book: pilgrimages (chapter 1); personal prayers (chapter 2); moral poetry (chapter 3); and spiritual virtuosos or leaders (chapter 6). And *mística* also now has a more secular twentieth- and twenty-first-century life beyond the church proper, for example in the Landless Rural Workers' Movement (which I explore in chapters 5 and 6).[44] All of these connected concepts have shaped my thinking about the mystic of friendship. However, I probably wouldn't have repurposed the idea of "mystic" if Michael B. Smith, the English translator of *The Mystic Fable*, hadn't also devised his own rather different notion of *mystics* first.

At the beginning of *The Mystic Fable* Smith tells readers that he had run up against a problem of translation: what Certeau studied, "*la mystique*," was not captured by the English word "mysticism" (which translates *le mysticisme*).[45] So Smith chose *mystics* to translate *la mystique* to help specify the emergent field of inquiry Certeau studied, which sought experimental, and experiential, knowledge of the divine. Crucially, Smith kept *mystics* always in italics, "to distinguish it from the plural of 'a mystic'" (Smith 1992, ix–x). As I read on, I was further interested to see that themes addressed by Certeau had analogs among people I worked with in Amazonia.[46] Most importantly they both shared in a "strange historicity," where the search for the other "continues to reappear, like an ethical requirement, like a 'song' whose returns defy history" (Certeau 2015, 20). This similarity made me realize I could adapt Smith's neologism to help me capture the problematic of friendship that I was trying to convey. Specifically, I realized that repurposing Smith/Certeau's *mystics* by singularizing and de-italicizing it would allow me to foreground this form of historicity, which resonates with recurrences: from will and longing to senses of loss and impossibility. I was aware that switching the reference of the term mystic from a person to an internal movement of will to relation—even a movement of will to transcend relation through unity—was somewhat awkward, including because it was understood that this will could never be fully realized. Yet I considered this awkwardness a good thing: it could better capture the motility, the unresolvable nature, and ultimately the insatiability of this longing(-*saudade*) for relation and more.

It must be said that Certeau was a pioneer of reflections on Catholicism and desire, though I am mostly avoiding that term because of its weightiness in Euro-American theory, and I question its appropriateness in the Amazonian settler context.[47] Certeau was also less interested than I am in the more anthropological questions of why such *saudade* and senses of impossibility recur, why they expand beyond Catholicism, and what such longing and will to unify effect in the world. Instead, Certeau was most invested in producing a history in the wake of a ruptured mystical body, and so he used the term *corpus mysticum* sparingly. Moreover, he claimed that *mystics* obsessed over an absent body due to an increasing sense of distance from the divine (see also note 43, below). For me, however, something else is evident: without the general idea of the unified body of God and community, prevalent during the period Certeau studied, the longing for union with this "body" would not have been there in the first place.

What this means for my own account is not trivial. The longing for unity with the divine and others recurs into the present. As I conceive it, the mystic of friendship still resonates with centuries of theological reflections, ritual enactments, and allegorical images of mystical unity. This brief discussion should begin to flesh out what has shaped the mystic movements at the heart of this book. But there is more to say; other more contemporary forces continue to shape the mystic of friendship.

SECULARITY AND RECENTERING RELATIONS

Let me be clear: when I acknowledge resonances of past colonial theology in the mystic of friendship, I am not contending, as Camara Cascudo and others have, that the Brazilian *povo* "retain a faith from before, during and after the Councils" (cited in Hoornaert 1997, 121). I emphasize that this is not an account of mere continuity. However, I can't affirm radical discontinuity, either. Rather there are recurrences, the "partial reinscriptions, modified displacements, and amplified recuperations" (Stoler 2016, 27), that are non-identical both because repetition never quite repeats, and because broader cultural changes eventually intersect with the reinscriptions. In cultural terms, then, one of the most evident differences between contemporary Amazonia and early modern Portuguese America is how settlers today produce, live with, and negotiate a more elaborate discourse on the *possibility* of a distinct and legitimate political domain, separate from "religion." Of course, many ultimately reject this possibility even while participating in politics, something I return to at various points in this book.

Let me elucidate this point by recalling Olina. Olina didn't fully reject politics (her husband ran for office, after all). Still, it is not a coincidence that when I asked her to explain what she meant by "hell is on earth," she offered me a political tale. The story was overtly about a candidate for mayor who blared jingles at her house all day while she was bedridden and forced to listen. However, it was also an allegory for how God punishes, "burns," the evil on earth. Indeed, the candidate got sick enough himself ("sick, sick, but *so sick*") that he was reduced to begging for charity, including from Olina's husband, his erstwhile opponent. Her story, in other words, reveals what many of my interlocutors often said: evil is everywhere but appears *especially* in the realm of human governance—politics and also law—because this is where humans struggle to exert power and authority over each other. This is why human governance is actually a special allegorical problem. While the political sphere can reflect the divine and the good, which is why people do not absolutely abjure it, politics is ultimately illegitimate because God is not merely the only true friend; he is also the only true authority. Humans who seek power, my interlocutors would say, are trying to usurp God's real power, yet they can never be the true leaders of this world because evil runs through them, as it does with all creatures of the fallen world.

Benjamin would say that this sounds like the problems facing the baroque kings of *Trauerspiel* who, like all humans, were fallen and therefore unable to properly decide or truly lead (2019, 56). The difference, however, is that early moderns rarely, if ever (at least openly), considered the possibility that the political sphere could be *legitimately* autonomous from "religion." Certainly, a more secular idea of sovereignty was taking shape during the baroque period, but kings retained the divine right to rule, at least officially. In short, there was no "politics" in the sense that we use it now: an exclusively human sphere through which all public and private rights can theoretically be negotiated. This is why we need to see the mystic of friendship, while retaining echoes of early colonial Catholicism, as both driving and being conditioned by something else: what I call an intensifying secularity.

To explain, let me return to the discussion that I suspended earlier: how the secularity I refer to in this book cannot be understood through the predominant frames of "secularism." Scholars have tended to describe secularity simply as the condition secured by political/state secularism, which comes after an official colonial period, and which manages and produces distinctions between religion and politics (see Mahmood 2015, 181; Agrama 2015, 307). This understanding emerged from a certain reading of Talal Asad's *Formations of the Secular* (2003), which responded to the perceived failure of the "secularization hypothesis," the assumption that the continual progress of the modern state and science would make religion disappear. While this hypothesis guided a good part of social science in the twentieth century, work on secularism inspired by Asad, including scholarship on Brazil, hoped to show that, far from disappearing, religion was produced and regulated, often unfairly, by states managing their citizens (Agrama 2012; Giumbelli 2013; Montero 2013). Some scholars also showed that secularism monitored other "private" practices alongside religion, like marriage, gender, and sexuality (Fernando 2014; Mahmood 2015; Scott 2017; Selby 2012).

This scholarship produced vital insights. Yet its focus on secularism has had some unintended analytical consequences. First, wishing to avoid the secularization hypothesis, the scholarship occluded one of Asad's key points: that if we understand secularization as the expansion of a domain of thought and practice distinct from religion, not as the rise of unbelief, it is clear that secularization *happened*, and that it *preceded*[48] and continues to exceed the ("postcolonial") secularist state (see also Lebner 2015, 2019). The other consequence of this occlusion follows from the first. In ceasing to reflect on the secularization hypothesis, scholars have inadvertently reproduced an assumption embedded in it, namely that the state, or "politics," is the cause of whatever happens to religion and the private sphere more generally.[49]

In other words, although this scholarship has contributed important reflections on religion, it nevertheless reinforces the premise of colonial histories of the present that I discussed earlier, which are founded on an uninterrogated secularization of knowledge. Although studies of secularism are generally aware of unselfconsciously secular thought, they nevertheless still privilege the secular, the political, and the public as more truly causal than those relations consigned to the private sphere—especially religion itself. The solution, as I see it, is not simply to reverse the privilege, establishing, say, the causal force of the private over the public, religion over politics. Scholars of Brazil sometimes assert something of the kind when they argue that secularism never had much effect on Brazilian religiosity (Montero 2006). Although I agree with Paula Montero that secularism in Brazil didn't make religion decline, changes did occur in the conditions and understandings of Brazilian religion and politics in various places and times, even before the First Republic. I make space in my description for these changes while being honest about where, under conditions of secularity, the relative powers of both religion and politics come from: interpersonal and conceptual negotiations and struggles, which are never only private and which are never only human. By this I do not (just) mean "material," "animal," or "object-oriented." Rather, I also mean that the conceptual, and especially the interpersonal, might be animated by divine persons or forces. Meanwhile, by "never only private" I mean that, while these divine interpersonal forces might be described in retrospect as private or religious, they are not necessarily only that; they may also be public, even political.

My argument—that the flow of relations, especially the practice of kinship and friendship, is more vital than secularism for understanding how distinctions among religions and between religion(s) and politics are animated on the ground—might appear obvious.[50] But it is a necessary argument, especially since scholars hoping to capture how it feels to live with secularity, and who focus less on political causality, have tended to sideline relationships and their everyday challenges. For Charles Taylor, for example, secularity is a condition of modern belief, the lived experience of which has been shaped by a "nova effect, the steadily widening gamut of new positions—some believing, some unbelieving, some hard to classify" (2007, 423). Taylor's detailed account of pre-Reformation Christianity's mutations as the root of secularity is an important counterpoint to the secularization hypothesis, and it complements the present account in many ways. Yet the interpersonal relations that propelled these changes appear infrequently in Taylor's history, making Taylor's understanding of secularity narrower than the one I am developing here.[51]

A few scholars have begun to call out the neglect of kinship in studies of secularism. Susan McKinnon and Fennella Cannell, for example, note in their pioneering volume *Vital Relations* (2013) that the two main debates about the nature of modernity never intersect. Discussions of secularism rarely contemplate the move from status to contract—from the rule of kinship to the primacy of commerce and freer forms of association. While McKinnon and Cannell's volume as a whole only begins to explore such an intersection,[52] others have since published monographs on these topics (Ramberg 2014; Lemons 2019). None, however, have seriously addressed the question of friendship,[53] or explored the idea that secularity may not be a characteristic of "society" in some way determined by the state. The difference that I am suggesting is this: secularity *starts with and necessarily includes* persons in relation negotiating distinctions among religions and between religion and politics. This is why secularity can even exist in states without secularism, and why negotiations between religion and politics can increase in intensity under certain conditions, leading to what I call an intensified secularity.

Secularity, in other words, is a tool that both helps describe an experience and supports the wider aims of this book: to recenter relations in the study of religion and bring politics (including colonialism) into greater dialogue with relations, religions, and their extensions alike.[54] For while "secularity" as I use it helps capture how persons in relation negotiate connections and distinctions among religion(s) and politics, it also reminds us that relations—more vitally than state secularism or society—produce religion and politics in the first place. The state might have a hand in arbitrating what officially counts as religion, for example, *but persons receiving, conceiving, debating, and embodying this issue (i.e., in various kinds of relation) have always preceded state decisions*. Moreover, they are what make such decisions about religion—and even secularism itself—possible. In chapter 6, for example, I show that the experience of secularity both preceded the republic and arguably intensified in the years around its founding.

SECULARITY IN BRAZIL AND ALONG THE PA-150: A PRELIMINARY LOOK

One place where the experience of secularity became most intense was Canudos, the name of a town that will figure prominently in chapter 3. Founded in 1893 in the state of Bahia by an itinerant preacher and his followers, Canudos soon attracted some thirty thousand people from across the Brazilian Backlands, including recently freed slaves. Canudos became famous for an unfortunate reason. It was the site of the republic's first war, which proved so fatal—practically no residents survived—that it inspired a firm denunciation by the journalist Euclides da Cunha (2003 [1902]), who is celebrated for his masterwork *Os Sertões* (The Backlands), the first work of Brazilian social science. *Os Sertões* reveals that at least some people in Canudos were motivated by millenarian hopes and fears. Writings found in the rubble of the town after the war suggested that at least some, if not many, residents rejected the secular republic as evil and died fighting for their independence or for a return to the divinely sanctioned monarchy and empire.

While few subsequent struggles over religion or politics in Brazil were as extreme as they were in Canudos, that is precisely my point: secularity can be more or less intense in different places and in different times and can have more and less devastating effects. The period that this book covers— the 1960s to the present, especially between 2004 and 2016—was marked by intensifying concerns different from those in Canudos. Namely, people worried about how, along the PA-150, families and friends were seeking unity and friendship and to that end were increasingly negotiating "new" politics and "new" religions. I use quotation marks here because the Marxist and secular politics and the Protestant and Afro-Brazilian religions in question have been practiced openly for at least one hundred years in Brazil, and covertly for longer. Yet not only is the contemporary configuration of settler Amazonia relatively new, it is also new that these religions and politics are increasingly viewed as separate and viable options, as well as competitors and even antagonists.

Let's look briefly at the politics first. I am not speaking about electoral politics but rather the politics around land that settler comrades, brothers, family, and friends both created and had to negotiate. These struggles over settlement began in the early days of the PA-150 during the military dictatorship. They had the support of liberationist clergy who came to the region to promote a more politicized Catholic fraternity, reigniting worries about the relationship between religion and politics that have continued intensifying up to the present day. Liberationists worked against traditional aversions to politics by trying to reunite it with religion. While they were successful for a time, these discussions diversified as traditional workers' unions became more independent, as military dictatorship ceded to civilian rule, and then especially when the MST arrived in Pará. I will leave discussion of this mostly to chapters 2, 5, and 6. Still, it is important to note here that while the MST was founded in 1984 in the south of Brazil with the support of liberationists, a year later it had become an autonomous and officially secular and Marxist movement. My point for now is that participants in the MST might be religious, but they and their families and friends still have to negotiate the possibility of a purely secular politics. In other words, whether people embrace MST politics or not, those who do have contributed to the intensification of secularity along the PA-150.

Let us turn more squarely to religion now. Remember that people are negotiating not only religion's relationship to politics but to a diversifying religious field as well. The antipathy of Protestants toward Afro-Brazilian religions is well known. Somewhat less commented on, however, is that Afro-Brazilian religions were practiced quietly within, or at least alongside, Catholicism by many faithful for decades without the need to acknowledge their separate religious status. Changes in the visibility and viability of Afro-Brazilian religions are especially interesting because they are at least in part effects of race-conscious activism in other regions of the country.

Nevertheless, while Afro-Brazilian religions are gaining presence along the PA-150, people rarely practice them *because* they are committed to maintaining "Afro-Brazilian" practices (although this is a common motivation elsewhere in the country). In my experience, practitioners rarely even referred to these religions as "Afro-Brazilian." This might be due to an important condition, sometimes noted by activist friends: that the Movimento Negro, the Black Movement, was still quite weak in Pará, while a colorist racism was rife. As Aurora, who appears in chapter 1, explained to me, many people distanced themselves from Blackness, not considering themselves Black despite acknowledging African descent. Aurora pointed out that Pará has the highest percentage of mixed-race (*pardo*) people in Brazil, at 70 percent of the population, while only 7 percent identify as "Black" (IBGE 2010). The 2022 census shows near identical numbers, although 9.8 percent identify as Black (IBGE 2022). LaShandra Sullivan, working elsewhere in Amazonia, has called this "Black invisibility" (2017). In short, during the time of my research race was not an overt concern of my interlocutors, and the present ethnography reflects that.[55] The everyday challenges of relating, along with the negotiations of religion, politics, and settlement, were objects of far more worry and discussion. This is why the mystic of friendship, and how it animates both settlement and the intensification of secularity, became the main theme of this book.

TRAVELING THE HIGHWAY

The rest of this book moves along the PA-150. Echoing the divining of my interlocutors, I have eschewed following a strict chronology. Instead, the chapters move back and forth between scenes from before the highway's construction to the Eldorado Massacre and its aftermath. Between chapters, further disrupting chronology, I have placed "Visitations," which include memories, apparitions, prophecies, and allegorical poetry and prose from the seventeenth to the twenty-first centuries. These are all forms that Certeau would include in what he calls "mystic poetics," a "thousand-year-old tradition that passes . . . from place to place and age to age" (1992, 298), and whose recurrence, Amy Hollywood reminds us, is also "one of a rupture, of an impossibility, of a wandering and an excess that cannot be contained by the very tradition of which it is a part" (2012, 198; see also Moore 2012).

The six chapters further elucidate the visitations, and they also tell two intertwined stories. Each chapter recounts tales from the lives of distinct groups of settlers, revealing moments in the process of the highway's settlement. But they also capture the force of the mystic of friendship, investigating how the movement between a will to friendship and a sense of its impossibility has vitalized key transformations in religion, politics, and settlement.

This also means that each chapter sheds light on broader processes and contributes to a series of conceptual interventions. The aim of the first three chapters, for example, is to offer multiple perspectives on the mystic of friendship and its connection to religious transformations.

Chapter 1, "Goianésia do Pará: The Recurrence of Allegory," conjures the landscape and religious history of the PA-150 while conveying settlers' unique ways of divining the world and their relationships—and indeed their very personhood in the process. It achieves this through an ethnography of the Pilgrimage of Liberation, the Romaria da Libertação, a devotion that has grown with the settlement of the PA-150. The Romaria has been celebrated every September 17 since 1983 in honor of two "little saints," Elizabete and Elineuza, who were viciously murdered as toddlers in 1980 and whose spirits, according to the faithful, have since performed many miracles. The ethnography describes my experience with a group of pilgrims traveling by bus and foot over two days to reach the saints' tomb on their commemoration day, a "repayment" to the saints for catalyzing a miracle. Pilgrimages are usually studied as rituals, while miracles are treated as supernatural phenomena; rarely are they both seen as reflections of everyday patterns of interpersonal and conceptual relationships (though see Coleman 2021a).[56] This chapter takes a different tack. It shows how the practice of pilgrimage, as well as the related search for miracles, entails allegorical ways of divining persons and relations. It has long been this way: even missionaries in early Portuguese America saw pilgrimage as a real and allegorical journey toward God and others, which would catalyze further help, friendship, and unity—or even a miracle, that sure evidence of divine friendship. Still, as my pilgrim companions taught me, allegorical practice also produces uncertainty. While one may search for God in the world, one can never be *quite* sure of finding him; one can certainly never be sure of the constancy of persons who appear to be his messengers, your friends. The chapter thus introduces the divining person and the recurrence of allegory, which are vital parts of common Catholicism that have shaped the mystic of friendship. At the same time, the chapter begins to decenter "materiality" and recenter "relations" in the study of religion.

Chapter 2, "Marabá: The Intensification of Secularity," shows how recent religious transformations are animated by the mystic of friendship. The chapter tells this story of religious change through an Amazonian settler family I call the Solanhas, many of whom live on the periphery of Marabá, the regional hub town at the intersection of the PA-150 and the Trans-Amazon Highway. The chapter begins with a puzzle about two secret prayers that were found among the family patriarch's effects after his death. Unsure of how to use the prayers, the Solanha children feel the loss of their father's spiritual protection as their relationships with kin, friends, and others become increasingly fraught and disunified. I mobilize the Solanhas' allegorical readings of their father's loss alongside accounts of a series of "conversions"—both religious and political—perceived as solutions to social, economic, and spiritual fragmentation. While two Solanha sisters convert to different Evangelical Christian churches, two others deepen their connection to newly visible and distinct Afro-Brazilian religions. Meanwhile, a Solanha brother joins the secular and Marxist Landless Workers' Movement after years of activism with the Catholic Church. I show that the draw of different religious and political communities for the Solanha children, their move toward new friends and away from their birth family, is evidence of how the mystic of friendship, that longing (*saudade*) for an elusive unity, is implicated in the late twentieth-century proliferation of new kinds of politics and religion—an intensifying secularity. This is also where I first show how conceiving secularity anew helps us recenter relations, reminding us to acknowledge how friendship and kinship animate everyday distinctions among religion(s), theologies, and politics even more vitally than does state secularism.

While the first two chapters include reflections on how past Christian and Afro-Brazilian theologies resonate in the present, chapter 3, "Cleusa's Settlement: Poetry and the Devil's Arts," foregrounds these transtemporal theological echoes. The chapter begins with an ethnographic account of Cleusa's childhood in the region before the highway's construction. When she was a child, her family accompanied her father through the forests collecting nuts from Brazil-nut trees (*castanheiras*), which were once the motors of the local economy. Cleusa told me about how every night her father would sing Catholic moral *cordel* poems to her; this memory continues to inspire her own struggles for land in adulthood. To understand Cleusa's inspiration, I examine several exemplary *cordel* from the turn of the twentieth century, including some verses found in the rubble of the Canudos war. Through an analysis of this poetry, I first argue that the implications of *cordel* for understanding past and present backlands Catholicism and mystic relational dynamics has been all but ignored since *Os Sertões*. Second, I show that the resonance of these *cordel* in the present means that, like the *Canudenses* before them, Cleusa and other backlanders along the PA-150 worry, or submit, that a secular politics that they read allegorically is always potentially devilish. This chapter expands on a critique of materiality and mediation begun in chapter 1 and shows that recentering relations—and, crucially, acknowledging their mystic vitality—can help transform both the terms of our analyses and the politics of our descriptions.

The last three chapters, while still charting different moments in the story of settlement, foreground how the mystic of friendship is implicated in struggles to build a new politics and a new distribution of land and power along the highway.

Like chapter 3, chapter 4, "Jacundá: The Cry and the Silence of Unity," excavates a "past" theology that resonates in the present: liberation theology, or "liberationism," as I call it for short. Liberationist clergy arrived on the highway in the late 1970s and helped propel—and politicize—the early struggle for land, a crucial step toward liberating the poor from oppression along the PA-150. Relatively little has been written in the social sciences about liberationism since the 1990s, when scholars sought to explain its decline. This chapter offers another kind of analysis. It shows how liberationism's legacy echoes today in how settlers oscillate between an embrace and rejection of politics, much like how they move between a will to friendship and a sense of its impossibility. The chapter makes this argument through an analysis of images that were published in the first year of *The Cry of the PA-150*, the liberationist newsletter produced in the town of Jacundá from 1980 to 1986. Through these images, especially of crucified individual peasants on the one hand and "unified" peasant collectives retaliating against oppressors on the other, *The Cry* promoted peasant organizing through a new kind of politics. It called for a politics of "fraternity" rather than "hierarchy" and of "equality" rather than "individualism." Yet I demonstrate that these images, and liberationism more generally, which both passionately promoted the value of "unity," allowed older allegorical associations between disunity, evil, and the devil to persist. This, I argue, has shaped understandings of friendship as divine, while division, which is the essence of politics and enmity, always remains potentially diabolical. This in itself is not the cause of liberationism's decline, but it does indicate a certain failure to sow seeds for sustainable transformation. I conclude with a diagnosis, that a theology aiming to support intentional political transformations over time must be able to articulate how difference and division are integral to unity. Otherwise, it is vulnerable to being neutralized when utopian discourses around unity are belied by division and its allegories.

Chapter 5, "Fazenda Peruano: Law's Enmity," extends the insights of previous chapters, showing how mystic dynamics can provoke resistance not only to politics but also to secular law. Here, my ethnography focuses on one of the largest land occupations, or camps (*acampamentos*), in Pará, which was created on the illicit Peruano estate by the MST. I show that the MST, as a secular successor to liberationism, retains a rhetoric of unity but seeks to facilitate political solidarity differently. For example, it replaces the more Catholic language of friendship or "fraternity" with *companheirismo* (comradeship). Significantly, I show how unity and *companheirismo* began to erode once the camp leadership began to enforce internal laws. Satisfaction plummeted as the months wore on, until one day a group of residents decided to create a new organizational structure, "an association of friends" that employed more Christian rhetoric and directly threatened the MST's control of the camp and its idea of *companheirismo*.

Brazilianist anthropology long ago established that Brazilians of all classes are wary of the law; specifically, being subject to the law is seen as depersonalizing, even as evidence of social worthlessness and friendlessness, hence the popular saying "for my friends, everything, for my enemies the law" (DaMatta 1991 [1979]). While insightful, these accounts have essentially excluded Catholicism from their analyses. This ethnography is particularly groundbreaking for showing how Catholicism is crucial to understanding what I call "law's enmity." First, it adds ethnographic depth. Being subject to the law in Brazil—being marked as a relationless enemy—can generate a sense of evil and of alienation from (Christian) society. Second, a still deeper understanding emerges when we consider older Catholic theologies, especially St. Augustine's attempt to protect the church from the evils of secular Roman law. In addition to contributing to Brazilian debates, this ethnography comes to light at a time when "for my friends, everything, for my enemies the law" has gained new visibility not only in Brazil but more generally in Latin American public life. In the last five years, politicians and commentators in Mexico, Peru, Colombia, Guatemala, and Uruguay have claimed this saying as part of their cultural and political heritage. This chapter concludes that, not only is law's enmity not uniquely Brazilian, we might consider its Catholic underpinnings to have resonance well beyond Amazonia and Brazil.

Chapter 6, "Eldorado do Carajás: Divining the Event," finally turns to the Eldorado Massacre. Eldorado has long been read through secular lenses, most commonly as evidence of the class war that has been waged against the Brazilian poor. Without contesting this analysis, this chapter offers another perspective: that of survivors, who are aware of the secular reading of the Massacre, yet also entertain alternative, more Christian allegorical readings. The chapter focuses on an example of this, briefly mentioned earlier in this introduction. Osias Martins, one of the wounded survivors, awoke from a nap one day to discover that he had written a prophetic text. Osias's prophecy, like Olina's dream, described the end of the world, projecting an allegorical image that evil was everywhere on earth. Osias, then a militant with the MST, decided to share his prediction with his "friends" and "*companheiros*" because it contained "a lot of reality" that he wanted them to reflect upon. The chapter explores what conditioned Osias's decision to share his text. Beyond Osias's experience as a wounded survivor, three other conditions, explored at various junctures of this book, emerge as determining: first, common Catholicism and its latent allegorical and millenarian features; second, the challenge to Christianity from the MST, whose Marxist pedagogy trains militants to grasp and transform the "real," "material," and "historical" conditions of the landless working class; and third, the mystic of friendship, the will to find unity in others and God. Of these, Osias's encounter with the failure of unity after the MST's powerful initial promise of a new collective was the most devastating. It ultimately led him to reject the land that he had struggled so hard to secure and leave to find another place to settle.

The conclusion reminds us of this book's main lesson: that the ongoing colonization of Brazil's frontiers is not fully conveyed through histories of the present that focus exclusively on human politics, materials, laws, and bodies. On the contrary, my chapters show that common Catholic theologies and relations continue to inspire religious and political movements along the PA-150, animating the dynamics of settlement. Furthermore, the conclusion reflects on how allegory, the mystic of friendship, and the ambivalence toward politics they produce shed light on the rise of the right wing in Brazil. In fact, the success of former president Jair Bolsonaro's anti-state rhetoric is much less surprising if viewed in light of one of my main arguments: that the critique of secular politics and law is not only a recent Evangelical import. Rather, it is part of a long-established tradition of ambivalence in Brazil, connected to historical Catholicism. Yet as this book also shows, the mystic of friendship and the allegorical disposition from which it arises is not perennially conservative. Instead, it is always inherently radical vis-à-vis institutional power. It thus can nurture radical democratic activism as well.

That is why this book, though in the first instance a scholarly endeavor, holds interest for activists, especially in Brazil. Works employing more recognizable critical traditions are evidently useful. But while such studies might be convincing to scholars and to already committed activists, they often only partially translate to the people on the ground whom activists are trying to mobilize.

In fact, well before the rise of a terrifying right wing in Brazil under Bolsonaro, my years of research with the MST showed me what is now increasingly obvious in Brazil and elsewhere: that as cogent and appropriate as the left-wing critiques of inequality might be, they do not always turn into mobilization. And yet, much critical scholarship is presented as if such critique is all that is needed to spark the flame of consciousness and action. *The Mystic of Friendship* argues that activists, especially young activists working on the front lines, need a variety of perspectives to help them relate to the masses whose consciousness they hope to raise. Predominant political theory, while offering important insights, often does not offer a recipe for success in recruiting and mobilizing, especially because it is so focused on transformation, even revolution, that it is often not elaborated in view of apprehending—and learning to address—epistemologies other than its own.

What I mean, in short, is that in addition to conventional critiques of structures of power, we also need relationally informed, ethnographically inspired research that local thinkers and activists can use to better reach their audiences, help harness their political potential, and avoid predictable pitfalls. What this fully implies will become clear, I hope, by the end of this book. For now, suffice it to say that along the PA-150 awareness of the mystic of friendship and of mystic relational dynamics more generally—including their baroque resonances—has something new to teach us not only about religion and politics in settler Amazonia but also about the possibilities for transforming politics more generally.

FIRST VISITATION
Jacundá, Pará, 1985

FIGURE 2. First page of the "History of the Church of the PA-150." São João
Batista Parish Archives, Jacundá, Pará.

HISTORY OF THE CHURCH OF THE PA-150: STRUGGLES, SUFFERING, AND VICTORIES OF A PEOPLE WHO WALK TENACIOUSLY TOWARD LIBERATION

The journey of the Church and the people is one and the same.[1] It is a
history written with sweat, sacrifices, persecutions and martyrdom, in a
cruel battle for land that belongs to God and his children forever.

Today, the 28th day of June of 1985, eve of the feast of Saint Peter, we want to register and plant on this land, on which we built a Church, this testament which is already marked in the memory and veins of the migrant people (*povo retirante*), who conquered this land with heroic tenacity.

It is at the heart of the Amazonian jungle that this people gave birth to life and hope after years of pilgrimage, like Abraham and Moses, in search of the promised land.

In the year of our Lord's grace, 1977, the PA-150 highway ripped through virgin forest, opening places until then unpenetrated, so that the migrants could confront the hard work of clearing and exploring the land of Liberty. This migrant people came principally from the states of the Northeast and also the South with the aim of improving their lives.

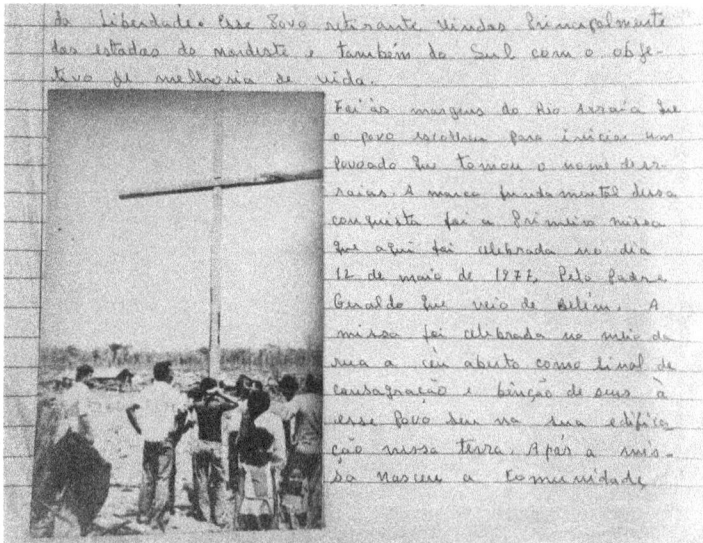

FIGURE 3. Page from "History of the Church of the PA-150." The birth of the town, Arraias, and the first Mass on May 12, 1977. São João Batista Parish Archives, Jacundá, Pará.

It was on the banks of the Arraia River that the people chose to start a settlement that took the name of Arraias. The founding mark of this conquest was the first Mass that was celebrated on the 12th of May of 1977, by Father Geraldo who came from Belém. The Mass was celebrated in the middle of the road under the open sky as a sign of God's consecration and blessing of his people and their edification on earth. After the Mass the community was born, gathering in people's houses, celebrating God's Word, and taking a position in face of the persecutions that had by then already begun.

Sister Dorothy[2] was the first who also arrived here, coming from the PA-70, to sow the first seeds of resistance among the *posseiros* (smallholder claimants) through the creation of the [ecclesial base] communities, in her tireless and happy work, and the *povo* began organizing for various struggles.

In the year 1978, the arrival of new migrants increased greatly and they spread out and set up along the margins of the highway and at the end of August of 1978 the village of Goianésia was born at kilometer 162.

That same year, the conflicts began, because the *grileiros* (wealthy land-grabbers) with their thirst and greediness for land, imposed a whole calvary of persecutions to stop the Children of God from living and staying on the land. . . . The Church of the PA-150 from the beginning stood in solidarity with the poor *posseiros*, taking up their struggles as a demand of the gospel. For this reason she [the Church] was always slandered, persecuted, for example:

Thirty-nine workers were subpoenaed (*intimadas*) to appear in São Miguel de Guamá, the Church accompanied them and the CPT [the Pastoral Land Commission] also offered support through its lawyer and defended the cause of the *posseiros*, which left the *grileiros* filled with hate. It was a trip of 1400 kilometers of dust, sun, and cold nights on the back of a "parrot perch" truck [the famous *caminhão pau de arara*, with a bar in the middle which travelers held onto to steady themselves]. For food there was only farofa [fried manioc flour, often with some protein] but the courage of the *posseiros* with the force of God led us to victory. On the part of the *grileiros* who wanted to take everything, they began the harshest persecutions, using the police, groups of gunmen, surrounding houses at night to kill someone, invading and burning huts, shooting into pots and killing children, and putting fake news in newspapers, slandering pastoral Church agents. But this never made us afraid.

On the 25th of March of 1979, after the celebration of Mass, the community chose a patron saint for Jacundá. All present were unanimous, and Saint John the Baptist was chosen, the great prophet who was not afraid of Herod and offers an example of how we should not be afraid of the Herods of today. . . .

In 1980, the conflicts continued and grew in force, with violence and assassinations. On the 17th of January [sic] the Association for the Defense of United Workers of New Jacundá was created, with the aim of protecting the rights of the smallholders. . . . The newsletter *O Grito do PA-150* ("The Cry of the PA-150") was also born as a tool for denounc-

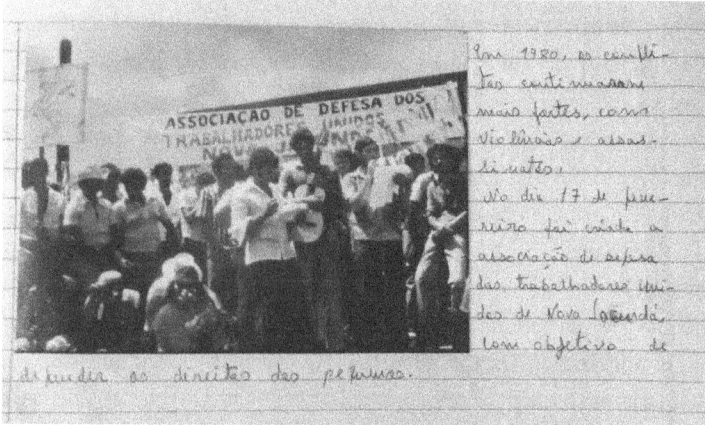

FIGURE 4. Page from "History of the Church of the PA-150." The founding of the Association in Defense of the United Workers of Nova Jacundá. São João Batista Parish Archives, Jacundá, Pará.

FIGURE 5. Page from "History of the Church of the PA-150." The text reads, "The pilgrims walk with firmness and hope to conquer the promised land. On the pilgrimage we regularly stop to reflect on God's word and our own situations today." São João Batista Parish Archives, Jacundá, Pará.

ing injustice. On the 25th day of July [1980], once again, the day of the
worker was commemorated and this time it was very moving, as the
whole Diocese of Marabá came, [including] Dom Alano, inseparable
brother and *companheiro* in the struggle . . . who [used] his prophetic
gift . . . to denounce . . . all the violence directed at the rural workers . . .
(Livro Tombo 1–4, 8–10).

Many pages later, after covering other major events, violent crimes,
public denunciations, and celebrations along the PA-150, a new section
begins: "Signs of Resurrection in the Journey of the People of the PA-150."
Compared to the previous section of the testament, this contains relatively
little description, but its first seven photographs are dedicated to the first
three Pilgrimages of Liberation.

01

GOIANÉSIA DO PARÁ

The Recurrence of Allegory

I started thinking seriously about Catholicism in Pará and how it was entwined with the mystic of friendship when Aurora invited me to go on a pilgrimage. We had met for our usual Brazil-nut shake on São Francisco Plaza in Marabá's New City, a few neighborhoods away from our houses. It was September, the hottest month of the year—even hotter than August, the month of controlled forest-burning that leaves the city air hazy.[1] Now, through the butter-colored streetlights, I could see that the plaza was busy (*agitado*), both because it was a Saturday night during election season and because it was so hot, around 30°C. I saw couples young and old milling about, groups of teenagers clustering in corners, children chasing each other under the eyes of their parents or grandparents. Most people were there to see and be seen and to enjoy the night air, but those with some money consumed snacks or drinks from rickety stalls or meals at the family-friendly restaurants concentrated near the bus stop at the plaza's northeast end. The parish church, St. Francis of Assisi, stood opposite, on the darkened southwest side.

Aurora was one of the first people I had met in the region. She was the best friend of Vanda, a cousin of a Brazilian friend of a friend of mine, who had kindly facilitated my entry into her network upon my arrival. Vanda took me in first during a short visit in December 2002, then again briefly in the twilight of 2003 before I found a base and began full-time fieldwork in 2004. Aurora was an involuntary outsider to the region, as she herself put it, especially compared to other migrants. A single, educated, dark-skinned Black woman from Brazil's Southeast Region in her late thirties, she was different from most migrants, who came from the Northeast, especially from Maranhão and the backlands. She was one of the few people who alerted me to a phenomenon that LaShandra Sullivan, working on another Amazonian frontier, has called "Black invisibility" (Sullivan 2017). Aurora didn't use this term, but she knew the feeling. She made clear that although people of color are visibly the vast majority, most people in the region see Blackness as "other" and something to distance themselves from. Aurora wryly told me how, after she arrived in the late 1980s, people had sometimes stopped her on the street, peered into her face and asked, "are you from Africa?" Some even exclaimed, "you must have lots of money [to be able to travel this far]!" As Aurora noted, this assumption that she was not from Brazil confirmed the existence of racism despite widespread "racial mixture." The general elision of Africanness is also one reason why, she explained, the Movimento Negro in the region never quite got off the ground. Most people, although of African descent, did not see the Black Movement as being about them.

Aurora's almost anthropological perspective on Pará meant that she knew what would be interesting for a researcher to learn. This was one reason she had invited me on the pilgrimage, she explained. She was happy to have the extra company, she said, since she sometimes felt like an outsider, even among friends. But she also thought I would *and should* be interested in this. Religion, after all, was among local residents' most pressing concerns, certainly more than questions of race. The intensity of this interest in religion, especially Catholicism, is why I emphasize the theological layers of common Catholic relations in this chapter and elsewhere in this book. We will see the importance of Catholicism for African diaspora peoples in Pará and Brazil, whether deemed native or colonial, and whether they consider themselves Black or not.[2]

"It is a pilgrimage that began in the 1980s as a protest against a terrible massacre—of two little girls and almost their entire family—by a policeman," Aurora explained. I shook my head at the story; Aurora nodded back. We were both accustomed to accounts of violence. Still, stories of murdered children remained especially devastating. These deaths so upset local residents, Aurora said, that lay members of the Catholic base communities, which gathered to worship and reflect on liberation near the town of Goianésia, soon began walking to the site of the massacre in prayer and protest. And then some people began making vows (*promessas*) to the spirits of the little girls, believing that their innocence and intense suffering positioned them to intercede with God. Aurora didn't know more background than that, but she emphasized that participation in the pilgrimage—the Romaria da Libertação, the Pilgrimage of Liberation—had continued to grow ever since.

Aurora was right; I was intrigued by this regional pilgrimage and began to consider her invitation even more seriously when she explained that a friend, Rosa, had invited her. Rosa, who worked as a cleaning lady at the school where Aurora taught for some years as a substitute teacher, offered to promise the saints on Aurora's behalf that she would make the pilgrimage every year if she found love. All Aurora had to do was join in with Rosa and her other friends and participate in the pilgrimage with faith and prayer.

I was fascinated that Rosa had made a promise for Aurora. "But that is uncommon, no?" I asked.

Aurora tilted her head. "Well, not really, people make *promessas* for others, especially family members, all the time. Rosa started going because her best friend Carmela, also a cleaning lady in the school, made a vow for her!"

"Oh, I see," I said, feeling slow—clearly, I didn't know as much as I should about common Catholicism. "Does everyone promise to go on the *romaria* if they are granted a miracle?" I asked.

"Not necessarily. Technically, vows can offer anything to the saint, though they often include something to bolster the saint's following and visibility," Aurora said. "For example, a supplicant can promise to print saints' images and distribute them. Or, if there is a pilgrimage, like in this case, the supplicant can promise to make the pilgrimage."

At this point, a beat-up black car that had been inching around the plaza blaring campaign jingles finally reached us. Aurora and I had to stop talking, as conversation would be futile until it passed.

I contemplated Aurora's invitation: should I go with her or should I stay focused on studying friendship discourses in the municipal elections? I had been doing the latter for weeks, though I was getting the sense that there was something beyond the politics I was missing—something that gave politics its force. With the campaign jingle blaring at me, my thoughts quickly shifted. I recalled the political march (*passeata*) that had passed through my neighborhood that afternoon. It had been led by Elza Miranda, a candidate for mayor with the Brazilian Social Democrat Party, or PSDB. I had never seen anything like it, though I was told such marches were common fare. In fact, like many other happenings in the "time of politics," as it is called in Brazil, these marches were social events. Locals knew in advance about the *passeata*, and on the designated day they stood outside their houses to meet the candidate and party activists (*militantes*), chatting among their neighbors as they waited. This contact with politicians—the conversation, handshakes, and especially the hugs—apparently made the difference, as one veteran of the neighborhood told me later. "The people here are in such need (*tão carente*)," she said. "It helps to feel that connection, that friendship." I certainly noted the hugs and how a PSDB activist lingered to tell me that Elza was an old and great friend of hers, "a true woman of the countryside."

What impressed me most, however, was the image of the march itself. It was an arresting group meant to inspire others to join. I can still see them now, walking in loose formation behind Elza down our hot and dusty street in their crisp yellow PSDB t-shirts and hats. Some of them brandished flags. I also remember Elza's blonde bob and broad smile, and how she dove into the crowd of onlookers—my neighbors—hugging them while offering political promises and encouraging words.

The experience and image of the *passeata* stayed with me and inspired a series of reflections on Catholicism and Brazilian colonization that helped give shape to this book. As I later discovered, contemporary processions draw from early Portuguese colonial forms, including marches for both God and king that promoted the unity of the empire with the mystical body of Christ (Santos 2005).[3] As I turned processions over in my mind on the plaza that night, I remembered how important they remained in Brazilian public life. As a scholar-in-training I had encountered their significance in Roberto DaMatta's (1991 [1979]) classic *Carnivals, Rogues, and Heroes*, which despite critique[4] continues to influence political anthropology, sociology, and even recent Latin American political discourse (e.g. Lomnitz 1999, 2001; Holston 2008; see below and especially chapter 5). DaMatta shows that processions dramatize and help produce the popular social types that animate Brazilian society: he lists the *malandro* or rogue, the martyr, the ruling hierarchical superior, and most importantly the socially and hierarchically configured person. DaMatta argues that such dramaturgical processions offer insights into what he calls the "Brazilian dilemma": the simultaneous longing for, and ambivalence toward, the rule of egalitarian law. In fact, the kind of socially and hierarchically embedded person celebrated in such processions is challenged, even offended, by the individualist premise of modern law: that all individuals are equal and therefore equally subject to the law.

But then I remembered that for DaMatta, the Brazilian dilemma was captured by the popular phrase "For my friends everything, for my enemies the law." Given what I knew by then—that "no one has friends, only acquaintances"—I realized that the stability of friendship and enmity that DaMatta conveyed was rather simplistic, especially for this corner of Brazil. Did this one-dimensional view have to do, I wondered, with DaMatta's limited attention to Catholicism?[5]

My decision to go with Aurora on that pilgrimage was based on little more than these questions and a growing hunch consolidated by an earlier encounter with Otávio Velho and his brilliant essay, "The Peasant and the Beast" (1995 [1991]).[6] I needed to attend to the connections, distinctions, and overlaps among common Catholicism, friendship, and politics to understand what was shaping the contemporary settlement of the region. The validity of this intuition became clearer while I was on the pilgrimage. Pilgrimage and the vow are among the most pervasive practices in common Catholicism. Both offer insights into how persons see and relate to the world. Specifically, pilgrimage and vows open a window onto the allegorical way of seeing that is at the heart of common Catholicism, a way of divining images to find the good and evil animating persons and relations, including the instabilities of friendship.

The following ethnography of the Romaria da Libertação brings to life this allegorical way of seeing—this practice of divining. I focus especially on the eventful second pilgrimage I made with Aurora's group in 2006, which really threw the mystic of friendship into relief when it became clear that one "friend" of the pilgrims was likely not the person she claimed to be. I also move through the archival traces of the Romaria, which help shed light on the distinctions among common and official Catholicism—especially the ambivalence of official Catholicism toward vow-making and miracles. The archive also contains a story that many pilgrims don't remember now: how liberationist thinking within the Catholic Church, powerful in the region until the late 1980s, initially framed the Romaria as an act of faith and a protest of violence. Finally, I recall the recurrence and transformation of allegory in medieval and early modern Europe and Portuguese America to show how its practice continues to recur in Brazil and southeast Amazonia, powerfully reshaping relations, especially notions of friendship and enmity.

Benjamin's (2019) *Origin* can help shed light here. Certainly, *Origin* points to a modern Christian tradition of reading allegorical images, and to the distinct instability that it can produce. But there are other reasons that make *Origin* relevant here: Benjamin's baroque "political anthropology"— including the tyrant, the martyr, the plotter/rogue, and what we might call the fallen yet always *divining person*—is strikingly similar to the Brazilian typology that DaMatta offers. Although DaMatta neither draws on Benjamin, nor does he discuss allegory or what I am calling the divining person, the resonance of their inventory of characters means that *Origin*, and the baroque, is uniquely relevant to both the study of Brazil and the history of the study of Brazil.[7]

In mentioning how Benjamin elucidates a classic of Brazilian anthropology—which continues to resonate[8]—my aim is not merely to justify more attention to Catholicism, pilgrimage, and allegory in the study of settler Amazonian relations and of Brazil more generally. By this chapter's end, I will show that focusing on friendship with Catholicism in clear view adds another chapter to the critique begun by Benjamin of Carl Schmitt's authoritarian theory in *Political Theology*. In other words, I conclude by showing that the mystic of friendship and allegorical ways of seeing both elucidate life on the PA-150 and outline a potentially emancipatory political disposition—which demonstrates less a stable DaMattian "Brazilian dilemma," than a Northeastern, Paraense, and potentially Brazilian radicalism whose powers have only partially been explored to date.

SETTING OFF, A FIRST IMAGE

We had agreed to meet at "The Six" bus terminal, o seis, at 8:00 a.m. on September 16, the day before the official Romaria, to catch the bus to Goianésia. The station's nickname, "The Six," reflected its point on the highway when "PA-150" still referred to the 190-kilometer highway built in 1977 between Marabá (then kilometer "0") and what became Goianésia—the town whose founding was mentioned in the First Visitation. The Six retained its popular name even after 353 kilometers of highways south of Marabá were added to the PA-150 (in 2010, the latter stretch of highway was federalized and its name changed to BR-155). Another highway that The Six services has always retained its name and composition: the Trans-Amazon Highway (BR-230), the Transamazônica, which intersects with the PA-150 only 240 meters south of The Six station.

I always loved the morning moto-taxi ride to The Six on the Trans-Amazon, especially crossing the bridge over the Itacayunas river. There, I was reminded that I was still in Amazonia: lush greenery hugged a dark river that reflected the dazzling morning sunlight.

Staying straight on the Transamazônica, that is, not turning off to Old Marabá, which had been settled around the turn of the twentieth century, brought us to New Marabá, a 1970s–80s expansion of the city.[9] The commercial buildings along this stretch were typical of cement houses of the region, painted all manner of colors beneath roofs of ruddy clay tiles. The occasional larger and more block-y modern structures also conveyed that Marabá was a key regional city, especially the shopping center "Verdes Mares" (Green Seas) and the buildings of Marabá's Federal University campus.[10]

I liked The Six, too. It might have needed a new paint job, but there was something inviting, even cozy, about it. Nestled between two small hills, the station was a world unto itself: travelers descend into a commercial space with a handful of stores and a corridor of homemade food stalls, all straddled by a semitransparent ceiling that let in a warm light.

As I arrived, I saw Aurora, Rosa, and Carmela, their rayon bags and bundled hammocks stacked on the station's orange plastic benches. We greeted each other with hugs and Rosa brought me up to speed: this trip promised to be exciting on a number of counts.

First, our host for the night, the widower of Carmela's late niece, was throwing a party at his *chacra*, a small farmhouse and garden near the city. The next day, we would wake up around 4:00 a.m. and be driven to the pilgrimage's starting point eight kilometers from the site where the "little saints" Elizabete and Elineuza were killed. Second, Rosa went on, seventeen of us were traveling together (the last time I went we had been only ten). I waved at a few people I recognized, seated nearby. We were still all women, of all ages, except for one ten-year-old boy who was coming with his aunt because he felt an affinity for the little saints, who had helped his cousin recover from an illness.

But the really big news, I was told, was that one of the new pilgrims, Julieta, was the paternal aunt of the little saints. No members of the family, not even the surviving mother, had ever made a public appearance at the pilgrimage. It was *uma bênção* (a blessing) for all of us, Rosa said on introducing me to Julieta.

In her soft high voice, Rosa went on, "And it will be so nice to have at least an image of the little girls! At the moment there is nothing really, just these paintings of two little blonde-haired angels." Rosa was referring to the banner of the little saints made in the 1980s, which used to grace the promotional literature and decorate the stage where Mass is celebrated at the site of the saints' death. I had noticed during the earlier pilgrimage that the image was a typical reflection of colorism, even racism—since the girls in life were almost certainly not blonde.

"But look at these pictures!" Rosa gestured at the photo album Julieta was holding open on her lap. I looked down at a black-and-white photograph of two dark-haired and dark-skinned girls, who appeared to be about four years and eighteen months old, respectively—about the ages of Elizabete and Elineuza when they were killed. "Well, the whole of this picture might

FIGURE 6. Left: The old image of the "Little Saints" used for the *romaria*, from the front page of the flyer sold on-site, which details the murder of the little saints. Right: The back page of the flyer sold on-site, with an old image of the chapel and the tomb.

not do, of course, they *are* completely naked. Are there others?" Rosa asked. "My mother might have some more that my brother sent before they died," Julieta said, talking slowly, looking down and passing her fingers gently over the next photo. "This is the mother," she said. "I met the family together only once. See how pretty she was?" She showed a picture of a young woman with long black hair, pale skin and bright red lipstick. "We were living outside of Xambioá, Tocantins, and they came to visit. He was a traveling salesman. I had just finished high school and arranged to go visit them in a few months. But when I arrived in Marabá to visit them, I found no one home. I was told by the neighbors what had happened—that they had all been murdered by the side of the road, that the mother had survived to tell the tale, but no one knew where she was now. I grew afraid, and I went quickly back to Xambioá. My mother spoke to his wife once after that, but we were never in touch again."

Julieta's story rang true. Recall that this was before social media, and few people even had cellphones. I had heard many stories of families losing track of each across this enormous country.

It was time to leave. As we embarked, some of us bought snacks from local vendors who were hawking peeled oranges, candies, nuts, and other goods. We were all hoping for an enjoyably swift and uneventful ride. Traveling these roads always came with some degree of apprehension due to the regularity of armed bus robberies. But the little van was full, which meant that our driver would not be tempted to pick up extra passengers on the road, which was apparently when assaults happened. We could almost relax, as we sat in the cool wind blowing hard through the windows.

I settled in next to Aurora, who asked Julieta if she could see the photographs again. Placing the album on her lap, she looked reverently through them. Like Rosa, Aurora was fascinated with the beginning of this new chapter of our collective story. It was as though Julieta and the photos she brought were special signs from God, blessing the pilgrims' physical and spiritual journeys, bringing them closer to the little saints, and making the miracles, the *milagres* they prayed for, more likely.

When we think about pilgrimage, especially in Brazil, the search for miracles is often the first thing that comes to mind. Miracles figure prominently in this chapter, especially since my fellow pilgrims considered one to have brought our group together and made the pilgrimage grow. However, I also hope to broaden this perspective. I show that my fellows' pursuit of miracles, and the vows made to secure them, grew out of the shared Catholic longing for God's help and friendship, which in turn is entwined with understanding life—and the person as well—as a persistent allegory for divine (and possibly evil) action. This divining has two senses: on the one hand it assesses or reveals the always-near-but-not-quite-complete divinity of the person, and on the other it interprets instances, images, of everyday life and ordinary social relations. The presence of Julieta and her photographs in our little group is a case in point: that a relative of the little saints joined us was a sign that our travels were "blessed," as Rosa said. Her statement also conveyed the possibility that the divine was coming closer to the members of our group, guiding and preparing us for the miracles each pilgrim had prayed for.

While any constellation of relationships can be turned into this kind of image, we should not forget their connection to the conventional figurative images and statues to which the faithful pray. In this light, Julieta's own pictures mattered. Indeed, a more accurate image of the little saints, as Rosa later explained, would both improve the aesthetic of the Romaria da Libertação and possibly even make the pilgrims' prayers more effective. Specifically, pilgrims would find it easier to visualize and "attach" themselves to the little saints, while making the sincerity of their faith known.

This process of attachment, *apegar-se* in Portuguese, is key to the making of vows and consolidating human and divine friendship. I had learned about it and its connection to settlers' allegorical lives on the previous pilgrimage, when I asked about how the pilgrimage started. The story I was told also taught me about the differences and overlaps between official and common Catholicism.

THE ROMARIA'S BEGINNINGS AND GROWTH

I vividly remember Rosa telling me about how devotion to the little saints began and grew. We were sitting on the spacious front porch at Olina's. All ten of us traveling that year had come to Olina's by bus from Marabá that day, and by late afternoon we had strung up our hammocks on the covered porch that encircled the house. Rosa and I were sitting on blue plastic-string chairs facing the dusty red town road, which was partially hidden by a white slatted wood fence. During a lull in activity before dinner I asked Rosa about how the pilgrimage began.

R: When these little girls died, there was a woman, her cattle were dying, they brought medicine, they brought a veterinarian, and nothing. And so they say that the woman remembered the little girls, she attached herself to them (*apegou com elas*), by herself, without anyone telling her to. They were innocent children; they had not sinned. In the middle of such a barbarity, of course they were going to be saved. She became attached without out even knowing their names. But she attached herself to them, saying, "help me, my animals are dying . . . every year I will pray a *terço* (a third of a rosary) and I will give a breakfast, or a meal, I will give something to the *povo* (the people of her town)."

A: Was this after the first pilgrimage?

R: It was November, December, some three months had passed [since their deaths]. And she made the promise with great faith, that those children should help her, with God's blessing and pronto! Her animals did not die anymore—not the chickens, the pigs, or the cattle—and so she started milking the cows and began giving it away: milk to people with small children who had no milk. And her animals began to multiply. And the next year it is said that she killed a chicken and her animals went on multiplying and multiplying. And then she began telling people. And then another person made one, another promise, which was validated [with a miracle] and [the saints' following] began to grow. The next year she also killed a pig, and her animals continued to thrive. . . . People told me this, Dona Angela [Dario's wife] who died. She told me that it was her *comadre* (godmother) who made this promise.

Rosa's description is striking for many reasons, not least because she didn't mention, or didn't seem to know about, the first pilgrimage, a spontaneous decision by the community to walk to the site of the little girls' deaths a year after their murders. Perhaps Rosa assumed I knew that story already. She was right, though it wasn't until the next day, my first walk (*caminhada*) with the pilgrims, that I learned more details through "official" materials sold on-site. And here I also began to see the difference between the official and the common Catholic view of pilgrimage—and of miracles. Since the difference between these accounts will be important for my analysis of attachment, let's look first at the official story, as explained in a little flyer sold at the pilgrimage site:

In the early hours of September 17, 1980, Vicente de Pádua Justo, together with his wife, Delcimar, their two children Elizabete, four years old, and Elineuza, one year and four months, and a friend of the family known as François, were victims of a terrible crime. Delcimar survived the slaughter and revealed in detail the cruelties committed.

Vicente was a traveling salesman and was bringing merchandise to sell at an agricultural fair. He was traveling with his family in his own vehicle. During the trip, Vicente stopped to give assistance to another vehicle, apparently broken down, where the policeman Aragão was with another two men. Aragão asked for a tool from Vicente and when he went to get it he was shot dead. Next, Aragão also killed François. The bodies were thrown on the side of the road, in the brush.

Delcimar and her two daughters were taken farther on, some eight kilometers from Goianésia. She was traveling with Aragão. Her two daughters were traveling in the other vehicle [that had been stolen from the family], right behind them, with the two other men. When they stopped, Aragão went to get Elineuza and brought her in front of their mother. After he went to get Elizabete, who was learning to walk. He brought the girl in his arms. The men raped the mother and stabbed the little girls in front of her. As Elineuza was still moving, Aragão stabbed her again, this time the knife passing through her whole body until its point entered the ground. Delcimar was stabbed fifteen times. They then threw the three, who they considered dead, into a fire and abandoned the scene. By a miracle, the mother survived to denounce the terrible facts.

One year later, on the 17th of September, more than 300 people got together to celebrate a Mass where the slaughter occurred. Since then, every year pilgrimages depart from various cities. Thousands of pilgrims, many dressed for penance, bring crosses and objects that commemorate the graces received by the intercession of the Little Saints. [All] are welcomed by the population of Goianésia. The Pilgrimage of Liberation is a manifestation of faith of the people who believe in life and can sing, as in the first Letter of Saint Paul to the Corinthians: "'Death has been swallowed by victory. Death, where is your victory?' Thanks be given to God, who gives us victory by means of our Lord Jesus Christ. Thus, dear brothers, be firm, constant; continually make progress in the work of the Lord, knowing that your weariness is not useless in the Lord" (15,54s) (Romaria da Libertação 2004).

This horrific account of rape and murder always gives pause. Although it was already a period marred by violence, as described in the First Visitation, one can understand the local anger when the story came out—and an eventual need to do something to mark this terrible event. The indiscriminate murder of a whole family by a former policeman, and especially the vicious treatment of a mother and her two children, were clearly both terrifying and enraging.

These two accounts of the start of the pilgrimage draw attention for another reason: they show different approaches to vows and miracles. While Rosa and her friends called the effects of their attachments and vows "miracles," the church account refers merely to the "graces received by the intercession of the Little Saints." The church account notably does not even mention a "vow" and uses the word "miracle" only once, with reference to the survival of Elizabete and Elineuza's mother.

The differences are significant. Grace implies God's "free giving," which is how Dona Delma, a lay Romaria organizer in her fifties, explained it when I spoke to her later at her home. In contrast to the unconditional generosity of divine giving, Delma said as she relaxed into her bright blue sofa, vows made in hopes of receiving miracles recalled a transactional "relationship of exchange" with the divine. An aversion to exchange is why the church discourages practicing faith in these terms, whether with the little saints or otherwise. "Our priest does not really like it," Delma said with finality. Delma herself had never made a vow, although she admitted that this was a very common way of praying among her fellow Catholics well beyond the Romaria—and that many believed in its effectiveness. Indeed, she added, careful of what she left on the record, she was sure that if someone made a vow with sincere faith to the little saints it would be "validated."

What Delma didn't mention was the other reason that the church might be loath to refer to "miracles" in the context of the Romaria. Miracles are officially only sanctioned by the Catholic Church after investigations prove that the phenomenon in question is "beyond the order of all created nature." This is a quote from Thomas Aquinas, who nevertheless had a broader understanding of miracles than what miracles have become since David Hume: mere "residue . . . after scientific explanation had whittled away all that it could" (Sallnow 1987, 54). While Delma did not cite Aquinas or Hume, she knew that the miracles celebrated by common Catholics in Brazil are often rather more mundane than miracles should be. Rosa's account of the first miracle, in which the little saints saved the woman's animals from whatever was plaguing them, is an example. This miracle, like others my pilgrimage group talked about, had no one concerned as to whether or not the outcome had a scientific explanation. The point was that a request for divine help had been made with a sincere attachment and a vow—and the vow had been heard and validated by the divine.

If the discourse on vows and miracles marks one difference between common and official Catholicism, positions on pilgrimage mark another. The Catholic Church has long had an ambivalent relationship to pilgrimage, especially after the Reformation, both because of the connection between pilgrimage, vows, and miracle-seeking and because of its independent, non-institutional, sometimes even profane character.[11] Pilgrimage nevertheless was a popular form of worship in medieval and early modern Europe, and it came with the Portuguese to the Americas, where, as I noted in the introduction, few of the Tridentine reforms were instituted until the twentieth century. Today, like vows and miracles, pilgrimage remains a traditional pillar of Brazilian common Catholicism, and small shrines to local saints dot the country.[12] There are also major shrines across Brazil that draw many thousands of faithful each year (Steil 1996).[13]

Although it is useful to have a sense of the differences between official and common Catholicism—and that the church hierarchy tries to guide and control where possible what its flock does—of course there is no strict division between them. In fact, there wouldn't be one without the other, and they certainly overlap. One site of overlap is in allegorical ways of divining human lives as the work of God's friendship and love.

ALLEGORICAL LIVES

———————

To understand my fellow pilgrims' allegorical lives and the connections between allegory and the mystic of friendship, let us first examine the practice of attachment. Rosa used "attachment," derived from the Portuguese verb *apegar-se*, to describe the origins of the pilgrimage. She said that the first supplicant "remembered the little girls, she attached herself to them (*apegou com elas*), by herself, without anyone telling her to." Everyone I spoke with used *apegar-se* to describe the act of promise-making (a usage that extends beyond Pará; see Menezes 2004). I asked Rosa what *apegar* meant, and she first responded that it meant "to ask." In common Portuguese usage, however, it means to become emotionally attached to a person, to feel affection for, to secure oneself to, or to unite with someone or something. When I inquired about the emotional and unifying connotations of the word, Rosa was quick to answer: "Yes! To join with the heart. Ask with faith first of all in God and then in the [little saints]." She further explained, "You have to *feel* that faith inside when you attach yourself, otherwise you aren't in real union (*união*), and it doesn't work." Many other pilgrims echoed this. They also reiterated that when walking on the pilgrimage they tried to stay in constant contact with God and the little saints, in hope that the promises they made for themselves, for family members, and for friends would be borne out.

What this implies, first, is that making and keeping vows activates and enacts a certain unity and friendship with the divine, which includes intimate, affective connection. The connection is intimate not only because it implies feelings of closeness, but also because it is an internal, almost somatic process. You approximate and attach yourself to "God first and then the little saints," as Rosa explained, and then ask with faith from deep *inside* the heart, so that the truth of your unity with the divine will be recognized and reciprocated in the form of help. Josefa, who joined us while Rosa was explaining attachment to me, described her motive for participating in the pilgrimage: "I always seek ways to know myself better. Don't we lack knowledge of ourselves? When we ask and wait, we can hear the voice of God, he cures us, he is our internal mystery, our best friend. He always helps us for our own good." Josefa's pilgrimage, then, wasn't only a search for a miracle; it was also a way to better know herself and God. Josefa expressed what many other interlocutors would corroborate: humans' *primary friendship* is with the divine. This is the case not only because God always helps but also because God has access to and even resides in our interiority. If we are patient, we can come to know this and become one with it, and then miracles can happen.

This interior divinity, which as we will see later can also become diabolical, is one reason we can speak of the "divining persons" of common Catholicism. That is, Catholics are always potentially animated by supernatural forces, though hopefully good and Godly ones. The other reason to speak of divining persons is because Catholics are always divining the world, reading divine signs in the constellations of relations around them—which I have been calling images. But to fully understand how common Catholics lead allegorical lives, it will help to explore further the vows and miracles, the divine and human friendships, that brought my pilgrimage group together.

Rosa described the constitution of our pilgrimage group this way: Sofia, Angela's mother, had been at her *comadre*'s prayer feasts from the beginning. Although Sofia had never made a promise to the little saints, over time she met many people who had, especially in cases that concerned children, and their promises had been validated with miracles, too. In 1990, when Sofia discovered that her niece Carmela was concerned by a strange mark on her daughter's leg, she urged her to make a promise to the little saints as well.

Carmela herself jumped in at this point and elaborated further: she had promised the little saints that if her daughter was healed by the treatment that she was receiving, she would make the pilgrimage every year for the rest of her life. "That was how I began participating in the pilgrimage," Carmela affirmed, "and my four children grew up healthy." From the time of her first vow, Carmela had made six promises for others. Only one of these was for a family member: her granddaughter, who began suffering convulsions in her seventh month of pregnancy. Both mother and child survived.

One of the friends for whom Carmela made a promise was Rosa, when she broke her leg in 1998. After healing perfectly Rosa became a firm believer in the little saints and began to accompany Carmela on the pilgrimage every year. Rosa subsequently made four promises for others, one of which was for Josefa to participate in the pilgrimage in exchange for a cure for her general weakness and vascular problems. When I met Josefa, she was in her early sixties, like Rosa and Carmela, and had children and grandchildren. Josefa was a Spiritist and vendor of lottery tickets, originally from the Brazilian state of Piauí. She had also been the prayer healer (*rezadeira*) for Carmela's father when he was alive. Besides Josefa, Aurora was the only other one of Rosa's promisees who made the pilgrimage in the years that I went. The others who had joined us were either friends or relatives to Carmela or Rosa, and not all of them had made promises. Some were hoping to find love, like Aurora, or a new job, or a cure for illness. Or, like the woman whose husband had been in a land occupation further down the PA-150, they were seeking protection from a dangerous situation (for more on land occupations, see chapter 5).

This brings us to a crucial detail: miracles often happen because God intervenes through webs of relationships. For example, the right doctor can be a *part* of the miracle that saves a life; encountering the right employer can help you afford that cement house; finding a husband involves meeting the right person at the right time. This means that God works miracles not just through one person who made a promise but through many people. God's capacity to intervene in human lives is why human worlds and relationships are allegories of divine action and divine friendship. Still, it is important to remember that outside of the promise-making context it is not always easy to read allegorical images, especially when what happens is not good. At that point the question of evil arises, which I will return to after expanding a bit more on allegory.

If the common Catholic miracle seems to "lack orthodoxy" today, this is not the case with the more general practice of allegory, of which miracles are a part. The Catholic Church has long cultivated allegorical thinking. For example, earlier I mentioned the importance of allegory in medieval Europe and how attention to allegory began to change and intensify in the wake of the distinction made around the mid-twelfth century between the *corpus mysticum*—a unified church and community—and the Eucharist, newly designated as the *corpus verum* or "real body." Allegory transformed again after absorbing other shocks to the mystical body of the church: the Reformation and the colonization of the New World. Now many mystical bodies—especially of the church and growing empires—were considered to be increasingly under threat, whether from heretical Protestants or a proliferation of other evils, especially in the colonies. The persistent specter of enemies, of evil, is why in Portuguese America all public forms of devotion, especially public processions like pilgrimages, were meant to both really and allegorically reinforce the "mystical connection"—the friendship and unity—among king, kingdom, subject, church, and Christ (Santos 2005).

Still, though mystical-body theology resonates in contemporary settler Amazonia, it has not gone unchanged. In the introduction I already offered an example of how the mystical body—and allegorical ways of seeing—were given fresh incarnations in the early twentieth century. The PA-150 was built many years afterward, however, by which time a postconciliar Catholicism was taking shape that soon morphed into a powerful new theology: liberationism. Liberationism distinguished itself by embracing solidarity with the poor and speaking of a new spirituality grounded in political and material liberation. Although liberationism was trying to modernize Catholicism in the spirit of Vatican II, it retained traditional Catholic forms, especially allegory and invocations of unity.

I will address liberationism at length in chapter 4, but it is worth pausing briefly on it here, both because of the liberationist origins of the pilgrimage and because liberationism's allegories were assimilated by common Catholics. That is, liberationism continued to shape understandings of human relationships, especially friendship.

LIBERATIONIST ALLEGORIES

The First Visitation, with its account of the migrant struggle for land and liberation on the PA-150, was clearly written in a liberationist key. When I first read it, however, I found it odd that the Romaria da Libertação didn't appear more centrally, especially given the size of this pilgrimage by the mid-2000s when I first went. At the time, people said that some ten thousand pilgrims participated. But once I started working through the slim archive of the Romaria, composed of a stack of newspaper clippings and four typed and hand-drawn newsletters (1983–86), I realized that the testament had been written in June 1985, when the Romaria had occurred formally only twice—and when no one knew its future. When people walked to the site of the children's death for the first time in September 1981, it had been a spontaneous, informal visit. In 1983, the first formal pilgrimage was planned well in advance of its September date and, as the second newsletter of the Romaria noted, "no one thought it would happen again" (Romaria da Libertação 1984, 2). The 1984 newsletter further explained that the Romaria was planned to honor the 1983 Fraternity Campaign against violence, inspiring the walk "to the tomb of the stabbed and burned little girls, Elizabete and Elineuza" (Romaria da Libertação 1983, 2). The year 1983 was also significant as "the Holy Year of the Resurrection of Jesus, which happened 1950 years ago" (Romaria da Libertação 1984, 2). This jubilee year was a time when many Catholics went on pilgrimage to Rome. The communities of the PA-150

FIGURE 7. First and second covers of the Newsletter of the Pilgrimage of Liberation. Santa Maria Parish Archives, Goianésia, Pará.

therefore considered themselves to be joining those pilgrims "to bring the Reign of God to earth, in Peace, in Justice, and in Fraternity" (Romaria da Libertação 1984, 2). The call of the communities to repeat this pilgrimage again in September 1984 came as a surprise.

This account of the Romaria's founding was news to me when I read it. Regular pilgrims like Rosa, Carmela, and Aurora, who were not active members of the Goianésia church community, had only a vague sense of the church's role in formally catalyzing the pilgrimage in 1983. Moreover, most pilgrims did not know that the church's criticism of the violence of those years reflected the "liberationist" theological trend predominant in Brazil at the time.

Of course, my interlocutors were familiar with the allegorical images the church employed to inspire struggles in the 1970s and 1980s—especially the image that appears in the First Visitation of the "people of God" crossing the desert in search of the promised land. Such images are no longer invoked much by the church or by contemporary pilgrims. But regardless of changing official church discourse, there are clear resonances among common Catholic pilgrims' allegorical ways of seeing in the 1980s and today, and they have similar relational implications.

One example of how the 1980s resonates with today is the 1984 "Message of Thanks" from a pilgrim named Maria Santa:

> I am thankful for the long journey, for so many calloused feet . . . for so many ways that you [all] had to show your love. . . . I am proud of so many friendships (*amizades*), I wax poetic (*fico prosa*) . . . with respect to that. Because one of the most beautiful things is that God evidently doesn't intend for all of us to be rich or powerful or big (*grande*), but he truly intends for us all to be united and friends. I thank God and I thank all the people [here]. . . . I am thankful for the love of a great love (Romaria da Libertação 1984, 5).

Second, a 1983 letter from the community of Kilometer 18, though more overtly liberationist in tone, also echoes in the thinking of contemporary residents of the PA-150—and is similarly allegorical:

> Our brothers by love, the universe is calling out, crying, yelling and the earth groans because this land drank your blood spilled by the assassins. Many of these live among us with faces like little saints, isn't it so? They are nothing less than the ancient Lucifer and the ancient serpent.
>
> Our pilgrim *companheiros*, it is hard to say everything that we feel. But what crucifies us most are facts like this: of the death of Elizabeth and Elineuza. These innocent martyred girls, are a case that has entered our hearts and the hearts of all Christian communities (Romaria da Libertação 1983, 6).

Taken together, these letters[14] show the allegorical underpinnings of both sides of what I am calling the mystic of friendship: both the profound longing for friendship along with the sense that it is often difficult or impossible to identify the divisive evil among us. The latter is clearly referenced in the second letter, through the image invoking evil people with "faces like saints." If biblical references to Lucifer and the serpent are heard less often among common Catholics today (people prefer the more colloquial "devil," "evil," or even "snake"), this will to friendship coupled with a sense of uncertainty about it continues to resound in contemporary reflections that I encountered along the highway. As Maria Santa's message suggests, friendship is an accomplishment, and something to be proud of when there is success. As we will see, this same unity was sought, but imperfectly achieved, on the pilgrimage that I made in 2006 with Aurora, Rosa, Carmela, and others.

THE ROMARIA DA LIBERTAÇÃO

On the bus to Goianésia I was reminded that the heat of this September was the worst ever. Some of the pilgrims claimed that they had wanted to use fans for the *first time in their lives* in the evenings as they slept. I didn't argue—I had been mysteriously bedridden for a few days due to the heat and was only just recovering. Looking out of the van window, it was evident that the weather had taken its toll on the landscape, too. Although never an Irish green, the bristly pastures along the highway had yellowed notice-ably since I had last seen them. Everything else was the same: the highway view offered an empty, monotonously undulating landscape mostly devoid of trees, with the occasional blackened Brazil-nut tree stump standing alone in a field, a survival of the slashing and burning required to make pastures for cattle or cultivation. This familiar landscape of Amazonian ranching and farming—which follows most of the PA-150—provoked an equally familiar melancholy. I knew it was a ravaged landscape, a razed forest, as well as a product of land conflicts made especially violent by the rich *grileiros* who drove smallholders off the land to claim ever-larger holdings. A few sawmills still remained along the highway, and they smothered us periodically with a stench that can only be likened to a giant basket of sweaty socks.

After about three hours on the road, we arrived at the Goianésia bus station, composed of a few bus bays covered by a high roof, under which ticket sellers, vendors, and travelers awaited new departures and arrivals. Goianésia is only about a tenth the size of Marabá, and the station is small, its platform only a few steps away from the equally small, closed part of the town market where fish and meat are sold.[15] Nearby, the yellow and orange steeple of the municipality's main Catholic Church rises impressively above the town.

Soon our lift arrived: an old white pickup truck with high guards around its back flatbed. Josefa and I were sent into the cab (I was still a bit weak) with the driver, Edson. The rest stood or sat in the truck's bed. The road was bumpy, especially once the paving stones ended, some way out of the town center. Josefa and I discovered that Edson was not more than thirty and, to our surprise, not a pilgrim. He worked at a local bar and was doing a favor for our host, Dario. But Edson was going to join us at the party that evening and had promised to also drive us to the start of our eight-kilometer walk to the pilgrimage site before sunrise the next day.

Before I had a chance to ask about the party, Josefa piped up: "Many people start out this way, you know, Edson. They offer different kinds of support to pilgrims and then one day, in a moment of difficulty, they remember the little saints and become devotees (*devotos*) themselves." Edson, who seemed very even-keeled, even impassive behind his mirrored wraparound sunglasses, tilted his head, smiled a bit, and replied with a simple assent: "É," keeping his eyes on the road. "In any case," Josefa went on, turning back to me as I tried to readjust myself on the seat we shared, "God is always working so that we take the right path. Life itself is like a pilgrimage, you might face obstacles and get very tired, but with faith, you will reach your goal, God willing (*se Deus quiser*)!" I remembered that this was how Josefa liked to talk—to make insightful pronouncements on spiritual matters. But what she said was not exactly surprising; any of our fellow pilgrims would have agreed and would have been intuitively aware that "life as a pilgrimage" was a historic Catholic image, an allegory.

Moreover, any of our fellow pilgrims would also have known that this image was not necessarily shared by Protestants. The Catholic practice of pilgrimage to saints' shrines was denounced by Brazilian Protestants, who roundly condemned the cult of the saints more generally.[16] Regarding this Protestant opposition, some of my more judicious fellows would say, "There will always be people who oppose you; you just have to learn how to manage that—and not lose your faith. We all believe in the same God."

Although this sounds like a platitude, it is no trivial insight. The need to manage differences was important among Catholics, whether on pilgrimage or not. After all, being in communion or simply "united"—a state of mutual support, sameness of intent, friendship—was an allegorical image of divine presence and will. This means that although Catholics expected divergence, there remained a certain anxiety about it, especially when unity seemed to unravel.

Emphasizing this anxiety around unity does not mean I am recentering the question of conflict, which a generation of pilgrimage scholars did as they tried to counter the romanticism of Victor Turner's *communitas*.[17] Rather, I want to flag how social friction, or "challenges along the path" as Josefa described it, coexists with and even fortifies allegorical readings, redoubling the longing, the *saudade*, for unity. But the converse is true, too. Faith in unity as divine sanction does not do away with unity's mystery, or even with its elusiveness, which can lead to reflections on evil, as we will see.

We finally arrived at Dario's *chacra*, and as we piled out of the truck Josefa and I remembered to thank Edson in advance for the lift he would give us the following morning.

Stiff and a bit dazed from travel, I dropped my things on the porch. Aurora then suggested that we take a quick look around the house. It was a small house made of local wood and clay roof tiles, with a similar layout to others in the region: there were three bedrooms in the back with paneless windows that looked out onto the hills, a small kitchen, and a living room. The only extras were a small gas stove and small mobile stereo—there was no fridge or television. I had never seen a house without a television in Brazil, no matter how poor, though this house probably lacked one because no one lived here continuously to protect its contents. The covered porch was the only architectural feature not entirely common in the Marabá region, though people with the interest and resources sometimes built one.

Dario, the owner, was nowhere to be seen, so we decided to stretch our legs and walk a bit. Unlike other *chacras*, Dario's had no gardens. The surrounding land was hilly and relatively bare except for some low-lying greenery and a few common tall trees, like palm and mango. Everything had yellowed slightly in the heat and had been dulled further by a thin layer of dust.[18] Behind the house was another hill covered in dusty brush, which sloped down to a small pond. There we found Rosa and a few other pilgrims, who told us we could bathe in the pond before dinner.

After we walked back to the house, Carmela introduced us to Dario, his new girlfriend Cornelia, and his talkative eight-year-old daughter Nalia. Both adults were in their forties. "You should go set your hammocks up and take a bit of a rest," Dario said. He took us over to a little house a few meters away, but because all the sleeping spaces had been taken by our fellow pilgrims, he set us up outside, sticking a post into the ground between two trees for our hammocks. I was quite pleased with this arrangement, as was Aurora, until we discovered that the post wobbled whenever either of us moved.

I appreciated the metaphor of the shared moving post, however, and recalled with a chuckle Josefa's warning about the challenges we would face. Before dinner I would be reminded of Josefa's prediction again, when it became evident how pilgrimage, while promoting unity with God and other humans, also generated concerns about disunity.

Pamela, a woman in her forties originally from Maranhão, was given the task of collecting donations from everyone in the party to buy food for dinner. She was a second cousin by marriage to Dario's first wife, the late Angela, who had encouraged Pamela to make a promise. Each of us gave her about three reais (then approximately one dollar), and off she went with Dario and Cornelia to buy food for a typical meal of chicken, potatoes, rice, beans, manioc flour (farinha), and some cabbage and tomatoes for a salad. Upon returning they went straight to the kitchen and gave the food to be prepared to Renata, the cook from last year, who had returned to thank the little saints after they had successfully helped her husband to survive and succeed in his land occupation.

A number of us sat chatting on the porch as we waited for dinner. Speaking in a raspy whisper, Carmela said, "We think that Pamela has kept the change from the food." She allowed her voice to slowly rise. "You don't do that, you are not supposed to profit from others on an occasion like this, we are all supposed to be *united*." The specter of disunity was, in this case, soon dispelled. Pamela had given the change to Dario and Cornelia, which we all approved.

We ate sitting where we could, on chairs, stools, tree stumps, or resting on the house walls. Once many paper plates had been emptied, Dario rubbed his hands together, proclaimed that the party was about to begin, and disappeared. He reappeared on the bed of a black pickup truck parked next to the house, where he was connecting his stereo to a large amplifier. Once connected, he let the music rip. And from that moment on, Brazilian music, like *brega*, *forró*, and *música sertaneja*, popular among Amazonians and Northeasterners, was played at such high volume that each bass note reverberated through my chest.[19] It seemed that the party was more for the young men like Edson who, although not participating in the pilgrimage, had been arriving since after dinner to drink. Conversation was out of the question.

Our group of mostly middle-aged women was surprised and disappointed. For a while we sat around near the house, smiling and tapping our feet, but despite the high volume the energy was low. Eventually many of the young men left to go to a small rickety bar, nothing more than a one-room wood shack, a few minutes' walk from the house. I went to take a peek and soon left, finding it no better for conversation than Dario's, for the music was just as loud and everyone seemed glued to a large television playing DVDs of Brazilian country duets. Carmela walked back with me, offering me the only conversation I'd had since the party had started. "Well," she said as we stepped carefully along the dusty path in the gathering dark, "Here we are, all of this ba-ba-ba is a bit much, no? Some partying is good, but we should be more reflective, we are on a spiritual journey. . . ." She stopped herself, clearly not wanting to say anything specific about our host, and waved her hand at me: "Anyhow, get some rest and strength for tomorrow." Despite her restraint, it was obvious that she was a bit irritated. Yet she wasn't quite shocked. Rather, she conveyed the sense that you had to resign yourself to some mixture of the sacred and the profane. Not only were most of the young men at the party not pilgrims—so one couldn't expect reverence from them—but people in Brazil are used to such blurring, as other scholars have noted (Fernandes 1982; Maués 1995). In any case, although my fellow pilgrims were disappointed by the profane affronts to the sacred nature of our journey, it didn't amount to an outrage or *mal* (bad or evil), as Pamela having kept the change would have done.

Other disappointments the next day would provide opportunities to further reflect on the "meaning" of what was happening—was it evil?

SPECTERS OF EVIL

It felt like I had only lain in my hammock for a few minutes before we were wakened to prepare for departure. I must have slept, though, because when I got up the music was no longer on, just ringing in my ears.

After a light breakfast of coffee and steamed rice bread (locally called *cous cous*) we were ready to go. But no one was there to take us. Where was Edson? We waited and waited. Dario and Cornelia were still sleeping, so we could not ask them. Although the clouds were low—it was a "smothered day" (*um dia abafado*), as locals call it—we could tell that it was after 5:00 a.m., and the sun had risen. Carmela stiffened. "OK, that's it, this man isn't coming. If we keep waiting here, we will never get there! Let's go!" That presented us with two new challenges: a much longer walk to the site *and* carrying our bags.

We set off. Yellowed and dust-covered scrub hugged the sides of the unpaved road, which stretched out far and red before us under thick gray clouds. It was slightly cool, enough so that a number of us still long-sleeved shirts and closed shoes, although many still wore their Havaiianas, literally "Hawaiians," the most famous flip-flop brand in Brazil. I wondered how many hours would this add to our walk. I didn't ask, but just hoped the sun would stay behind clouds until we made it there. Josefa came up to me and asked, "Do you know what this means?" I shook my head. "Well, we never know for sure, except when God speaks directly to us. Which he does sometimes. But we often just have to decipher events. They are messages, you know." Carmela walked up beside us with another pilgrim, Maria Antonia. "I am talking to Ashley here about what this all means," Josefa said, smiling.

"Well, don't talk too much; it means that we have to keep walking!" Carmela replied brusquely. "That is so (*é mesmo*)!" said Antonia. Neither Carmela nor Antonia said anything more, but they stayed close to listen. "You see, they also know what this means," Josefa said. "We must keep walking. It was designed for all of us here [as a test and an opportunity], especially those of us who made promises, to show our devotion, to demonstrate our faith that God first and then the little saints will help us. God made that man [Edson] stay away to remind us that we will always encounter people who are not good or not doing things right, who want to stop us from achieving our objectives."

"That's right! (*com certeza*)," Aurora sidled up to add, while Antonia turned her head to say, "It means we must keep going, there is much still to be done," and Josefa added, "And we must stay close to those good people (*povo do bem*) whom God brings to us."

That kept me thinking as I walked. Taking Edson's failure and its consequences as an image, Josefa had expanded on what she had said to me in the truck: challenges, including evidence of human divisiveness, although not good, should be read positively as divinely crafted opportunities to seek further unity. Still, when she hinted that Edson had not done right, she did not completely exclude reflections on evil, either.

Pilgrims, and other people I spoke with along the PA-150 generally, did not talk obsessively about evil or the devil. In fact, some avoided it because even saying the devil's name might conjure his presence, as we will see with Mona in chapter 6. Still, it never seemed too far from people's minds, especially in the context of this particular pilgrimage, whose prelude, most would agree, was a murder of diabolical proportions. As I walked, I remembered a discussion I had with Carmela after my last pilgrimage about bad spirits:

> Some good souls have died, my daughter, but a bad spirit doesn't help anyone, only does evil. They say that whoever was bad on earth will always be bad. I think I agree, if you are a bad person, when you die you will be the same. You will go about tempting people, leaning (*encostando*) on them, entering them if you can, to make them do bad things. Hell is here on earth itself. Here with us! When one person needlessly kills another, is this not Satan (*Satanás*)? My daughter, right here in Marabá, there was a man, Sebastião, he used to throw children up in the air and let them fall on the point of a knife. Is this a person? He was taken prisoner in Belém and died little by little. And the one who killed the [little saints] lived right over here in Cabelo Seco [a neighborhood of Old Marabá] for a time.

Here, Carmela was categorical: bad souls and spirits, here in "hell on earth," have interpersonal effects. Drawing on idioms often associated today with Afro-Brazilian and Kardecian Spiritism[20]—but not alien to Catholicism or new charismatic Christianities—spirits "tempt" humans by leaning on them, influencing them, or entering them. The verb *tentar*, which means literally "to tempt," refers not necessarily to the temptation to "sin" in a strict sense (a concept I found was rarely used in everyday conversation),[21] but the temptation to do things improper or abhorrent to good, sociable persons. Carmela's question about Sebastião, the man who killed children, is telling in this regard: "Is this a person? Is this not Satan?" The personhood of anyone who commits unnecessary violence is dubious; any person who is successfully tempted, Carmela suggested, abandons their divine nature, their appropriate personhood, and is transformed into an evil "other"—at least temporarily. This is where the everyday idiom of committing a *besteira*, a bestial act, comes from, especially when it is used to describe a person saying or doing something violent, though *besteira* is also commonly used to describe something stupid. In other words, in everyday life people can be quickly transformed into the beast.

After some two hours of walking, and fearing that we would miss the Mass, we decided to flag down lifts. Aurora and I hopped in with a nice man who was helping to set up the site for the day. Carmela and Julieta joined us.

It was early, thankfully. Still, as we neared the site, the density of pilgrims was rapidly increasing. Their vows were made visible in various ways: some wore smocks of brown or white; some carried stones; others bore crosses; others still carried their children, dolls, children's clothes, flowers or other objects, like wooden legs, arms, heads, hearts and other sculptures (ex votos) that represented their validated vows and their relationship(s) to the divine.

From the advancing car, the shrine's thin cross became visible above the thickening crowds; then the tomb came into view. The tomb, in the middle of a dusty field beside the highway, was surrounded by a small fence. Pilgrims crowded in close; they were each waiting for a chance to touch the cross and directly offer their prayers and their gifts to the little saints and to God. Two assistants accepted whatever the pilgrims handed over the fence—flowers, plastic dolls, wooden ex votos representing miracles received—and stacked them on the coffin, which was raised on a foundation of steps already covered with offerings. Some way off from the tomb to the right, the smell of wax thickened the air. Pilgrims were praying and lighting candles, often burning whole boxes of candles at once, which blackened the shrine walls and left ash and other remains on the adjacent grounds.

FIGURE 8. Pilgrims burning candles and honoring their vows. Photo: Ashley Lebner.

FIGURE 9. The chapel of Santa Elizabete and Santa Elineuza, 2004. Photo: Ashley Lebner.

Only three more areas of activity were evident on the otherwise flat and condensed site, which covered no more than an acre or two. Stalls and ambling vendors crowded close to the road, selling drinks, food and trinkets like keychains, t-shirts, and other objects depicting images of the little saints as blonde angels. Plywood latrines had been placed at the back of the site.

At the site's center, between the tomb to the right and the newly painted

FIGURE 10. Ex votos inside the chapel, marking the miracles received from the little saints. Photo: Ashley Lebner.

pastel shrine to the left,[22] was a wood and aluminum-covered stage where the bishop and priest would celebrate Mass. A banner painted with the blonde images of the little saints hung in front of the stage. A children's photographer was making his rounds with a stuffed polka-dot pony.

Sometime after we arrived, the official *romaria* appeared, with a priest leading a procession of the faithful carrying an image of the little saints. Then the bishop of Marabá,[23] Giuseppe (José) Foralosso, took the stage to celebrate Mass. He employed a measured tone and recalled the importance of family, of respect for children, and of the need for continued struggle against violence. After his homily, he said the Eucharistic prayers, and then lay attendants waved tall white flags above the crowd, announcing communion wafers (without wine) accompanied by a hymn, "Vamos Comulgar" ("Let's Take Communion"), led by *comunidade* leaders onstage.

After this the local priest gave a sermon of some twenty-five minutes, echoing the themes set out by the bishop, and ended with an invitation to the thousands present not just to participate in pilgrimage "and one-day celebrations," but to worship at church regularly. By the close of the ceremony, no pilgrims had been invited on stage to discuss popular miracles, which had apparently been the norm the previous seven years. Still, there was going to be a special story on this occasion, an invitation to our own Julieta! The priest called her to come onstage and speak to the crowd as the aunt of the little girls! Unbeknownst to me, Carmela had taken Julieta to see the priest after we arrived on-site, and apparently she had agreed to say something to the crowd. Everyone in our group was excited to see what she would say, especially me. I hadn't been able to talk to her the previous evening, given all the blaring party music.

The priest called out for Julieta a few times, introducing her as the aunt of the little saints. But to everyone's surprise, he received no response. A low hum rippled through the crowd as we waited, but after a time he was forced to move on. To change the mood, the musicians decided to play one of the most popular hymns of the pilgrimage, "In the 1980s." Aurora and I looked at each other in concerned astonishment, then over at Rosa and Carmela, who looked worriedly back at us. Julieta was nowhere to be seen. The Mass was at its end and soon we would all make our ways back, grabbing lifts where we could. In the meantime, we sang along:

1. In the '80s two children were martyred.
And today I spill my blood and sweat,
Your death seems like my life.

**Refrain: O saintly children bless these gifts that are on the table
And sanctify, Saint Elizabete and Saint Elineuza.**

2. Time has passed, on continues our strife
Our routine seems like the cross and your life.

As I read the hymn on the page, I noted with some irony that the lyrics, while drawing attention to the similarity between humans and the divine, also recalled their difference: while they *seemed* the same, human and divine weren't *quite* the same. This deceptive similarity—humans who weren't quite one with the divine, though they were supposed to be—carried the sense that Julieta's disappearance had left with us as well. We realized that she might not be quite what, or who, she was supposed to be.

THE MYSTIC OF FRIENDSHIP

_____

I did not travel back to Marabá with my fellow pilgrims. I stayed on in Goianésia to visit and do some interviews. But immediately upon my return to Marabá some days later, I called Aurora. She hadn't traveled back with the women either, I was surprised to hear. "What did you think about Julieta?" I asked.

"Well, it was very strange," she said.

"Do you think she was lying about being a relative?" I asked.

"I mean, it is possible, everything is possible in this-here Marabá," she responded. "Carmela will surely have something to say about it, she often reads things—remember how Rosa chastised her for worrying about getting punished (by God or the saints) for not walking the whole way? But then again, she might not say much for that very reason—she doesn't want to be criticized." I remembered what Carmela had said, and thought it was a fascinating example of how the church's campaigns to root out common Catholic "superstitions" had been going on for centuries with only relative success.

Days later, I went to visit Rosa, Josefa, and Carmela, who were all neighbors, in hopes of understanding more about what had happened with Julieta. The women all lived across town in New Marabá, in a neighborhood as poor and as peripheral as mine on the edge of "New City." I talked to Rosa first, and then with Rosa and Josefa in the latter's festively colored and decorated wooden house, which contrasted with the sparseness of Carmela's and Rosa's cement houses. I brought up the topic of Julieta carefully—much more so than I had with Aurora. They responded carefully in turn, saying they found it comprehensible enough. "She said she was scared," Rosa said, shrugging and stopping there, though not looking entirely at peace. Josefa's and Rosa's responses were strangely measured, unconvinced even. Then it hit me: they were using the evasive speech that people in this region deployed when they wanted to imply a degree of suspicion without fully articulating it. Of course this was all very strange. But I still had to try to talk to Julieta. When we had finished our discussion, they took me over to her house.

She invited us into a recently built front yard covered in sparkling tiles and offered us green plastic monobloc garden chairs. Her house looked more affluent, but she did not invite us inside—not that we expected that. As we began to talk, she seemed struck by a fear that she barely managed to control. She answered my questions in succinct phrases, speaking slowly and almost in a whisper. Maybe the tape recorder was inspiring this semi-paralysis, but judging by the looks on Rosa and Josefa's faces, Julieta was making everyone else uncomfortable, too. And so we all sat around for a bit with tentative, closed-lipped smiles. Our discussion revealed little. "I just couldn't go up there," she repeated a few times. I didn't press, and I soon ended the interview, to everyone's relief. Rosa and Josefa then took me to Carmela's house—she was only then returning from her own *chacra* outside of Marabá—and Rosa and Josefa went back to their daily tasks. Rosa had spent nearly half a day with me and had to prepare dinner for her husband. Josefa had to contact the lottery managers.

Carmela did not elaborate much about Julieta either. They had only recently met: "What did we really know about her?" Carmela asked. "She wasn't even really a friend," I said. While Carmela agreed cautiously, I soon realized how the mystery of Julieta was already assimilated to the broader mystic of friendship that I had been tracking. Carmela kept talking about friendship when I asked her to elaborate:

c: A friend is, I don't know. A friend is a person who helps me, who I like, I don't wish ill for. [Yet] I don't know if he does not wish me ill because the heart of another is land that nobody walks, right? Sometimes I know that I don't wish [him ill] and he wishes [me ill]. But I know that I don't wish [ill] for him. . . . I think he is my friend but I don't know if people have friends. The word could even be wrong. I think that he is but maybe he isn't. *Minha filha* (my daughter), even the clothes you wear aren't your friends. . . . Our friend is only him up there [she pointed to the sky]. . . . Everywhere I go people say that we don't have friends, only acquaintances.

a: But Rosa is your friend?

c: I consider her a friend, but I don't know if she is. I cannot guarantee that she is.

a: But it has been how many years, twenty years that you are friends!

c: Twenty-four years.

a: And you see each other [almost] every day, and even then. . . .

c: I consider her a friend, but I don't know if she is. I don't wish her ill, in no way. I only wish her well. I know that she doesn't wish me ill, it isn't possible, she is my comadre, the godmother of a child of mine. If she wishes me [ill] I'll pull her ears [chuckles]. But still [now serious] . . . any one of us can, at any moment be influenced by other interests, other forces. We can do things we never thought we could do, how can we know others? We never fully know ourselves. How can we be friends?

Carmela echoed a refrain that I had heard many times before. But here, in the context of a discussion of pilgrimage, its "Catholicity" profoundly struck me. Indeed, the sense of the impossibility of consistently knowing the intentions of others—and thus of ascertaining their friendship—existed in the shadow of a primary friendship with God, who was always acting for people's good. Moreover, Carmela's explanation here, how "any one of us can, in a moment of weakness be influenced by other interests, other forces," also entailed her position on evil, discussed above, which she reiterated later in this conversation: "Bad spirits can lean on, enter, influence the living, and make them do things they might not otherwise do."

In other words, the mystic of friendship, this longing for friendship and a sense of its elusiveness, is entwined with allegory: the sense that God's action in the world, as well as the actions of bad spirits, even the devil, is always happening behind the scenes. Attributing good to God is relatively easy, as we have seen, but when bad things happen, people often wonder about their source. Were they "allowed" by God as punishments, or were they the actions of some evil entity trying to attack God's work? Either way, one conclusion remains the same: faith helps stabilize and even improve relationships, yet the work of faith must continue, since uncertainty always remains.

CONCLUSION

When Aurora and I next met on the plaza, we returned to the subject of Julieta. "Maybe she thought she could gain something from being related to the little girls," Aurora said. "What we know is that she couldn't go through with it, whether she was lying or not."

It must be intimidating to get up in front of thousands of worshippers to declare your kinship to saints, even if you are not there to defraud. As I mentioned earlier, the little saints' mother never publicly went on the pilgrimage, although it is rumored that she went once, in disguise, after the murderer Aragão was shot dead. Although Aragão was sent to prison after the mother survived to tell the tale, he had escaped in 1981, went into hiding, and kept committing more crimes. His death nearly ten years later during a shootout with police in Santarém (some 862 kilometers northwest of Goianésia by road and ferry) became instant news. It drew so many people to the central police headquarters in Santarém that military police had to be called in to control the crowds of onlookers wanting to see the corpse of the "super-hit man" Aragão (O Liberal 1990).[24]

I told Aurora about my discussion with Carmela, including about how Carmela chuckled when she said she would pull Rosa's ears if she wished her ill. Aurora chuckled herself, but she knew that Carmela had been serious. "*Pois é*": "That is the way people here think." I already knew that Aurora had identified Carmela as being on the "superstitious" side and that Aurora didn't *quite* think about friendship the same way that Carmela did. "I believe in friendship," Aurora once said, "but real friends are hard to find, and it is true that you can never *really* know someone else." Aurora here emphasized part of her difference: as an educated woman from Brazil's Southeast who had been a lay liberationist activist before leaving her home state, she wasn't quite *povo*. Since she had an undergraduate degree and was studying toward a master's in education, one could even call her "elite." She certainly made an above-average salary, which had afforded her a home in a neighborhood known to be a bit more upscale, albeit only relatively so, as her street was unpaved. Thus, the difference was one of degree rather than kind. The affirmation that you could never *really* know another person remained a shared position, even though, with her studied liberationist tendency to downplay evil (see chapter 4), Aurora was less inclined to ascribe the inability to know others to evil. This did not stop her, however, from describing acts of violence as manifestations of the devil or Satan, or from viewing her life allegorically. Ultimately Aurora, like her fellow pilgrims, attached herself to the saints in hope of convincing them to intercede with God to grant her a miracle. In other words, Aurora, too, was a divining person who propelled the recurrence of allegory along the highway.

In the first instance, this chapter set out to describe the Pilgrimage of Liberation and the vows and miracles that animate it, in an effort to bring to life the early days of this settler frontier and the common Catholicism that has shaped it. In particular, I underscored the pervasiveness of promise-making beyond the pilgrimage to help shed light on the widespread recurrence of allegory, the perennial divining of persons in relation, and their mystic relational implications.

But this chapter had broader aims as well: to begin opening our minds to the possibility that the mystic of friendship can hold radical democratic promise. This point needs to be underscored because Aurora's reluctance to affirm that "no one has friends" indicates a sense—shared by other activists and allies in the region—that this could essentially be a negative position. They might, for example, be concerned about the political message such a description could send, that it could frame those struggling for rights as somehow less capable or desirous of solidarity, community, and political transformation. Indeed, such a description might be especially worrying in a Catholic space where solidarity and community are generally marks of the good and even of humanity itself. However, I propose to see this otherwise: rather than consider this allegorical desire for an always elusive friendship a flaw to be hidden, it should be recognized as holding the power to challenge any and all structures of power, including authoritarian forms.

This power to challenge can be elucidated by turning to one of Benjamin's quiet aims in *The Origin of the German Trauerspiel*: to reveal the untenability of Carl Schmitt's arguments in *Political Theology* (1985 [1922]). There, Schmitt famously asserted that "all significant concepts of the modern theory of the state are secularized theological concepts . . . whereby, for example the omnipotent God became the omnipotent lawgiver . . . [and] the exception in jurisprudence [became] *analogous to the miracle in theology*" (36, my emphasis). Schmitt affirmed that these analogies developed in the Counter-Reformation/baroque period, to both explicate the state as well as legitimate its grounding in sovereign decisionism. Yet Benjamin unraveled two of Schmitt's aims by describing how *Trauerspiel* kings *failed* to make decisions. First, although Benjamin was writing about plays, he was still making a historical point. By showing that baroque sovereigns were seen as unable to decide to avoid disaster, he complicated Schmitt's account of the rise of the concept of sovereignty. That is, he showed that the idea of sovereignty emerged when sovereigns were considered not very sovereign after all. Second, Benjamin rejected the fascist decisionism that Schmitt sought to legitimate. Samuel Weber (1992) was among the first to make this argument, usefully noting that the indecisive sovereigns of *Trauerspiel* showed one way that Benjamin took "exception to the decision."

However, like subsequent commentators, Weber neglects how Benjamin's focus on allegory was a key part of his challenge to Schmitt.[25] Indeed, where Schmitt draws attention to *analogies*, Benjamin notes that *allegorical* practice is what connects terrestrial sovereignty to the divine, and also makes sovereignty impracticable, a pale replica of divine power. Instead, the creaturely, fallen nature of the king makes him similar to all humans. While he is supposed to be God's representative on earth, he is not omnipotent; he can never be quite sure of the "good" of his decisions. In short, *Origin* shows how allegorical practice threw into question the supposed "absolute" powers of post-Reformation imperial/state sovereignty and reminds contemporaries of their powers to do the same.

Benjamin's suicide in 1940 meant that he never completed his major work on the rise of the Paris Arcades in the nineteenth century. Still, before he died he returned to the critique of fascism and to questions of allegory. In particular, he was keen to document allegory's recurrence in the nineteenth century, especially in Charles Baudelaire's work. Few have noted, however, how Benjamin's early critique of fascism through allegorical practice later inspired his most famous essay: *Theses on the Philosophy of History*, subsequently retranslated as *On the Concept of History*. This disregard may be due to the neglect of *Origin* in scholarship, compounded by the fact that Benjamin does not mention "allegory" in *Theses*. Yet placing *Theses'* concern with images, theology, messianism, and redemption in the context of his wider work and correspondence, there is little doubt about the convergence of his early and late work. This is relevant here because Benjamin makes explicit in *Theses* the implicit political critique of *Origin*. The reading of images, Benjamin suggests, can help the oppressed grasp the time of the now and find redemption.[26] It is true that allegory is unstable and dangerous. It can call into question not only fascism but any human form, project, or relationship—and we will see this happening within the left-wing Landless Workers' Movement in chapters 5 and 6. But my point is that this instability, this readiness to critique, can also be made into a democratic virtue.

In his late work, Benjamin doesn't cite Schmitt's 1932 *The Concept of the Political*, but he most probably knew it. He was likely aware, too, that *The Concept of the Political* extended the authoritarian bent of *Political Theology* by defining true politics as the decision to exclude (and potentially kill) a political "enemy" deemed beyond a group of political friends. My ethnography in this chapter has shown how an allegorical way of seeing can unravel any material process, including the difference between friends and enemies, as Carmela's comments suggest. And this is where the democratic virtue of the mystic of friendship lies: it reminds us of the crucial fact that the enemy is never only "other." Indeed, it teaches us that we must seek friendship, both despite and because of the enemy's potential to be in our intimate circle or to even be *us*. This doesn't mean that we shouldn't try to engage the enemy and sometimes use conflict to do so. But it can mean that if the fluidity of the friend-enemy distinction is valued more than it is lamented, if communities remember that differences will always proliferate, communities can become more resilient. In other words, agonism within groups of friends can be normalized and dealt with accordingly, rather than be taken as a sign of evil and a reason to end relationships.

We will return to these more speculative political points later in this book. We will return to DaMatta too, whose mostly secular interest in processions and Brazilian (baroque) figures inspired me to explore Catholicism, Benjamin, and Schmitt. In the next chapters, for example, we will continue to see divining persons in action, and we will consider how friends and enemies are less stable than DaMatta's discussion suggests. This engagement with DaMatta will be oblique until we revisit him squarely in chapter 5, especially on the question of law's enmity. For now, it is important to consider that the mystic of friendship reveals a dynamic radicalism in Pará—rather than a static DaMattian "dilemma"—that has not been fully acknowledged or channeled to date. It will take more ethnography to flesh this idea out. First, we must continue to explore Catholic relations, especially their power to shape an intensifying secularity: a growing religious and nonreligious pluralism.

When I was a baby, I was healthy, until strange things started happening.[1] At four months old I was talking. Then, at seven months old I started to seem sick. I started to see things that no one else could see—I would cry out loud, have fevers, and generally was afraid of everything. My parents always brought me to Mr. Arunes, a *cientista* (medium) my father trusted. I was treated by him throughout my [early] life.

After I got married, I went to work with Mr. Arunes for a while. I would read the medical scripts that he wrote while he was incorporating spirits [possessed]—in fact, I had a gift: that I could read any handwriting.

But I always knew that I wouldn't stay there with Mr. Arunes. And then one day it happened: a big handsome white man came up to me while I was at work with Mr. Arunes—no one else there saw him but me—and the man showed me an open Bible, citing a passage from Matthew, but I can't remember which one. And I saw from that moment that I was going to leave Mr. Arunes and, of course, the spirits.

I stayed on for a few more months, and then one day I told them, the spirits, that I was going to leave. I told them that I had nothing against them but just wanted to do my life differently. And would you know it, they still got mad? They did! One day I was at home alone and they threw a full plate of food out of my hand. And so I spoke out to them: "I TOLD YOU that I had nothing against you, but that I am going to do my own life—and I am going to eat this food—I will!" . . .

But somewhere I just always knew that I would be an Evangelical, and an Evangelical to me is just someone who believes firmly in God. There are actually only a small number of real Evangelicals. But being among Evangelicals in church feels so good, they lift you up. It feels especially good to cry in church. You can't go around talking to so many people like that—about your problems and such. So it is good to go to church, pray, cry, and get raised back up.

02

MARABÁ

The Intensification of Secularity

"I killed my father," Ina Solanha said as we moved our conversation inside. I stopped walking, suddenly aware of the buzzing houselight and the evening Amazonian cricket song. "*Como assim?*" I managed to say, an innocent Portuguese "How so?" you can use to subtly suggest you don't understand. The house was empty. Only a bare bulb in the kitchen was on, and its sheen inched into the front room where we stood, illuminating the right side of Ina's face. "No one else in the family had been able to bring themselves to do it," she explained, turning to me. "After a year of illness, my father just couldn't die. He couldn't talk, he had sores on his body, he had to be moved around every day or so. It was so painful to watch. My mother was exhausted." Ina shook her head. "So I went to visit Mr. Arunes, the *cientista* (medium) who had treated the family for years, and asked him to cut the spirits' connection to my father. His spirits were too strong." Mr. Arunes gave her a thick silken cord he had prayed over. He told her that if she placed it around her father's neck he would die on June 20, 1995. "I came back and put the cord around his neck. And he did in fact die on June 20."

Ina motioned for me to sit, and we relaxed into the plastic-string armchairs behind us. I was relieved. Rather than suddenly confessing to a crime, Ina had just wanted to add dimension to her family's story and give me a little shock—and a mystery to contemplate. She leaned forward, squaring her shoulders to the smooth cement floor. "After he died, I found two prayers and a *patuá* (amulet) in his wallet." How long her father had carried them was difficult to say. He had never spoken about them. But for Ina, they validated her decision; they were clearly what had strengthened her father's connection to his spirits, and only someone with the right knowledge could have helped him die. I asked Ina if I could see the prayers. The next day, she brought two yellowed and unevenly folded papers from her sister's house. The amulet could not be found.

I try to capture the prayers' inconsistent grammar, punctuation, and spelling in the translation below:

> Prayer of the just judge of Nazareth, Son of the virgin Mary that in Bethle-hem was born. Remembering Lazarus, I ask you, my Lord. Through yours, on a certain day, that my body should not be captured nor wounded nor killed. Nor in the hands of justice in your passion of Christ. Therefore, give to the disciples that if the enemies will come to take me they will be taken. Eyes will not see me. If they should have ears they will not hear me. If they should have a mouth they will not speak, with the arms of St. George I will be armed with the swords of Saint Abraham I will be cov-ered by the milk of the Virgin Mary I will be surrounded by the angels of my Lord Jesus Christ I will be baptized in Noah's Ark . . . God is my father, the Holiest Virgin my mother with the arms of St. George I will be with the sword of Saint James I will be guarded for ever amen . . .
>
> Jesus
>
> Fim

This prayer was the more elaborate of the two. Yet both were clearly meant to generate protection for the bearer and those near to him. Both called on Christ and saints in the Catholic pantheon, requesting their protection from dangerous situations and from enemies—the most important point for this chapter. The other prayer ended: "Whoever prays this prayer will not die of disaster, will not be offended by enemies. Will not die drowned, nor will his wife die of a dangerous birth, with this prayer. . . . Offer yourself to the wounds of Christ and the pains of Saintliest Mary."

At the time, all I knew was that these were not usual prayers. But Ina wasn't interested in their religious source. She focused on a specific prob-lem: "No one in our family knows how to use these prayers anymore. This, I am sure, is one of the reasons why my family has faced increasing disunity, among ourselves and with others, with friends outside the family. We used to be so *unido* (united). We need to do more spiritual work. . . ."

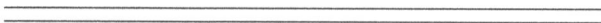

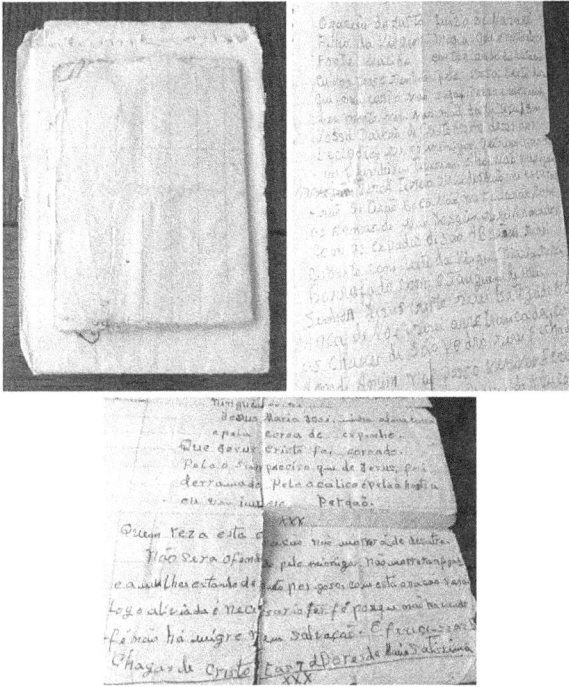

FIGURE 11. Carlos Solanha's prayers. Photo: Ashley Lebner.

I open with these prayers not because I will offer a detailed exegesis of their content. Instead I am interested in them as an image of a concern which, as Ina indicated, persisted among the Solanhas even after the prayers became obsolete: how to protect oneself, and one's family and friends, not only from harm, but from division and instability, from becoming enemies?

By now readers know that these concerns with enmity and the general unpredictability of others were not particular to Ina and her family, although I first encountered them as common Catholic phenomena.[1] This instability made friendship, always defined as a relationship of "help," seem problematic, almost impossible, especially "outside the family" as Ina often put it. But people also faced challenges of friendship among kin, who were supposed to be one's primary circle of support.

As I noted in the introduction, at first it seemed logical to assume that this mystic of friendship was an artifact of a people affected by the events of the region's volatile recent (post)colonial history: from the dictatorship's colonization and development projects to the gold rush and the ongoing

struggles for land. After all, the scars of these processes were visible everywhere—on the endless clear-cut lands along highways, in the dusty frontier
towns and peripheries, and in state-approved rural settlements, often forgotten by the state once they were established. Locals moved through and
shaped all of these spaces with their struggles.

Yet my encounter with these prayers was one of the moments during
my first sojourn in Pará when I realized that the concern about others, the
mystic of friendship, was not merely a product of material conditions or
violent recent events, but rather came from farther afield and had more
wide-ranging effects. Specifically, the mystic of friendship was shaped by a
once-encompassing Catholicism and it was now driving a major religious
transformation. Indeed, by the 1990s settlers along the PA-150 and Brazilians
more generally had begun to see their predominant Catholicism, with its
incorporation of officially "unorthodox" practices, give way to a condition
in which family and friends were often allegorically reading, negotiating,
and inspiring hardening religious and political differences.

This chapter describes these shifts, focusing first on relations and transformations within Catholicism to shed new light on how Protestantism and
Afro-Brazilian religions gained prominence alongside new concerns with
politics and perceptions of unbelief.[2] Settler Pará, of course, has its own
particularities, including a greater "Black invisibility," which as I have mentioned affects the recognition of what elsewhere are readily described as
"Afro-Brazilian" forms.[3] Ultimately, what the Solanhas help us see is how
proliferating religious and political differentiations, as well as the mystic
relational dynamics that partially propel them, constitute the PA-150's intensifying secularity.

By foregrounding the mystic of friendship (and kinship), this ethnography begins from a different premise than most studies of secularity and
of colonial situations. Scholars have tended to describe both as a condition
secured by political/state governance. Meanwhile, "secularity" is generally
tied to a "secularism" that comes after the "colonial." Here, I argue that attention to the flow of relations,[4] especially the practices of kinship, friendship,
and other interpersonal relations, is more vital than attention to colonial or
republican *states* for understanding how religions and politics, including
the distinctions and overlaps between them, are animated on the ground.[5]
To this end I show that when kinship and friendship are viewed together in
(post)colonial Pará, we begin to see how they are both key sites of knowledge formation; how they share a concern with constancy; and how they can
be considered as grounded in—and their problems solved by—adherence

to forms of devotion, whether more religious or more secular. Keeping all relations in view, we can see how concerns with the instability of kinship and friendship in Pará, once shaped by Catholicism, are now driving differentiations among religions and between religion and nonreligion. In short, mystic relational dynamics are generating, and further entailed by, a condition that I am calling an intensifying secularity.

To me, the Solanhas had always epitomized the settler history of the PA-150. The family were descendants of northeastern migrants to Amazonia, with African, Indigenous, and white heritage, who had successfully navigated the violence that characterized the dictatorship's hostile recolonization of the Amazon. But my encounter with Ina's father's prayers and their social effects helped me grasp how the unstable relational dynamics of Paraense Catholicism were propelling more recent religious and political transformations and negotiations—an intensifying secularity. That story is the focus of this chapter. I begin by describing how I learned of the Solanha prayers after a Christmas party gone wrong. I use this event and allegorical interpretations of it to make a point about life along the PA-150: that kin and friends are key sites of knowledge about the inconstancy of others and the need to protect oneself from enmity.

I next offer an account of the background to the Solanhas' fight on Christmas day: Ina's father Carlos's life, beginning with the time when the prayers may have come into his possession. His life allows me to shed light on how Catholicism once constituted understandings of kinship and friendship, as well as their shared problems and solutions.[6] In particular, I show how Carlos's Catholic devotions were the source of his power to turn enemies into friends, assuring that his familial and social life remained healthy and stable. From this, I draw the lesson that Brazilian Catholicism, shaped by four hundred years as a pillar of imperial governance *prior* to secularism, entailed the idea, still powerful today, that social stability was best sought through devotional practice.

The remaining parts of the chapter focus on how Catholic relational concerns animate the intensification of secularity along today's PA-150. Tracking Ina's brother João's move from Catholic youth activism to Brazil's largest secular agrarian movement, the Landless Rural Workers' Movement (MST), I show that the Catholic commitment to fraternity ("brotherhood") over "friendship" generated increased concerns with religion and its others, especially with politics and the possibility of unbelief.[7] Through João, I show that Catholicism, rarely recognized in the literature as the "fraternity" long dear to Catholics,[8] helped disseminate ideas about politics, religion, and the absence of religion—and the impossible-to-stabilize relations and distinctions among them. Ultimately, this chapter explores an account of how secularity along the PA-150 is generated by all of these intersecting impossibilities, which are mediated by the mystic of friendship operating especially (but not only) outside the family.

A CHRISTMAS FIGHT

My field notes from the early hours of December 26, 2004, show that I had observed something significant that I did not yet understand. Exhausted and shaken, I attempted to sort out on paper how the fight that broke up the Solanhas' Christmas party had started. Ina's twenty-seven-year-old brother, Carlinhos, was drunk and melancholy, and he wanted to leave the party. His mother asked his cousin Zé, who was around the same age, to stop him. Soon, the cousins were chasing each other, first around the yard on Ina's lot where Emelza and I lived in small houses, and then on the street. I followed them out and watched the fight unfold under the purple-blue street lights that lined the dusty unpaved road.

The memory is still vivid. I can see Zé running after Carlinhos with a large branch in his hand, the older cousins Antônio, Sandro, and João running after them, multiple configurations of all five in various standoffs, verbally threatening and throwing branches and stones. I also see their mothers—Edna (mother of Carlinhos, Ina, João, Larissa, Camelia, Emelza and Lilia); Emelza (mother of Zé and Antônio); and Lilia (mother of Sandro)—watching from beside the gutter, crying out to their children to stop. I remember Ina, in a white t-shirt, wrestling Carlinhos to the ground, his face crumpling into his red collar as they both fell into the dust; Sandro throwing a brick at Camelia and Larissa, though with little apparent attempt to harm; and Camelia, tall and imposing like Ina, but pale, "the whitest one in the family" as they occasionally called her, charging after him in her short white sports shorts. Shortly after all this, Ina told me to take the younger girls into my house. The girls and I were awed and a bit afraid, though sometimes we giggled when we caught each other's eyes. We listened to the sounds on the other side of the shutters until Ina knocked to tell us that the fighting had stopped, that everyone was safe, and that we could go to bed.

The next day, I walked around the corner to Ina and Larissa's house for lunch, as I did nearly every day. Weekly, I bought meat and vegetables for the house, and Ina would prepare them and add rice and beans. We would eat lunch with whoever else was around—Larissa's children, sometimes Larissa (back from her work at the supermarket), Carlinhos or João, and occasionally some of João's *companheiros* from the MST. "What happened last night?" I asked Ina when I arrived. She was too busy and too annoyed with her kin to answer. But we talked it over on two subsequent visits, sitting as we often did on plastic-string chairs under the mango tree that towered over the backyard.

"When they fight like that," Ina explained in our first conversation, "they are not the ones doing it." I asked her what she meant. She replied in her cryptic way: "It is the things that follow them." I began to catch on. She had spoken about spirits following her before, calling them *eles* (them). "You mean *eles?*" I asked. She nodded, smiling a bit. She didn't know if spirits followed Lilia and Emelza's sons Sandro and Zé, she explained, but they followed Carlinhos and Antônio. But any kind of spirit could enter anyone: "A spirit of a person who used to kill people, or who has not left the earth. You know, they take advantage, do things with people, especially when people drink. Bodies are more open when people drink." I asked again about the spirits that followed her brother and cousin, and she grew serious, offering me an allegorical reading of her family's recent history and specifically of the Christmas fight.

> You know that my father had very strong protection. Not that he ever had the *coragem* (courage and wherewithal) to tell anyone. . . . But once my father got ill everything changed. Before that, everyone was *unido* (united)—these kinds of fights didn't happen and no one wanted to treat my mother badly. But before he died, they were practically hitting her in front of him! He couldn't do much by that time anyway. . . . But there is a special thing between *eles* and my mother. My mother, like the other mothers that night, was the source of the fight. Something goes into my mother and starts to bug her children (*implicar com eles*) and then, eventually, they lose control. You saw the whole story! This happens to me. But after I explode, my mother becomes "good" again. I know that it is not fully me or her, though, it is "them." *Eles*. But still, it affects us.

"How?" I asked.

"Well, it gets harder to be together, to help each other. We won't go to Lilia's house for a while now. Sandro was terrible." Ina was called away at that point, but we resumed the next day. When I asked her to talk more about her father's protection and its relationship to her family, she told me about the discovery of her father's prayers and her own role in his death.

Once I had the prayers in hand, Ina began to tell stories of her father's early life and her own. These stories were fleshed out over years of retellings, with Camelia, Larissa, or another of her sisters adding details. Beyond the particularities of Carlos's spiritual life and death, which I highlighted above, his life otherwise reflects the lives of many other poor residents of Brazil's Northeast who came to the Amazon in search of a better future, especially after the military initiated major development projects like the Trans-Amazon Highway, which runs in a near-direct line from the northwestern-most Brazilian state of Paraíba across four thousand kilometers to the states of Pará and Amazonas. The aim was to promote Amazonian colonization, and thousands of poor Brazilians streamed into Pará, either through state-directed settlement schemes or on their own. Rich land-grabbers, capable of hiring militias to secure claims to large tracts of public lands, came too. Pará became famous for its land conflicts and political violence—an unfortunate notoriety that has stayed with the region ever since. Since 1970, the population along the Trans-Amazon Highway system has exploded from around seventy thousand to one million (Neto 2019). Although Carlos came before the real crush of migration began, the family, like thousands of others, was eventually settled on land that abutted the Trans-Amazon, and like everyone else, they navigated the region's volatility. But the Solanhas' story is exemplary in other ways, too. Their varied forms of religious devotion tell us much about Catholicism, its allegorization of mystic relational dynamics, and the ways Catholicism has produced the religious and political transformations that create an intensified secularity.

AN ENCOMPASSING CATHOLICISM

To bring the devotional, relational, and political forms encompassed by Catholicism into view, we begin with Ina's father Carlos. Carlos was born in 1948 in the Northeastern state of Maranhão, which neighbors the Amazonian state of Pará. Carlos had been raised in a devout, churchgoing Catholic peasant family with African, Indigenous, and white ancestry. As he was about to become a teenager, he became very ill. He was eventually treated by a blind man, who was a local spirit medium—a *cientista* or "scientist." The *cientista* was an eclectic figure who used herbs, prayer to various Catholic entities, and spirit-channeling to cure ailments. Though no one is certain, many of his family members thought that Carlos received the prayers to control the powerful spirits that caused his illness during his encounter with the local *cientista*. The *cientista* probably told him never to reveal that he carried those prayers.

Carlos needed the prayers' protection when he decided to strike out on his own in search of fortune in the Amazon, Ina and her sisters explained. Many young men were making their way to the Amazon on the promise of its abundant land, gold, and other resources. In Pará Carlos met his wife Edna, then the thirteen-year-old daughter of an Indian woman who had left her village and married a white man. Once Carlos had secured a plot of land, the couple started a family. Edna had ten children, and, as Camelia pointed out, "none died in childhood, as the prayer promised." The children were raised as churchgoing Catholics, but they all still went to the local *cientista* when cures were necessary. Meanwhile, Carlos said his own prayers regularly and mostly alone, at night.

It was Lilia who first told me about his nightly prayers. "My father was a very pious man," she said. "He prayed a lot, even outside church. And sometimes when he prayed at night it would affect me (*mexia comigo*)." By using the verb *mexer*, literally "to stir," Lilia was telling me that her father's prayers worked on her, especially on the spirits around her. But she needed lots of prayers. She told me that strange things began happening to her as a baby (see the Second Visitation), and she began to be treated by the family *cientista*, Mr. Arunes. Ina, who is some seven years younger than Lilia, tells it slightly differently: Lilia began to behave very strangely in her late teens, apparently affected by *eles*. As an example, Ina recalled a bizarre instance when Lilia was once walking past a neighbor's house. She abruptly stopped, grabbed the neighbor's collar, and peered into his face. "Suddenly, all of the buttons fell off the man's shirt, just like that." After that, Ina explained, Lilia began serious treatment with the family *cientista*.

This glimpse into the early life of the Solanha family points to a well-documented fact about mid- to late twentieth-century common Catholicism: it encompassed a variety of officially heterodox religious forms and ideas. While this remains the case today, Catholicism is no longer as hegemonic as it once was. Whereas 95 percent of the Brazilian population declared itself Catholic in 1940, since 1980 the Catholic population has fallen precipitously from 88.3 percent to 56.75 percent, with likely lower rates in the north, including Pará state (Coutinho and Golgher 2014; IBGE 2022; and see note 21, below). To understand this change in Amazonia, I will not focus on the particularities of the "new" religions that have come on the scene (Protestant sects and the increasingly visible "Afro-Brazilian religions"). Nor will I turn to state secularism, which has had relatively little effect on the common Catholic religiosity of local people across Brazil since its formal inception in 1889 (Montero 2006).[9] Instead, I am interested in the role of Catholicism in the intensification of secularity, in particular how Catholic socialities, and especially their mystic dynamics, have contributed to the multiplication of religion(s), politics, and shades of unbelief.

COMMON CATHOLICISM AND
THE MYSTIC OF FRIENDSHIP

Carlos's prayers shed light on Catholic sociality precisely because they helped regulate its perennial instability—even its danger. The prayers were powerful, Ina, Larissa, and Camelia assured me, and not only because they kept all Carlos's young children healthy, a serious feat in the early years of the Trans-Amazon when they lived hours away from the nearest clinic. The prayers were also powerful because, like magic, they "turned enemies into friends."

Recalling the prayers' powers to ensure that Carlos and the Solanha family "would not be offended by enemies," Ina told me how people who bad-mouthed her father around town would shed their anger as they entered the house. When I asked her for an example, she explained that she was young at that time and couldn't possibly know about her father's business. Still, she remembered a story about a man who was upset about where Ina's father had put a fence separating their ten-hectare lots. "He went all around town talking, trying to build up animosity against my father, to intimidate us. When my father heard about this, he decided to invite the man over to visit. The day he came over, we saw him striding angrily toward our house, but by the time he walked through the door, his demeanor had totally changed. . . . We never had more problems with him. He became a friend."

The sisters' allegorical account of the prayers' power to keep their family healthy and safe from enemies and land disputes recalls the struggle for land in Southeast Pará, while also evoking how Catholicism helped both to produce the longing-*saudade* for friendship and to manage the inconstancy and danger of others. As I noted in the introduction, I call this striving for unity and concord amid divergence a mystic dynamic, a mystic of friendship, especially because this language also captures how the "past" of this problematic—that is, its commonness in early modern Portuguese America (Luz 2007)—recurs in the present.

Significantly, this framing also allows me to include kinship. That is, I do not marginalize or exclude it, as some treatments of friendship tend to do.[10] While the people I spoke with generally considered friends outside the family more problematic than kin—less constant, dependable, or "knowable"— they used "friend" (*amigo*) simply to mean someone who helps. Kin are expected to help, to be friends. Yet kin frequently disappoint, throwing their true amity into question. Crucially, the mystic of friendship is also grounded in the essential inconstancy of the person. As we have already seen in Ina's descriptions of her family, persons are permeable, always potentially open to animation by other agents, including agents of ill intent. Others say that anyone, even someone who does not believe in the devil, can be the devil at any time. In short, personal actions, whether good or evil, can lead to unity or to division and conflict, which interrupts the flow of mutual support.

The changeability of human persons stood out as a major concern, especially in relation to the constant friendship of God and his agents. Parents were often spoken of as the "next best friends, after God" for having given their children "breath." Yet there was no consensus on how far into the family this support extended. In theory, people could count on their families: their brothers, sisters, children, uncles, aunts, and cousins. But this did not always happen, my interlocutors explained, because other interests, other agents, got in the way. Compared to the divine, friendship among humans appeared essentially impossible—and impossible to achieve without the help of the divine.

The Solanha family's story, beginning with Carlos's prayers, illustrates how Catholicism shaped sociality in Pará while encompassing a range of devotional forms now associated increasingly with other "religions." The Solanhas, like other families, recognized the problem of instability in social relations and sought to mitigate it through prayer and devotion. They sought to convince God and his agents to bless them with love and grace, with help (that is, friendship), but the broad applicability of this concept also made it a problem: "Everyone is my friend," some would say, "but no one is." While I was doing fieldwork, this appeared to me to be a long-standing social orientation. But it was also clear that the religious field was changing, as people like the Solanhas embraced new religions or distanced themselves from religion altogether.

What occasioned this change? While the return to civilian rule in 1985 played a role, the religious and political differentiations began well before that transition and were propelled in good part by a reforming Latin American Catholicism after the Second Vatican Council (1962–65). Ina's brother João helps illustrate this Catholic "fraternal" reform and the religious and political transformations it helped bring about.

FROM LIBERATIONIST CATHOLICISM
TO AN INTENSIFYING SECULARITY

"When I joined my Catholic youth group in 1986, Brazil was still trying to leave the dictatorship behind and start a proper democracy," João explained to me in his yard one Sunday. "Although this began before the dictatorship ended, after 1985 people in the church were openly talking about how to transform social relations, how to mobilize communities to deal with widespread hunger and violence." The church devoted its most visible ritual work to this end, João suggested, through the annual Fraternity Campaigns, which had been held by the Catholic Church each year during Lent since 1966. The aim was to promote more positive, equal, solidary, and kinlike relationships, which (it was assumed) would be more stable. "I still remember the [Fraternity Campaign] motto of 1986," João told me: "*Terra de Deus, Terra de Irmãos*" (Land of God, land of brothers).

João was recounting this more than a decade after he had left the church and become an activist, a "militant," with the MST, Brazil's largest agrarian movement. It made sense that he foregrounded what others on the Brazilian left celebrate: that this period was defined by the church's resistance to the dictatorship and its mobilization of the people, *o povo*, against its oppressors. I do not contest this; it is well known that in Latin America the Second Vatican Council's concerns with human well-being and freedom developed into a theology of liberation, which was focused on freeing societies from the "social sin" of inequality and exploitation (Boff and Boff 1986). The liberationist call for a revolutionary politics of faith became powerful in Brazil and, even though it was cut short by a conservatizing Vatican under Pope John Paul II and Cardinal Joseph Ratzinger (then head of the Congregation for the Doctrine of the Faith), João's narrative suggests that this new Catholicism had already had effects. While drawing on traditional Catholic concerns like stabilizing relationships through devotion and kinship-as-fraternity, the new Catholicism also transformed these concerns through its engagement with "politics." In other words, and this is my focus here, liberationism's politicized devotion among brothers helped propel the political and religious transformations—the intensifying secularity—we see in (post)colonial Amazonia today.

João initially mentioned Catholic brotherhood and the Fraternity Campaign in passing, but once I asked him to elaborate, it became clear that the campaigns of 1985 and 1986 had politicized him. The Solanha family had just moved from their settlement on the Trans-Amazon Highway, and as João attended Mass with his family in his new Marabá city neighborhood, he encountered church activists aiming to galvanize social and political consciousness through Catholic brotherhood. For example, the Fraternity Campaign of 1985, which specifically addressed the problem of hunger, ran discussion groups, workshops, and special liturgies. The 1986 Fraternity Campaign in turn promoted a solution to hunger: the mass redistribution of land through agrarian reform. João was referring to this call for a more egalitarian landowning structure when he recited the 1986 Fraternity Campaign motto "Land of God, Land of Brothers." And this more egalitarian fraternity, this mystic longing for unity, is what eventually brought him to politics.

FIGURE 12. Covers of Fraternity Campaign booklets (1985 and 1986). Left: "Bread for Those Who Are Hungry." Right: "Land of God, Land of Brothers." Archives of the National Council of Brazilian Bishops, Belém, Pará.

The lessons João learned during those early Fraternity Campaigns, he explained, deepened as he participated in Catholic youth activism in the early 1990s. Brazil was one of the only countries in Latin America to retain colonial-era landownership patterns (Guimarães 1964), and the Brazilian left took up the demand for land reform again after twenty years of dictatorship. Even though at the time liberation theology was being curtailed in Brazil, liberationists continued to work in Amazonia, where many liberationist priests and nuns had moved in the 1970s and early 1980s to support the struggle for land. João learned from some of these clergy that the current structure of social relations in Brazilian society was problematic and characterized by severe inequality. He remembered an especially effective tool they used to catalyze his understanding, "the pyramid method." This, João explained, "was an analysis of society drawn in the shape of a pyramid. You had the miserable at the bottom, then the poor, then the middle class, then the upper middle class, and there on the tippy-top were the rich. The priests [who taught us] used to emphasize the ugliness of poverty, and they urged us to see that *we* were the poor, suffering physically and socially. And they would ask us: What do we have to do to change this? And one of the answers being discussed in those days was . . . how to redistribute the land to those who could work it." The pyramid method was meant to inspire activists to devote themselves to forging fraternal, solidary relations in order to confront the oppressors and transform society from a steeply unequal hierarchy to more stable equality for all. Accompanying the traditional message of fraternity was the more radical idea that devotion should not be limited to prayer; it should include active, collective engagement in politics. "Sometimes [our group] didn't talk much at all about religion," João said with a chuckle, "but the underlying message was that religion and politics should come together—I distinctly remember a theme of a workshop I attended in those years on 'faith and politics.'"

João hadn't kept any documents from that time, but he suggested that I look in the archives of the Commissão Pastoral da Terra (Pastoral Land Commission) in both Marabá and Belém cities. One booklet that I found there, from the late 1970s or 1980s, was directed especially at youth.

The booklet's cover calls on youth to bring their faith (*fé*) to politics (*política*) in order to achieve justice and liberty and to gain land. Inside, there is a dialogue between two youth with the same message. One says to the other: "Politics is a way of honoring God. Do you agree?" The other responds, "No! We shouldn't mix things. Politics has nothing to do with God." The text concludes: "This is the kind of faith we need to free ourselves

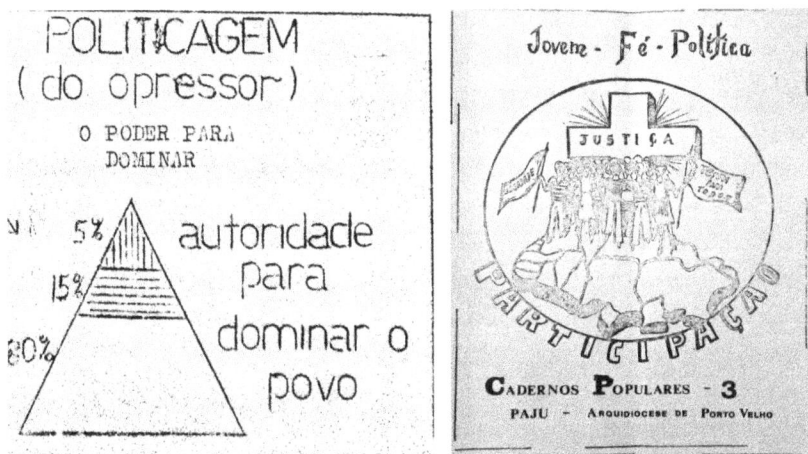

FIGURE 13. Left: "The politicking of the oppressor, the power to dominate . . . the people" (*The Cry* 1981h, 7). Archives of the Pastoral Land Commission, Marabá, Pará. Right: Faith and politics to be studied by Catholic youth (PAJU, n.d.). Archives of the National Council of Brazilian Bishops, Belém, Pará.

from. We need to find a transforming faith that . . . does not accept injustice." The point is simple: youth should use faith to bring real-world problems and politics into view to solve them. Those who don't do this, the text says, are embracing an "anesthetic-faith." These "alienated" youth are the kind of people "who say that priests speaking of politics is a sin."

The Catholic clergy who wrote this handbook identified an ambivalence toward "politics" among their flock. And indeed, such wariness remains widespread among Brazil's Christian public, conditioned by centuries of warnings against the spiritual dangers of indulging in worldly action. Some scholars have argued that liberationism's concern with politics even drove people away from Catholicism (Burdick 1993; Mariz 1994). Here, I am less interested in engaging in this debate than in highlighting how Catholic discourses, even before the transition to democracy, intensified the public's experience of secularity, its relational negotiations of religion and politics. In particular, the privileging of fraternity mediated the promotion of politics while elevating kinship by conjuring Christianity's historic ambivalence toward friendship (as a highly valued classical "pagan" concept).[11]

The mobilization of these distinctions—faith and politics under the rubric of fraternity—ultimately reinforced the possibility of their difference, even if the church's aim was to bring them together. Indeed, João and his fellow youth group members came to learn that there were limits to the forms of fraternity, equality, and political comradeship they could practice within the church. "I probably began to know I would leave the church a few years into [my involvement with the youth group]," João said. "Take this moment. The church wanted us to pray more. But we were very rebellious. From the moment the nun said we should speak *less* and listen *more*, well, then [we felt that] she didn't have to participate with us anymore." João smirked, remembering his group's youthful insolence, but then he turned serious. "There were still struggles in the church itself, you see. Some priests and nuns didn't accept this talk of agrarian reform, didn't accept the talk of rights . . . of speaking out, saying what we thought. The very issue of participation was still an issue . . . but *o povo*, the people, started . . . organizing for the struggle within and also outside the church. And I began to see that I could only pursue what I believed had to be done outside. But then again," he added with a smile, "I also joined the Movement because it was *fun (era bom)*! And I have been working with the MST ever since. Although you can't be friends with everyone, you know, we are *companheiros*, like a family."

As this account implies, it was not only João who realized the limits of the church. He arrived at this conclusion in dialogue with members of his group—who became "lifelong friends," in his words—and some decided to join the MST with him. But the transition wasn't all smooth; it was marked by the hope and longing for unity, accompanied by fissures, among kin and friends. Indeed, drawn in by new friends, he also had to negotiate with his kin, who doubted his decision *and* his new friends, and were themselves confronted by the perennial question about how best to live their lives. The various results of this navigation contributed to a condition increasingly shaped by what Charles Taylor might describe as a nova effect: "A widening gamut of new positions—some believing, some unbelieving, some hard to classify" (2007, 423). Yet we must remember the role of kinship and friendship in this intensifying secularity—kin and friends negotiated among themselves and generated these new positions, whether religious, secular, political or otherwise.

AN INTENSIFYING SECULARITY

Neither the church nor the MST alone produced this new "gamut" of positions. Rather, the ways João and his family variously, and often ambivalently, responded to the changes in his life gives insight into how mystic relational dynamics animate the intensification of secularity. As I have been emphasizing, we cannot understand secularity without the relations that drive it; indeed, my redefinition of "secularity" is precisely meant to help us see interpersonal and conceptual relations better. If João's departure for the MST was catalyzed within Church spaces, the move was ultimately made with his new friends-turned-kin who collectively began to privilege secular political solutions to unstable relationships rather than the traditional religious solutions—a position with which many in his family did not agree. That is, João's story shows how he, his parents, and his siblings began negotiating the suddenly shifting interpersonal and conceptual relationships among religion, politics, friends, and kin, which deepened their experience of secularity.

The possibility of unbelief played an important role in these conceptual and interpersonal negotiations. To understand this, we must grasp what the MST was: an agrarian reform movement fostered by the church in the early 1980s that intentionally though amicably separated itself from the church in 1985. The hope was to radicalize its activists (henceforth also "militants," after the local term *militância*) while retaining church support to better achieve its goals for land reform. If after this secularizing move the divine was carried ever more rarely into the MST's political struggles, this does not mean that people in the MST stopped believing.[12] João, for example, emphasized that he still believed "in a higher power, though this power is not something that humans can understand." He went on to insist that fundamentally "the MST is very religious. Everyone in the MST believes in God." But I protested. I had heard a number of activists either admit their disbelief or complain about how others did not believe in God. "They say they don't believe, but they believe!" João insisted, his eyes bright in the dusk. "Just watch. When the going gets tough, people turn quickly to God."

João's assertions were instructive, though not because they established the truth of belief beneath a secular exterior. Of course, whether João, or anyone, "truly believes" cannot be ascertained. Yet João's comments point to a condition in which his fellows were experimenting with the possibility of nonreligion or unbelief, even as he tried to obscure this by asserting that MST members are fundamentally religious. It isn't surprising that João minimized this problem. The MST's image requires continuous curating and, as most in the movement know, some people find the MST's seeming ambivalence toward God troubling.

João learned about these concerns regarding belief both from his friends in the MST and also from his kin, who for the most part kept their distance from the movement. When João joined the movement, his parents and siblings began to worry about his more secular devotions and his new political friends. "Our mother didn't like when her children spent too much time with their friends," Ina often remarked. "She always bugged us when we did." These concerns were amplified in João's case since his new friends, with their avowedly secular political commitments, were taking him away from his family. Indeed they were becoming his family, just when João's mother needed help with his ailing father. By all accounts his mother was hard on João. "She was especially critical of his new friends, sometimes to their face," Camelia said, chuckling as she remembered the sharp-tongued barbs her mother could shoot people's way.

João's siblings also criticized his new friends. João had already known some of the militants from church, but many were new; some, rumor had it, were unsavory gangster types. Some of these rumors were fed by a social discourse that construed the MST's politicized land occupations as a shoddy cover for criminally "invading" land that was owned by others. Hoping to recruit his family to the movement, João tried to explain that these lands, especially in Amazonia, had been illegally appropriated by wealthy land-grabbers (*grileiros*). He tried to convince them that smallholders should claim back this stolen land, that the MST was there to help see justice served, and that the political organization of the poor and the redistribution of wealth were the only path to bring about the social stability and equality everyone craved.

João's siblings and their spouses were not convinced. Family members had heard about the exploits of his new friends, and though it was normal to be wary of friends, João's family was shocked by stories of promiscuity, struggles for power, and even violence among them. For the Solanhas, all this confirmed an irreligious orientation to the world and made it impossible for them to have faith in this path to landownership, let alone in the MST's promise of social stability. None of them ultimately joined the MST, despite João's efforts.

Instead, five of João's sisters consolidated their religious commitments: Emelza kept frequenting the Catholic Church; Lilia and another sister, Bininha, converted to the Pentecostal Assembly of God; Ina joined what she called both "Spiritism" and "Umbanda," confounding scholarly distinctions between Spiritism and African-derived religions that do not always hold (see also Hayes 2011). Finally, Camelia joined another kind of "Spiritism," the Valley of the Dawn. And all his siblings concurred that politics—especially transgressive politics—was not the proper means to obtain economic, social, or moral improvement. On the contrary, although some, the Evangelicals and the men in particular, were reluctant or too shy to affirm that their father's prayers had protected and unified their family, they all agreed that they now had to find their own ways, their own supportive communities and friends. They all agreed that work and faithful religious devotion in community were better ways to stabilize, protect, and transform their lives and relationships. "It certainly isn't politics that will protect us from the devil!" Bininha once said.

I told Ina about my exchange with Bininha, and rather than merely concur as I had expected, she exclaimed, "Sure, politics is dirty but Evangelicals (*os crentes*) always claim that *others* are the ones conjuring the devil, but *they* are really the ones talking about the devil all the time! For them it is the devil *this*, the devil *that*, but we Spiritists don't call on the devil at all! Instead, we work to keep the unruly spirits in line, without bringing 'the devil' into it." This brief commentary clarified a lot for me. It showed me first that, as in other contexts, the devil was a term in the Christian lexicon that could be mobilized to identify spirits who may not be deemed officially acceptable or "good" in the Christian world, but who still continued to exist and matter (Chestnut 1997; Meyer 1999). But it also showed me that the Solanha Evangelicals knew—as much as the Spiritists or Catholics did—that there would always be some spiritual and social disruption. Such devilish instabilities were ultimately impossible to contain completely and must be consistently worked on in one way or another.

Ina's commentary returns us to the arguments I have been developing. First is how the perennial interplay of friction and *saudade* for unity among kin and friends—a mystic that was once understood in the language of Catholicism—is not incidental to the social transformations along the PA-150. Rather, the will to unity has clearly begun to inspire engagement with "new" religions, with politics, and the possibility of unbelief. Second, Ina helps us see how this condition, a condition of secularity, is a context of reflection and action on both religion and the challenges of relating. Indeed, it is significant that Ina became an adept of Umbanda, choosing to join none of her siblings in their devotions, whether João in the MST, Bininha in the Assembly of God, or Camelia in her Spiritist practice with the Valley of the Dawn. Certainly, Ina's choices were shaped by religious and political concerns, but they were also perhaps first informed by her relationships with her siblings and their respective friends—and crucially, they were also shaped by *eles*. When I once asked her why she never wanted to participate with Camelia in the Valley of the Dawn, for example, she said,

"I don't know—something always stops me," which was her euphemism for the spiritual forces that oriented her and even made her do things against her will. But it was clear that she also wanted to escape her siblings' influence and not tie her fortunes to theirs or to the fortunes of their friends. In fact, Ina didn't believe that any of her siblings' communities could help her—or could even help *them*.

If Ina often questioned the authenticity of Evangelicals, whose religious fervor seemed more performed than sincere to her, she still thought it better to *have* a religion help keep one's life and relationships on track. This is where she differed fundamentally from João. "João needs a religion, he's my father's son after all," Ina said. "Take for example, this supposed friend of João's, who was challenging João's authority and turning people against him in the MST. João came to me and asked me to mobilize *eles* to make him leave Pará."

"Wow, did you succeed?" I asked, surprised at this intersection of Marxism and Umbanda.

"I did!" Ina answered. "I put his picture there and every night I did my work." She motioned toward the little altar she had installed behind a satiny curtain that separated her bedroom from the room that had once been the kitchen. She had filled the altar with candles, images and statues of saints, photographs and other items, and she prayed over requests from relatives and friends twice a day, at noon and at midnight. "João was very happy. But it isn't enough, you see? You have to keep it up. Of course, I work hard to protect him and all my family and friends, but to really be sure he should be involved [in the rites] himself a bit more. I mean, people are free to do what they want, but it isn't good to stay away from religion, as João and many of his friends—even some of my other brothers—do. You see, it can't just be politics, or nothing," Ina argued. "You have to *choose* a religion."

CONCLUSION: THE POLITICS OF SECULARITY

"Religion" was Ina's choice, in a way, but it also wasn't a choice. Spiritual forces were there working whether one believed in their power to help or not. Instead, what Ina was saying is that if you begin to practice a religion, you are in a better position to control these forces. At the time, Ina was trying to teach me about religion, but for our purposes she helps put the final point on my argument here: that when reflecting on secularity, colonial or otherwise, the effects of the potential differences and overlaps among politics, religion, kin, and friends must all be considered in tandem while we remain alert to the impossibility of fully living or fully describing any of them. In other words, secularity is not just about transformations in politics and styles of managing religion. It is also, and more vitally, a matter of kin and friends negotiating their relations and distinctions, finding ways to either render politics an other to religion, or to reconnect religion and politics. Moreover, it is also about kin and friends developing distinctions among other religious and nonreligious forms. This brings us back to the assumption raised at the beginning of this chapter: that states, and politics more generally, whether independent or colonial, are the primary causes of social and religious change. As an alternative, I have tried to offer a perspective often occluded by the focus on the state or on politics. This is that the necessary flow of relations—including kinship, friendship, their imbrications with religion (in this case Catholicism), and the interpersonal questions and impossibilities they all produce—has vital transformative power, including the power to produce politics itself. To this end, I have shown that in Southeast Pará both liberationist and common Catholicism promote kinship and marginalize or problematize friendship, even as (or perhaps because) what remains the ideal is friendship as a relation with a God who "helps." I have used the stories of João and Ina to describe how religious and nonreligious transformations entail openness to new friends who become like kin even as original kin have misgivings about them. And I have emphasized how, for the various members of the Solanha family, both kin and friends can disappoint, confirming the sense of friendship's instability inside and outside the family, an instability that itself generates new spiritual and political action.

I can also elaborate here on what I began outlining above: it is debatable that state secularism has been a consistent determinant in the Brazilian context (see also Montero 2006 and the introduction to this book), not least given that the Brazilian state has never officially been defined as secular (Zylberstajn 2012). This does not mean that secularism is irrelevant or that some of its principles have not operated in Brazil. Indeed, the first Brazilian Republic's constitution formally separated church and state and recognized increased religious freedom, influencing all subsequent constitutions. Yet scholars also remind us that collaboration continued between church and state even in this early period and has continued into the present, although the churches concerned may no longer be only Catholic (Leite 2011).

The wider literature on secularism has certainly explored the impossibil

ity of knowing whether a state is secular. One of the most creative elabora-
tions of this argument asserts that secularism is not merely a doctrine of
governance but is also a "questioning power" that constantly asks where the
line between religion and politics should be drawn, which in turn generates
and destabilizes the two domains and reinforces the need for a sovereign
decision on the matter (Agrama 2012). Yet the proposal to study secularism/
secularity as a set of questions connected to state sovereignty, and to seek
ways to resist it by finding spaces of "asecularity" where we can suspend
questions about the distinction between religion and politics, obscures two
crucial facts. First, it hides how the distinction between religion and politics
relationally precedes and exceeds the state in both history and ethnography, including in Egypt, where Agrama conducted research (Lebner 2015,
2019). Second, it does not acknowledge that distinctions from religion (and
therefore secularity) are difficult to escape in many contexts, perhaps especially for scholars. Indeed, scholarly language will continue to be haunted
by the fact that academic writing is generally distinguished from religious
discourse, whether or not this distinction is foregrounded.

Being unable to escape a distinction, however, does not mean that how
and when a distinction is drawn will always be the same. Certainly, in many
contexts the relationship between religion and politics is constantly being
negotiated, especially in the Catholic tradition, and I have tried to show
this happening in Pará. While Catholicism is now on some level in retreat
in Brazil, the impossibilities it helped promote—the impossibilities of fully
knowing oneself, of fully believing in the friendship of others inside and outside the family, of accepting the reality of religious un/belief, or of trusting in
the good of politics—have driven the proliferation of religious possibilities.
Moreover, they continue to animate these new "religions," if perhaps less
in more secular developments. I have tried to capture how all of these relational impossibilities and religious and political differentiations are essential
to what I have called the intensification of secularity in Pará and Brazil.

These arguments also further mark my difference from Taylor, who, as
noted, has neglected the role of interpersonal relationships. Bringing relations back in and looking especially at friendship alongside kinship allows
us to see secularity anew: not only as a condition in which a society of "buffered selves" can choose rationally between religious options (Taylor 2007)
but as a condition in which persons are permeable, animated by human and
nonhuman relations that both trouble their kin and friends and problematize their religious and political commitments. Granted, Taylor's account
focuses on the North Atlantic. Yet this ethnography of secularity in Pará is

not an effort to merely highlight a "different kind" of secularity; it is also an invitation to reflect back on the forms of secularity that Taylor describes. One of Taylor's aims was to denaturalize the buffered self and the individual, showing that they are products of history, even a history of Catholic reform. In light of my description of secularity in Pará, however, where both common and official Catholic social forms have had a role to play—and are now animating and transforming into other religions—one wonders whether Taylor's elision of relations still unduly reinforces the idea of the autonomous individual. It is conceivable that, if we were to look more closely at the place of kin and friends in the North Atlantic too, another picture, another person, another secularity, indeed another history might emerge.

To say this does not mean that, like Taylor, I am advocating that we necessarily tie secularity to an exclusive "age" in particular places. Nor does it imply that, like many students of secularism, I wish to identify one modern globalizing project. Instead, I see secularity as a tool to help scholars stay attuned to the fact that many religious and secular projects, states, realities, politics, beliefs, differences—whatever they might be called—though connected, are engaged and continuously transformed by persons through relations. I draw inspiration here from Strathern's diagnosis of the ongoing effects of early modern philosophy, which divorced "personal identity" from relationships (Strathern 2017b, 25; see also Strathern 2020). This produced the concept of the individual agent, Strathern argues, which emerged alongside a concept of relation as *external* to entities that ultimately reinforced ideas of individuality. Prominently citing John Locke (not incidentally a father of secularism), Strathern's conclusion is clear enough. The forgetting of relations, especially kinship/friendship, has not only affected anthropological description; it has given us our current political predicament, at whose heart lies the individual (see also Lebner 2016a). This is why redescribing secularity with the flow of relations in view, including relations of kinship and friendship, can help us see the North Atlantic and elsewhere in new ways. Distinctions between religion and politics never just appear on their own. They are always lived and negotiated by persons through relations, variously conceived, experienced, and problematized.

It follows that while the rise of nonreligious phenomena, especially of an autonomous political sphere, might be tied to certain historical moments and places, this rise is not evenly or progressively distributed or experienced. In certain times and places, the experience of secularity may become more or less intense and have varying relational effects. Moreover, while secularity might be more pervasive in periods deemed modern, the possibility that there were pockets of secularity *before* modernity in Euro-America or else-where should not be excluded. Certainly, we should beware of conceptual anachronisms (e.g., of finding "religion" or "politics" before their time), but we should also be careful not to unselfconsciously reinforce conventional periodizations and spatializations that mark radical differences between the "modern secular West" and the rest (Davis 2008). In short, I am neither advocating the universalization of secularity, nor presenting a project of radical particularity. Rather, I am offering one way of admitting partial con-nections and helping us—with a conceptual tool—to describe distinctions from there (Cadena 2015; Strathern 2004).

Thus, my focus on relations, a nonpolitical site in the first instance by virtue of name and classification, can also be grasped as the politics of my description of secularity. If political transformations are to occur, it is essen-tial to understand the nature of relations and their contributions to these transformations. Which brings me to my final point here: it would be good to remember that, in writing secularity through relations, the aim is not only to identify secularism's contradictions (a common aim in anthropolo-gies of the subject). Instead, it is to acknowledge and work through multiple intersecting and shifting hopes and impossibilities—including the will to, and impossibility of, writing through relations in just the way we might wish (Lebner 2020). Of course, we might try to foreground how knowl-edge is made through interpersonal and conceptual relations, but powerful concepts will often get in the way, including the concept of relation itself (Strathern 2017b).

Throughout this book, I use impossibility synonymously with mystic, problem, instability, and paradox. All of these states share a lack of self-sameness, which is the essence of the relation. Some anthropologists have dismissed "impossibility" as a kind of philosophical ruse that is overcome in practice, arguing that despite logical impossibilities (say, of the free gift, of sacrifice, or of comparison), things are still done (e.g. Mayblin 2014; Bialecki 2017; Candea 2019). While this is one side of the argument, it remains vital to remember the impossibilities out of which conceptual and interpersonal relations are made, because they condition and limit what we can accom-plish as scholars. Historical anthropologists have recently advocated this point to useful effect (Collins 2015; Palmié 2014, 2023; see also Modern 2011). The present ethnography further underscores for me that these mystic rela-tional dynamics also come "before" any history at all.

I am not only saying that the intensification of secularity produces proliferating concerns with history (see Lebner 2019). My concern here is to also suggest that, especially in Brazil, we might do better to start with the mystic dynamics conditioning the relations we hope to describe before we can grasp the historical processes, including the politics or colonial processes, in which they are enmeshed.[13] This point complements my arguments above about the privileging of political causality in studies of colonialism and secularism, but it also builds on my early ethnographic realization that I could not analytically privilege the historico-political events of Amazonian recolonization to understand the forms of sociality that I was encountering. Indeed, local peoples' worries about the precarity, even impossibility, of human friendship were not merely shaped by the volatile events and after-effects of Amazonian settlement, whether it was the construction of the Trans-Amazon Highway, state-directed or spontaneous colonization, or the persistent conflicts over land and resources that followed. If the impact of such quintessential "events" cannot be discounted, what elucidated (and affected) the local social ambivalence in the first place were the relational tools that my interlocutors had come to Amazonia with, which, crucially, had a different kind of temporality built in. That is, not only did the Catholic divinities and their powers to shape relations arrive in Brazil from the earliest days of the colony, as we have already begun to see in the introduction and chapter 1. Crucially, they also themselves travel through time and will exist after "historical time" comes to an end. Once this Catholic temporality became evident to me, so did the force of the mystic of friendship, specifically its power to generate transformative processes, including the intensification of secularity along the PA-150 and beyond.

Here it is worth recalling the traditional Brazilian Portuguese meaning of *secular*—old, terrestrial, temporal, worldly. Though rarely used colloquially in Pará, incorporating this Portuguese sense into my description of secularity, itself a description of colonial heritage, helps further convey how I locate the mystic of friendship temporally. The secularity I am attempting to describe is not pure discontinuity but entails the ongoing negotiation of old conceptual and interpersonal relations that do not completely disappear as they transform. In other words, the longings and impossibilities that animate the mystic of friendship, while resonating with an earlier colonial moment, remain vital, moving, and transforming in modern settler Amazonia.

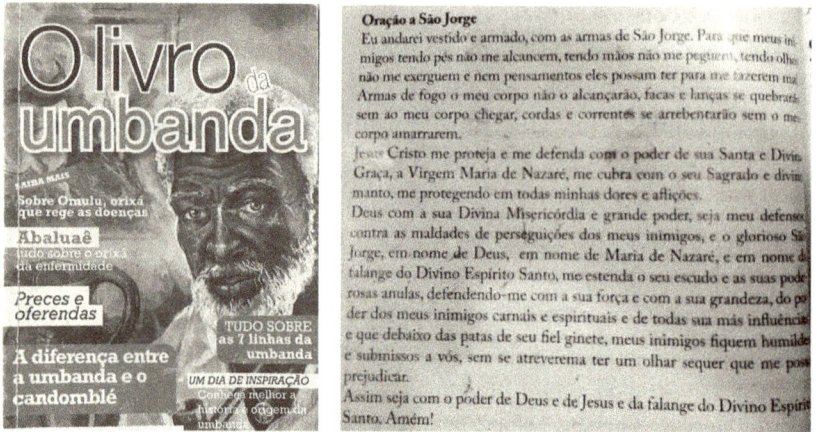

Oração a São Jorge
Eu andarei vestido e armado, com as armas de São Jorge. Para que meus inimigos tendo pés não me alcancem, tendo mãos não me peguem, tendo olhos não me exerguem e nem pensamentos eles possam ter para me fazerem mal. Armas de fogo o meu corpo não o alcançarão, facas e lanças se quebrarão sem ao meu corpo chegar, cordas e correntes se arrebentarão sem o meu corpo amarrarem.

Jesus Cristo me proteja e me defenda com o poder de sua Santa e Divina Graça, a Virgem Maria de Nazaré, me cubra com o seu Sagrado e divino manto, me protegendo em todas minhas dores e aflições.

Deus com a sua Divina Misericórdia e grande poder, seja meu defensor contra as maldades de perseguições dos meus inimigos, e o glorioso São Jorge, em nome de Deus, em nome de Maria de Nazaré, e em nome da falange do Divino Espírito Santo, me estenda o seu escudo e as suas poderosas armas, defendendo-me com a sua força e com a sua grandeza, do poder dos meus inimigos carnais e espirituais e de todas as más influências, e que debaixo das patas de seu fiel ginete, meus inimigos fiquem humildes e submissos a vós, sem se atreverem ter um olhar sequer que me possa prejudicar.

Assim seja com o poder de Deus e de Jesus e da falange do Divino Espírito Santo. Amém!

FIGURE 14. Ina's father's prayer, found in an Umbanda magazine.

On a lazy day in 2015, as Ina and I were preparing to go see her Umbanda spiritual master, her *Pai de Santo*, we found one of her father's prayers published in a magazine promoting this traditional Afro-Brazilian religion. She dismissed my excitement. The next day, on the bus, I tried to insist, "Ina! Now that you know where the prayers came from, now you can use them!" The Amazonian scrub sped by through the window behind her. "No, no, Ashley, this doesn't make any difference. I still don't know how to use them—no one does." She turned her eyes toward the window. "You can keep them."

After all of this, my understanding of the church changed—not my relationship with God, that has stayed the same.[1] I can explain it like this: Let's say I have my family, and my family loves me. But then tomorrow I discover that my mother always wished me ill (*mal*) and my sister always wished me ill (*mal*). So my understanding of my family changed, but it is still my family. My God is my God. He is who protects me and gives me strength, he is who gives health for my children and my family. Look. I don't miss a [Marabá] *círio* (saint celebration, which honors Our Lady of Nazareth). . . . I pray the rosary (*terço*) periodically here at home. . . . I call on my community to pray the *terço* here at home. . . . Perhaps it is because there are religious forces that have accompanied my family since 1800 and something—I will tell you that story afterward. So, my relationship with God—every night I pray, before leaving home I ask for protection from God in my prayers. I don't ask for anything from God, because if I do I am being selfish, I am being ungrateful, I already have so much. . . . My relationship with God hasn't changed, it is the same. I try to always, always, always be thankful. For example, I go to Corpus Christi Mass, all the way over there in [New Marabá], there are days of Mass I participate in here [at the church] with my mother, as I said my mother is a Minister of the Eucharist, so I meet [and pray] with my mother, in other communities, I go all the way there to the Sanctuary of Saint Nazareth, so nothing has changed [with God], my trauma is with Man. . . .

Let me now explain that other thing that connects me with God, to

Catholicism: my great-grandparents were Indians (*Indios*)—I mean, my great-grandmother was an *India*. It was in the South, Rio Grande do Sul, at the time there were *cacheros*, right? That person who went around selling in the interiors of the country and such. And then one of those days, my great-grandfather [a *cachero*] went into an Indigenous village, and he fell in love with [the woman who was to become my great-grandmother]. My great-grandfather stuck around for a time to see if he could run away with her. He had asked if he could take her, and she wanted to, but [her family] did not let them. So they stalled a bit, working things out, and my grandfather said one day, "We are going to run away. Let's wait until everyone is sleeping and let's run away." And so they did. They waited until everyone fell asleep and then [snaps fingers] they ran, they left everything, they left the merchandise and everything, he left just with her and the clothes on his back. When the sun rose they [the villagers] realized that [my great-grandparents] were missing and they went after them.

[Meanwhile, in the forest] my great-grandfather, running to escape, tripped and fell. My great-grandmother, who was behind him, fell on top of him. Both of my great-grandparents looked at what had tripped them, it was a like a stump, but a different kind of stump. They tried to pull it out, there was only the top of it, black—no not black, like a little bald patch, right? And they said, "It is an image (*imagem*)!" And they began to dig, and they pulled and pulled, tried to wedge it out with a stick. But then they decided to hire someone to dig this image out. My great-grandfather was thinking that he was going to *sell it*. Finally, they got it out, though they had broken the arm, and they ran away with that image.

They came all the way to Pará and wanted to start their lives here. They went to the church, to get married and to baptize the image—because at that time they baptized images, right? My great-grandmother didn't speak [Portuguese] that well at the time so my great-grandfather told the story to the priest—and the priest said that the image was St. Anthony the matchmaker (*casamenteiro*). . . .

My great-grandparents then decided that their first son would be called Antônio, and they would give him the statue. My grandfather was born, they named him Antônio and gave him the statue. Then my father was born, they named him Antônio and gave him the statue. Then my father got married. Three girls were born and then I came. And they named me Antônio and gave me the statue. ["Yay, how cool!" I exclaimed, and Antônio chuckled and walked away and brought the statue to show

FIGURE 15. Antonio's family's Saint Anthony. Photo: Ashley Lebner.

me.] So it has been in my family since 1800 and something. Here is where
they broke the arm taking it out of the ground. At some point it fell—
during my father's generation. Here is where they glued it. And now I
have a son, he is fourteen years old and his name is Antônio [and he will
be taking care of this after I am gone].

    This seems like just a stone statue. But for us, our faith is so strong.
Just so you have an idea of it, sometimes I would cough and my father
would take the saint and clean and clean it, and then put water inside of
it—I don't know if you saw that it is hollow here? Well he would put water

in it, and then pour it into a cup of water for us to drink and the cough would go away. He is our saint: every year I celebrate his feast [June 13]. And I will pass it on to my son. I tell him [each year]: "Soon, you are going to start making these celebrations too."

03

CLEUSA'S SETTLEMENT

Poetry and the Devil's Arts

I came here with my mother and grandmother in 1962 from the North-east. Once here, my mother married a Brazil-nut cutter, a drover (*tropeiro*) who led troops of animals carrying Brazil nuts through the lands with no owner (*terras sem dono*). Well, the "owners" were the major Brazil-nut barons who had arrived and simply said the lands belonged to them.[1] My father went wherever the bosses told him to go to collect Brazil nuts. He went with wife and children, sometimes even my grandmother. I remember my mother having children in the forest. Sometimes we went years without coming to the city. All these places, towns, settlements like the 26th of March, or this settlement where we are now, I passed through them all on the backs of animals on trails. There were no cars here, no cars in Marabá. After a time I remember there were two cars—a Jeep, owned by the Bezerra family, and a *Rural*, owned by the Rosa family. People just moved around [this region] on the backs of animals and on the rivers.

All the Brazil nuts my father collected were for the *barracão*, a warehouse and general store [owned by the bosses], where they sold coffee, sugar, kerosene—*everything*. They even sold rifles and cartridges. [You had to use your pay from Brazil nuts to buy other necessary items from the *barracão*, and] many people never had money to leave [or stop working for the boss]. Our luck was that my father really learned how to expertly cut open Brazil nuts [pods and shells] with a machete. [The seed pods and nuts themselves have extremely hard shells, and it is very difficult to extract them]. My father died [some time ago], and I had always meant to ask him where he learned to do that. Because he harvested and processed *a lot* of Brazil nuts [and fast]; he even won an award for it. And he was a good troop leader too, which made our situation a little better than others. Few could cut Brazil nuts [well], and many could never [pay off their debts with the *barracão*]. They became like slaves.

As a child I didn't have the opportunity to study.... We were so often in the forest. We didn't go to church. But my grandmother prayed the rosary and every night she would make us kneel with her and pray. She would also talk about a conformist God, a God who accepted that suffering. I always questioned that. One time, I remember it like it was today, I was praying and praying and I said, "Oh, I don't like this God anymore. I don't like him!" She said she was going to hit me because I was sinning, [but I insisted]: "I don't like him!" How can this God let me stay without sandals, how is this God going to let me stay in this place with no little friends (*coleguinha*)? But she thought that we had to conform to our life, because the poor existed to work for the rich. She said that, she did. She didn't know how to read or write. She was the descendant of slaves. And she still thought all that....

My father told lots of stories at night. So many. Despite arriving tired, he enjoyed it. Lying in little rooms in our hammocks, through walls of palm thatch, we asked him to tell us stories. Later we were ten brothers and sisters, but in the early days we were only a few, only four. He told us stories that used to be called "romances," but today they are called *literatura de cordel* [string literature]. I remember these stories—and he didn't only tell them, he sang them, too. I remember he told one about Alfredo and Lindalva, about an impossible love. You know, those romances of suffering and courage. There were others, "The devil and I-don't-know-who," "Zé goes to heaven with I-don't-remember-who-else." We each had our favorite. "Tell that one. No, tell that one!" The stories seemed like they were all true, they were realities that we were living. . . . Their suffering seemed like our suffering. But at the same time the struggles and victory of those impossible loves made it seem like we were going to succeed too. It is a lesson that still guides me today.

Cleusa shared these images of her childhood with me one day in 2015 as we sat beneath a small tree in her backyard in a settlement along the PA-150 highway around one hundred kilometers west of its intersection with the Trans-Amazon. Our aim had been to talk about Cleusa's Catholic activism in the 1980s during the recolonization of the region. As I later listened to this interview, I was captivated: I could see her traveling through the forests as her father worked his way out of debt bondage to the *barracão*, a common mode of "employment" in the region at the time. I was also struck by her youthful prayers with her grandmother and her anger at a conformist God. And I was especially fascinated by how common Catholic poetic tales animated her enjoyable nights and daily struggles, especially the perennial struggle with relationships: human, nonhuman, divine, and diabolical. Her references to this latter struggle reminded me that, although Catholicism may have changed since Vatican II (1962–65), grasping contemporary dynamics like understandings of the devil still requires attention to preconciliar forms. One such form was the *cordel*, a key genre of Brazilian print media, consolidated in the late nineteenth century and read and performed ever since, especially in the Northeast.

Although the religious aspects of *cordel* have long been recognized, it is remarkable how few studies approach this poetic genre as a source of knowledge about Brazilian Catholicism.[2] With this popular medium in hand, I first began to reflect on *mediation*, a scholarly concern that has inspired much twenty-first-century scholarship on religion. I soon noticed that the turn to mediation has mostly sidelined discussions of relations—especially the kinds of interpersonal relationships and mystic relational dynamics so important to Cleusa and other people I spoke with along the PA-150. Instead, the media turn has focused on how materials and sensing bodies produce and bind religious communities, publics, and politics. Initially, this occlusion seemed to be an inadvertent consequence of a salutary scholarly focus. After all, the original aims of this turn were to get beyond religion as belief and to better understand how religion became real (e.g., Meyer 2009, 5; Hirschkind and Larkin 2008). Yet it was instructive to find that some influential scholars of media have actively sought to replace the concept of "relations" with "mediation" (Grusin 2015, 128).[3] Of course, many students of religion are not so radical in their approach. Still, it has rarely been pointed out that a turn away from relations is deeply embedded in discussions of mediation. This might be due to how the interest in mediation converged with the new materialism, inspired in good part by the work of Bruno Latour, which has persistently, if quietly, valued the mediator (agentive object) above the relation (Latour 1993; see Strathern 2020). And the effects are visible. Across a range of scholarship, the idea of the medium has tended to expand, coming to stand in for relations, whether this is intended or not. More problematically, as Marilyn Strathern suggests, focusing on the agency of material media makes the medium into an individual, rather than helping interrogate the category of the individual, as is often assumed (2020, 173).[4] In short, in a world where all human and nonhuman actors have their respective, individual, agency, and affect others *after* they relate, relations become secondary, even incidental.

By pointing out the relative invisibility of relations in studies of mediation and their corresponding tendency to individualize persons and things, I am extending a recent critique of the scholarship on material religion: that a lack of attention to relationships has often produced a standardized individual "religious subject." Constance Furey, for example, has pointed out how the turn to the body, materiality, subjectivity, and society—precisely also the concerns of the "media turn"—has surprisingly made the religious subject appear to be "alone in a crowd" (2012, 10; 2017). As a corrective, and expanding on Robert Orsi (2005, 2011), Furey has called for new research on the role of intimate relationships such as "kinship, friendship, patronage, marriage, and other relationships less easily named" (2012, 10). Brenna Moore soon joined the conversation, suggesting that friendship is often key to cultivating religious sensibilities and communities (2015). Anticipating critique, both Furey and Moore assert that they are not calling for a retreat to "nonessential" practices or "inner worlds" at a remove from "power and politics" (Furey 2012, 9; Moore 2015, 439). On the contrary, Moore affirms that studying relations can keep "our studies of structure tethered to people's experiences. . . . [Relations offer] a crucial matrix for analyzing that intermediary realm between the individual and society" (2015, 439). In other words, focusing on relations allows us to stay critical while confounding the "impasses" produced by the academic trade in opposed approaches: practice versus belief, action versus meaning, materiality versus interiority.

Following these authors, I agree that a more relationally minded scholarship can shed new light on how religious sensibilities and communities are shaped. However, drawing on the work of Marilyn Strathern, I show that a focus on relations is more than just a supplement to, or a way to unite, current approaches (Strathern 1988, 2020; Lebner 2016a, 2017a). Studying relations also entails more than focusing on social or even intimate relationships, though the latter remain important. Indeed, when relations are grasped solely as social or intimate, it might seem plausible to say—even despite the growing consensus to the contrary (Dunn and Moore 2020)— that religious studies has been discussing relationships for a while, especially in Catholicism. Yet even if accounts of Catholicism began attending to relations following Orsi's (2005) call, relations have remained mostly secondary to other foci such as identity, experience, imagination, or agency (material or otherwise).[5] Most importantly, these accounts neither explore what relations can mean for the production of knowledge generally, nor do they help bring into view the ways individuals and other related conventions such as politics or mediation are conceived in, and emerge from, relations.[6] Treating relations as secondary may have also contributed to the surprising fact that few have explored evil, especially the devil, as a key part of Catholic relationality, including how God and the devil can be seen to perennially create and dissolve all media. Instead, material mediation has become a kind of orthodoxy that has "built in" the displacement of relations. All this, I argue, has contributed to the circulation of a relatively essentialized view of Catholicism as a religion mediated by materiality par excellence and of the media turn itself as more "Catholic" (than Protestant). Such a view has quietly undergirded thinking on religion and media for more than a decade (e.g., Engelke 2011a, 99, 101; 2011b).[7]

This book, in contrast, is committed to exploring a broader understanding of relations for the study of religion, secularity, and colonization. Here I can fully articulate how I am doing so with the help of Strathern, who has offered a powerful, if deceptively simple, account of relations. Though Strathern's writing is notoriously challenging, the ways she defines relations are also very colloquial, to the point that scholars have regularly misrecognized her project's difference from, say, Latourian or allied ontological approaches.[8] Simply put, for Strathern, relations are not just interpersonal connections among humans and nonhumans but also conceptual ones. In fact, she calls on us not to even distinguish between persons and things until we know how *persons* and *things* are conceived within the domain under analysis. This does not mean that everything is everywhere the same, as sometimes happens in Latourian-inspired analyses, where all entities are preidentified as "agents." Rather, a key part of studying relations is acknowledging distinctions. In truth, there *can be no relations* without distinctions. This means, to give a few examples, that relations are not only positive; that persons might not always be individuals; and that politics might not always be determining. Indeed, from a Catholic perspective, relations, persons, and politics can all be evil and consequently—as Osias, one of Cleusa's comrades, impressed on me—not ultimately real (see chapter 6). In short, attending to both interpersonal and conceptual connections and distinctions can help transform both the terms of our analyses and the politics of our descriptions.

I have already discussed how an unmarked faith in the causal power of political secularism has obscured the vitality of relations. Yet more can be said about why a focus on relations, and especially critical engagement with mediation and politics, is important for scholars, especially those concerned with their own politics. I am not suggesting that religious processes should not be read as potentially political; they certainly should, when ethnographically or historically relevant. I am arguing instead that more scholarly care is needed. We might miss something when we privilege material mediations and politics as both the sources and outcomes of transformation, as many studies of mediation do.[9] Remaining open to relations, which includes remaining open to their rarely discussed potential for evil in Catholicism, can not only tell us about political and colonial dynamics; it can also help reveal the power and limits of what politics, mediation, or materiality in a given context might be.

Although my readings of Strathern, together with important calls to think beyond mediation (Hirschkind 2011; see also Beliso-De Jesus 2015; Hovland 2017)[10] helped me think through these issues, it was ultimately my engagements with cordel, and with Brazilian Catholics more generally, that inspired me to reprioritize relations and be cautious with mediation and politics. What might appear as mediation for the scholar of the Catholic context I describe here is ultimately only important because of its role in relationships, or what it does to them, or how it is, in fact, *composed by* them. As Antônio said in the Third Visitation about the found "image" of St. Anthony: "This seems like just a stone statue. But for us, our faith is so strong. . . ." Antônio suggested that the statue had blessed his great-grandparents' marriage and subsequent generations of his family, and even that the water poured from its hollows cured their illnesses. Thus it is more than mere matter, more than a simple medium. For Antônio, at the very least it is an image composed by the divine powers of kinship and friendship. It is their family saint. My argument in this chapter is this: once we identify how relationships among these Catholics and their surroundings might always be potentially animated by relationships with divine entities, whether they are devilish or not, the material medium dissolves. That is, it becomes impossible to identify what or who is mediating what or whom. The challenge of this point can be easily obscured by those scholars foregrounding the medium, not least because of their avowed "essentialist" and "Catholic" starting point as affirmed by Engelke (2011a, 99; see note 7, above). Indeed, despite broader interest in where the medium dis/appears,[11] underlying and ultimately Protestant assumptions of Catholic religiosity as "mediated by materiality" make the particularities of various Catholicisms especially hard to see. When we begin instead from relations, we find that, even as relations remain troubled, both the "good" or causal force of the material medium—along with the political, defined as human struggles over governance—can be productively questioned.

To begin from relations with these *cordel* in hand—to understand them both on their own terms and their relational legacies for settlers along the PA-150 highway—I must start from the conceptual and interpersonal relations within *cordel*, not from *cordel*'s preconceived "materiality," despite what an observer can see and touch. *Cordel* are a kind of print media that emerged in the late nineteenth century and retain the same form and themes today. Although *cordel* are no longer technically "string stories," that is, mostly sold in outdoor markets pinned up on cords, they continue to be printed on fourfold newsprint pages and are made into pamphlets of four by six and a half inches, containing eight pages or multiples thereof.[12] The content of *cordel* is also the same: they generally recount moral tests of their heroes or heroines and are meant to entertain; sometimes they even evoke sex. But their moral concerns, and especially their concerns with evil, link them, as Candace Slater (1982) notes, to "religious tradition." Even though *cordel* might be understood as a material medium, then, beginning with the relations they dramatize reveals a Catholicism where the material dissolves and therefore cannot be relied upon to "mediate."

These dissolutions and their implications can be gleaned from four exemplary *cordel* from the late nineteenth and early twentieth centuries that I have selected for analysis here. I consider these *cordel* exemplary because, first, they represent the different kinds of *cordel* that Cleusa mentioned in my opening quotation: stories about impossible love, about the devil, and about journeying, struggle, and redemption. Second, they were widely distributed both in their day and after. And third, they shed light on a preconciliar Catholicism that still resonates strongly in Brazil today, even though this is rarely acknowledged.

I have chosen to examine *cordel* drafted in the years of the First Republic (1889–1930) because these years were defining. Early *cordelistas* produced the forms that later *cordelistas* elaborated on. This was literally the case for Leandro Gomes de Barros (1865–1918), the most influential *cordelista* of any period, whose work will be the focus of the first three sections of this chapter. The rights to much of Barros's work were acquired in 1921 by João Martins de Atayde, who reworked many of Barros's *cordel* and republished them under his name (R. Benjamin 2020). "The Force of Love" (1910) and "The Duel Between Manoel Riachão and the Devil" (1908), discussed in the next two sections, were published under Barros's name. These two poems show how love, friendship, and even kinship are constituted and destabilized by the perennial possibility of divine and diabolical intervention. "The Migrant," discussed in the fourth section, currently bears Atayde's name (Atayde 1946).[13] Expanding on what we learn in the first two *cordel*, this poem about backlanders fleeing drought and hunger tells us that as one seeks God, one might encounter the devil anywhere or in any*thing*, from the weather and the land to the estate foreman and the scythe that you wield against him—and thus even potentially in oneself.

The final poem I examine is the most famous of all. It is also the oldest, and it is less conventional, as it is composed in quatrains rather than sextains. It was discovered in 1897 in postwar Canudos, a backland town of some thirty thousand people who had gathered to live under the leadership of a radical preacher, Antônio Conselheiro. Soldiers found the poem in the ruins after the Brazilian Army leveled the town, and Euclides da Cunha, a journalist covering the war, copied it into his notebook. Parts of this *cordel* made their way into da Cunha's account of the war and its people, *Os Sertões* (The Backlands), which became one of Brazil's foundational literary and social-scientific works (Cunha 1984 [1902]).

I deploy an analysis of the Canudos *cordel* to bring to life the relational implications the other poems introduce. Crucially, the Canudos *cordel* shows how the perceived proliferation of the devil, evident in the other poems, played a role in one of the most dramatic events in Brazilian history: the first war of Brazil's republic. As we will see, the Canudos *cordel* proclaims the devil's triumph in the guise of the new republic, which separated church and state in 1889, instituting the idea of a political domain autonomous from religion. Although I do not argue that *all* backlanders came to believe that the republic was decidedly evil, reading across these *cordel* makes it clear that the generalizability of evil, its *potential* presence, was widely conceived as a possibility. Because this fact is elided in recent and predominant accounts (e.g., Hoornaert 1997; Johnson et al. 2018; Levine 1992), its social and political implications have remained obscure for the past as much as for the present. Focusing on relations allows me to foreground these implications and to consolidate the argument of this chapter: because all "matter on earth" remained in question for these Catholics, exclusively human authority, as manifest in the nature of republican politics, was also eminently problematic because it was always potentially evil.

As we have already begun to see, and will continue to see in later chapters, Amazonian settlers approach the topics of evil and politics in much the same way. In other words, this journey far beyond the PA-150 highway will bring religious and political dynamics along the highway into clearer view.

LEANDRO GOMES DE BARROS
AND *LITERATURA DE CORDEL*

[Leandro] was not the prince of the poets of the asphalt, but he was, in the eyes of the people, the king of the poetry of the backlands. . . . Leandro was the great consoler and animator of his compatriots . . . telling them as much about . . . the devil, as . . . about real . . . [rural bandits].

C. ANDRADE 1976, cited in *Revista Prosa Verso Arte*

Leandro Gomes de Barros was the author of three of our four *cordel*. He was widely recognized as "the poet of the people" and the "first without second" well before the celebrated modernist poet Carlos Drummond de Andrade wrote the description quoted above. Barros was born in the Northeastern state of Paraíba in 1865, and he had become the most prolific and widely known *cordelista* in Brazil by the time of his death at fifty-two—whether of Spanish influenza, the shame of prison, or an aneurysm—in 1918.[14] He wrote most of his poems between 1889 and 1918, as the genre of *cordel* was distinguishing itself from its most immediate precursor, the Portuguese chapbook, also sometimes referred to as *cordel*.[15]

Brazilian *cordel* came to differ from their European forebears thanks mostly to the influence of the improvising poet-performers, the *cantadores* (singers), on whom Barros modeled his career. Backlanders enjoyed these performers' spontaneous and quick-witted compositions in song and verse. The first and most famous school for such singers, the Escola do Teixeira, emerged in the eighteenth century in Paraíba's interior. The Teixeira group is credited with shifting poetic taste and practice from the four-line quatrain known as the *quadra*, used in Portuguese chapbooks, and instituting the *repente* (sextain), the predominant verse form of Brazilian *cordel*. *Repente* are generally six lines of seven syllables following a consonantal ABCBDB rhyme scheme. The success of backlands *cantadores* (who were sometimes called *repentistas* after the verse form) may have contributed to the consolidation of the *cordel*'s almost exclusive grounding in poetic forms, contrasting with Portuguese chapbooks, which often included prose.

Barros grew up in Teixeira, and his career emulated the model established by the Teixeira school. Like other *cordelistas* and poet-singers before him, Barros traveled widely to perform and sell his songs. He also improvised verses, even though he supposedly did not engage in the verbal dueling that made others famous. Barros's impressive productivity, coupled with the quality of his verses, consolidated his legacy and that of the *cordel* more generally. In approximately 1893, Barros founded his own press, Perseverance Typography (Typografia Perseverança) to publish his *cordel* in "all the genres and modes of the popular form: duel, romance, humor, satire and social criticism" (Gaspar 2009). Barros became one of the few *cordelistas* to live solely off the proceeds of his craft, and his birthday, November 19, is now celebrated as the "National Day of the *Cordelista*" (Gaspar 2009).

Despite Barros's acknowledged importance, his work has never been systematically studied,[16] which adds credence to the claim by Carlos Filho (2005) that scholarship on *cordel* has been patchy, particularly with regard to religion (see also note 2, above). Yet *cordel* offer insight into Northeastern conceptualizations of everyday relationships animated by Catholicism, that is, by divine and devilish agents shaping, challenging, and dissolving the mediating power of everything from the environment to love and marriage, friendship and kinship, and relationships of hierarchy, as we will see.

The Power of Love

To capture these Catholic relational challenges, I begin with "The Power of Love" (A força do amor), which was published by Barros in 1910–12 and republished many times until at least 1975 under the title "The Power of Love, or Alonso and Marina." It is a story of "impossible love," as Cleusa would call it, which is significant for our purposes, as it introduces us to the power of God to make impossible relationships possible for the faithful. Though some of what follows might seem familiar, my hope is that readers will come to see the implications of these forms and themes anew.

"The Power of Love" weaves a tale about the daughter of a baron and a poor boy who met and fell in love when they were children but whose marriage was cruelly forbidden when they came of age. After their love comes to light, the baron runs Alonso out of town. Yet when he tries to force Marina to marry, she refuses since she can't marry Alonso, and she finally and dramatically stabs a fiancé at the altar. The poem mentions God regularly, but God's supremacy over the lovers' relationship becomes clearest at the climax of the story, when Alonso and Marina have been reunited, only to face death at sea. Marina prays:

> Jesus Christ, Redeemer,
> God and true man,
> . . .
> For your innocent blood
> That in drops from the cross came down
> . . . Pardon these crimes of mine.
>
> I ask you, my Lord! help me
> . . . If you wish
> To punish me with penance
> Make the waters open
> So that we drown in them
> Saving Alonso is enough
> I am satisfied to pay (Barros 1910, 27–29).

The extent of this prayer is impressive. It runs six stanzas, not all reproduced here, detailing and celebrating sacrifice and suffering for others, from Jesus Christ who died for humanity's sins, to Marina's willingness to die to save Alonso's life at God's hands. Most significant for our purposes is the *fact* of this prayer at the climax of the story, coupled with God's intervention as a result. When God answers Marina's prayer, the audience is shown how all loves are made possible by the grace of God, who attends to the requests of the worthy. This is not only a scholarly interpretation. As Cleusa's account suggests, a tale of impossible love like Alonso's and Marina's can both reflect one's own faith and provide a hopeful example.

While *cordel* teach their public to remain faithful to God, they also call for wariness of the devil, who is always poised to disrupt human relationships with God, with his agents, with other humans, and with natural places.

The Struggle Between Manoel Riachão and the Devil

One of Barros's most famous *cordel*, "The Duel Between Manoel Riachão and the Devil" (henceforth "The Duel"), brings into relief the potential for evil in common Catholic relationships. In other words, although God makes good, loving relationships possible, the devil can appear at any time

FIGURE 16. Reprint of Barros's "The Duel Between Manoel Riachão and the Devil." Published originally in 1908, with this reprint from 1974 in open access format from the Biblioteca de Obras Raras Átila Almeida.

as anyone or anything, especially as a person posing as a new friend. Published first in 1908 and then repeatedly throughout the twentieth century, "The Duel" tells the story of a guitar player who is approached by a poorly clothed Black stranger who wants to sing a competitive duet or "duel" with him. Riachão rejects him, not because he thinks he is the devil, but because he might be an "escaped slave." The palpable racism here reveals the deep prejudice against Afro-Brazilians that persisted after abolition in 1888 and was conveyed in numerous *cordel*. Others have discussed this, including in a reading of "The Duel" and another of Barros's *cordel*, which describes the relationship between the devil and Protestants (Lacerda, 2014). However, because the devil does not always appear in *cordel* as a Black man and because the devil is associated with religious difference and numerous other "deviations," it is worth reading "The Duel" for its more general warning against engaging with the devil.

That the devil repeatedly tries to convince Riachão that he is worth trusting as a friend suggests that the audience should remain attuned to the threat posed by potential friends. The *cordel* also models how to face such dangers: think with the Bible and stay on God's side. Riachão begins thinking with the help of biblical figures such as Joshua and Moses, who appear in the eleventh stanza. Yet it is only after twenty-eight more stanzas, when Riachão sees the stranger is able to do things that no person can do, that he begins to doubt whether this stranger is human.

For example, when the man claims to know Brazil so well that he can tell anyone how to travel safely thousands of miles from the Northeast to Rio de Janeiro, Riachão finally begins to think that he is not heaven-sent (Barros 1908, 7–8). "This Black man is damned," Riachão says to himself. "He came from hell / by the demon he was sent / to trick me. . . ." Yet Riachão does not speak his thoughts out loud for twenty-six more stanzas, when he exclaims:

> Now I finally believe
> You are the enemy. . . .
> But I believe in God
> I cannot run the risk (Barros 1908, 13).

The "enemy," as we have already seen, is a common name for the devil in Brazil. The devil is the enemy because he tries to appear to be divinely sent, a friend who helps, while doing evil. The devil responds to Riachão's accusation:

> Riachão, you love God
> But are badly recompensed
> God made Paul a monarch
> And Peter a simple soldier. . . .
> Your neighbor and relative

> Got rich without working
> Your father worked so hard
> And could never get richer
> He didn't go to bed for one night
> Without praying (Barros 1908, 14–15).

The devil is the enemy because he seeks to divide, to destroy human lives and human relationships with God and other people. The devil, it is implied, can raise Riachão up where God has kept him down. But Riachão does not lose his faith. "If God made Paul a king," he says,

> it is because Paul deserved it. . . .
> If it wasn't necessary
> our great God would not do it. . . .
> My father died in poverty
> He was faithful to God. . . .
> It is a happy man
> Who is consoled by his lot
> I can die in poverty [too] . . . (Barros 1908, 14-15).

The devil looks at Riachão with hatred and disappears, leaving the stench of sulfur in his wake.

Riachão passes his test, falling neither for the devil's initial attempt at deception nor for the promise of power he made once Riachão discovered his true identity. Beyond the racism in Riachão's initial fear of the man's Blackness, this *cordel* tells readers to constantly stay aware that the devil can appear at any time as anyone, perhaps especially as people claiming to be friends. Of course one might also say that this *cordel* carries a political message, since it can be read as a comment on the order of things, on governance. "The Duel" certainly calls on its audience to uphold God-given hierarchy, inequality, and even poverty. Yet the *cordel*'s stated concern is not political. Instead, its primary message is relational, namely, that you must always be on your guard against devilish persons and practices that might shake your faith in God and cause you to question or break with the human relationships that make you and your world. As we move through the next two *cordel*, it will become clearer why this difference in message matters. These divine and devilish powers are the reason Catholics might question the true power of any medium, political or otherwise.

The Migrant

It is the devil in mourning
in the year that in the backlands
if at the end of the month of January
no one hears thunder
the backlander does not take
his eye off the wanderer (Barros and Atayde 1946, 1).[17]

These lines begin the *cordel* whose title I have translated as "The Migrant," though the Portuguese title (*O Retirante*) employs a term used specifically to describe Northeasterners who leave (or retreat from) their land to escape drought and poverty. The Northeastern backlands had severe periodic droughts that set off successive waves of migration to other parts of Brazil, most notably in 1877, 1915, 1932, 1958, and 1983 (Nys et al. 2016, 25). The drought, associated in the verse above with the devil, is referenced there by the absence of thunder. "The Migrant" is therefore uniquely resonant for our purposes: it helps build a vivid image of the everyday lives, suffering, and Catholicism of Northeasterners, deepening our understanding of the powers of God and the devil presented in "The Duel."

I should emphasize that whereas "The Duel" merely *suggests* that the devil can appear anywhere, in "The Migrant" we see the devil threatening persons and things. The devil can animate the weather, the land, and even the backlanders—a distribution of evil that ultimately dissolves the difference between mediator and mediated. This will echo in the Canudos *cordel*, as we will see.

Of course, "The Migrant" also reminds readers of the power of God and his agents to shape, redeem, and save human lives. Take the second stanza:

And he [the backlander] says to his wife
prepare the carrying-baskets,
tomorrow I am leaving
if our good God wishes (Barros and Atayde 1946, 1).

In the next stanza, another divine entity, Padre Cícero, who often appears in *cordel* (Filho 2005), joins God in blessing the hungry migrants' journey. Padre Cícero (1844–1934) was an important religious and political leader during Barros's lifetime, and millions of faithful across Brazil continue to

venerate him as a popular saint. Padre Cícero reappears again in the fif-
teenth stanza where the poem describes the "thousand promises" (Barros
and Atayde 1946, 5) or vows made to Cícero, exemplified by the backlander
who promises to pray daily in exchange for rain and a safe journey home.

This devotion to divine entities notwithstanding, what is most significant
here is that the backlanders see no end to their suffering; they receive no
response to their prayers. Instead, the *cordel* describes the devil's torment-
ing presence—including the ways he animates or even infuses the lands
to which the backlanders have traveled as they search for work, food, and
redemption:

> Oh! Saintly father take us
> from this country of mosquitoes
> nights here are so ugly
> the days so strange
> in contrast to the backlands
> where the fields are so pretty. . . .
> in the forest and mountain
> not a cricket chirps
> there is no joy. . . .
> loneliness remains
> it is here that the devil
> lost his spur (Barros and Atayde 1946, 6).

A stanza later the devil appears again, this time no longer as a being who
has marked the land with his spur—a word which in Portuguese (*espora*)
conjures "spore" (*esporo*) and thus the capacity to penetrate and infuse even
more than it does in English.[18] Instead, the devil appears as the figure of an
estate manager as well as the backlander he oppresses:

> Sometimes my mouth froths
> with the anger I have
> the mill owner has this manager
> he is the devil
> worse than a dragon
> I truly intend
> to one day take him out
> to put to him to an end
> on the scythe of Satan (Barros and Atayde 1946, 6–7).

If the devil is the cause and end point (on the scythe) of one's own anger, then the devil is not only potentially everywhere, he is also possibly in one-self. The *cordel* ends in dejection:

> This is the result
> of the poor man who leaves
> without even a cent
> displaced from his lands
> he finds not a damn
> doors will not open
> what gruesome luck
> with too many children
> and his wife behind him
> leading a goat (*cabra*) (Barros and Atayde 1946, 8).

The poor man's bad luck seems to go beyond finding all doors closed. If the backlander is able to kill a man with "the scythe of Satan," his family also seems damned—he is followed everywhere by the devil, as his wife trails behind leading the most devilish animal of all, the goat.

"The Migrant" thus helps flesh out the problem of Catholic relations. If the first *cordel* we examined, "The Power of Love," showed the power of God and his agents to secure good and loving relationships against all odds, "The Migrant" displays the challenges confronting the faithful: the devil can truly be everywhere. Although one can always try to steer clear of devilish temptations, "The Migrant" shows us that this might not always be possible. Evil is everywhere, potentially in others, in ourselves, or in the environment. The first lesson I draw from this, as I discussed at the beginning of this chapter, is that when evil, as much as the divine, might be animating any person or thing, it is not only the medium as material that dissolves. What also disappears is any clear sense of who or what is doing the mediating, whether the person, the object, God, or the devil.

Yet I not only question our capacity to properly identify "the medium" in this context. I also hope to show what happens when we begin to take what we learn from studying relations seriously. In the Northeastern Catholic world, where the good of one's relations, both human and nonhuman, is always potentially in question, it follows that doubts regarding exclusively human forms of governance, of politics, should arise. Although I phrase this idea here as the logical outcome of a mode of thought, the next section grounds it in verses that narrate a key event in Brazilian history, in

fragments of a poem found in the rubble of Canudos. These verses will further historicize our understanding of how fears of worldly materialized evil
animate a radical anti-political strain within Brazilian Catholicism, already
visible in the *cordel* described above.

CANUDOS

In the last days of the campaign, when permission was given to enter
the shattered huts, the victors met with painful disappointment. . . .
The most abundant war spoils to be found were mutilated images and
coconut-shell rosaries, and what the victors most coveted in the end were
the letters, whatever writings, and principally the graceless verses they
unearthed. . . . They recorded the preachings of Antônio Conselheiro. . . .
What resonates in each line is the same diffuse and incongruent religiosity, very little political significance, which would allow them to be
lent easily to the messianic trends expounded. The rebel [Conselheiro]
attacked the constituted order because he imagined that the promised
reign of bliss was imminent. He pronounced the republic . . . a supreme
heresy indicating the ephemeral triumph of the Antichrist. And the rustic

FIGURE 17. Hut at Canudos, Flavio de Barros, 1895. Public Domain.

FIGURE 18. Follower of Antônio Conselheiro in front of a hut in Canudos. Flavio de Barros, date unknown. Public Domain. Coleção Canudos, Acervo Museu da República / IBRAM / Ministério da Cultura.

> poets, rhyming their deliria in colorless quatrains, lacking the spontane-
> ity of backland improvisers, nevertheless left a . . . rude and eloquent . . .
> second Bible (Cunha 1984 [1902], 119).

This is what Euclides da Cunha wrote in *Os Sertões* (The Backlands) to introduce a series of excerpts from a poem found in the rubble of postwar Canudos. "We will copy a few of them at random," continues Euclides (as he is generally referred to in the Brazilian scholarship). He also adds framing commentary, which I have put in italics below:

> Dom Pedro II was sent
> To the kingdom of Lisbon
> The monarchy ended
> Adrift Brazil went!

> *The republic was sacrilege:*

> Protected by the law
> Are those we know are evil.
> We have the law of God
> They have the law of the devil (*do cão*)!

How wretched are they
When elections come around.
It's down with the law of God
And up with the law of the hound!

They are marrying the people
Just to deceive
They are going to bind (*casar*) everyone
Through civil marriage!

The demonic government, however, will soon disappear:

Dom Sebastião has arrived
With a mighty regiment.
He put an end to civil unions
Making us content!

The Antichrist was born
To govern Brazil.
But here is the Counselor
To save us from his will.

Sebastian our king
To visit us is bound.
Woe be to sinners
Living under the law of the hound![19]

I have quoted Euclides at length to contextualize these verses, which I analyze to consolidate the argument of this chapter: that attending to interpersonal and conceptual relations in Catholicism, especially evil relations,
can denaturalize concepts that contemporary scholars of Catholicism and
religion rarely question—from mediation to politics. Yet to offer this analysis I must untangle these verses from the weave of more than a century of
debate, which has mostly effaced the relations and distinctions they convey.

    In the early twentieth century, Euclides was considered an authority on
Canudos. But more recently, scholars have called his readings into question,
even actively seeking to "deprivilege" them due to biases he revealed despite
his sympathetic account (see Amory 1999, 667). Indeed, while Euclides condemned the brutal fourth and final campaign waged against the backland-

ers, famously calling it a crime, he seemed to mock the religious proclamations in the writings he found. Therefore, in part because of Euclides's descriptions, Canudos has often been remembered as the war that a rational republic had to wage against religious fanatics. Then, in the mid- and late twentieth century, analyses started moving away from Euclides. Scholars employing a traditional materialist approach to the uprising focused, contra Euclides, on its "political"-economic and material-environmental causes as opposed to its religious ones (de Queiroz 1965; Cava 1968). More recent studies allowed more space for Catholicism, though most still remained keen to de-exceptionalize the Canudos rebels. To this end, they chose to downplay the millenarianism, monarchism, and anti-republicanism described by Euclides, instead depicting Canudos as a place where more terrestrial, docile, and conventionally Catholic concerns prevailed alongside the active political resistance there (Levine 1992; Hoornaert 1997; Johnson et al. 2018).[20]

Although I reject Euclides's religious biases, my agenda is not to privilege or deprivilege his interpretation. My aim is not even to reopen the debate regarding what motivated *all* residents at Canudos to wage war against the republic. Contrary to many recent reevaluations that hinge on such global interpretations, I can only return to these poem fragments and analyze them for what they are: an indication of a strain of monarchist, anti-republican,

FIGURE 19. The last survivors at Canudos, most of whom were executed not long after this photo was taken. Flavio de Barros, 1897. Public Domain.

FIGURE 20. The 40th Infantry Battalion (coming from Pará province) in Canudos. Flavio de Barros, 1897. Public Domain.

and millenarian thought that circulated in the late nineteenth century among Catholic backlanders whose primary worries were the religious and relational order of things.

Whatever one's position, and keeping in mind Barros's three *cordel* analyzed above, one cannot maintain that religious and relational apprehensions, including with the devil, were unique to the Canudos poet or poem. Moreover, the verses invoke well-known events that inspired a range of responses across Brazil. These verses come from a nearly complete poem that Euclides copied into his field notebook and are published in *Os Sertões* in a specific, and different, order from the one in the field notebook.[21] In *Os Sertões*, the first three verses address the fall of Emperor Dom Pedro II, the rise of the new republic in 1889, and the institution of elections, which are connected directly to the devil and convey clear monarchist and antirepublican positions. The last four verses discuss the decree of civil marriage in 1890 and extend anti-republican positions by adding explicitly millenarian references from the coming of the Antichrist to the promised arrival of the long-disappeared Portuguese king-Messiah Dom Sebastião. I begin discussing the first three of these verses below. A separate and final section focuses on the last four verses, where I also discuss the implications of my analysis for religious studies more broadly. Across these two sections, I turn regularly to Conselheiro's recovered writings, as well some of the stanzas that Euclides left unpublished in his notebook, to flesh out the verses' central religious and relational concerns.

The first verse quoted above introduces Dom Pedro II, Brazil's second and last emperor, who was expelled by a military coup in November 1889, which radically changed the constituted order. In the verse, Pedro escapes to Lisbon, Portugal's capital, which local audiences all knew was Brazil's colonial "owner" until autonomy was declared in 1822 by the king of Portugal's son, Pedro I, who would become Pedro II's father.[22] The end of the monarchy is lamented because, the poem claims, it left Brazil *atoa*, which in Portuguese means "to be pointless, directionless, adrift."

In the longer poem in Euclides's notebook, this verse citing Pedro II appears as the third stanza, and it is followed by three others that continue to discuss the fall of the Brazilian empire. Only then does the poem come to the second quatrain quoted above, which deepens its monarchist message, condemning the new republic for being of the *cão*, which literally means "hound" but clearly refers to the devil. As we saw in my discussion of "The Duel," Catholics of the time would readily know the grounds on which the secular republic would be called evil: it had abolished a divinely ordained monarchy and instituted exclusively human governance, threatening the traditional order. For many Catholics, the republic stood against God and so was diabolical; it established an illegitimate and socially and spiritually dangerous government in their name.

The third quatrain above gives further evidence to this effect. It is directly anti-republican insofar as it describes where the law of the hound originates: in the new words and practices, especially the "elections," that constitute the republic. In fact, the original Portuguese verse in Euclides's notebook shows that the very term "election," which the poet writes (incorrectly) as "*aleição*," calls up the devil's law: *a lei cão* (election in Portuguese is written *eleição*). I am not the first to notice this (Levine 1992). And anthropologists have also documented talk among Northeasterners of the "law of the beast" (Velho 1995 [1991]) and politics as a "painful" thing (Palmeira and Heredia 2009 [1997], 167; see also introduction, note 11). However, few have made the important next step: to think seriously about the scholarly implications of the rejection of the republic and its exclusively human struggles over power and governance—what scholars normally refer to as *politics*.

REREADING RELATIONS, DENATURALIZING
POLITICS—AND MATTER

When we note that recent work on Canudos continues to sideline these verses, their relations, and thus their radicality, rereading them brings their broader implications into view. Robert Levine (1992) discusses lines here and there. Then, Paul Johnson, in his essay "The People and the Law of the Hound at Canudos," who quotes Euclides's verses in full, simply states:

> The verses reinforce the sacred king Dom Pedro II's link to the sixteenth-century Portuguese King Sebastian who disappeared fighting Muslims in Morocco, but who will one day return. All legitimate kings, the lyric suggests, are part of one body represented by Sebastian, the disappeared meta-king. One stanza likewise points to the emptiness of marriage and, by extension, law, when presided over by a mere civil judge. It points to the ways the verses of everyday folk reproduce in simpler terms the same ideas as the sermons of the Counselor, an organic circuit (Johnson et al. 2018, 59–60).

Johnson's overview remains silent on important aspects of the verses, excluding any mention, for example, of the evil of the republic or that Dom Sebastião had for centuries been a widely known messianic figure in Portugal and Brazil, who even affected people's dreams (Lima 2010).

It is worth noting that, although this silence accords with the scholarly tendencies to overwrite the fanaticism that I discussed above, Johnson's descriptive strategy can also be explained by a broader theoretical goal shared with other religious studies scholars: to establish the study of "churchstateness," or *ekklesia*. Alongside Pamela Klassen and Winnifred Fallers Sullivan, Johnson promotes a scholarly focus on the "necessary entanglement" of church and state, to stop "excluding . . . the messiness of religious and political life, giving too much . . . distinctness to entities only ever imagined as separate" (Johnson et al. 2018, 1, 5). However, the limits of this conceptual investment quickly become evident. To argue coherently that Canudos, as much as the republic, is a "churchstate," Johnson has to minimize signs of the distinction between church and state, the perceived differences of "religion" from the republic. As a result, his analyses and translations labor against the call of voices from Canudos, which clearly decry the republic as evil.

Like so many other discussions of Catholicism, Johnson's account of

Canudos rarely mentions evil, even when confronting Conselheiro's rhetoric. In the opening lines of Conselheiro's sermon on the republic, also discovered in the ruins, he portrays the republic as "uncontestably a great evil for Brazil," invented for "the extermination of religion (*religião*)" (Conselheiro 1978, 175). Johnson quotes this sermon but does not translate this line and avoids mentioning the distinction between *religion* and the *republic* that Conselheiro repeatedly draws. Again, the intention is to minimize Conselheiro's radicalism and assert that Canudos, like the republic, is an *ekklesia* where *religion* and *politics* are so entangled that they are not worth distinguishing (hence the need for a concept like "churchstateness") (Johnson et al. 2018, 39, 58). Although I am sympathetic to scholarship that recognizes conceptual fluidity, replacing two unstable concepts with a more stable one might obscure more than it reveals.

Similarly, Johnson's related focus on how material and sensorial practices produce *ekklesia* expands this blind spot. Indeed, Johnson elides how Catholics were anxious both about the instability of worldly matter(s) and the republic's relational—and ultimately damning, even world-ending—effects. In short, it brings us back to my argument about how foregrounding material mediations in the study of religion, can obscure the vital relations, both interpersonal and conceptual, that animate religion.

To explore one key occlusion, and to bring this chapter's argument for relations to a close, I turn to the republic's civil marriage decree, which is denounced directly in the fourth and fifth verses quoted above. Clearly some Canudenses, including Conselheiro, were worried about much more than "the emptiness" of civil marriage and law (contra Johnson in Johnson et al. 2018, 60). Specifically, the fourth stanza quoted by Euclides indicates a certain disquiet regarding the republic's "deceit" on the issue of civil marriage, which became the only form of marriage recognized by the state as of January 1890 (Costa 2006). Crucially, it should be noted that *casar* in Portuguese has a broader meaning than matrimony. Being united with another also means being bound or captured, making it deadly serious: being captured could be a sign of the Antichrist.

The connection between the Antichrist and the republic is clearly stated in the sixth stanza quoted above, but the republic's connection with captivity appears in the stanza just above that in Euclides's notebook, a verse he did *not* publish in *The Backlands* and which has mostly been forgotten. There, the poet accuses the first republican president of Brazil, Marechal Deodoro (written "Liodoro"), of wanting to "capture" the people (Cunha 2009 [1897], 147). Crucially, captivity (*cativeiro*) is a historical and biblical-apocalyptic reference to slavery. It has circulated among Northeastern farmers well into the contemporary period, especially via the final book of the New Testament, Revelation (Velho 1995 [1991], 15). In other words, while we know that Conselheiro preached against slavery even before abolition (1888) and the end of the republic (1889), his concerns with slavery and captivity should not be simply read as a desire for social justice (cf. Levine 1992; Johnson et al. 2018). Rather, the first and greatest slavery to resist was slavery to the "demon (*demônio*) who wants to put an end to the faith of the Church" and to institute governance without God, beginning with civil marriage (Conselheiro 1978, 176).

Along with the terror of such "captivity" there was a more specific fear associated with the universal requirement of civil marriage, namely its threat to a key Catholic sacrament. Although sacraments are not mentioned in the poem cited by Euclides,[23] Conselheiro did discuss the threat to the "sacrament" of marriage in his sermon on the republic (1978, 178). Conselheiro prophesied that civil unions would "invade" and "corrupt" people's very "conscience and soul" and even their "hearts," fatefully breaking their relations with God and kin (179, 178). "The father of a family . . . who has given in to the sin of that law [civil marriage]," Conselheiro wrote, might no longer be capable of "tenderness or compassion. . . . How can the beauty of faith before God dominate, if you obey such a law? How can you reconcile yourselves to the affect[ion] you owe your daughters[?] . . . So that the tenderness of this truth can rule in your heart, it is necessary to sustain your faith" (178). Conselheiro called on families, especially fathers, to intervene in this moment of "crisis" against their "enemies." But of course, Conselheiro also knew that humans are already flawed. "How," he asked, "can divine law and human law be reconciled, taking from [He] who has the right, to give it to he who does not?" (176). The question is rhetorical; of course, the divine and the human could not be reconciled, especially not under the republic. "There is *nothing absolute in this world, everything is subject to the saintly Providence of God, which dissipates the plans of men and confounds them* however it wants" (179, my emphasis). In other words, the republic, like all (material) things on earth, is no match for God's omnipotence.

What the opposition to civil marriage by Conselheiro and his followers helps us understand is that their most vital concerns were relational, religious, and transcendental, not political—including because God (and the devil) animated, and could dissolve, all worldly materials and plans. Crucially, this transcendent Godly power both mocked and pointed out the dangers of claims for the legitimacy of human governance.

I am not saying that these worries cannot be grasped or translated as political; the republic's agents certainly saw them as political, at the cost of the Canudenses' lives. However, many residents of Canudos were not merely resisting a new law, a new government, or a new political regime and suggesting an alternative. Rather, they were resisting an evil order, the application of which would undercut a key sacrament and thus cut humans off from God's love, wither their souls and hearts, and disconnect them from kin.

Finally, Conselheiro's affirmation that there is "nothing absolute in this world," that everything dissipates, together with his and his poet's anxiety about the spread of evil under the republic, connects the radicality of Canudos with the more everyday Catholicism that I discussed with reference to Barros's *cordel*. Indeed, the messages of all the poems converge on a position that their audiences knew well: because God or the devil is always potentially working through the world (relating through persons and things), nothing in this world is absolute; everything can be dissolved by God, or indeed by the devil. Therefore, to protect ourselves, we must be wary of the things of this world: all earthly materials and all humans who seek power and deny God.

I have argued that these Catholic dispositions, which have animated historic rejections of exclusively human politics, should give scholars pause. There are contexts, even Catholic ones, where the analytics of material

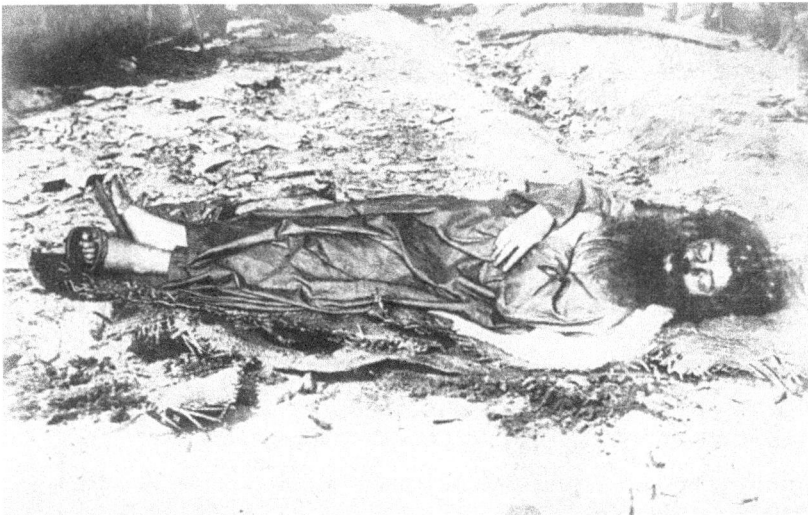

FIGURE 21. The body of Antônio Conselheiro exhumed after the war. Flavio de Barros, 1897. Public Domain.

mediation or politics should be more carefully problematized, so that the vital interpersonal and conceptual apprehensions of our interlocutors—the relations that animate them, whether with humans or nonhumans, saints or the environment, God or the devil—can be described more faithfully. In the case of Canudos, the people were not seeking to shore up yet another vision of politics, government, or law. Instead, many were willing to die to resist what they saw as an exclusively human form of governance—the political itself.

CONCLUSION

Cleusa's childhood memory of lying in her hammock listening to her father sing *cordel* through palm-thatch walls was, like *cordel* themselves, more than just entertaining material for a story. It was an invitation to understand Catholicism by reading relations first, by seeing and listening to the connections and distinctions that emerge from them. Instead of focusing on the Catholicism of Cleusa's day, here I have followed *cordel* back to the late nineteenth and early twentieth centuries, when the genre was first consolidated, and studied it on its own terms. In doing so, my hope has been to encourage the apprehension of Catholic particularities both past and present. Indeed, reading closely has brought me to my most general conclusion: that we should attend carefully to moments when Catholics (or others) challenge what scholars routinely affirm to be mediating or determining, whether it is politics, materiality, or mediation itself.

Yet it was Strathern who helped me articulate why starting with relations holds broad significance for the study of religion. Indeed, for Strathern studying relations entails more than focusing on social or intimate relations. Rather, studying relations entails attending to interpersonal and conceptual relations, where "interpersonal relations" involves not only humans, and "conceptual relations" means that concepts never stand alone in people's heads. They are always interrelated, even as they have distinct particularities that need to be studied (see also Lebner 2020).

A key point where Strathern intersects with the religion scholars now thinking through relations is in her interrogation of the individual. However, because Orsi, Furey, Moore, and others have already clarified many of the problems associated with methodological individualism, I have turned my attention elsewhere, to how a focus on relations can help us more readily identify and free ourselves from the limitations of other conventional analytic concepts.[24] In addition to the limits of material mediation, I was concerned with the "political," a concept most scholars still rarely question, in part at least because it is seen to be vital for proving scholarly relevance. Some scholars of religion certainly recognize that a predominant focus on the secular and the political has led us *away* from the study of relations and toward the "intellectual habit of not taking religion seriously" (Moore 2015, 440; Hirschkind and Larkin 2008, 1). Despite this, the political has remained a remarkably stable concept, even when its boundaries are blurred.[25] Thus, while not all scholars of mediation study politics directly, they often still assume that material conditions produce, and are produced by, politics (Stolow 2005, 134).

Reading *cordel* closely has revealed that our analyses can be otherwise. Although "The Migrant" and "The Duel" contain powerful hints of the problems associated with both human hierarchy and politics, the problem of politics emerges vividly in the Canudos *cordel*. Of course, Canudos has widely been read as political, and tens of thousands died because of such a reading. But since the writings Canudenses left behind in the ruins did not recognize the republic—and never mobilized under the banner of any politics—we can see that many denied the power and legitimacy of the republic in particular and rejected the primacy of politics in general. The main worry expressed in the Canudos verses and Conselheiro's sermons was that participating in exclusively human struggles over governance might corrupt human relations from the inside, slowly making the Canudenses captives of the devil. This rejection of politics and the prioritization of relations, especially family relations, may not be unique. My point is that this historically contingent episode can encourage us to begin to denaturalize not only mediation but also politics as analytics.

The denaturalization of politics can extend far beyond the case of Brazil, for the meaning and practice of politics has continued to transform across time and space. In the North Atlantic, broadly speaking, the concept of *politics* was reintroduced in the Middle Ages via the recuperation of Aristotelian thought, and its meaning regularly shifted thereafter. Most significantly for our discussion, *politics* only fully took on the meanings it has in our scholarly languages today during the establishment of the First Republic in the wake of the French Revolution, when king and church were dramatically severed from the political, and a whole "new political language" emerged (Guilhaumou 2008, 150). The new "metaphysic of politics" that gained ascendency at that time was fundamentally connected to other modern, secularizing concepts, especially that of the individual, which continue to haunt contemporary analyses (see also Guilhaumou 2005). Just because these concepts gained ascendency in modern Europe does not mean they should be taken as givens, and we should certainly not take them as *necessarily* stable causes of social process, in Europe or elsewhere. Denaturalizing politics does not mean always avoiding it as a term or simply blurring its distinction from religion. Rather it means taking care about where and how it appears, whether it appears alongside religion, or whether it might be rejected in religion's name.

This means that I would not simply assert that Barros, or the Catholic audiences of his *cordel*, would wholly reject politics, as many of their Canudense compatriots did. But I would say that, as with earthly material media animated uncertainly by God and the devil in a radically uncertain world, politics—a realm of human governance—is a site of ambivalent legitimacy, ambivalent "good," and ambivalent power. One might be tempted, as was Antônio Cândido in a related context, to describe such a world as operating on a principle of "reversibility" (2002 [1957], 134). But even here I would be cautious. The perennial potential for evil also has irreversible effects, for it leaves one unable to consistently know with what or whom one is dealing.

To say that some Catholics wrangle with irreversible uncertainties vis-à-vis worldly things does not negate the possibility of change. Cleusa's story presents an example of such change, as does the postconciliar liberationist movement that inspired her as a young woman. As chapter 2 began to show, and as the next chapter continues to demonstrate, liberationist Catholicism sought precisely to make politics acceptable for Catholics (C. Boff 1987), and it is perhaps not incidental that liberationists often downplayed the devil, like many other consciously modernizing Catholics. In fact, Cleusa remarked on how strange it was for her to hear a liberationist priest talk about politics in his Sunday sermon, with little mention of the usual message about "heaven and the devil."

The fact that many Catholics have considered traditional notions of an embodied "devil" to be an antiquated part of the faith to be abandoned, especially since Vatican II, is particularly relevant to my argument. It might also help to explain why scholars of Catholicism have not encountered the devil or simply may not want to write much about him. However, it is vital to remember that this is not the perspective of all Catholics, nor is it even the position of the contemporary Vatican. In fact, the contingent of Catholics hoping to "say farewell to the devil" (the title of a notorious 1969 book) became so powerful that in 1972, Pope Paul VI gave a homily that repudiated this new trend with assertions like "Evil is not only a privation but a living, spiritual, corrupt and corrupting being. A terrible reality, mysterious and frightening. . . . The devil is the enemy number one" (quoted in Ratzinger and Missori 1985, 136). By 1975, the Congregation for the Doctrine of the Faith published "Christian Faith and Demonology," fleshing out Paul VI's statements and establishing that "the existence of the demonic world" is "a dogmatic datum." And then-Cardinal Ratzinger, who had just become the prefect of the Congregation for the Doctrine of the Faith under John Paul II, reaffirmed Paul VI in no uncertain terms: "Satan is the absolute destroyer, undermining every relationship: man's relationship to himself and men's relation to one another. Thus he is the exact opposite of the Holy Spirit, who is the absolute 'mediator' who guarantees the relationships in which all others are rooted and whence they spring: the trinitarian relationship by which Father and Son are One, one God in the unity of the Spirit" (Ratzinger and Messori 1985, 151).

In short, it should not be controversial to say that Catholics often have irreversible, or ineradicable, worries about the pervasive arts of the devil, whose agency, in many ways like God's, can put any medium into question at any time. But of course the Vatican does not have the last word. I have focused here specifically on how some Brazilian Catholics at the turn of the twentieth century considered an autonomous politics divorced from God to be the epitome of evil, even a sign of the end times, with the capacity to corrupt and undermine all worldly media and all the relations these media contained.

Grasping this vital concern with relations in the world, as well as the divine and diabolical agencies working through them, should lead us to a fuller understanding of what we might call the mystic orientation to the world expressed by the Catholics discussed in his book. A focus on relations should also help refine our approaches to Christians in other places and times. Indeed, as Furey (2017) rightly points out, recent discussions of motile modes of post-Reformation sacramentality, defined as modes of seeking unity with the divine beyond the traditional sacraments, have not led to further study of interpersonal relationships—even as they show that both Catholics and Protestants have sought the Christian divine through others (e.g., Schwartz 2008). Here, adding to Furey's call, I argue that a focus on Catholic relationships should also contemplate their mystic component, including the dangers of evil. This means that scholars should be attentive to the fact that while Catholic modes of seeking unity with others do not necessarily exclude politics, they do not necessarily include politics either.

This brings me to my final point: specifically, what a call to attend to relations means for the study of religion, and even for the politics of scholarship on religion. To say that scholars might have a political stance while being open to interrogating the political is not a contradiction. Focusing on relations is a way to disentangle state discourse from analytical practice to show just how variously relations—conceptual, interpersonal, terrestrial, or transcendental—sustain human life, religious or not. That is, a focus on relations positions scholars to more clearly see not only what makes people different, but also what connects them amid differences. Rather than focusing on the universal existence of religion and politics, or on their universal fusion, I have offered another perspective: that a strain of turn-of-the-century Catholic thought in Northeastern Brazil provoked worries first about relationships and then only maybe about the politics that relationships animated. If this description now makes Canudenses' Catholic thought appear more similar to other religious—and even nonreligious—actors, this was part of the point. Too often accounts that emphasize the universality of the individual, of materiality, or of politics are also critical of studies that highlight differences, as I have done here, worrying that they may exoticize others or even deny a common humanity. Yet it is becoming increasingly clear that denying difference can be oppressive and even dehumanizing (Kendi, 2019; Crosson 2020). Instead, as I have endeavored to show, displacing assumed starting points and then rereading and writing through relations will allow us to rediscover, if not oneness or sameness, then the intersections, the partial connections, where we can meet and differentiate at once.

The next chapter turns to liberationism, which intersected with this preconciliar Catholicism and tried to differentiate itself from it by avoiding direct discussions of evil and sin while embracing a fraternal, liberatory politics of force and unity. If *cordel* help us see the preconciliar source of this abiding concern with relations and the threat of evil to corrupt and break them, liberationism, I will show, further shaped the mystic of friendship and the settlement of the PA-150.

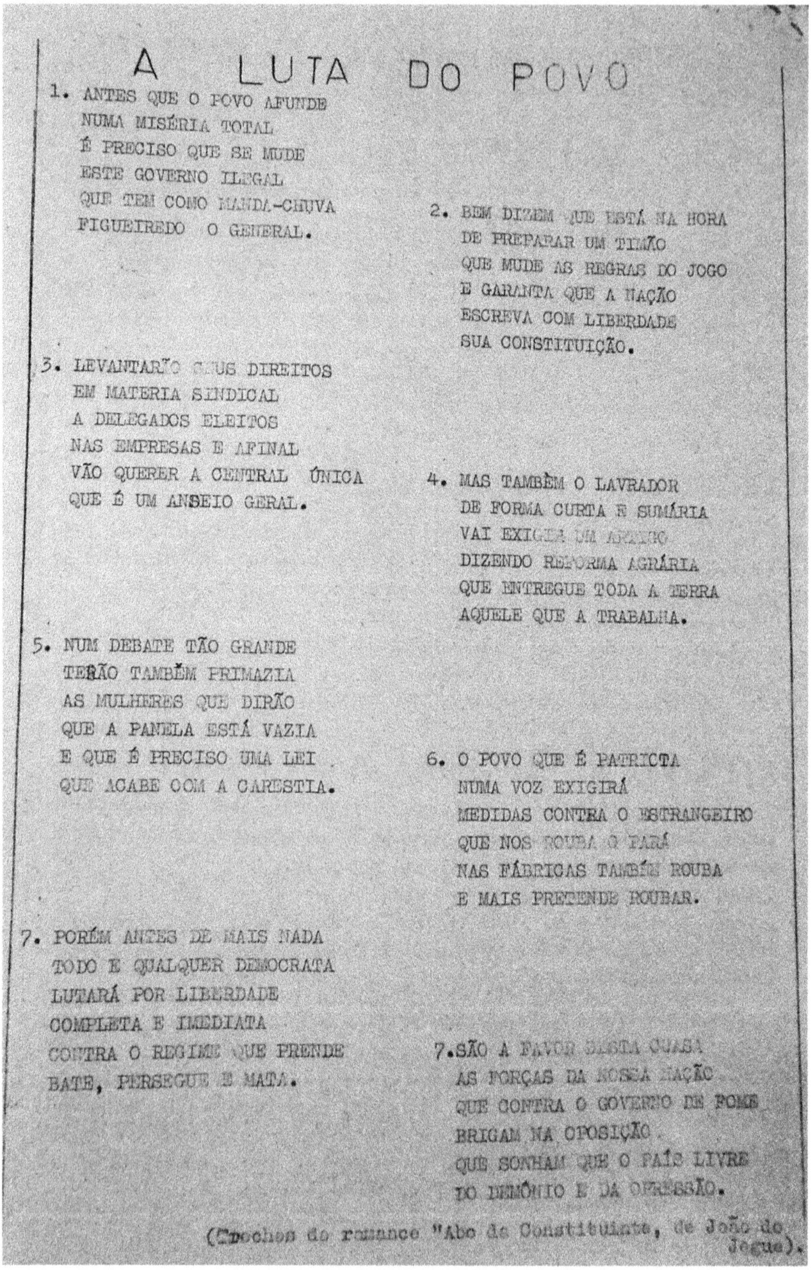

A LUTA DO POVO

1. ANTES QUE O POVO AFUNDE
NUMA MISÉRIA TOTAL
É PRECISO QUE SE MUDE
ESTE GOVERNO ILEGAL
QUE TEM COMO MANDA-CHUVA
FIGUEIREDO O GENERAL.

2. BEM DIZEM QUE ESTÁ NA HORA
DE PREPARAR UM TIMÃO
QUE MUDE AS REGRAS DO JOGO
E GARANTA QUE A NAÇÃO
ESCREVA COM LIBERDADE
SUA CONSTITUIÇÃO.

3. LEVANTARÃO SEUS DIREITOS
EM MATERIA SINDICAL
A DELEGADOS ELEITOS
NAS EMPRESAS E AFINAL
VÃO QUERER A CENTRAL ÚNICA
QUE É UM ANSEIO GERAL.

4. MAS TAMBÈM O LAVRADOR
DE FORMA CURTA E SUMÁRIA
VAI EXIGIR UM ARTIGO
DIZENDO REFORMA AGRÁRIA
QUE ENTREGUE TODA A TERRA
AQUELE QUE A TRABALHA.

5. NUM DEBATE TÃO GRANDE
TERÃO TAMBÉM PRIMAZIA
AS MULHERES QUE DIRÃO
QUE A PANELA ESTÁ VAZIA
E QUE É PRECISO UMA LEI
QUE ACABE COM A CARESTIA.

6. O POVO QUE É PATRICTA
NUMA VOZ EXIGIRÁ
MEDIDAS CONTRA O ESTRANGEIRO
QUE NOS ROUBA O PARÁ
NAS FÁBRICAS TAMBÉM ROUBA
E MAIS PRETENDE ROUBAR.

7. PORÉM ANTES DE MAIS NADA
TODO E QUALQUER DEMOCRATA
LUTARÁ POR LIBERDADE
COMPLETA E IMEDIATA
CONTRA O REGIME QUE PRENDE
BATE, PERSEGUE E MATA.

7.SÃO A FAVOR DESTA CUASA
AS FORÇAS DA NOSSA NAÇÃO
QUE CONTRA O GOVERNO DE FOME
BRIGAM NA OPOSIÇÃO.
QUE SONHAM QUE O PAÍS LIVRE
DO DEMÔNIO E DA OPRESSÃO.

(Trechos do romance "Abc da Constituinte, de João do Jegue).

FIGURE 22. A selection of the *cordel* "ABC of the Constitutional Assembly" by João do Jegue (*Cry* 1982). Archives of the Pastoral Land Commission, Marabá, Pará.

FOURTH VISITATION
Jacundá, Pará, 1982

THE PEOPLE'S STRUGGLE[1]

1. Before the people drown
In total misery
We must make fall
This illegal government
Whose big gun
Is Figueiredo the general

2. They say that it's about time
To prepare a super team
That will change the rules of the game
And guarantee that the nation
Writes with freedom
Its own constitution.

3. Their rights will be raised
In syndical terms
Delegates will be elected
In companies and then
They will want a central union
Which is everyone's ken.

4. But the worker too
In a short and summary form
Will demand an article
About agrarian reform
That will hand over the land
To all of those who work it.

5. In such a big debate
The women will have primacy
It will be them who will say
That the pan is empty
That a law is necessary
To end the woe of the needy.

6. The *povo* that is practiced
In one voice will demand
Measures against foreigners
Who rob Pará
Who rob factories
And will rob more again.

7. But before anything else
Each and every democracy
Will fight for liberty
Complete and immediately
Against the regime that arrests,
That hits, pursues, and kills.

7 [sic].
The forces of our nation
Are in favor of this cuase [sic]
They fight in opposition
To this government of lack
And they dream of a country free
Of oppression and the demon.

04

JACUNDÁ

The Cry and the Silence of Unity

Marabá, 25.05.1980

Exmo.Sr.
Gen.Bgd Manoel de Jesus e Silva
Cmdr of 23rd Brgd Jngl Inf

Mr General:

I have just received a report from Father Paulo, with reference to the serious conflicts now growing on the PA-150, involving numerous *posseiros* (would-be smallholders, squatters) and some *grileiros* (land-grabbers) like Misters Basílio, Geraldo Veloso, Dão, Osanir, and the Capixabas.

These tensions are reaching a climax, and the responsible authorities are acting very little, or very slowly, in search of a just solution.

The *grileiros* feel increasingly empowered; they can interact as equals with the authorities, with soldiers, and etc, which gives them leeway for all kinds of offenses, abuses, and barbarities, which, of course, they will never acknowledge.

The *posseiros* live constantly under the eye of the law, always threatened, because they don't have any way to talk to the authorities, and out there in the middle of the forest they are exposed to all kinds of cruelty, seeing the murder of some of their *companheiros* go unpunished.

This situation can no longer be sustained, Mr. General. . . . What kind of regime of ours is this that only efficiently resolves the problems of the rich? . . .

Mr. General, the situation of the PA-150 is crying out to the skies, it is injuring the image of God, present in these *posseiros*, and it is weighing on the conscience of those who have the authority in this region. Mr. General, you call yourself a staunch Catholic. That is good, and as a pastor I tell you that in the face of this situation, which has been worsening every day for some time now, your sleep cannot remain tranquil, and your faith cannot remain inactive. . . .

Of one hundred cases, only one is more or less resolved while the others grow in gravity. . . . The judges, . . . before any . . . objective examination of [local land] conflicts, always side with the rich. BASTA (ENOUGH). There has been ENOUGH infamy, Mr. General, there has been ENOUGH venality and corruption. Today, the day of PENTECOST, I suggest that you place your spirit in prayer to the Divine Paraclete [the Holy Spirit] and ask for the necessary strength TO ACT with sharpness and firmness to once and for all end the abuse and arbitrary acts of this group of *grileiros* of the PA-150.

It is the minimum that can be demanded of each one of us, Christians, who consider ourselves disciples of Jesus Christ, who spilled his own blood to liberate men from the forces of Evil.

This true subversion merits an active combat that has been necessary for a long time now.

Respectfully,
+ Fr. Alano Maria Pena op[1]
Bishop of Marabá (*Cry* 1980b, 6).

Dom Alano Pena, bishop of Marabá, wrote this letter during Brazil's military dictatorship, addressing it to the highest regional authority in 1980, Brigadier General Manoel de Jesus e Silva, commander of the 23rd Brigade of Jungle Infantry. The letter was printed in the first issue of *The Cry of the PA-150*, a lovingly homemade newsletter published with declining frequency from 1980 to 1986.[2] At the helm of *The Cry* were the priests and nuns of the PA-150 Evangelizing Committee, which was established in the town of Arraias (now Jacundá) shortly after the highway opened in 1977.

I begin with Dom Alano's letter because it exemplifies many of the aims of *The Cry*, although I also admit that it is something of an anomaly. Indeed, it is one of only four places in *The Cry* that explicitly mention the devil or evil—the poem quoted in the Fourth Visitation is another rare example. Dom Alano's letter to the communities along the PA-150, published in the second issue, is more representative, as it emphasizes unity rather than tension and dissent.

[June 1980]

Dearest brothers [and sisters] (*irmãos*)[3] of the communities of the PA-150, may the Grace, Force and Light of Jesus Christ reside in your heart and help you to keep growing in unity, in faith, in hope, and in love.

During [the week of June 17–24] I visited the various communities of the region of the PA-150, from KM 12 of the PA-70 to Goianésia. They were blessed days, in which God allowed me to listen more closely to the voice of his beloved people, who are you my brothers. In each community I encountered, I felt great joy, the work of God's Holy Spirit in our brothers' hearts. I perceived the great effort being made so the community can meet, can better learn the Word of God that is the Bible and celebrate in faith and prayer the journey of life. I could also perceive how you are ever more illuminated by the truth of God, and how you, in the communities, are seeking to keep illuminating the problems of your life—especially the problem of land—with the Light of the Word of God. From right next to you, I felt how your prayer rises to God like a cry of pain and anguish, so great is the suffering that surrounds you.

I also noticed that you have realized there are things to improve, for example, more unity among everyone in the communities and between communities. This is of the greatest importance, because without sincere and strong (*forte*) unity we cannot be saved nor can we triumph. This unity needs to keep growing because without it the community cannot triumph. I know that some brothers have let themselves be vanquished by fear and left the battlefield. [Others are no longer with us] because they sold their land or because they left the community. This makes people suffer, without doubt. But it also increases our unity and it should make our courage and force grow to continue the struggle. These small failings (*falhas*) should be corrected with patience and firmness, because we cannot lose time and energy to small things, between us, when the powerful are reuniting to crush the People of God for once and forever.

I want to say to you as well that it made me very happy and hopeful to see how the testimony of the Gospel is being inspired among you by our brothers, Father Humberto, Father Paulo, Sister Dorothy . . . all

of them dedicating the best of their energies to serve you all, looking
for the paths of God with you, the paths of justice and Truth. They all
have my support to continue their work and all of those who spread the
calumny that they are communists, agitators, subversives, God will have
to punish those who think that way severely.

The communities are growing like God's beautiful garden. This is
comforting and encouraging.

+Fr. Alano Maria Pena
Bishop of Marabá (*Cry* 1980e).

These two letters by Dom Alano will serve as guides through the account
below to one of the final points I wish to make in this chapter: that the
relative silence on questions of evil compared to the importance placed on
unity has helped shape the mystic of friendship along today's PA-150. It will
become clear in what follows that *The Cry*'s relative backgrounding of questions of evil, an approach common in post–Vatican II theology, reflects the
tendencies of liberationism. I will suggest that this tendency to privilege
unity over questions of evil also unintentionally allowed conventional perceptions of evil to flourish, even while deepening and refreshing a collective
longing for unity. Although a relatively experimental point, it does illuminate the development of the mystic of friendship, which is undergirded by
concerns with both unity and widespread evil.

It might seem paradoxical to claim that a reluctance to foreground evil
helped perceptions of evil to flourish. To help explain how this happened, I
will move in stages. First, I must attend to liberationism as a whole, a theology crafted by Latin American clerics to help their flocks free themselves
from oppression by learning to see and struggle against a diffuse social-
structural sin. So in the first section below, I will begin by using Dom Alano's
letters to help introduce liberationism. Then, in the following sections, I will
turn to other content from *The Cry*. Specifically I will show that *The Cry*, following liberationist practice, used allegorical images to inspire the faithful
to "see" and "judge" the sins entailed in oppression and then "act" to create
a new fraternal unity and a new politics along the highway.[4] I will attend to
the subtle absent-presence of questions of evil throughout, fleshing out the
broader effects most fully in the conclusion.

INTRODUCING LIBERATIONISM

———————

Dom Alano's letters can teach us much about liberationism. First, they demonstrate something fundamental: how liberationism built on the post–Vatican II image of the church as the "people of God." Dom Alano's letter to the PA-150's communities referred to this explicitly: "The powerful are reuniting to crush the People of God once and forever." His letter to the general referred to this image of the church more figuratively, mentioning that the violence is "injuring the image of God" in the poor *posseiros*, an injury that should weigh "on the conscience of those who have the authority in this region." Few social scientists have discussed the implications of the new "people of God," image and even fewer have engaged with how it contrasts with the previously dominant ecclesial image of the church as the "mystical body of Christ." I spoke at some length in the introduction and chapter 1 about the early modern and twentieth-century incarnations of mystical-body theology. Here it is worth noting briefly why the clergy began to abandon the "mystical body" in favor of the "people of God." This will give us insight into how liberationism built a unique theology and pedagogy that it hoped would transform Catholicism in Brazil, Latin America, and potentially the world.

The most common explanation of why "the people of God" became a preferred image for the Catholic Church is that it conveyed greater egalitarianism (Cavanaugh 1998; Dulles 2002 [1974]; Walden 1975).[5] For many, the mystical body of Christ evoked hierarchically valued parts working together to support the divine God/head, and it was widely felt that the postwar, post–Vatican II era needed a more horizontal, more democratic social vision: an image that rendered everyone an equally valued member of the Church, whether laity or clergy, powerful or weak.[6] Joseph Ratzinger, before he joined the church hierarchy, added flourishes to this view. By the 1960s, he said, calling the Church a "mystical body" was increasingly seen as "incapable of doing justice to the true realities" (1972, 108–9). The mystical-body image might disfigure the humility of the pilgrim Church, Ratzinger argued, by falsely glorifying it and cloaking it with an "individualist mystique." Of course, this didn't mean that the people of God weren't constituted through the body of God, the Eucharist. But there was simply no reason to think of this body as "mystical." Ratzinger's assessment was less critical of hierarchy than those of other post–Vatican II theologians, but it still supported the feeling of the time—that the people of God image would communicate a realistic church that carried its tradition while being engaged with the world and its problems.

Liberationism formally emerged in 1968 and radicalized this popularizing post-mystical vision of the church. Under this new influence, Latin American bishops at the 1968 Episcopal Conference of Latin America (CELAM II, held in Medellín, Colombia) called on the church and faithful to remember God's preference for "the poorest and most needy sectors" (Gutiérrez 1988 [1973], xxv).[7] At CELAM III, held in Puebla, Mexico, this preference was dubbed the "preferential option for the poor" (xxvi). Although a primary commitment to the weak is communicated in the Old and New Testaments, the renewed preferential option for the poor called on Catholics to identify with the disenfranchised in order to free them—and society—from the suffering and sin of oppression.

This brings us to the second thing that Dom Alano's letters teach us about liberationism: that it was not merely a call to *defend* of the rights of the oppressed. More fundamentally, it deployed a theological pedagogy to produce Catholic *unity* with and among the poor. This unity was meant to defeat the evils of disunity, which liberationists believed to be a "social" or "structural" sin, caused by oppression, inequality, and injustice. Dom Alano's letters do not explicitly mention this new theology of sin, and *The Cry* as a whole is similarly silent on the matter—although I will show later how the newsletter powerfully invoked "structural" sin through images of the crucified peasant. For now, I simply want to underscore Dom Alano's letters' more overt aim: to exemplify a pedagogy called the "see-judge-act" method, intended to produce unity.

See-judge-act was not invented by liberationists, but liberationists gave it their own radical twist with the preferential option for the poor and what came to be called "Ecclesial Base Communities."[8] Liberationists encouraged Catholics to form small local communities within larger parishes to worship together, to critically evaluate real-world inequalities in light of the Bible, and to try to abolish those inequalities through acts of unity (Comerford 2003; see also introduction, note 42). Dom Alano's letter to the communities of the PA-150 invoked unity consistently, even repetitively. Two successive sentences in the letter say almost the same thing: "This is of the greatest importance, because without sincere and strong (*forte*) unity we cannot be saved nor can we triumph. This unity needs to keep growing because without it the community cannot triumph." Meanwhile, Dom Alano's letter to the general turned more obviously to the see-judge-act method. His letter was structured to first make visible the injustice along the PA-150, then invite the general to pray "to the Divine Paraclete [the Holy Spirit]," and finally ask for the necessary strength "TO ACT" against the rich land-grabbers who committed violence against the poor. Dom Alano's demand was not just a call to act against the violence from his position of authority. Instead, he told the general to ask for divine guidance to understand that the violence was "injuring the image of God present in these *posseiros*."

While liberationist invitations to "see" situations of injustice reflected a new and more realistic church, we should not lose sight of the allegory this pedagogy also deployed. Dom Alano compounded his demand to act in unity with the needs of the poor by telling the general that acting against injustice on the PA-150 was "the minimum that can be asked of each one of us, Christians, who consider ourselves disciples of Jesus Christ, who spilled his own blood to liberate men from the forces of Evil." In other words, as disciples of Jesus, Christians had to act, to truly and allegorically reflect Jesus's work and sacrifice to remove evil from this world.

Admittedly, liberationists didn't often use the concept of allegory. In fact, one of the reasons for their elision of allegory overlaps with a reason behind their limited discussion of evil: both allegory and evil might invoke a transcendent, otherworldly, "mystical" kind of Catholicism, while liberationists, even more than the broader church, were trying to emphasize historical and terrestrial realities.[9] Still, their use of see-judge-act was clearly an allegorical practice, which used one story to tell another (the simplest meaning of allegory; see Tambling 2018). While liberationists called for a certain empiricism in their injunction to see concrete situations, judging and acting was always done in God's light, as Dom Alano notes in his letter to the communities. That is, they encouraged the faithful to see and then judge contemporary events in light of the historic actions of Jesus Christ and then act with the force of this legacy to unify, combat evil, and redeem sins in the present. This leaves us with an insight we will track as the analysis here proceeds: the recurrence of allegorical practice can help begin to explain how concerns with evil persist even when evil is not labeled as such. In short, because it tells divine stories through human stories, Christian allegory necessarily evokes the evil against which humans perennially struggle.

Still, my focus below will be on understanding liberationism in the first instance, specifically on how liberationists worked along the PA-150. I will draw attention to the allegorical images deployed in *The Cry* to mobilize the pedagogy I have just sketched out. The structure of this discussion in four different sections—according to *The Cry*'s concerns with "seeing," "judging," "acting," and "politics"—is somewhat artificial, since each was present in some way in every item of the newsletter, as was the allegorical message that unity with others and God was the religious and political way to defeat evil and injustice. Nevertheless, each issue of *The Cry* tended to emphasize one of these four principles, especially in the newsletter's first two years of production. For example, I will discuss next how the inaugural issue focused more on *seeing*—that is, simply making visible the problem of land on the PA-150—rather than calling directly for biblical judgment and unified action. My description follows suit, leaving discussion of the allegorical content, and discussion of sin and evil, for the remaining sections.

THE CALL TO "SEE"

A PRESENTATION

Companheiros, this little newsletter intends to be a vehicle of information regarding everything that happens on the PA-150. Not only to inform, but to also be of service to the people's struggles in this region, denouncing the violence and injustices committed against the *povo* (people), impeding their growth and the development of their rights and dignity.

   We hope that it can truly be a voice of the popular causes of this region and others . . . (*Cry* 1980a, 1).

This was how the *Newsletter of the PA-150*, which became *The Cry* in its second issue, introduced itself in May 1980.[10] Two drawings consolidated this image of the newsletter's support for the struggle against "the violences and injustices committed against the *povo*": one of a man in a wide-brimmed straw hat with his left arm raised and another of two hands breaking chains. These images, which were not yet obviously allegorical, were deployed to diagnose the situation, namely how the *grileiros* or *grandes*, the big and powerful men who build large estates, had the tacit support of the government to use violence and intimidation against *posseiros*, the little guys searching for land and a living.

   It was no coincidence that the events recounted in the newsletter's first issue included the actions of the *grileiros* called out by Dom Alano in his letter to the general: "Misters Basílio, Geraldo Veloso, Dão, Osanir and the Capixabas." These refer to the region's most extreme, unresolved cases of landholder violence against the *povo*.

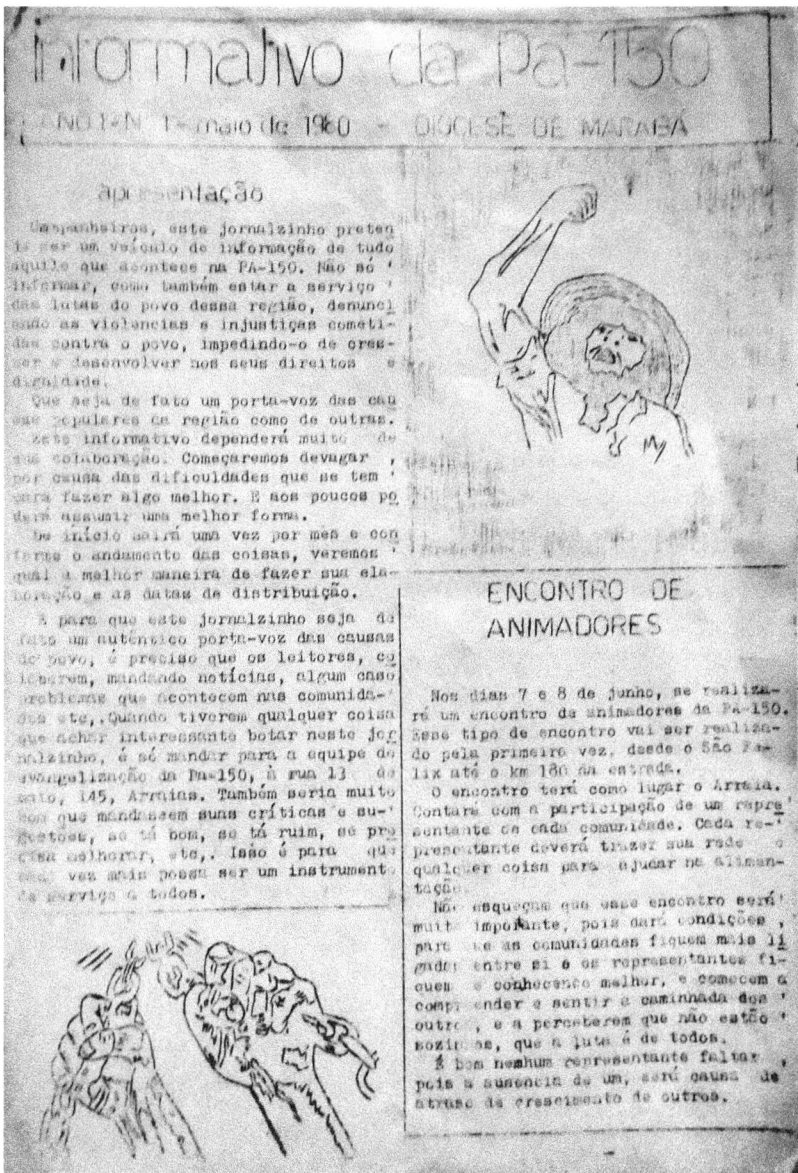

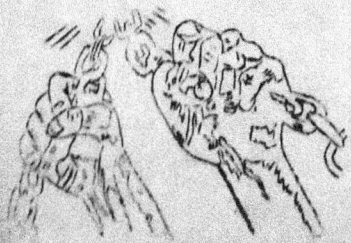

FIGURE 23. The first page and first issue of what would become *The Cry of the PA-150*. Archives of the Pastoral Land Commission, Marabá, Pará.

The newsletter's first article reported the murder of a rural worker named Lourival on the orders of the *grileiro* Osanir (*Cry* 1980h). The story of this murder, which shocked and outraged the local communities, also appeared in the testament I quoted in the First Visitation. The article tells how Osanir's bodyguards murdered Lourival in December 1979 and gravely injured a second worker, Alcebíades, who was left paralyzed. It relates that five months later, a messenger from Osanir arrived at Alcebíades's house and told his brother-in-law Joaquim that he intended to *acertar contas* (settle accounts, that is, finish the job). Meanwhile, witnesses to Lourival's murder reported it to local authorities and gave testimony to the police. The police did little more than make empty promises and "tell people to be careful." "Osanir has now come from his den (*toca*) accompanied by his children and a truckload of forty people from Espírito Santo," the article concluded. "The workers of the area are all petrified by this new move by the *grileiro*. The competent authorities have not taken any precautions, and the *povo* continues in its insecurity." In a drawing that illustrates the story, a huge man tells a tiny man that he "needs to disappear from this laaaand."

FIGURE 24. Drawing accompanying the article "The Lourival Case" (*Cry* 1980h, 2). Archives of the Pastoral Land Commission, Marabá, Pará.

The Cry's description of Lourival's case did not recount the specifics of the land conflict in question, but other news items elaborated on similar disputes. I have selected one exemplary article from *The Cry*'s first issue that, for our purposes, achieves two things at once. On the one hand, it offers images of violence, intimidation, and governmental disregard along the PA-150. On the other hand, it depicts the kind of "spontaneous colonization" common in the region and the conflicts that ensued. I will quote the article in full to give readers a more complete view of how *The Cry* sought to help readers "see." I have tried to reproduce the newsletter's direct, simple, and unpolished language in my translation.

CRICKETS AND *GRILAGENS*[11]

Very close to the village of Arraias, at KM 90, some 6 KMs away from the road, there is another area in dispute.

The *fazendeiro* [estate owner] Geraldo Veloso received from "Dão" [a *grileiro* and frontman of the *fazendeiro* João de Freitas] an area of 100 *alqueires* [500 hectares] in exchange for protecting Dão's lands [from further invasion]. And in this area [given to Geraldo Veloso] there are *posseiros*. Veloso decided to sue the *posseiros* and one day he brought a written piece of paper to them saying that it was an eviction order from Judge Rosa in Tucuruí.

The *posseiros* went to Tucuruí to check to see if this was true, and they were told that the judge had not issued any order. Geraldo had just used the name of the judge to threaten and expel the *posseiros* with the help of policemen Josafá and Luis.

On the 23rd of the month, as some of the *posseiros* walked to Marabá to denounce this, Geraldo Veloso decided to act on his own. He took advantage of their absence and knocked down the *posseiros'* shacks with a chain saw (*Cry* 1980f).

This article was accompanied by a drawing that reinforced both the image of inequality and the problem that *The Cry* was trying to shine a light on: how small-scale subsistence laborers, who needed land to support their families, were being disregarded and marginalized in favor of the rich and powerful. The drawing depicted a rural worker shouting *ABAIXO O LATIFÚNDIO! TERRA PARA QUÉM TRABALHA NELA* ("DOWN WITH THE LATIFÚNDIO! LAND FOR THOSE WHO WORK IT"). These were common slogans of the left, even before the dictatorship. Unlike other major Latin American countries,

GRILOS e GRILAGENS

Logo perto do povoado do Arraias, no km 90, uns 6 kms fora da estrada, há outra área em confusão.

O fazendeiro Geraldo Veloso ganhou de "Dão" (grileiro e testa de ferro do fazendeiro João de Freitas) uma área de 100 alqueires para vigiar as terras de "Dão" (Sidney Barreto). E nesta área tem posseiros. Geraldo Veloso, abriu processo contra os posseiros e trouxe um papel escrito dizendo que era ordem de despejo. Arranjou a polícia e foi despejar os posseiros dizendo que era ordem da juíza Rosa de Tucuruí.

Os posseiros foram em Tucuruí verificar se era verdade, disseram que a juíza não expediu ordem nenhuma. E Geraldo Veloso usou o nome da juíza para ameaçar e expulsar os posseiros, acompanhado dos policiais Josafá e Luis.

Dia 23 deste, enquanto alguns posseiros caminharam rumo à Marabá para denunciar o fato, Geraldo Veloso resolveu agir por sua própria conta, aproveitou a ausencia deles e derrubou os barracos dos posseiros de motoserra.

ABAIXO O LATIFÚNDIO

TERRA PARA QUEM TRABALHA NELA

FIGURE 25. "Grilos and Grilagens" (*Cry* 1980f, 4). Archives of the Pastoral Land Commission, Marabá, Pará.

Brazil had never had an agrarian reform. With land distribution patterns still reflecting those of colonial times, Brazil has retained one of the most unequal distributions of land in the world: approximately 1 percent of land-owners control almost 50 percent of the land (Guimarães 1964; Mueller 2018). Calls to reform the system that upheld such inequality and poverty began turning into governmental plans for a massive agrarian reform during the left-wing presidency of João Goulart (1961–64). Together, the calls for justice and reform programs led to a violent response from the right: the 1964 military coup (Dezemone 2016). As is evident here, liberationists and others on the Brazilian left had again begun to call for agrarian reform during the dictatorship's final years. Liberationists (in the south of the country) eventually went on to help found the Landless Workers' Movement, which we explore in the next chapter (Stédile 2002).

Let me underscore that the article and the accompanying drawing depicted a main mode of early settlement or "spontaneous colonization" along the PA-150, while also acknowledging the wider political, legal, and economic context. As I have already noted, spontaneous colonization was a byproduct of the construction of roads and industries and of many failed "directed" colonization schemes developed by the Amazon Development Superintendency (Hébette and Marin 1977; Moran 1990). While there were no directed colonization programs for smallholders along the PA-150, people were attracted to the highway by the possibility of claiming cheap or "free" land. Thus, many settlements began with smaller groups, or even solitary *posseiros*, simply settling on relatively isolated and unused plots of land which they hoped to secure as their own.

These settlement processes weren't entirely sui generis: the Land Statute of 1964 had made such possession practices legal. That law gave the state the power to expropriate lands that were not fulfilling their "social function" and redistribute them to cultivators without compensation to original land-owners.[12] The Land Statute was the military dictatorship's main concession to the clamor for agrarian reform that had helped inspire the 1964 coup. The slogans that demanded land for workers and the elimination of the *latifún-dio* referred precisely to this political and legal context.

To implement the Land Statute, the military government founded the National Institute of Colonization and Agrarian Reform (INCRA)[13] in 1970—which made its commitment to agrarian reform seem at least somewhat serious (Penna and Rosa 2015). Still, little in the way of actual reform was forthcoming, even when state agencies got involved. This was due to conservative colonization policies, also called "counter-agrarian reform," that favored the creation of large landholdings over small-scale agriculture (Ianni 1979). *The Cry* denounced this tendency, suggesting a critical stance toward the lack of reform in general. The newsletter documented case after case where *posseiros*, who had already settled on the land, sometimes even *with INCRA's permission*, were attacked by *grileiros* hoping to claim the land themselves.

Like most of *The Cry*, these documentary articles said nothing particularly "religious." Nevertheless, the Evangelizing Committee strategically added religious topics to incite judgment and action in light of God's word. Recall that Dom Alano's letter to the general was published at the end of the first issue. This letter was deliberately included to produce reflection on how the secular authorities were not going to help. *The Cry*'s editors then consolidated that message with a comment on the letter: "The General received [Dom Alano's] letter and returned it to the Bishop because he didn't like it, and he even sent this note: 'I return to your Revered Excellency the letter dated 25 May 80 because I disagree with the terms that seep from it, showing my surprise and regret at how different it is from other solicitations made previously to this command'" (*Cry* 1980b, 6).

Beneath the general's signature, the editors asked, "Well *companheiro*, that's all. What do you think about these things? How do you think this situation should be resolved?" (*Cry* 1980b, 6). With this question, the newsletter challenged their *companheiros*, the communities, to look closely, pass their own judgment, and decide what to do. Yet in light of Dom Alano's letter and God's word and image, they would clearly have to act. Christians, followers of Christ, as Dom Alano said, could do no less. This message remained in the background of the articles that preceded it in the newsletter and much that was to follow.

THE CALL TO "JUDGE"

I noted earlier that Dom Alano's reference to the struggle against evil in his letter to the general was relatively anomalous: it was one of only a handful of places in *The Cry* where evil, the devil, or sin were mentioned. Even so, *The Cry* quietly relied on standing notions of evil and sin. It did so specifically by placing biblical-allegorical images at strategic points to make it clear where sin, evil, and the enemy lurked and to demonstrate how contemporary and

FIGURE 26. GETAT crucifies a worker (*Cry* 1980g, 2). Archives of the Pastoral Land Commission, Marabá, Pará.

historic events should be judged. To exemplify this point I want to look closely at the most arresting biblically inspired drawing published in the newsletter's first year: a worker crucified by the Executive Land Group of the Araguaia-Tocantins (GETAT), which took over INCRA's land regularization operations along the PA-150 in mid-1980.

This image was printed in the newsletter's September 1980 issue (1980m). It depicts a worker crucified atop a hill or platform on the central "T" of GETAT—T also standing for *trabalhador* (worker). The audience gathered below appears to be mystified by what is happening: "What did he do?" one man asks. "He wanted to work," another answers. Meanwhile, the dying worker cries out, "Father, they told me that they were going to do agrarian reform, and they deceived me again." Of course, this illustration refers to Christianity's founding moment: Christ's betrayal by Judas and his subsequent crucifixion. This worker too has been betrayed by an ally, who promised to help him secure land. The accompanying text, "Politics of Land," rounds out the message:

> In Brazil, the land question, for a long time now, has been resolved
> through the concentration of land. It has been nearly 500 years of a sys-
> tem of *latifúndio*, of domination, and of the exploitation of Indians, slaves,
> and workers. This domination always had the support of those governing.
> Once in a while, the government would create entities to resolve land
> problems, which happens until this day. . . .
>
> INCRA was created . . . to change the agrarian structure via AGRAR-
> IAN REFORM. This objective was achieved only on paper, as we know that
> the number of smallholders and *posseiros* has diminished more and more,
> ceding space to large estates and businesses and expelling man from the
> countryside, which will inundate the suburbs of large cities . . .
>
> GETAT wants to regularize lands by reconciling *grileiros, lati-
> fundiários*, businessmen and *posseiros*. But this is nothing if not an attempt
> to deceive the workers and distort their opinions . . . to repress the growth
> of the working class and in this way to implant what has always interested
> the military regime, *latifúndio* and capitalist enterprise (*Cry* 1980m).

The passage does not mention Christ or the crucifixion. However, the text is
clearly supposed to be read through the drawing of the worker's crucifixion.
What did it mean that this worker was crucified on the cross of GETAT?
Answering this question will help us understand how *The Cry*'s readers were
invited to judge and then act against what was happening around them.

It might come as a surprise that, despite being a central "datum of the
Christian faith," the crucifixion appeared relatively infrequently in theological reflection during the 1970s (Sobrino 1978, 179). Nevertheless, after German Protestant theologian Jürgen Moltmann published his breakout book
The Crucified God (1993 [1974]), which identified the cross as the site of
Christian hope, Latin American liberationists began to respond by turning
to the crucifixion as a way to understand their own historical task alongside
that of the poor. The first extended reflection on "the crucified people" was
"El Pueblo Crucificado: An Essay in Historical Soteriology," by Salvadoran
liberationist Ignacio Ellacuría, published in a volume prepared for CELAM
III (Ellacuría 1978). Ellacuría began by acknowledging Moltmann's book,
but chose not to polemicize, noting that his own title simply expressed "a
reality . . . that the greater part of humanity is literally and historically crucified . . . by historical and personal oppressions" (49). This reality, Ellacuría
added, had a specific soteriological value. The crucified, the poor, and the
oppressed could be seen as acting historically to realize Jesus's work to save
and liberate the world.

This was not just a gratuitous claim: the idea that the crucified can be the liberators of the world was based on the new liberationist theory of sin, which identified sin's origins in unequal social structures rather than solely in individuals. Ellacuría's focus was not so much on "social sin" as on how Jesus's death was "in history." This focus implied a certain distancing from the mystical, reflecting the move away from the mystical body I discussed earlier.[14] Yet Ellacuría also helped explain why liberationists were creating a new way to understand sin and evil:

> In moments when consciences were oppressed or consciences felt oppressed by a Christianity centered on the idea of sin, of guiltiness and of eternal condemnation, the structure of forgiveness, in which an offended God would forgive the guilt and annul the consequences, was indispensable. But this structure with its valid points underscores neither the collective objectivation nor the human action—destroyer of injustice and creator of love—that are historically "necessary." A new theology of sin should overcome expiatory schemes, but should not allow us to forget the existence of sin. To forget it would be, among other things, to leave an open field for the forces of oppression that massively reign in our world and it would also neglect the area of personal conversion (1978, 62).

Ellacuría admitted to the possibility that Christians have been, or might have felt, "oppressed" by a Christianity that revolved around sin. He agreed that an "expiatory scheme" was essential in earlier incarnations of Christianity, in which an "offended God" absolved a worthy penitent. Yet he argued that this was not enough—there should be a new theology of sin.

Building on decades of change in moral theology that preceded Vatican II, a change in the understanding of sin was already under development in wider theology (Keenan 2016). In the early 1970s Gustavo Gutiérrez, the avowed founder of liberationism, was following suit, developing a specifically liberationist approach to sin:

> Sin—*a breach of friendship with God and others*—is according to the Bible the ultimate cause of poverty, injustice, and the oppression in which persons live. In describing sin as the ultimate cause we do not in any way negate the structural reasons and the objective determinants leading to these situations. It does, however, emphasize the fact that things do not happen by chance and that behind an unjust structure there is a personal or collective will responsible—a willingness to reject God and neighbor.

It suggests, likewise, that a social transformation, no matter how radical
it may be, does not automatically achieve the suppression of all evils (1988
[1973], 24, my emphasis).

Here, Gutiérrez defines sin simply as the "breach of friendship with God and
others," and he is careful not to say that social structures *cause* sin. Instead,
he notes that a personal or collective will acts *through* an unjust and unequal
social structure to produce sin. Gutiérrez is clearly calling for social transformation to combat this social or structural sin, even though he concedes
that it might not put an end to all evils.

The notion of social or structural sin, embodied in the image of the
"crucified people," gained increasing traction within the church in subsequent years (Baum 1989). But as Derek Nelson has noted, even as the church
accepted that social, political, and economic structures could be considered
sinful, "the specifics of how this was to be so conceived escaped consensus" (2009, 96). Some theologians and clergy went further than Gutiérrez
to claim that the structures, being sinful, *produced* sins themselves. One
source of this radical conception was Leonardo Boff, Brazil's most famous
liberationist.[15]

A complete account of Boff's theology lies beyond the scope of this chapter. However, even a brief look at his most notorious book, *Church, Charism,
and Power* (1994 [1981]),[16] brings us back to the question of Jesus's crucifixion
and more precisely to a liberationist understanding of the sinful "pagan"
structures that continue to oppress the poor. Christianity, Boff wrote, "is not
against power in itself, but against the diabolical form in which it usually
comes historically clothed, the domination and subjugation of others" (1994
[1981], 106). This statement comes from chapter 5 of *Church, Charism, and
Power*, "The Power of the Institutional Church: Can it be Converted?" Not
incidentally, this was one of the chapters that caught the attention and censure of the Vatican, leading to Boff's silencing for one year in May 1985, a
fairly shocking punishment (see Cox 1988). Boff was a highly prolific theologian and had been head of the premier Brazilian journal of theology, *The
Brazilian Ecclesiastical Review*, since 1972—a post he had to leave after the
Vatican's judgment. The Vatican did not single out for censure Boff's assertion that structures of domination were "diabolical" (one of only four places
in the 367-page book that refers to the "devil" or the "diabolical").[17] Instead,
Cardinal Ratzinger, who was head of the Congregation for the Doctrine
of the Faith, quoted a phrase from the same page as an example of Boff's
problematic position: "The exercise of power in the Church followed the

criteria of pagan power in terms of domination, centralization, marginalization, triumphalism, [and] human hubris beneath a sacred canopy" (L. Boff
1994 [1981], quoted in Ratzinger 1994 [1984], 274). Ratzinger expressed "serious doctrinal and pastoral reservations" regarding Boff's proposed remedy
for the Church's problems—a new egalitarian, less "hierarchical" way of
"being Church" (1994 [1984], 274).[18] But Ratzinger clearly was also bothered
that Boff saw structures of domination, and by implication the devil, acting
through the Church in its "pagan" hierarchical structure.

Boff's description of the pagan and diabolical nature of hierarchical
power resonates with the image of GETAT's crucifixion of the rural worker.
Moreover, Boff's infrequent but powerful deployment of images of sin, evil,
and mystery can help us understand how *The Cry* enjoined its readers to
allegorically "judge" their current situation. The newsletter called on readers
to see the recurrence of evils that led to the historical sacrifice of Jesus. It
thus required Christians to *act*: to transform contemporary sinful oppression into liberation.

A CALL TO "ACT"

The Cry's first issues referred to "action" in a relatively vague way. It wasn't
until October 1980 that the newsletter offered its first major articulation of
action, which it inevitably joined with seeing and judging in the light of God
(*Cry* 1980i). October was the month of the annual assembly of the Marabá
diocese, which representatives from all PA-150 communities were meant to
attend. The June issue had already announced the upcoming assembly as an
occasion when communities would come together to discuss "the problems
of our Church and the directions that it will follow" (*Cry* 1980j). Expanding
on this, the October issue opened with a report that recursively reflected the
pedagogy of seeing and judging and called explicitly for a divinely infused
fraternal unity to move forward into action.

Without repeating the image of the crucifixion or mentioning evil or
sin, the report recalled Ellacuría's proposal to re-found the people of God
in order to liberate all from the reign of sin: it reiterated Boff's call for a
new kind of church and repeatedly invoked the image of a unified people.[19]
The report began by introducing the "Assembly of the People of God." This
gathering had been held annually in the region since 1977, "to construct a
new way of being Church, at whose front is our God, who acts in the lives

A Assembléia do Povo de Deus, iniciou como história na Igreja de Marabá no ano de 1977. Esta Assembléia, tem a finalidade de ser a REPRESENTAÇÃO MÁXIMA desta Igreja. Quer dizer: todo o povo junto com o Bispo Diocesano, padres, freiras e agentes pastorais leigos, caminhando e tomando decisões em conjunto, dando testemunho de uma Igreja Peregrina, que prega e busca o Reino de Deus anunciado por Cristo, Senhor da História e dos homens.

Com a Assembléia participada por todo mundo, começa-se a construir um novo jeito de ser Igreja, tendo a frente nosso Deus que age na vida dos homens e nos acontecimentos da realidade, nos chamando a ser Povo.

CHAMADOS A SER POVO

HOMEM NOVO

É NECESSÁRIO CRIAR NO HOMEM LATINO-AMERICANO UMA CONSCIENCIA SADIA, UM SENTIDO EVANGÉLICO CRÍTICO DIANTE DA REALIDADE, UM ESPÍRITO COMUNITÁRIO E UM COMPROMISSO SOCIAL. TUDO ISSO TORNARÁ POSSÍVEL UMA PARTICIPAÇÃO LIVRE E RESPONSÁVEL, EM COMUNHÃO FRATERNA, COM DIÁLOGO, PARA A CONSTRUÇÃO DE UMA NOVA SOCIEDADE COMO MODELO CRISTÃO. ELA SEGUIRÁ O MODELO DA COMUNIDADE DO PAI, FILHO E ESPÍRITO SANTO, E HÁ DE SER A RESPOSTA AOS SOFRIMENTOS E DESEJOS DO NOSSO POVO, CHEIO DE UMA ESPERANÇA QUE NÃO PODERÁ SER ILUDIDA (cf. Rm 5,5) (Puebla, 1068)

FIGURE 27. "Called on to be *povo*" and the "New Man" (*Cry* 1980c). Archives of the Pastoral Land Commission, Marabá, Pará.

of men and in the events of reality, calling upon us to be *povo*" (*Cry* 1980c, 2). A drawing consolidated this image: a shepherd raised his staff before a diverse flock, including men, women, children, and even a person with rabbit ears. This mandate to re-form the *povo* ended with an emphatic call to cultivate the New Man.

> IT IS NECESSARY TO CREATE IN THE LATIN AMERICAN MAN A HEALTHY CONSCIOUSNESS, A CRITICAL EVANGELICAL SENSE IN FACE OF REALITY, A COMMUNITARIAN SPIRIT AND SOCIAL COMITMENT. ALL THIS WILL MAKE POSSIBLE A FREE AND RESPONSIBLE PARTICIPATION, A FRATERNAL COMMUNION, WITH DIALOGUE, FOR A CONSTRUCTION OF A NEW SOCIETY ON A CHRISTIAN MODEL. IT WILL FOLLOW THE MODEL OF THE FATHER, THE SON AND THE HOLY SPIRIT, AND IT HAS TO BE A RESPONSE TO THE SUFFERING AND DESIRES OF OUR PEOPLE, FULL OF HOPE THAT CANNOT BE IGNORED (CF. RM 5,5) (PUEBLA, 1068) (*Cry* 1980c, 2).

Here, the report offered a practical discussion of *how* to foster the fraternal communion necessary to make a new society "on a Christian model." The second page fleshed out how to achieve this new man and his communitarian spirit and elaborated on the concepts and strategies explored at the assembly.

The previous three assemblies had focused on how to achieve basic needs, expand evangelization, and understand inequality, the report noted. But the 1980 meeting discussed key conceptual practices of liberationism, via the questions "What is COMMUNITY?" and "What is CONSCIENTIZA-TION?" (*Cry* 1980c, 3). The report described community as a "form of organization" of the church, providing detail by paraphrasing answers apparently arrived at during the assembly: "Community are [sic] groups of people struggling, whether in the fields or in the city, embracing a just cause, moving in only one direction, conscious of their rights and duties, [and] *struggling in fraternity*. Groups that agitate, that pressure the powerful (*grandes*) so they can conquer their rights, that testify to their faith as Christians, illuminated by the word of God, that *walk united* and are responsible for what they do, never allowing themselves to be drawn away by fear" (*Cry* 1980c, 3, my emphasis).

The text went on to explore the conceptual practice of conscientization, which further supported the existence of unified fraternal communities who acted in pursuit of liberation. "Conscientization," it said, is seeing reality and its problems discovering the causes and consequences

[It is] knowing about one's rights and duties, acting and demanding together, illuminated by the WORD OF GOD.

[It means] TO STUDY and clarify the situations[.] To discover the causes and consequences of problems, with conscientized leaders, not like big men, but by being *companheiros*.

[It means] TO MEET, participating in groups, bringing *companheiros* to add to the community, exchanging experiences with other communities and dividing tasks as everyone is responsible.

[It means] TO ACT on the religious, political, and social planes, with Biblical Circles, studying the situation with new parties, elections, becoming interested in the Union, Youth Groups, etc.

[It means] TO DEMAND AND CLAIM a response from AUTHORITIES, denouncing in newsletters, making petitions, letters, and public protests (*Cry* 1980c, 3).

The drawings that accompanied this text consolidated the image of conscientization and unity-building, both of which follow the see-judge-act script. One drawing depicted "the *povo*" carrying the weight of "Hunger, Illness, Illiteracy, Poverty, and Dependency." Another showed someone helping a man remove a blindfold. And a final drawing showed the desired result: a trinity of Brazil's poor and weak (an industrial worker, an Indigenous man, and a rural worker) demanding entry to a door marked "social life and politics" (*Cry* 1980c, 3).

The final page of the report set out the method for unified Catholic action in a set of powerful drawings under the headline, "In the assembly the issues of capitalism and socialism also came up" (*Cry* 1980c, 4). A see-judge-act sketch—where "practical life" was "observed" and "critiqued" in light of the gospel—indicated how to read the drawings on the top of the page. One illustration showed a large man held up by layers of smaller men, depicting capitalist oppression. Text around the graphic described this as a system supported by the government, police, and laws, so that "wealth remains in the hands of the few." To the right was a contrasting drawing of people all the same size holding hands under signs reading "participation" and "the decision [and] government of the people," entailing "more equality,

FIGURE 28. Three drawings from the report (*Cry* 1980c). Archives of the Pastoral Land Commission, Marabá, Pará.

distribution, [and] socialism." In the center of the page, a note read, "And how to organize to bring about a change in the situation?" The first of a list of sixteen items in response was "increasing unity." The items that followed all supported this overarching goal in one way or another: from "participating jointly in discussions . . . and courses" to learning how to "study and live the gospel" and "improving the community (doing away with the idea of the big chief)" (*Cry* 1980c, 4).

The image was clear: fraternal, communal unity in light of God was the proper condition for, and outcome of, seeing, judging, and transforming reality. Reality, of course, meant many things. First and foremost, material reality was an allegory, in the sense that it contained divine meanings—a point we will return to in chapter 6. But reality *also* meant unequal access to resources, whether economic or political. And this reality, the report suggested, must be changed through living properly, in unified egalitarian communities. To consolidate this image, *The Cry* regularly printed drawings depicting the power of unity.

NA ASSEMBLÉIA SURGIU TAMBÉM A QUESTÃO DO CAPITALISMO E DO SOCIALISMO

dinheiro
governo
terra
policia
juiz
fábricas

lucro
tudo na
mão so'
de
alguns

opressor

oprimido

capitalismo

participação
decisão e governo
do   povo
mais igualdade

distribuição

socialismo

E COMO ORGANIZAR PARA FAZER A MUDANÇA DA SITUAÇÃO?

- aumentando a união
- participando junto nas discussões
- criando equipes de luta
- planejar, decidir e agir
- fazendo encontros com pessoas de fora que podem prestar ajuda
- promovendo atividades de interesse do povo.
- criando Associações
- fazer ligações com entidades de apoio.

- fazendo cursos de base para:
  - conhecer as necessidades
  - conscientizando dos direitos e deveres
  - melhorar a comunidade (acabar com a idéia de chefão)
  - estudar e viver o evangelho
- Procurar a justiça e denunciar as injustiças
- não esperar pelos outros quando se tem condição de agir.

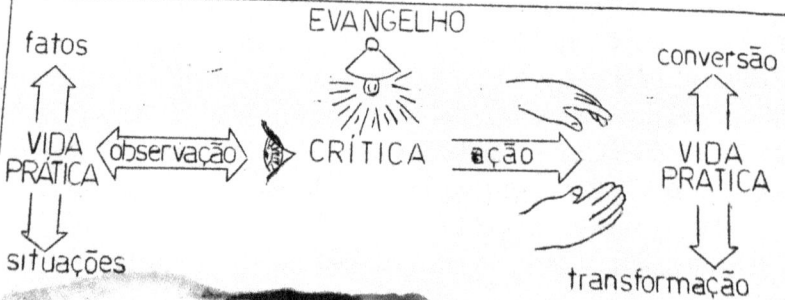

EVANGELHO

fatos   conversão

VIDA ⟨observação⟩ CRÍTICA ⟶ação VIDA
PRATICA   PRATICA

situações   transformação

FIGURE 29. The final page of the report, showing readers how to see, judge, and act to change their situation (*Cry* 1980c, 4). Archives of the Pastoral Land Commission, Marabá, Pará.

FIGURE 30. "Do you understand the meaning of this drawing? Does it have to do with recent events?" (*Cry* 1980k). Archives of the Pastoral Land Commission, Marabá, Pará.

ENCONTRO DE LAVRADORES

Nos dias 27,28 e 29 de outubro, em Belém, houve o 1 ENCONTRO ESTADUAL DOS TRABALHADORES RURAIS DO ESTADO DO PARÁ. O encontro contou com a presença de quase 400 participantes, que se reuniram com o objetivo de discutir sobre SINDICALISMO e REFORMA AGRÁRIA.

Resultados do Encontro:

Sindicalismo: pontos aprovados
. associar-se ao sindicato mesmo que seja pelego
. pela participação das mulheres e dos jovens nas lutas sindicais e políticas.
. bandeiras de lutas
. sindicatos só de agricultores e não de patrões
. diretoria que defenda os agricultores e que seja composta realmente de agricultores.
. ganhar as delegacias sindicais
. mensalidade decidida pelo próprio sindicato
. desenvolver lutas concretas

A LUTA É NECESSÁRIA PELA REFORMA AGRÁRIA

Reforma Agrária: pontos aprovados
. reforma agrária radical e imediata
. dividir as terras de acordo com o seu tamanho e qualidade e conforme o tamanho da família
. dividir as terras devolutas e latifúndios
. defender as terras com armas se for preciso

FIGURE 31. "For agrarian reform, struggle is necessary" (*Cry* 1980l, 7). Archives of the Pastoral Land Commission, Marabá, Pará.

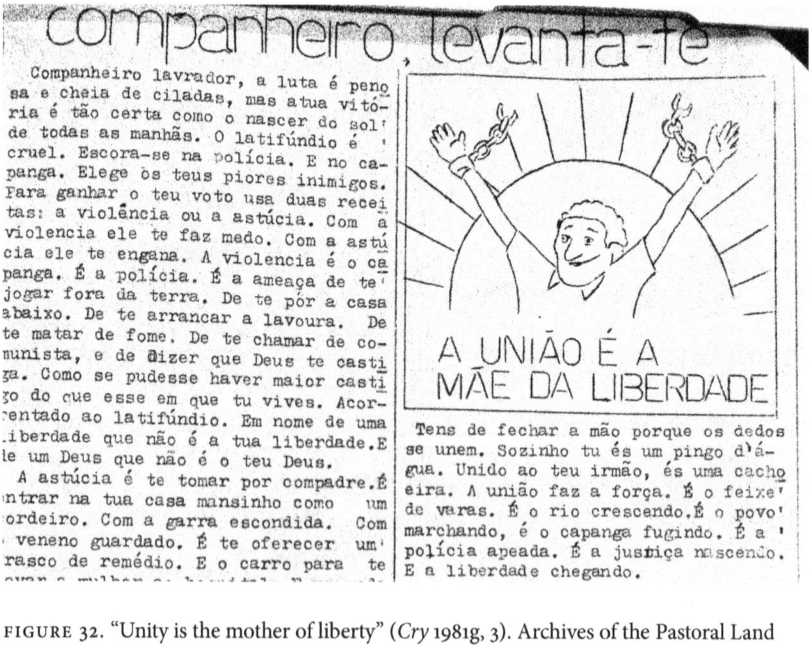

companheiro, levanta-te

Companheiro lavrador, a luta é penosa e cheia de ciladas, mas a tua vitória é tão certa como o nascer do sol de todas as manhãs. O latifúndio é cruel. Escora-se na polícia. E no capanga. Elege os teus piores inimigos. Para ganhar o teu voto usa duas receitas: a violência ou a astúcia. Com a violência ele te faz medo. Com a astúcia ele te engana. A violência é o capanga. É a polícia. É a ameaça de te jogar fora da terra. De te pôr a casa abaixo. De te arrancar a lavoura. De te matar de fome. De te chamar de comunista, e de dizer que Deus te castiga. Como se pudesse haver maior castigo do que esse em que tu vives. Acorrentado ao latifúndio. Em nome de uma liberdade que não é a tua liberdade. E de um Deus que não é o teu Deus.
A astúcia é te tomar por compadre. É entrar na tua casa mansinho como um ordeiro. Com a garra escondida. Com veneno guardado. É te oferecer um rasco de remédio. E o carro para te ...

A UNIÃO É A MÃE DA LIBERDADE

Tens de fechar a mão porque os dedos se unem. Sozinho tu és um pingo d'água. Unido ao teu irmão, és uma cachoeira. A união faz a força. É o feixe de varas. É o rio crescendo. É o povo marchando, é o capanga fugindo. É a polícia apeada. É a justiça nascendo. E a liberdade chegando.

FIGURE 32. "Unity is the mother of liberty" (*Cry* 1981g, 3). Archives of the Pastoral Land Commission, Marabá, Pará.

FIGURE 33. "A united people goes far!!!" (*Cry* 1981f, 7). Archives of the Pastoral Land Commission, Marabá, Pará.

My description so far has shown how *The Cry* used allegorical images of sinful structural relationships—between the big and the small, the rich and the poor—to catalyze a new Catholic unity and a new Catholic politics. While emphasizing unity, the report said little explicitly about sin and even less about politics. Unlike sin and evil, questions of politics would surge onto the stage the following year as the dictatorship further eased its repression in view of returning to civilian rule. Before concluding, then, it is worth detailing the unique Catholic politics that liberationists were promoting, in which evil was a fundamental problem.

LIBERATIONIST POLITICS IS TO CAPITALIST POLITICKING AS "FORCE" IS TO "POWER"

The uniqueness of the liberationist concept of politics—its difference from the "politicking" of the powerful, for example—was most clearly articulated in *The Cry*'s October 1981 issue, during the fifth annual meeting of

FIGURE 34. Little fish against sharks: stronger united (*Cry* 1981d, 1). Archives of the Pastoral Land Commission, Marabá, Pará.

the Marabá diocese. That issue's opening article justified a need for politics among "us Christians of the communities [who are] seeking and working for the Kingdom of God through our works and organizations" (*Cry* 1981a). The authorities, the article stated, had refused to help communities with even small initiatives, from building a health clinic or a school to securing a piece of land. The article continued the conversation begun during the previous year's meeting about not being "let in" to the domain of politics and concluded, "It is as if a COMMUNITY were walking until encountering a BARRIER. A WALL that no one passes through. THE PEOPLE WHO HAVE POWER IN THEIR HANDS ACTUALLY SAY NO" (*Cry* 1981a, 2). The next page raises the question, "What will be our attitude, as a small community, in face

COMEMORANDO as lutas e vitórias

25 de julho se aproxima. Esse é o dia especial dedicado ao TRABALHADOR DO CAMPO, o camponês. É um dia pros trabalhadores festejarem. Afinal são muitas lutas enfrentadas, e nelas há ensinamentos e vitórias dos trabalhadores, principalmente na dura luta pela terra.

Na Pa-150, área de grande interesse dos grileiros e grupos capitalistas, tem sido bastante tensa a questão da terra. Os lavradores têm passado por muitos apertos, perseguições, espancamentos, prisões, torturas e até assassinatos, e tudo isso com a cobertura do governo que nada faz para que o homem do campo possa gozar dos direitos que lhes pertence. Mas os trabalhadores, apesar de todas as pressões, conseguiram algumas vitórias, ganharam a terra e fizeram sair fora o grileiro. Por exemplo:

Na área localizada entre os rios Cametaú e Cametauzinho, logo às proximidades da entrada da Pa-150, 130 posseiros ganharam a terra pretendida pelo grileiro NELITO(Manoel Cardoso Neto)que apenas queria a terra por ser área de bastante castanha e só estava tirando pra vender. E os posseiros já com o direito de posse garantido, tiveram que resistir às pressões do grileiro, procurando seus direitos através do Sindicato até que botaram o grileiro pra fora.

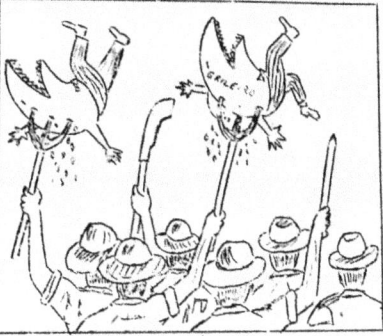

Em outra área, próxima ao Arraias, onde era de cobiça do grileiro Antonio Abreu, cerca de aproximadamente 200 posseiros estão agora localizados, já sendo feita a medição pelo GETAT, depois de 4 anos de luta.

Mais adiante no km 121, numa área denominada Globo Pitinga, pretendida pelo grupo grileiro de pixaba " Condomínio Espiritosantense", hoje há cerca de mais de 700 posseiros, que tiveram que enfrentar muitas pressões tanto por parte do grupo grileiro como pelo GETAT que até hoje enrola com as medições da área.

Nas proximidades de Goianésia, à altura do km 150 da Pa-150, área de pré tensão do grileiro ANTONIO FERNANDES, estão apossados calculadamente cerca de 400 posseiros a mais, que também a algum tempo já vêm lutando contra as investidas do grileiro, que já usou da polícia para mandar prender e espancar lavradores. Mas bravamente os posseiros vem resistindo e estão firmes e praticamente seguros nas posses.

Também próxima a essa área, mais de 100 posseiros ganharam as terras cobiçadas pelo grileiro GENERVINO, depois de muitas ameaças e investidas de pistoleiros. Mas os posseiros reagiram na mesma moeda fazendo correr os pistoleiros e o grileiro perdendo.

Na Pa-263, na Agra do Gavião, também mais de 15 posseiros conseguiram ficar na terra que a ELETRONORTE estava querendo impedir.

E há muitas e muitas outras vitórias que os lavradores conseguiram e muitas outras que os posseiros ainda estão em luta porque ainda têm muitos grileiros na região e agora apareceu o GETAT pra dar apoio aos grileiros. Resta a força e união e organização dos trabalhadores, para fazer valer os seus direitos.

FIGURE 35. Unity trounces the *grileiro*/shark (*Cry* 1981e, 2). Archives of the Pastoral Land Commission, Marabá, Pará.

of this wall?" (*Cry* 1981a, 3). Addressing the possibility of knocking the wall down, the text cautioned, "Sometimes it can fall on top of us. ISN'T IT BETTER TO TRY TO OPEN A DOOR? The door is the political space of communities. There is no other alternative for work that advances [objectives] than participation in politics" (*Cry* 1981a, 3). In other words, what was prescribed was not violent action or armed uprisings, but rather the simple opening of a door to a common political space.

        À Associação dos Trabalhadores Unidos e ao Sindicato   dos
Trabalhadores Rurais, dois braços de um mesmo corpo, o meu agrade
cimento à vocês e o meu reconhecimento e apoio por serem as ferra
mentas verdadeiras e segura na luta do povo pela Libertação. Não
esmoreçam, mas creçam e não se cansem na defesa dos oprimidos.

        Enfim quero testemunhar que não levo mágoa de ninguém. Não
tenho ódio de pessoas. Levo sim, é uma revolta que me doi no pei
to e na alma pelas estruturas injustas e corruptas do poder político; pervesso e podre em nossa região .

        Em nome de Jesus Cristo deixo o meu apêlo:
- façam a Justiça !
- defendam o direito do fraco .
- não torturem mais na cadeia .
- não pisem no pobre .
- vivam e pratiquem unicamente a verdade .

FIGURE 36. "Land and Justice on the PA-150" (*Cry* 1986, 3). Archives of the Pastoral Land Commission, Marabá, Pará.

Over five more pages, *The Cry* developed a concept and an image of a politics gently animated by allegory, emphasizing the good while subtly reminding readers of evil. The second article opened: "Politics is what most influences our lives. Politics is a great weapon we have to create a future world that God wants. What we have today is POLITICKING and not POLITICS. One way to do good politics is via POLITICAL PARTIES. But we shouldn't be afraid to enter into politics. WE SHOULD BE SIMPLE LIKE DOVES AND SHREWD LIKE SNAKES. WE MUST FIND FORCE (FORÇA) FOR THE STRUGGLE WE ARE ENGAGED IN" (*Cry* 1981c, 3).

This issue was composed while discussions were underway in the National Congress about reinstituting elections for governor for the first time since the 1964 coup. In preparation for redemocratization, *The Cry* and liberationists elsewhere in the country[20] were keen to address and change the *povo*'s well-known aversion to politics, which had long preexisted the military government's repression. As in the liberationist texts we saw in chapter 2, the article in *The Cry* referred to the common Catholic sense, adopted by the *povo*, that human governance is evil. *The Cry* used explicitly allegorical images to argue that its readers should not fear participating in politics, since it did not have the power to touch their moral cores. People can remain "simple like doves," the article said, "even as they are shrewd like snakes" (*Cry* 1981c, 3). While local readers might not know the quote from Matthew 10:16 upon which the above is based,[21] they would recognize the biblical images readily, especially the serpent who, with his deviousness, brought about Adam and Eve's expulsion from Eden and the fall of humanity. The liberationist claim was that if you are "organiz[ing] to serve" the oppressed by drawing on the "force" of unity, like Jesus, you will be doing proper politics, a politics of the oppressed, which was fundamentally opposed to the politicking of the powerful (*Cry* 1981c, 5, 3, 6).

As early as Christmas 1980, *The Cry* made evident the difference between force and power. The first article begins by affirming:

> Christmas—is Christ being born to renew the hope of the oppressed. Hope and *força* (strength, force) in the struggle for Liberation. . . . It is when the oppressed, the poor and weak, unite and organize against their oppressors that the Father surges like the hope and force that nourishes the poor in the journey toward liberation. . . . [CHRIST] DOES EVERY-THING WITH THE STRENGTH OF HIS ARMS / HE EXPELS THE ARROGANT / KNOCKS DOWN THE POWERFUL FROM THEIR THRONES / SENDS THE RICH AWAY EMPTY-HANDED / HE LOOKS WITH LOVE AT THE HUMBLE . . ." (*Cry* 1980g, 2).

A 1981 issue then reiterated "the force of unity" (*Cry* 1981b, 9). While implying that Catholic unity was a unique politics, the newsletter made a point to distinguish force and unity from party politics. "POLITICS ALSO COMES

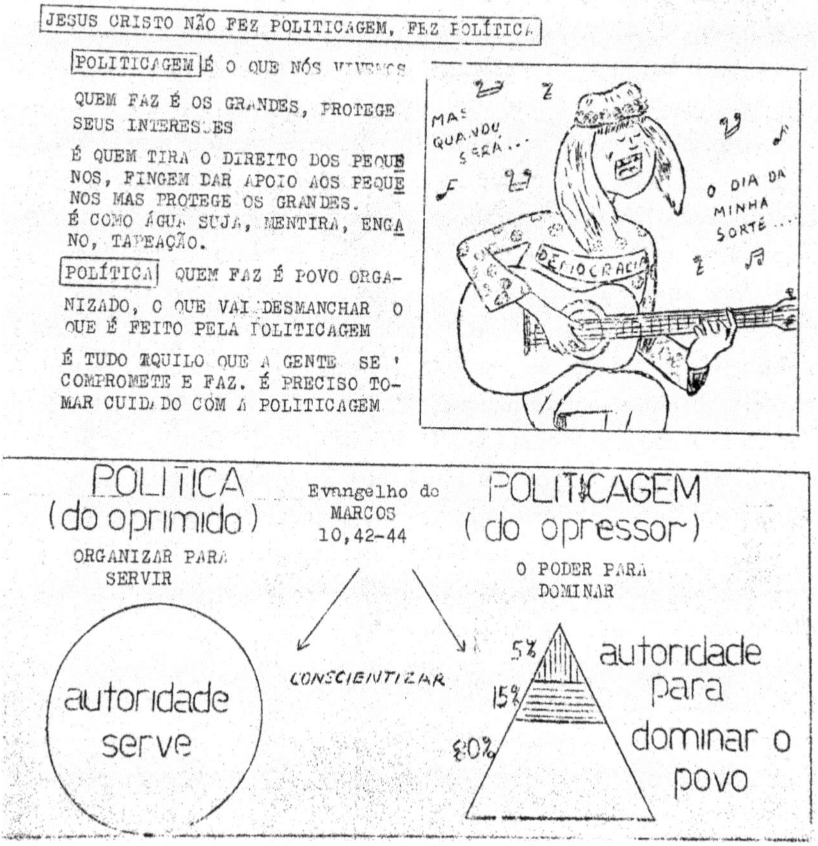
JESUS CRISTO NÃO FEZ POLITICAGEM, FEZ POLÍTICA

POLITICAGEM É O QUE NÓS VIVEMOS

QUEM FAZ É OS GRANDES, PROTEGE SEUS INTERESSES

É QUEM TIRA O DIREITO DOS PEQUENOS, FINGEM DAR APOIO AOS PEQUENOS MAS PROTEGE OS GRANDES.
É COMO ÁGUA SUJA, MENTIRA, ENGANO, TAPEAÇÃO.

POLÍTICA QUEM FAZ É POVO ORGANIZADO, O QUE VAI DESMANCHAR O QUE É FEITO PELA POLITICAGEM

É TUDO AQUILO QUE A GENTE SE COMPROMETE E FAZ. É PRECISO TOMAR CUIDADO COM A POLITICAGEM

POLITICA (do oprimido)
ORGANIZAR PARA SERVIR

Evangelho de MARCOS 10,42-44

POLITICAGEM (do opressor)
O PODER PARA DOMINAR

FIGURE 37. A page from the October 1981 issue of *The Cry* (1981c, 6). Archives of the Pastoral Land Commission, Marabá, Pará.

INTO RELIGION and ALSO INTO COMMUNITIES," the October issue proclaimed, but "this does not mean that Community is the same thing as Syndicate or Party" (*Cry* 1981c, 5). In other words, while religion and politics remained different, force and unity still applied both to what happened in the church and to the formal political practices that Catholics engaged in.

Now we are ready to understand the specificity of *politics* as opposed to *politicking*, which was what those in power do to "dominate." Politicking "take[s] away the rights of the little guy, pretend[s] to give them support while protecting the powerful. It is like dirty water, lies, deceit (*engano*)." Jesus Christ, the text noted, "did politics, not politicking" (*Cry* 1981c, 5).

The tools to undo politicking, *The Cry* explained, were "ECCLESIAL BASE

COMMUNITIES, SYNDICATES AND ASSOCIATIONS, AND OTHER ORGANI-
ZATIONS OF THE PEOPLE, POLITICAL PARTIES," and, most importantly,
the Bible. The diagram illustrated "the politics of the oppressed" in which
"authority serves," versus "the politics of the oppressor" where "authority is
for dominating." The image suggested that the Bible was the way to "consci-
entize" regarding the difference between politics and politicking (*Cry* 1981b,
6). The diagram referred to the Gospel of Mark, which is worth quoting
(although *The Cry* did not provide the quote): "And Jesus called them to
him and said to them, 'You know that those who are supposed to rule over
the Gentiles lord it over them, and their great men exercise authority over
them. But it shall not be so among you; but whoever would be great among
you must be your servant, and whoever would be first among you must be
slave of all'" (Mark 10:42-44, RSVCE).

Here we see an echo of the crucified worker, the current system of domination likened to the Gentiles, the Romans who killed Jesus as a result of
their domineering brand of authority, the essence of evil and sin. Liberationist Catholics, *The Cry* maintained, must do things differently. Like Jesus
they had to use force to expel the "ARROGANT" and to "KNOC[K] DOWN
THE POWERFUL FROM THEIR THRONES [AND] SEN[D] THE RICH AWAY
EMPTY-HANDED" (*Cry* 1980g, 2). But force, again, was not power or politicking. Force was generated through unity with others and God—which we
should recall could also be conceived as friendship—and was as important
for Catholic communal religious practices along the PA-150 as it was vital
for politics.

CONCLUSION

In 1984 Joseph Ratzinger, as prefect of the Congregation for the Doctrine of
the Faith, the agency once in charge of the Inquisition, published a sharp critique of liberationism (Ratzinger 1984). Elsewhere Ratzinger went so far as
to suggest that heresy lurked in liberationism's new politicization of Catholic
unity (Ratzinger and Missori 1985). Ratzinger's denunciation was followed,
as noted earlier, by the Vatican's silencing of Leonardo Boff as punishment
for his book *Church, Charism, and Power* (Cox 1988). The Vatican softened
its critique of liberationism somewhat in a follow-up statement (Ratzinger
1986), but the die had been cast, and the movement went into decline across
the Americas. The most substantive wave of social-scientific scholarship on

liberationism debated what led to this fate, although it barely addressed the theology (Burdick 1993; Mariz 1994; Vásquez 1998; for an earlier social science perspective, see Lancaster 1988). This lopsided attention is one reason that the waning of liberationism has not been my concern here. Another is that I am more interested in the *practice* of liberationism than its decline, for the movement clearly had a deep impact on the faithful during its decade and a half of predominance. To understand its legacies beyond its institutional continuities, I began by exploring movement theology as it was put into practice along the PA-150.[22] The first issues of *The Cry* illustrate how the newsletter sought to influence its readers to see and judge the world around them and to act to change it for the better.

My focus on liberationism via *The Cry* has generated some lateral insights as well. At the most general level this chapter has offered an image of the early dynamics of colonization along the highway. Would-be smallholders who arrived in search of land settled in large and small groups, both close to the highway and deep into the forest. Smallholders had to compete for land with each other and with *grileiros* who retained the support of state agents as well as private militias. The *grileiros*, *The Cry* showed in each issue, often used violence to intimidate smallholders, and did so with impunity.

Yet these stories of colonization also served as allegorical images that inspired the newsletter's readers to see, judge, and act. The descriptions were reinforced by occasional drawings, for example of crucified peasants and egalitarian communities, that were meant to inspire judgment based on a liberationist understanding of social or structural sin. The prescription for action against sin and evil was to enact fraternal unity and thus invert the political-economic hierarchy that reproduced inequality and disunity. This unified action was potentially revolutionary, since it was to serve as the grounds for a new kind of church, a new kind of politics, and a new nonhierarchical, noncapitalist society.

While the image of the "crucified people," reflecting the notion of social sin, was meant to guide judgment and action, we have seen examples of how *The Cry* generally avoided direct mention of sin or evil, or even *dis*unity. In its entire seven years of publication, the newsletter mentioned the devil four times, and sin and evil remained implicit, to be inferred by readers.

I noted that this backgrounding of sin and evil was not an exclusively liberationist tendency. Indeed, despite the Vatican's urging not to forget the devil, by the 1980s talk of sin and evil had been receding in Catholic discourse for some time—as had invocations of mystery and especially the "mystical body." This can be put in broader perspective with another example. Immediately after Vatican II, *The Brazilian Ecclesiastical Review* published one article on evil, a deeply considered piece titled "The Problem of Evil and Its Contemporary Pastoral Relevance" (Tepe 1966). The author, Valfredo Tepe, was a Brazilian-trained German priest who would be promoted to Auxiliary Bishop of São Salvador da Bahia in 1967 and then to Bishop of Ilhéus, Bahia, in 1971. But Tepe's was the last essay in the *Review* to mention evil in its title until at least 1985, when Boff had to relinquish his editorship of the journal and liberationism began to wane. With these changes in mind, Tepe's call to address the profound sense of evil with which the Brazilian *povo* lived is arresting:

> In our vast country . . . the sayings that [truck drivers] write on their bumpers express the emotional and "philosophical" life of the *povo*. The following sentence, which we found on a truck, is a challenge to our pastoral ministry: "If the world was good, the owner would live here." The world is here compared to a large estate: the owner left and handed over the hard work to those remaining behind. . . . If the phrase of the driver reflects the experience of large swathes of our *povo*, of the "Christian *povo*," we should acknowledge the failure of our pastoral ministry. . . .
>
> [We] wan[t] to bring men to salvation in Christ. To achieve this, first it is necessary to feel how today's men live and experience evil and then it is necessary to find ways to present, in a convincing way, Christ as today's salvation. . . . But will our pastoral ministry secure the "conscientization" of the *povo* regarding these truths? Will . . . [it be] the ferment for the eschatological transformation of the cosmos, of the person, of society? (Tepe 1966, 871).

Tepe's essay adds a dimension to my ethnography, offering further evidence of how a pervasive sense of evil persisted among the *povo*.[23] But this text—especially its call to recuperate the "eschatological promise" of the future—is also a kind of prefiguring of liberationism. While Tepe's rhetoric was decidedly tamer than later liberationist discourse, the eschatological orientation to the "promised land" was precisely what the movement would espouse (Tepe 1966, 866). And as I have noted, liberationists did develop an explicit theology of social or structural sin, which remained implicit in much of their work. Still, whether in *The Cry* or in academic scholarship, Brazilian liberationists avoided an *overt* focus on sin and evil.

Which brings me to my final argument: liberationism's intense focus on unity, its relative silence on evil, and its diffusing of sin into a collective structure all echo today in the mystic of friendship. Specifically, these tendencies helped intensify the Catholic longing for unity and a sense of pervasive evil, while offering few new resources for understanding horizontal, everyday divisions among the people of God. In other words, we can say that liberationist ambivalence about the overt discussion of evil allowed older anxieties about evil to persist, anxieties that have continued to recur ever since a mystical-body theology in the service of empire first landed on Brazilian shores.

The critical edge to my argument is not that liberationism "failed to change" this mode of relating because it failed to oust old understandings of sin and evil forever. On the contrary, I am more concerned that it failed to address how traditional understandings of evil recurred and shaped everyday relationships and failed to work this into their theology in constructive ways. For indeed, the mystic of friendship alerts us to the fact that achieving and maintaining unity is truly hard work. In contrast, while liberationists affirmed the value of unity openly and regularly, it was rare to find in *The Cry* or elsewhere advice on how to achieve unity in spite of whatever might bedevil it.

To flesh out this final point on liberationism's silence on disunity, evil, and sin, let us return to Dom Alano's letter to the communities of the PA-150. Though Dom Alano found a problematic sense of disunity in the communities, he did not dwell on it. Instead, he instructed his flock to reduce the time they spent thinking about the people who had abandoned the struggle. People left, Dom Alano said, for any number of reasons: maybe they were "vanquished by fear," or maybe "they sold their land" and moved. Alano acknowledged that communities might "suffer" as a result, yet he suggested that these departures should just be seen as opportunities to increase communal force and unity. They were but "small failings," he added, "that should be corrected with patience and firmness" while communities remained focused on the "powerful" who were "reuniting to 'crush the People of God for once and forever.'" After the analysis presented in this chapter, we know what Dom Alano implied, even if he didn't say it explicitly: the powerful were the "real enemy," the real evil, that communities should focus on defeating.

This was where local communities might have had questions. If common liberationist ideas maintained that sin was "a breach of friendship with God and others," a basic "refusal to love one's neighbors and, therefore, the Lord himself" (Gutiérrez 1988 [1973], 24), the question remained: how can only *some* people (i.e., only the powerful outside the community) who fail to join in solidarity with the people of God be the enemy? Wasn't *any* disunity, the failure of *any* instance of friendship with God and others including among the struggling *povo*, the essence of sin? The faithful weren't given coherent answers to these questions. Instead, beyond repeated injunctions to unify, they were given few new resources to help them address the immanence of division and disunity in their communities and daily lives.

The message of this chapter and the chapters that follow is not only for scholars of religion and politics. It is also for activists, theological and otherwise. Liberationism unquestionably offered vital support to the poor who had come to the PA-150 to struggle for land. Still, it seems clear to me that a theology—or for that matter any political theory—that aims to support intentional political transformations over time must be able to articulate how difference and division are integral to unity. This is especially important in common Catholic communities in Brazil, which can quickly be inspired to act through utopian discourses of unity but perhaps just as quickly become skeptical of them—as they divine the divisions, and the allegories, that continue to haunt them.

The next chapters explore more contemporary versions of the problems of unity and division through ethnography of the Landless Rural Workers' Movement, which many see as the more secular legacy of liberationism (see especially Burdick 2004).

The Province of Brazil, 1682

As confirmation of Predestined's reflections, what happened next, I am
not sure whether by chance or by heaven's destiny, was that a great uproar
suddenly began, & with banging Palace doors & Observation arriving to
see what it was, there came running an illustrious Lady, who came in a
great miserable rush to take refuge in Obedience's house, like someone
escaping a wild beast, or like the same wild beast escaping the hunter
chasing it.[1] [The Lady] had a lavish golden crown on her head and & it
was resting on two bases made of saintly bread (*pão santo*). She was being
pursued by a detestable old woman, who looked like a Hag (*Arpía*), who
came with many young men & many young women throwing stones at
her, & she wanted to find refuge in the house of a powerful Prince or Lord,
to defend herself from such vile rabble. Soon that old woman [Arpía]
who was pursuing her came in behind her & she was thrown out of the
house. . . .

   Shocked, Predestined asked Observance what Lady was this who was
being pursued in such a villainous way? That Lady (responded Observance) who is being pursued in such a way is Divine Law, the crown on
her head is the Dictate of Reason, which gives its power to all of the Law,
the base on which it rests, made of saintly bread, is Natural Law and the
Law of the peoples (*das gentes*), in which lies the Law of God. That evil
hag who pursues her is the Law of the World, the young men & women
who are throwing stones at her are Human Respect & Reasons of State,
due to whom respect for the Law of God is very often lost; & because she
should be and is defended, and supported by powerful people & Lords,

the opposite happens, because the Law of the World & Human Respect
come with them, and soon the Law of God is reviled, & the Law of World
esteemed.

O how correct and how true this verdict is, exclaimed Predestined!
How despised is the Law of God, how trampled on in the Courts & Pal-
aces, how flattened by these respects, & by these reasons! How many times
when placing divine respect alongside human respect, we cut the divine
so as not to lack the human! How many times for a point of honor, for
respect for the King, to reciprocate with a friend, for a point of courtesy,
for the emblem of a nobleman, we knock down Divine Law, & we lose
respect for God! O accursed reasons of state, how beyond all reason you
are! O infamous Law of the World, how contrary you are to all the Law
of God! O accursed human respect, how worthy you are of all disregard!
O accursed Law of the World, to how many Pilgrims you have closed the
doors of Jerusalem, to how many you have opened the doors of Babylon.

05

FAZENDA PERUANO

Law's Enmity

The coordinators' meeting had been tense. Sensitive subjects had been raised: the unsanctioned occupation of the highway, the problem of the militant Gabriel, the death threats received by coordinators. They used a kind of evasive speech characteristic of these MST meetings and other delicate public discussions of people's behavior. "*Perigoso mesmo*" (truly dangerous), one coordinator commented of the situation.

The meeting ended with a *grito de ordem* (chant): *"Patria livre!"* Coordinators quickly went back to their *barracos* (huts) in the light drizzle, knowing that a downpour was about to begin. It was November 2004, the beginning of the rainy season in Southeast Pará.[1] I decided to stay a little longer with a few other stragglers. It was my first visit to the camp in a while.

The rain began to thicken. Voices hummed. Black tobacco was rolled into notebook paper. Smoke curled beneath the palm-thatch roof of the meeting hut. A man whom I did not know, perhaps a new resident, sidled up to me. "I think that you will be interested in this," he said, showing me a clipboard and a letter. "This is something that we are thinking about, a way of organizing the camp better." "Can I copy this down?" I asked, surprised at my own boldness, given the tension of the meeting. "*Claro!*" "Of course!" he said. I copied the paper into my notebook as the rain began really pounding the roof. Timoteo, who helped represent what is called the *militância*, the MST activist leadership (henceforth "militancy" or "militants") to the camp's coordinators, came up behind me as I copied, looked briefly, and then went off to talk to other people.

It was a declaration, shakily written, with mistakes that I try to capture below:

DECLARATION OF THE THOT OF OUR CAMP

This camp [Lourival Santana] is very well because it is one of the largest
in the south of Pará. In organization it is not going very well because
something needs to change. The coordination [committee] is very well,
altho not as it always should be, always up to date, yes it has to change
and even certain residents (*componentes*).

And he that does not want to change has to leave. And leaving he that
wants to work inside of our camp because the work of the *componente*
is following the norms of the MST. And within the nucleus follow the
enstruction of the coordinator and of security and discipline etc. Only
this way will our camp embetter every day. Each one doing his part. It
would be great, espelling he that doesn't want to work and leaving he
that wants to work for real. If each one thincks that, yes, everything will
change for real.

The declaration had three signatures. When I had finished copying it, the
man reiterated: "A few coordinators have gotten together to form an association of friends to help orient the people of the camp." I was intrigued, though
I didn't fully grasp the implications of his proposition.

"I am actually interviewing coordinators now; can I interview you later?"

"Of course," he said, smiling brightly. He introduced himself as Anton,
and we arranged a time to meet in the early afternoon when the rains usually
stopped. He invited me to stay through the first meeting of the group he was
forming, which would take place at 5:00 p.m. I then went to exchange a few
jokes with Timoteo and some other militants before braving the rain, which
wouldn't stop for hours. The militants didn't ask me about my conversation
with Anton, although they had been watching. I tried to reassure them about
our friendship with my jokes. I knew they had to stay extra sharp now; they
had to regain control of the camp after the coordinating committee had
decided to protest the militancy's leadership by occupying the PA-150, letting no traffic through. This protest was reminiscent of the one that had led
to the 1996 Eldorado Massacre, and it had made it onto the national news the
previous day, forcing the MST state leadership, headquartered in Marabá,
to rush to the scene. *Dangerous*, I thought, echoing the sentiment of the
coordinators' meeting. *Perigoso mesmo.* I ran out into the rain.

Halfway back to Mona's *barraco*, where I always stayed, I was forced to
stop to unstick my foot from the bottom of a muddy puddle. As I maneu-
vered so as not to lose or break my flip-flop, I overheard a man say, through

the thatch walls of the *barraco* a few feet away: "I don't like to fart where I am and choke on my own farts. I like to fart and have it stay far away from me." Well, that's another way of putting it, I thought, laughing to myself. I knew that this was a comment on the increasingly open conflicts in the camp, including how they were being aired at the meeting. Put otherwise, it was a creative reiteration of the ethic that helps manage the mystic of friendship. My faceless interlocutor was offering a graphic version of what I had heard many times before: one must be socially careful, "friendly," with those around you, otherwise one is cut off, one chokes, can even die. All this friction, and the talk about it, was, in short, *dangerous*. I managed to free my foot and keep running.

This chapter describes how the mystic of friendship, a longing for unity coupled with a sense of its precarity, animated a turning point in a massive land occupation led by the MST, the Landless Rural Workers' Movement.[2] In describing this process, I also shed new light on a persistent theme in Brazilian ethnography: a longing for legal equity coupled with a sense that law is "for enemies." Roberto DaMatta was the first to investigate how people in Brazil can be affronted by attempts to subject them to a law or rule (1991 [1979]). DaMatta showed that this dynamic can give rise to a variety of conflictual responses, from violence to "authoritarian rituals" that reassert relational hierarchy over impersonal law. DaMatta's classic study, written during Brazil's military dictatorship, explores one authoritarian ritual in particular: the wielding of the phrase, "Do you know who you are talking to?" While DaMatta focused on the upper classes of Rio and São Paulo, he did find that persons of all social classes used this phrase to assert their own status (or that of their bosses) when a rule stood in their way. Although DaMatta implied a generalized desire for the rule of egalitarian law, he foregrounded how this desire coexisted with a widespread suspicion around the application of law. This suspicion is captured, DaMatta argued, in the common Brazilian saying "for my friends everything, for my enemies the law."

Though DaMatta's findings are decades old, they continue to resonate widely, beyond my interlocutors in Amazonia and even beyond Brazil.[3] "Do you know who you are talking to" is used across the anglophone world (at least), while the phrase "for my friends everything, for my enemies the law," has recently gained a new life, deployed by politicians and commentators across Spanish-speaking Latin America to articulate their own heritage and political struggles. I suspect that this development was catalyzed by the Mexican president Andrés Manuel Lopez Obrador who, during his period in office (2018–24), sometimes quoted a nineteenth-century version of the phrase, attributed to Benito Juárez, the twenty-sixth president of Mexico (Sodi 2022). Lopez Obrador may have drawn inspiration from the US-based Mexican academic and public intellectual Claudio Lomnitz, who wrote about this saying and its resonance in Mexico in the late 1990s. Significantly, Lomnitz never claimed that the phrase originated in Mexico, instead engaging DaMatta on this "Brazilian adage," arguing that it captured only some aspects of Mexican citizenship and politics (Lomnitz 1999; 2001).[4]

Meanwhile, in Brazil DaMatta's analysis continues to be a touchstone for political anthropology. A salient example is James Holston's 2008 book *Insurgent Citizenship*, which found the sense that "the law is for enemies" undergirding and complicating both older legal structures and new demands for social justice among poor Northeastern migrants to São Paulo.[5] Holston argues that despite the emergence of new calls for justice, contemporary "insurgent citizens" continue to work with the idea that the law is for enemies as they struggle against laws and procedures made to exclude them while using laws against their enemies in turn. For Holston, insurgent citizens are not just of the left. They come from across the political spectrum: from neighborhood associations struggling to secure land titles, to gangs establishing their own (misrule of) law against police. Yet whatever side of the political aisle insurgents are on, they share the new language of rights. "If, in the past," Holston reflects, "the oppressed found expression in millenarian religious movements, today they have a secular voice and it speaks in rights talk" (2008, 308). That is, the oppressed are now insurgent, making secular calls on the law to bring them justice against their historic enemies.

I agree with Holston that this new talk of rights circulates in a secular register. We will see it circulating this way in the MST, one of the most important insurgencies, to use Holston's language, in post-authoritarian Brazil. However, relegating millenarian and religious thinking to the past oversteps the mark, at least for poor Northeastern migrants in the Amazon. As each chapter of this book has shown, Christianity echoes in and shapes local social and political life in settler Amazonia and elsewhere in Brazil. Although Holston puts more historical and political-economic flesh on the body of legalized Brazilian inequalities, in the end he does not go very far beyond DaMatta's similarly secular and therefore partial explanation as to why the law could be considered to be "for enemies."

Let's look more closely at DaMatta's reasons for what I dub "law's enmity," which he summarizes with the pithy counter-phrase "for individuals, the law; for persons, everything!" (1991 [1979], 186). DaMatta means that the law, supposedly applied equally and impersonally to all, transforms the "person" into an "individual" of inferior social value precisely because he has no connections to protect him from the law's sanction. DaMatta occasionally refers to Brazil's Catholic inheritance to explain this disposition, for example noting the Brazilian preference for vertical rather than horizontal solidarity in the style of religious fraternities. But DaMatta does little more than nod at these correlations, neglecting the key to understanding the persistence of the idea of law's enmity: that human law and justice are sincerely wanted but neither stable nor entirely "believed in" because of the immanence of terrestrial enmity, or evil. We can say, in other words, that law's enmity is an iteration of the mystic of friendship.

In what follows, I show how these mystic relational dynamics—once Catholic, now increasingly distributed among religions—helped undermine law in the camp, leading to Anton's insurgent proposal to reclaim unity by forming "an association of friends." But before we can fully understand this, I must show how an intensified sense of unity was created in the process of occupying Fazenda Peruano. This occupation was a momentous achievement. Some one thousand families, representing around four thousand people, packed up and moved from a temporary camp about twenty-five kilometers away and resettled on lands held by one of the most powerful families in Pará, the Mutran (see chapter 3, note 1).

Below I begin by describing the preparations for the occupation, focusing on the efforts to instill *mística*—an important conceptual practice for the MST, though it is not the same as the idea of mystic that I use in this book. I will consider at length the connections of *mística* to unity, to Catholicism, and to *companheirismo*, a secular relationship beyond friendship and kinship. My description emphasizes a central message: that a Christian hope for unity was inevitably carried into the camp along with the MST's versions of *mística* and *companheirismo*. This does not mean that there was no secular domain emerging in the camp. Instead, Christian hope operated alongside the primarily secular political solidarity promoted by the MST. Although researchers of the MST might sometimes say that there is no distinction between religion and the secular or political in the concept of *mística*, they are simply ignoring the emergent distinctions between Christian and non-religious views of the world that the MST has developed and introduced to many of its members as it became autonomous from the church (I expand on this below). The secular, recall, is also not entirely excluded when *mística* is said to be "spiritual" (Flynn 2013; also Rolemberg 2020).[6]

Keeping in mind the overlaps and tensions between Christian and MST organizational forms, the second part of the chapter shows how camp unity was fractured and so, too, were *mística* and *companheirismo*, even as God's friendship remained firm. Specifically, I describe the camp's organizational structure, homing in on the challenge that coordinators faced, namely, how they made enemies by applying the "law"—that is, by punishing and excluding neighbors for committing infractions. This inadvertently whittled away the camp's unity.

Although this is a Paraense, Brazilian, and Latin American story, it is not only that. In the conclusion I show that law's enmity recurs from even farther afield in time and place. I trace it to Christianity's beginnings with St. Paul, and later to St. Augustine, whose injunction to avoid pagan courts and to be wary of the world resonated in early Portuguese America, as already suggested in the Fifth Visitation.

THE FIRST CAMP

I climbed down from the little van and walked toward the *guarita*, the guarded entrance to the new camp. Though my bags were searched for arms and other illegal items, I passed through as easily as my fellow travelers. I would later learn that guards were letting everyone enter the camp for the next few days. The plan was to let as many people as possible in to ensure that it would be a massive occupation. It would be safer that way.

I asked the guards where I could find the *barraco dos militantes*, the hut for MST activists. It was late afternoon, and people were milling about on the long thoroughfare into the camp in the fading light. A few huts, covered in black tarps and palm leaves, had been erected on either side. The huts without leaves on their roofs gleamed in the afternoon sun. As the density of huts thickened, I noticed Bernardo, and he noticed me at almost the same time. We greeted each other warmly. "So you have come to accompany us in the preparations," he said. "Let's leave your things in the *barraco*." We made our way through the first row of *barracos*, and I remembered that this was just the beginning of an intricately laid out space, with huts along "streets" extending in all directions. Camps were often set up this way to dissuade invasions by the police, who found it difficult and dangerous to walk a camp's winding, densely settled paths. "The *povo*" can be fierce.

Bernardo and I arrived at a small *barraco* and entered, bending slightly to walk through the low door. "You can stay here. This is where most of us are staying. Sit." He gestured to a narrow wooden bench. The late afternoon sun glowed through the thatch onto the uneven earth floor. Wanting to impress on me that I was there to witness "a very special event," Bernardo explained: "This is one of the largest camps ever in Southeast Pará. There are more than 1,000 families here—that's over 4,000 people. Many of them have had contact with the movement already, some are relatives of residents of the 17th of April settlement, which, as you know, has been marked by the traumatic experience of the Eldorado Massacre. Moreover, many if not most have been gold-miners. And, as I often say, 'A man [human] can become a gold-miner, but it is hard for a gold-miner to become a man again.'" At the time, I did not realize that Bernardo's reference to the dehumanizing experience of artisanal gold-mining (*garimpagem*) reflected a worry among the militants over whether such a big camp of fiercely independent people would hold together through the occupation—whether, that is, the occupiers could develop a shared *mística* in time for the big day.

Of course, I knew that this camp had been set up differently from others. Camps usually came into being in the act of occupation (Sigaud 2000). But this one had started five months prior on the lands of another settlement to build up a critical mass. This was intended to help avoid the failures of the Fazenda Mutamba occupation. The Mutamba occupation of November 2003 (shortly before I moved to Pará) had a mere two hundred participants and had been conducted at night. This seemed to embolden the police to respond swiftly and with violence: They shot at the occupiers and took eight people prisoner as the rest fled into the forest. Some would not resurface publicly in the region for two years. Six of the prisoners were kept for four months without trial. They were released on probation months later, and authorities simply closed the case.

Before Mutamba, Bernardo reminded me, there had not been an MST-led occupation in Southeast Pará since 1998, and *that* occupation process had triggered the assassination of the historic leaders Fusquinha (Onalício Araújo Barros, 33) and Doutor (Valentim Silva Serra, 39). Hence, the success of the present occupation was particularly important. The MST leadership had waited until they had a large group, which would be more difficult and politically dangerous for the police to disperse. They hoped that a successful occupation would be a major affront to both the state government and the local oligarchies. Finally, the MST hoped to demonstrate their local power with the first occupation in the region since Luiz Inácio "Lula" da Silva was elected to the presidency in 2002 at the helm of the Workers' Party (PT), helping to signify the triumph of the left.

Bernardo did not tell me two important details. First, he did not tell me that we were occupying a farm owned by the Mutran family, which had been at the apex of the regional oligarchy since the 1930s, when they came to control large Brazil-nut groves (see chapter 3, note 1; Emmi 1999, 91; see also Petit 2003; Barreiros et al. 2017). He also didn't say that the occupation would "take place" in five days. I did learn, however, that six militants from other settlements had arrived to help organize two days earlier. The first meeting between the visiting militants and the camp coordinating committee was to be that very night. I was pleased. Perhaps this meeting might begin to answer a key question of mine: What did the militants perceive to be their biggest obstacle? And how were they going to confront it? There were many material difficulties, as we will see, but I would learn that the central challenge was how to create a unified, solidary community of *companheiros* (something like comrades)[7] out of mostly "unconscientized" strangers.

COMPANHEIRISMO

Just before 7:00 p.m. we headed to the football pitch near the gate under a dark sky. The faint light of tea candles stuck in the sand welcomed us. After more than a hundred coordinators positioned themselves in an oval shape on the pitch, Júlio began to play one of the MST's more earnest songs on a guitar: "Ordem e Progresso" (Order and progress). Many people knew the song and sang along. After we stopped singing, one of the resident militants, Timoteo, led a *grito de ordem*, the chant of a key slogan: "*Reforma agraria quando?* (Agrarian reform when?)" he asked. "*Já!* (Now!)" everyone cried. They repeated this call and response three times. Then Timoteo called out in his deep powerful voice, "*Patria Livre!!*" Once the crowd settled down, Timoteo began introducing the visiting militants. The seriousness with which the coordinators were treating the new militants' presence was palpable. Everyone was silent and paying close attention, knowing that we were about to receive important news about the occupation.

And so we did. The militants told the camp residents to begin preparing to move at last. They were to take only essentials. The MST had hired only ten trucks, which could not carry everything.[8] They also had to entrust their guns or rifles to the militants for safety; these would be returned after the occupation. On the morning of April 16, all residents would load their chosen belongings onto the trucks and set off on a march of approximately twelve kilometers to the S-Curve on the PA-150 highway, where the Massacre had occurred. They would camp there overnight, and protest for workers' rights on April 17, the International Day of the Peasantry and the eighth anniversary of the Eldorado Massacre. Friends and allies would also join from other MST camps, the PT (Worker's Party), the Catholic Church, the Federal University of Pará, and FETAGRI (the state syndicate of workers in agriculture). In fact, with the latter there would be a "historic synchronizing of calendars," which meant that the FETAGRI syndicates, directed by the National Workers' Syndicate (the Central Unico de Trabalho), would be organizing large mobilizations throughout the state on April 17 instead of on May 1.

Then Bernardo brought the discussion of the coming days to a close. "And then at some time and some day on or around the 17th, we will march again, this time to the land that we will occupy. We will just not say which way we will march, be it in this or that direction, until the time comes." That is all that could be said:

> We cannot give our secrets to our enemies, who are the *latifúndio* and the police. And what are our secrets? Our information. This does not mean that you are not the right *companheiros* to confide in, but because we are a popular movement that bars entry to no one, whatever their color, religion or political orientation, we do not completely know who we are. We do know that there are police informants among us, but that does not matter. We just caution you to tell the members of your family nuclei to be careful who they talk to and what they say.

The meeting concluded with another song and another *grito*: "*Che, Zumbi, Antônio Conselheiro: Na luta por justiça somos todos companheiros!* (Che, Zumbi, Antônio Conselheiro: In the struggle for justice we are all *companheiros!*)"

Everything that happened at the meeting, from the candles to the songs and *gritos*, was intended to energize and unify the camp residents in preparation for the upcoming occupation. And Bernardo clearly articulated that unifying the camp was one of the MST's main challenges. The MST's openness to "whatever color, religion or political orientation," he affirmed, made them unable to fully know "who we are." The solution, he suggested, was to foster a cohort of solidary, militant *companheiros* who would stand strong against "enemies," the *latifúndio* and the police.

It is significant that both the *latifúndio* and the police make it hard for the landless to claim their rights under the Land Statute, which allows for the appropriation and redistribution of land "not fulfilling its social function" (see chapter 4). However, this misrule of law, *pace* Holston, is not the only significant aspect of law's enmity. Another aspect will come into view when we examine the MST's attempt to maintain a community of truly unified *companheiros* after the occupation.

What are *companheiros*? As Bernardo explained to me in a later conversation, a *companheiro* is "someone who you share the struggle with," and though friendship can strengthen *companheirismo*, a *companheiro* is not necessarily a friend: "Friendship is a commitment to care (*carinho*) in every sense—that develops where you are rooted, in your everyday. Not every *companheiro* can be a friend, because you don't have that contact. But you know that they have some similar level of commitment to agrarian reform, the values of our organization and to others because of this."

The MST has various levels of formal training geared to strengthen *companheirismo* among its militant members, which (like friendship) takes time. As the privileged relation, *companheirismo* implies a certain wariness of friendship—a sense of its insufficiency for a mass political movement that aims to create a "new man" and a new society. In revolutionary Russia, Lenin felt the same.[9] As we have seen, in Brazil the language of friendship has been used to speak about religious and political relationships into the twenty-first century, from the infamous political bosses, or *coroneis*,[10] to today's politicians. It is thus already associated with conventional politics and the conservative, hierarchical, and exclusionary status quo. In short, *companheirismo* was necessary to make possible a *new* solidary set of relations beyond the usual coordinates of kinship, friendship, and brotherhood.

In everyday practice, however, the connection to the idea of friendship as unity cannot be fully severed, as we will see when we return to Anton (see also chapter 6; Comerford 1999, 2003). For now, the basic point is this: while within the MST *companheirismo* is a political relation created by a shared commitment to the struggle for agrarian reform, political ideas are not the only way to consolidate it.[11] As Bernardo suggests, and as all well-trained MST militants know, *companheirismo* must be cultivated through considered action across domains. This includes nonnarrative practices, like the tea lights, songs, and *gritos* that opened and closed the coordinators' meeting. In the MST, these are called *mística*, and are meant to consolidate *companheirismo*, which is itself a vector of *mística*.

MÍSTICA

Mística, the militant Soraya told me as we swayed in our hammocks that evening in our *barraco*, was one of the most important aspects of MST praxis. It was "the heart of the struggle, where it all begins." Soraya and Marilene had put tea lights in the sand that evening to heighten the sense of *mística* among the coordinating committee.

While *mística* is colloquially used to refer to the theatrical or artistic performances that accompany MST activities, Soraya and many others taught me it was much more than that. Indeed, while the *mística* sometimes seems trivial, a mere adornment—as in the candles, songs, and *gritos* of the coordinators' meeting—it plays a major role in the MST's self-conception and organizational theory. As an MST training text from 1994 puts it, *mística* should be everywhere, not least in *companheirismo*. "*Mística* is the animus that makes people combative and caring, open and persevering, but overall, *companheiros*" (Peloso 1994, 9).

A mística se manifesta:	Mística manifests itself:
- *Na vida pessoal*	- In our personal life
- *No companheirismo*	- In *companheirismo*
- *Nas atitudes*	- In our attitudes and behaviors
- *No trabalho produtivo*	- In productive work
- *Na participação*	- In participation
- *Na maneira de fazer as reuniões*	- In the way we do our meetings
- *Nas mobilizações*	- In our mobilizations
- *No zelo ao cumpricada tarefa*	- In the zeal with which we accomplish our tasks
	(Peloso 1994, 7)

While the ubiquity of *mística* makes it difficult to define succinctly, the title of this training text, "A Força que Anima os Militantes" (The force that animates militants), offers a compelling attempt.

Recalling our discussion of liberationism in chapter 4, the fact that "force" is used as a synonym of *mística* is not accidental. *Mística* originated in the liberationist Church that fostered the MST in the early 1980s. Beyond the mention of force, other traces of this influence abound in MST texts, notably their discussions of unity. "After every act [of *místíca*] people should be more confident and unified," Peloso says (1994, 6). And Ademar Bogo, an MST leader, poet, and culture theorist, describes *místíca* as "expressed by characteristics that guarantee unity, like passion, will, cordiality, honesty, etc." Without these, Bogo emphasizes, "the struggle dies. . . . Where there is mistrust there is no *místíca*" (2002, 57).

However, while there are clear connections to the church in the MST's version of *místíca*, there are vital distinctions as well. One of my aims in this chapter is to acknowledge such distinctions even while demonstrating how the two versions of *místíca* have influenced and shaped each other. Indeed, Peloso doesn't acknowledge the church at all, an approach that one of the MST's main spokesmen, João Pedro Stédile, later shed light on:

> [*Místíca*] came from the influence of the church, we had *místíca* as a uni-
> fying factor, of the living of ideas, but for being a liturgy, it came with a
> lot of baggage. . . . [The MST originally thought that] "the Church uses a
> specific mystical liturgy to maintain unity around the project of the evan-
> gelism." When we tried to copy this, it didn't work because people have
> to have the feeling directed for a certain project. From this understand-
> ing, in each moment, in each activity of the movement, we emphasize a
> facet of the project as a way of motivating people (Stédile and Fernandes
> 1999, 130–31).

This comes from a canonical interview in which Stédile outlined the past, present, and future of the MST. Notable here is that Stédile indicates that *místíca*, or at least a "mystical liturgy," was originally copied from the church, but that the MST eventually distinguished it, secularized it, because its Christian significance was not connected directly enough to the MST's project. Digging into liberationist publications has led me to conclude that the connection between the church's *místíca* and the MST *místíca* is actually more complicated than what Stédile (and the existing social-scientific literature) describes (Betto 1989).[12] However, Stédile's general description stands: there was a point at which the MST's *místíca* no longer made any direct reference to what they had inherited from the church. I have not been able to date exactly when this change occurred; Stédile does not mention it (and it may not have been a uniform process). But it was at least a few years after the MST formally separated from the church in 1985, possibly sometime in the 1990s. This doesn't mean there weren't alliances with the church. Rather, I am saying that we can be sure that by the time this interview was conducted in 1998, the MST had developed its more secular "theatrical" practice of *mística*, intended to fortify the struggle for land (see Flynn 2013). We can take the institution of this more secular practice of *mística* to be indicative both of the MST's secularizing—it introduced distinctions between religion and politics—as well as its embrace of secularism. That is, the MST was no longer just for Catholics. Like a secular state it sought to encompass everyone beneath its political umbrella, as Bernardo suggested, "whatever color, religion, or political orientation."

By invoking the MST's secularizing and secularism, I am *not* saying that MST militants are not or cannot be religious. In fact, militants are enjoined to respect religiosity, even if they are not religious (and some are decidedly not). For example, in a key MST text, Ademar Bogo's *The Vigor of Mística* (2002),[13] readers are told that if they do not know how to respect popular devotions, they "will never understand the reality they have to transform." *Mística*, Bogo continues, "should . . . [help] balance the contradictions between naïvete and political consciousness" (124–25).[14] Certainly, this demand for respect also implies a difference between a politically conscious MST militant and more "naive" (less politicized, more "religious") rural workers. Still, Bogo depicts religion as a resource for transformation, rather than excluding it.

Nevertheless, Bogo's interest in religion remains limited, including for the development of *mística*. A case in point is Bogo's discussion of Canudos, the millenarian movement discussed in chapter 3. Bogo explains why Canudos, and all historic popular struggles, continue to be important for fomenting *mística*: "It is possible to develop *mística* by rescuing each one of the struggles that have existed in Brazil, to help them symbolically conclude their victory, interrupted by repression" (2002, 59). Yet when Bogo recounts the poignant story of the last four survivors of Canudos who refused to surrender to the Republican army in 1897—an old man, two young men, and a child—it is clear that Bogo was ultimately less interested in the religious commitments of Canudenses than in the fact of their willingness to sacrifice everything to resist (59, citing Cunha 2003 [1902]). This ultimately more secular interest in past struggles is exemplified in one instance of *mística* that concluded the coordinators' meeting, the *grito de ordem*: "Che, Zumbi, Antônio Conselheiro, na luta por justiça somos todos companheiros!" This *grito* mobilizes Antônio Conselheiro, the leader of Canudos, as a *companheiro* in the struggle for justice, alongside Che Guevara, the revolutionary Cuban leader, and Zumbi, the last leader of Palmares (c. 1590s–1695), the largest and longest-surviving runaway slave community in Brazil's history. In

short, MST *mística* is a largely secular practice concerned with the struggle
for freedom from oppression, whose distinction from church rituals of uni-
fication helps produce a secularity from which the divine is not banished
but instead persists in the background, calling for continued negotiation.
This presence of the divine accompanying the *mística* of a unifying group of
companheiros will help us eventually understand law's enmity.

MORE WORRIES, MORE *MÍSTICA*

Following the coordinators' meeting, the camp began buzzing with excitement and anxiety. While residents were inspired by a hope for land, they
regularly speculated about what was to come, often openly discussing their
fears. "Some people think that this is war!" said Joelma, a woman of about
fifty from Pernambuco whom I had met on my first visit to the camp months
before. We were sitting below a thatch awning extending over an earthen
floor off her lovely *barraco* overlooking the Rio Vermelho, which flowed
alongside the far edge of the camp. "My husband and I entered this camp to
get a piece of land. We had friends who convinced us to join. I was happy
with the decision, my very own piece of land! That has been a dream since
we came to Pará twenty years ago," she said emphatically. "But what will happen if someone decides to pull the trigger? Will it be like *o Massacre?*," she
asked, referring to the tragedy at Eldorado. Like Joelma, many were anxious
finally to occupy their own land, and this is why they stayed, despite their
worries about the potential for police violence. Many believed that another
massacre was unlikely to occur. Yet nerves frayed, and some decided not to
participate in the occupation, leaving both the camp and the MST. The vast
majority remained, however, their fears calmed by others. The fact that I was
staying, for example, seemed to soothe Joelma. And so did the animating
activities of the militants. "*Faz bem*, it is good for us," she said, "to see them
give so much energy, to want to help."

The militants were working hard to ready the camp for the occupation,
to unify it both in form and in spirit. In the days following the coordinators'
meeting, the militants held meeting after meeting in huts, on the plaza, on
the football pitch, and at the *guaritas* to discuss procedure and problems
among themselves and with family nuclei, the camp coordinating committee, and members of the MST "sectors," such as the sectors for security,
discipline, health, education, and leisure.

In these meetings, camp residents were asked to make an effort to come together, to build resolve for whatever was to come, and to comply with the militants' rules and suggestions. As Bernardo had done on the football pitch, militants made apologies for not being able to disclose more information on exactly when and where the camp would move. And they reiterated requests for caution. The militants also engaged in lighter tasks, such as meeting with the *sem terrinha* (the "little" or very young landless) and the older youth of the camp. At these events, songs were taught and material was collected and prepared for the *místicas* that would commemorate the twentieth anniversary of the MST and then preface the final general assembly before the departure. While these efforts did not make everyone feel included, they nonetheless energized camp residents and helped mitigate tensions along the tightly packed streets.[15]

Animated though they were, the militants were working through their own worries, holding many camp evaluation meetings in their own *barraco* in the late hours. Camp residents "lacked political consciousness," Sidneidi, a veteran militant of ten years, told me, and this could interfere with the occupation's success. That is—and here we recall that *companheirismo* takes time—residents were not as aware as they might be about the need for agrarian reform and what is required to achieve it: commitment to the MST and to the "reality in transformation" accomplished by occupying land. That the camp members did not have "consciousness," militants told me, was due to the small number in charge of the camp and their insufficient exposure to MST training. Indeed, a mere seven militants led a camp of a thousand families, although young aspirants to militancy assisted. And most of these newer militants had not yet been to an *escola nacional* and were thus unable, or perhaps not yet dedicated enough, to impart political training to camp residents.[16] Of course, when Sidneidi spoke of a deficit of political consciousness, she was talking about a lack of *mística*.

The militants finally called the general assembly for Wednesday, April 14, at 5:00 p.m. When we arrived at the appointed hour, the plaza had been primed. It was outfitted with a generator for light and to power the sound system; the militants had set up a little stage with a microphone, and had prepared a *mística* on the ground. White-painted stones spelled out a large numeral 20 to mark the twentieth anniversary of the MST. Around that, small tea lights demarcated a larger area where a theatrical *mística* would be acted out. A large stack of wood sat at the plaza's far end. The famous Brazilian version of Bob Dylan's "Blowing in the Wind" began playing on the sound system, and five people with candles began slowly lighting the tea lights (quickly extinguished by the wind). They then set the pile of wood alight. As the five gathered in front of the fire, it became evident that they were supposed to represent a family. A young *sem terrinha* carried a sickle[17] to give to the family's father, and the mother began reading a poem, though her voice was carried away by wind and drowned out by music. Even so, the crowd was pleased with the *mística*. The pile of wood had become a bonfire, lighting up all our faces with a warm glow.

Other militants then took to the podium, spoke briefly, and offered a few energetic *gritos de ordem*, including the ubiquitous *"Patria Livre!"* Bernardo emerged from the crowd in a straw hat, reciting a poem as he walked. Though the poem was mostly inaudible, its message was clear enough, evoking a future of both struggle and liberation. Bernardo then delivered a well-crafted twenty-minute speech from the stage, attempting to consolidate the *mística* in words. That is, he was trying to inspire the camp's most fearful residents to strengthen their faith for the struggle.

An extended excerpt from Bernardo's speech exhibits one strategy for creating solidarity out of *mística*: to identify a shared project and the enemies who oppose it, while calling for unity and decrying division.

> Good evening *companheiros* and *companheiras*!
>
> [Response from the crowd: Good Evening!]
>
> We are all very happy to be in this very special moment for our camp. . . . Every time that we have the patience to listen to the ideas of our *companheiros*, this struggle is strengthened. And every time we meet to organize our dreams, those in power squirm. Because if there is one thing the bourgeoisie of this country, the landed class (*clase latifundiária*), which historically oppresses the workers, is afraid of, it is when we organize to speak and listen to our truths, and when we organize to plan our action. No *povo* is victorious if *companheiros* do not give each other their hands and if they cannot collectively plan.
>
> Therefore, *companheiros* and *companheiras*, I would like to discuss some issues with you this evening. The first of them is that we are going to occupy a great *latifúndio* in this region of Eldorado do Carajás. IS THIS TRUE OR NOT?? [Response from the crowd: It is!!] Well, then, our history is just beginning. We cannot wait to see if land falls from the sky, because our Lord Jesus, our God says, if we want land, we must struggle to liberate it.
>
> Another issue concerns our resistance.

Our enemy will attack us in four ways:

> One. Our enemy tries to divide us [by saying "the MST is trying to
> trick you"]. . . . We have to say NO!;
> Two. Our enemy tries to co-opt us. . . .
> Three. They can plant false information among us, and
> Four. Our enemy can try to defeat us by repression!

It is no secret that every time we occupy land—what happens? The *fazen-deiro* submits a dispersal request, then the police come and, depending on our numbers and firmness, either we stay or go. Is it a surprise to anyone that the police will come to visit us?

[Response from the crowd: NO!]

We have nothing to fear. The only thing that we must do is organize our forces.

We know that many of you are afraid. And walking around or lying in our hammocks at night we hear all kinds of [wild] stories. And I want to say that the Direction of the MST will not be irresponsible and put our *companheiros* in a tight spot (*enrascada*). We are going to leave here together, and we are going to enter the land together. If we have problems we are going to face them together. Those who are still doubting, do not fear. Because we are going to be victorious.

[A woman in the crowd shouts: Amen!!]

So to end. May this fire illuminate our nights and illuminate our dreams. Tomorrow we will depart for our promised land. Can this be our big decision?

[Response from the crowed: YES!!]

Bernardo closed by reciting "Peasant Dawn," a poem by the Amazonian poet Tiago de Mello (2024 [1965]). "Patria livre!," camp members shouted, left fists raised. They looked hopeful, excited, and nervous that the day had almost arrived. After Bernardo left the podium, one of the more musical militants, Alonso, led the crowd in songs until the assembly ended.

Bernardo clearly crafted his speech to address the fears of the camp residents, especially fears of violence and police repression. More broadly, however, both the speech and the *mística* that accompanied it were intended to bring the camp together. On the one hand, Bernardo wanted to reassure them that the MST would not abandon them; that they would face all problems together.[18] On the other hand, and more importantly, he wanted to ready the camp to resist their shared enemies, "the *latifúndio* and the police," who would seek to divide and demobilize them.

Bernardo was a highly trained and skilled MST spokesman. If we compare his speech with the discourse on liberation theology mentioned in chapter 4, we might notice that it was much more secular, and indeed the MST produces mostly secular rhetoric. Still, Christian references do occasionally animate it. I was surprised that Bernardo slipped in references to "Lord Jesus, our God" and the "promised land." I had not remembered such a thing being done before, but it showed me that the *mística* of the MST does not entirely foreclose Christian rhetoric, perhaps especially when the stakes are high. They were certainly high on the eve of the coming occupation. Thus we might understand the MST as crafting the secular, cultivating a sense of its possibility, while acknowledging the force of Christianity, even sometimes touching on it in direct ways because of the *povo*'s own faith. We need only remember that a woman called out "Amen" when Bernardo said "We are going to be victorious" to begin to grasp how secular events coexist with but also unfold in the Christian understanding of many of my interlocutors' collective devising—and divining.

THE OCCUPATION

The following days put Bernardo's suggestions to the test. Everyone had to work to maintain unity in face of the tensions and challenges they were facing. I saw a number of fights, some physical—the result of fears that had to be continually assuaged. But the occupation was coming. Everyone knew that on Friday at 4:00 a.m., each family nucleus, akin to a neighborhood of the camp, would load their possessions onto the trucks and leave without knowing exactly where or how they would land.

On Thursday, after the last meetings of the coordinators and the neighborhoods, the militants held their final meeting. Tasks still unassigned until then were allotted, and the camp hummed around us. Bernardo had given me my usual task of taking photographs to document the process.[19] After the militants' meeting, Nuncio, an older militant, saw that I was waiting to see if there was anything more to do. "It's late," he said. "You should get some sleep, and so should I. There's nothing more to do. If we're lucky we can get five hours of sleep. Tomorrow you can take more photographs." Our hut had already been dismantled, so we strung our hammocks on the exposed wooden frame of a now abandoned *barraco* close to the plaza, feeling close enough to the action in any case. "This camp has been organized very loosely, Ashley," Nuncio said in the dark. "I hope that it is going to be OK."

"Me too," I replied. As I drifted off to sleep, I still heard residents speculate about the process while finalizing their packing in wooden crates, suitcases, and cloth and plastic bags. I awoke intermittently when excited residents interrupted the energetic hum with *gritos*. Sometimes just one person cried out; sometimes a few called out in succession: "*Paaaaatria liiivre!*"

Around 4:00 a.m., I woke up with a start. Nuncio had gone. I quickly folded up my hammock, stuffed it into my bag, and made my way to the main street leading out of the camp to see how close we were to departure. Residents lined the street beside their bags, their faces caught in the lamplight as they waited to load their possessions onto flatbed trucks. There was still time, so I made one last sweep of the camp, wandering among the mostly dismantled huts taking photographs and encountering militants as they rushed to fulfill different tasks. Some ran to put out a fire that threatened to spread through the camp after a resident had dramatically and mindlessly set his old *barraco* alight to mark his departure. Once that catastrophe had been averted, militants and security volunteers went out to the highway with large MST flags to stop any traffic, to help the marchers make their way out of the camp safely.

We started the march silently, two single files lining up in the dark.

As dawn broke, we saw the pastures on either side of the highway. As ever, I tried to imagine the forests. "Everything here was once forest," I remembered countless interlocutors saying. Militants tentatively began a series of *gritos*. "*Liberdade o morte!*" This was energizing, if a bit ominous, given that it means "liberty or death." I didn't think most of the marchers really shared that sentiment. Some of them held large flags by their four corners and watched them billow in the wind. Others lifted flags high on poles. As the sun grew hotter people began to smile at each other, but they said little. We were all so focused on the physical demands of the march that there was nothing to say until we would stop at some point in the future. The clear blue sky held out promise for the day.

At around 11:00 a.m. we approached the S-Curve, where the Eldorado Massacre had taken place in 1996. The monument to the Massacre came into view under an already blistering sun. It consisted of nineteen blackened Brazil-nut trees that volunteers in 1999 had cut from the nearby pastures[20] and placed in a circle to honor the memory of the nineteen MST protestors whom the police had killed instantly on this spot (see Baron 2004).[21] Hot and worn out, we found our things and sought places to rest: under trees, in temporary *barracos* of branches and black plastic tarps, in the little museum honoring the memory of the Massacre. MST militants served us a delicious meal of beans and rice complete with *farofa*: fried manioc flour of the hard, large-grained Amazonian style called *farinha de puba* or *farinha d'água*. An evening of music and film about the Massacre followed before everyone went to rest.

The next morning was April 17. We watched the commemoration ceremony for those killed and injured in the Massacre, held every year on this date. Many people had arrived from elsewhere to participate—not only MST members but also farmers from rural syndicates throughout the region, people from the Pastoral Land Commission, the Worker's Party (PT), and even students from the Marabá campus of the Federal University of Pará. Both lanes of the PA-150 were nearly covered with people, though they left a narrow space for cars to slowly pass. All had come to support the marchers and participate in the annual commemoration ceremony. Militants also performed a *mística* reenacting the Massacre—police shooting down *sem terra*—within the towering monument of burned Brazil-nut trees.

Next, the bishop celebrated a Mass, and MST leaders, PT politicians, and religious activists gave speeches. Of particular interest to me was the speech given by Batista, once a seminarian, now a member of the CPT (Pastoral Land Commission) national coordination committee and the chief lawyer of the CPT-Marabá. Significantly, Batista used language inspired by liberation theology to describe what needed to be done and what was to come:

> Beyond the nineteen who were assassinated, dozens of others were injured and now continue to suffer the mental and physical effects of their injuries. Eight years on, the perpetrators remain free. We have to remember the blood of our *companheiros* and *companheiras* and keep struggling for the freedom that they were fighting for. We should also never forget what can be read in Deuteronomy, which speaks of the people of God who were camped in the desert. Before they had been kept in slavery, but they walked through the desert to the promised land. You will all go to the promised land. You must go to the promised land and there be free.

As we have already seen, MST members rarely employed elaborate Christian or biblical references to generate *mística*, though they did sometimes make such references in passing. Batista's speech, however, is an example of how Christian activists used biblical images to give allegorical meaning to the contemporary struggle for land: specifically, the Hebrews' exodus from Egypt and their journey across the desert. The speech also helps us understand why even a brief reference to "the promised land" or the freedom of "slaves" might have invoked God for listeners or readers. Indeed, many rural workers along PA-150 and throughout Brazil had been exposed to liberationism and were aware that these images could also refer to the contemporary struggle for land.

Beyond rhetoric, rural workers throughout Brazil knew that marching was a key ingredient of liberationist Catholic practice (see also Chaves 2000). As I discussed in chapter 1, pilgrimages and processions have been a popular form of Catholic devotion since the Portuguese first came to the Americas, and *romarias da terra* have been held throughout Brazil since liberationism's zenith in the 1980s. Marching in protest and marching to occupy land could not be separated from Christian references to pilgrimages even when secular language dominated their description. These acts were replete with memories of faith. Although most MST occupations in Pará were not preceded by large commemorative events at which church activists were present, many participants would nevertheless have remembered the image of God overseeing the passage of landless pilgrims on the road to freedom from slavery. In short, the acts of marching and struggling collectively recalled the beauty of God's unifying agency.

After the speeches and *mística* concluded, MST militant Eli announced that the march would continue. A huge *trio eléctrico*—a mobile, bus-shaped sound system with a top deck on which musicians performed—had appeared to lead the march. Many of those who had been present at the commemoration of the Massacre followed the march south along the PA-150. We walked twelve kilometers from the S-Curve, approximately four hours in the crackling heat, until Bernardo motioned to one side of the road. This gesture was all it took: a flood of people began running euphorically, jumping, whooping, and shouting *gritos*, as they crossed over onto land they hoped would be theirs.

The land descended quickly from the side of the road, and a few acres of scrub stretched out before us. A river ran parallel to the highway, crossing the land to the right. Beyond the scrub a forest extended far enough that we could not see to the other side. We were instructed to go into the forest beyond the cleared land, to wait and see if police came to enforce a *reintegração de posse* (repossession) via *despejo*, a dispersal often ordered by a judge after a land occupation. Amid the tall trees we found logs and large branches to sit on, and we cooled off in the thick air, swatting mosquitoes and talking quietly. Two hours passed, and when it was clear that the police were not coming, we assembled to watch the MST flag jubilantly erected on the top of a palm tree and to get instructions on what to do next. The MST leadership told us to go and set up camp temporarily by the road.

The leadership also told us to stay as close together as possible in the following days in case the police arrived. People used trees and logs to spread tarps and erect hammocks wherever they could. We ate sitting on the ground around small fires lit for each neighborhood, surrounded by our things, which the trucks had delivered. A night of tension and excitement passed as we continued to wait.

The next day, I walked around to ask people about their experiences of the occupation. People were smiling, excited and singing, proud and worn out. They no longer seemed quite so anxious. Instead, there was a renewed sense of community, accomplishment, and resolve. I found Amalia, a very large young woman, sitting together with Claudinha, Joelma, and Danilo in her small temporary shelter of sticks and black plastic tarp. "How are you all feeling?" I asked as I sat on my heels next to them. "What did you think?"

Amalia answered first: "Well, I couldn't do the walk, you know. Quite a few people couldn't. Some got sick. The march wasn't easy. But I was at the *curva* to see the march arrive. When I saw all of the people coming, I cried. To see all of those people, *que emoção* (I was so moved). You know, back in the other camp, I had my doubts, but now I am staying until the end, until where the end takes me, hopefully onto a piece of land that will help me and my family, *se Deus quiser* (God willing)."

"We have reached our promised land," Danilo (Amalia's neighbor in the previous camp) said, smiling. "There will still be struggle, but if we stay together (*unido*) like we are now, we will be rewarded with our land, with freedom, in God."

Joelma said, "I was so afraid that something would go wrong, *só Deus* (only God)."

I looked at Claudinha, who said pensively, "*Era tão bonito* (it was so pretty). Everything, from the way that the camp was prepared, the assemblies, the *mística*, the ceremony today. I was proud to be a part of it, and now the issue is to keep up our faith and remain united until we can all live freely on our own land."

The word Claudinha used, *bonito*, was often used to describe participa-

FIGURE 38. Beginning the occupation process. Photo: Ashley Lebner.

tion in the pilgrimage recounted in chapter 1. Indeed, people express appreciation not only for the aesthetic of those moments of unity but also for their significance: that participants are there despite differences and with a similar overriding purpose in mind, a unifying purpose ultimately overseen by God. "Only God," as Joelma said. For Amalia, the occupation signaled that God might be willing to give her and others land, and this is what filled her with emotion. In fact, all the comments I quote here reflect the Christian meanings that regular participants often gave to a secular MST process. Marching to this promised land generated a sense of Christian unity in view of a collective goal mediated by God.

I have been emphasizing how the process of occupation produced a sense of unity. But I have also aimed to show that this kind of unity was expected. It was considered a prerequisite for the camp's liberatory success, as both Claudinha's and Danilo's statements suggest. Yet, as we will soon see, the fact that unity is an indicator of faith in the struggle, in divine promise, and in liberty, means that any perceived disunity can be destabilizing in profound ways.

FIGURE 39. A photo of the march from the *Trio Elêctrico*. Photo: Ashley Lebner.

FIGURE 40. The monument—and *mística*—honoring the massacre of Eldorado do Carajás. Photo: Ashley Lebner.

FIGURE 41. During Mass at the S-Curve. Photo: Ashley Lebner.rch from the *Trio Elêctrico*. Photo: Ashley Lebner.

FIGURE 42. The first entrants in the rush to occupy the land. Photo: Ashley Lebner.

FIGURE 43. Inside the camp; a strange helicopter above. Photo: Ashley Lebner.

MST "LAWS"

The police never came to push the occupiers out of Fazenda Peruano. This was a boon for the camp, Aldo and others said, because violent police repossession often has immediately negative effects on the cohesion of camp life. In other MST camps I visited, people told me that residents became afraid after being chased out of the camp by police with riot gear, guns, and dogs in a *reintegração de posse* or *despejo*. Many move out for good, leaving those who return after the *despejo* with the task of trying to rekindle faith in the struggle for land. Although this camp was spared such violence, other aspects of camp life broke down the residents' resolve and unity. All the perceived divisions heightened the dangers of relating, recalling that friendship, solidarity, and especially *companheirismo* are fragile. As we will see, all these values eroded as the MST established strict internal regulations.

For the first few days after the occupation, the thousand-plus families camped precariously by the side of the road. After three days with no police response, an assembly was called. From the top of a water-supply truck that had been hired by the MST leadership to keep us hydrated as we stayed close together, militants announced that it was time to make more durable living arrangements. With spirits running high, work groups gathered to cut the grass and demarcate a grid within which *barraco* allotments would be distributed to each neighborhood, called the "family nuclei." These were redrawn after having swollen and shrunk haphazardly at the previous camp. Lots were drawn to distribute blocks from the camp grid to fifty-one family nuclei of twenty families each, and then *barraco* plots were assigned to individual families.

A few hardworking men could build a *barraco* in about four days, although not every household had that many men. Still, *barracos* got built, using wood and palm leaves collected from the forest. Each had a kitchen and at least one other room—and sometimes two or three—where residents slept in hammocks or on mattresses. Each *barraco* had a little yard and a stall for bathing.[22] A deep latrine and a well was dug for each nucleus. A primary school would be up and running after a month. And Catholic and Evangelical churches would be built later, haltingly, after many more months.

Each reconstituted nucleus had to elect two coordinators, a man and a woman, to represent them to the camp coordination committee and to organize nucleus meetings at 5:00 p.m. every day. One member of each family had to participate in these meetings, where problems of specific relevance to the nucleus would be discussed. Coordinators also passed on the information that they received at the 7:00 a.m. general coordinators' meeting. This often consisted of news from "outside" of the camp, like updates about the land, MST events, and other items for the agenda. Concerns from within the camp were discussed, too. Coordinators would sometimes discuss interpersonal problems in their nucleus that could only be resolved through consensus or with the coordination committee's intervention. These issues were called *picunha*,[23] which meant nitpicking complaints about the minutiae of relationships. But *picunha* (a noun clearly related to the English adjective picayune) weren't always trivial. *Picunha* were often relevant to making decisions about the most important issues of all, the rules that each camp member had to follow and the measures to be taken when rules were broken. Transgressions and their punishments were to become a key source of tension. Put simply, the application of camp rules gave rise to a sense of enmity.

The first rule was that everyone had to attend meetings of the family nucleus. Roll call was taken at every meeting. If anyone missed three meetings in a row they were supposed to pay a *pena*, literally a "penance." That is, a coordinator or militant had to make the guilty person do something that would benefit the family nucleus or the camp more generally, like cutting grass or picking up garbage. From the perspective of the MST, the logic of enforcing participation in meetings was both practical and political. It was practical because it strengthened the organization of the camp and kept everyone informed on how to behave vis-à-vis outside threats. It was political because meetings were considered the means to achieve the "conscientization" and emancipation of the landless. The process might also be called cultural, as Bogo did when he described MST camps as "founding a new culture . . . created around the virtues" (2000, 31).

For the first few months, most people I knew eagerly attended meetings. News that filtered into the camp contributed to maintaining enthusiasm, particularly because it appeared that the lands would be speedily appropriated from their formal "owners" and redistributed to the landless occupiers. The CPT lawyers, for example, discovered that of the 10,000 hectares that were supposed to belong to the *fazenda*, Evandro Mutran had titles for only 4,200 hectares.[24] The suspicion was that the remaining 5,800 hectares were public lands that had been illegally appropriated and were therefore available for distribution under the agrarian reform legislation. Bernadete ten Caten, the superintendent of INCRA Marabá, also considered the *fazenda* to be a model case for appropriation because it was clearly not fulfilling its social function: the use of modern slave labor (also known as "debt bondage," which is endemic in the region: see Esterci 1994; Geffray 1995; Rezende 2004) had been discovered there. Then the *ouvidor agrário* (national land ombudsman), Gersino Silva Filho, came from Brasília to see the camp with a commission of state and regional officials, journalists, and lawyers in late May 2004. At a meeting with CPT lawyers at which I was present, he agreed to intervene: he instructed Judge Kátia Parente of the Agrarian Court of Marabá to suspend her declaration of the *reintegração de posse* until INCRA had made proper cartographic and topographic assessments. All this activity, discussed subsequently at meetings, heated (*esquentou*) camp members' resolve and their connection to the MST, which they saw as honoring its promise to assist camp residents in acquiring both land and freedom. But as discussions dragged on, enthusiasm dimmed, especially as the coordinators were tasked with applying all rules with more stringency.

In the previous camp, the rules were often flaunted. The MST wanted a large occupation to assure its success, so the militants didn't press the coordination committee to track offenses. After the occupation, things were different. The peace of everyday life in the camp had to be secured, as did equal rights for all. And so, for example, the consumption of alcohol and drugs in the camp was prohibited, and a curfew required quiet after 11:00 p.m. Residents were also forbidden to sell goods in the camp, to avoid relations of exploitation.

Most importantly, camp members were supposed to maintain active residence in the camp and could not secure a place ("registration") in the camp for people residing outside. While the MST encouraged people to move into the camp with their families, only one member of each household had to be a registered resident who had to participate in official camp activities. Registered members had to request leave to be out of the camp, and they were allowed out only for short periods to work or buy provisions in the city. The length of this period changed over the months by collective decision, reaching a maximum of fifteen days per month once nuclei meetings were held less frequently. The unregistered members of the household, however, could come and go. They sometimes worked on *fazendas*, even though the MST discouraged this.[25] In doing so they helped support family members inside the camp who had limited opportunities for long-term employment. Many people could only stay in the camp because of this family help, especially because the monthly food baskets INCRA was supposed to deliver came irregularly. The majority decided not to plant their own food, so eating was difficult without a support network.

Still, the logic was to get as many people as possible to stay in the camp, so the MST could both politically educate the residents and show a committed and organized social entity to the broader Southeast Paraense public, which would in turn help pressure the authorities to appropriate and redistribute the land to a worthy community. This is why schools were built as soon as possible with the aid of the militants and the education sector. It is also why numerous other sectors were established, like security, production, health, and leisure, which ideally recruited one person from each family nucleus to meet regularly and organize the camp's responses to these needs.[26]

As the months wore on, besides the usual upkeep of home, hearth, and the camp, people had little to do but talk to each other. Entertainment was extremely limited, in a way unimaginable for most today in the age of smartphones. As one woman said to me, she found the quiet of camp life, with no electricity, no television, and no radio, "lonely," much like life in Pará when she had first arrived twenty years earlier, when there was only forest all around. It may have also been lonely because people were speaking less and less to people beyond their closest family, friends, and neighbors as social frictions increased. This threw into relief the *saudade* for, and the precarity of, unity—that is, the mystic of friendship.

DISUNITY, THE SPECTER OF ENMITY

———————

"Being a coordinator gets you many enemies (*desamizades*)," Mona said bluntly, when I told her about my intention to interview coordinators. She went on,

> I am a woman, alone, with no husband and not even one son here; and what, am I going to look for arguments? No. The problem is that a coordinator is the authority on their block, and they are supposed to make people follow the rules—rules that the militants tell us to enforce. But people don't follow the rules, and we're supposed to make them follow them. And when they don't, we have to inform the militants [and even discuss it at the coordinators meeting]. And then what? How many people have I seen leave this place angry at their coordinators, threatening to settle the score (*acertar*) with them outside of the camp (*na rua*)? There is this guy here who never came to meetings, never did anything, he even left for about three months, and then he comes back and wants to stay, and he thinks of himself as very brave (*valente*). No, so that's why

I stopped being a coordinator. I passed it over to a man, there are two men coordinators and it is better. That way it is iron with iron (*é ferro com ferro*), and I can be friends with everyone, with God's help. It is everyone for themselves, God for everyone.

Mona had become my closest interlocutor in the camp after I moved in with her following the occupation, easing the constraints of living with the all-male militants once the visiting female militants had all returned home. Mona was a savvy woman of forty-eight, originally from rural Maranhão, a mother of ten and a former gold-miner. Her analysis helps turn this chapter's ethnography toward its final task: to understand the move from unity to a growing sense of disunity that included the proliferation of enmities, leading to Anton's proposal to found an "association of friends."

I knew that Mona's analysis was not unique. I had been attending coordinators' meetings from the beginning, and I had spoken regularly to coordinators from family nuclei across the camp. Some coordinators, especially in the camp's early days, expressed happiness with their new positions. Zé, for example, who had had been a *garimpeiro* (artisanal gold-miner) for eight years after moving to Pará from Maranhão, spoke of how good it felt to always know what was going on, and to contribute to the process. With time, however, men and women began to confess to me that they disliked the position, because it meant they had to enforce the rules.

Mona's explanation captures the bind in which coordinators found themselves. They went from being equals—*companheiros*, neighbors, and friends—to becoming authorities who had to punish neighbors who broke the rules. In extreme cases, they had to request assistance from militants and the coordination committee, leading to potential expulsions. Mona's question indicated the complexity of this scenario: "How many people have I seen leave this place, angry at their coordinators?" As others also pointed out to me, it was both difficult and dangerous to enforce the rules. Many coordinators received death threats from enraged residents who had been told that they had to comply, pay a *pena*, or leave. In one case, a man threatened to kill his female coordinator if she did not relinquish her position to him. To resolve the issue, she transferred to another family nucleus, where people were happy to receive her as a coordinator.

But it wasn't only enforcing the rules that generated tensions; not enforcing them caused problems, too. Many coordinators, like Mona, had to overlook problems to remain "friends with everyone" to avoid trouble. But unlike Mona, most did not leave their positions, since no one else wanted to take on this role. So they remained and often simply turned a blind eye to infractions. Some family nuclei composed entirely of members of extended families apparently did not have such internal problems, since their coordinator-relatives never enforced the rules. Ultimately, the uneven application of rules made residents feel discriminated against when they were made to comply or pay a *pena* for infractions.

DaMatta's model helps explain how the *im*personal application of the law could make it a source of enmity in the camp. However, in ignoring Christianity, which was brought insistently into view by coordinators like Mona, DaMatta's account remains partial, and especially silent on the challenge of friendship.[27]

Recall that Mona gave up being a coordinator so she "could be friends with everyone, with God's help." She was emphasizing that while relations of authority complicate friendship, a social ethic practiced with God's help avoids seeking control over others, tames enmity, and facilitates unity and friendship. This did not mean that Mona considered friendship unproblematic. Her wish to be friends with everyone was intersected by one of the expressions she used most often: "It is everyone for themselves, God for everyone."[28] Though this saying indicated a perceived collapse in collective possibilities, displays of friendship were the protective armor against further—and potentially violent—ungodly divisions.

Mona often lamented the challenges of friendship. One day, sitting in the small kitchen in her *barraco*, Mona tried to explain what friendship was. Shorty, a young militant of about eighteen, was waiting to snack on the fresh corn that Mona was roasting on her wood-fired tinfoil-and-clay stove. Mona sat on her lone chair, tending the fire and turning the corn. It had just been harvested from the small plot of land she had cleared and planted. Shorty sat on a low bench, his back at an angle from the door, and I sat on a large truck tire next to him. Trying to make her point, Mona gave a spin on an expression famous well beyond Pará: "A friend is like your belly button" (*Um amigo é como seu umbigo*). "And what does *umbigo* rhyme with? Father (*pai*), of course!"

I hesitated and then diplomatically interjected, "But Mona, father doesn't rhyme with belly button," and Shorty concurred.

"It doesn't?" Mona looked unconvinced.

"But enemy (*enemigo*) does," I replied mischievously.

She looked at me knowingly. "Ah yes, not only do we not know who our friends are, but the enemy can be any one of us. But it means the same thing: we have to be friendly, not instigate problems (*não aprontar*) with others to avoid conflicts (*confusão*)." Her take on this rhyme reveals fundamental local assumptions about friendship and kinship, especially paternal relations, as well as divinity and enmity. *Pai* in Portuguese, like "father" in English, can indicate both a parent and God. Whether human or supernatural, a father is supposed to maintain a constant presence and provide benevolent support from the moment of conception. A father, moreover, commands respect. You are not supposed to argue with him or attempt to assert authority over him. In essence, Mona was saying that all this is expected of friends as well. A friend must be present, behave kindly, and provide support, while not attempting to argue or control you. When I introduced the possibility that belly button and enemy rhymed (*enemigo* referring to both humans and the devil), she responded that it boiled down to the same pragmatic message. One should not look for trouble or instigate arguments, because, like ourselves, others are always potentially evil and might respond violently.

I returned to the question of friendship some days later when Mona and I were alone, as we often were in the evenings when Mona's youngest son of thirteen, who still lived with her most of the time, was back in Curionópolis. This time she made clear that friendship might always entail violence. Sitting on the log outside her *barraco* as night fell, with the long row of *barracos* lining up into the distance, she said, "Look, we don't have friends, only *companheiros*. You don't know what your friend is going to do to you down the line. Look at my older son's friend who pretended to be so nice! He killed him, shot him dead." This was the first time Mona had brought up her son, whose name, call him O Grandão, I had known well before I met her. His murder had been all over the local papers in February 2004, just over a year after he testified that he had been recruited as a hit man by the most notorious mayor of the region, Sebastião "Major" Curió, from whom the town of Curionópolis derived its name. Shortly after I met Mona in the camp, Timoteo had told me that she was O Grandão's mother, but I was always hesitant to ask her about him. Now I asked her how he died. "He was shot in another camp," she said. "Not of the MST, but another one, where I was for six years prior to coming here. There are some bad elements there. . . . My son used to go back to the house [in Curionópolis] to watch a film. So off he went and, when he was gone, this other guy who had acted like such a good friend, who treated him so nicely, took his gun. Then, this guy was afraid he would find out, so he shot him."

I didn't press further. I imagined that Mona might be worried that I would be afraid, which I guess I was, a little. There is more to this story, and I will return to it to connect this apparently local account to law's enmity at the national level. But for now, it can remind us the dangers of friendship as much as the dangers of life in camps. As another resident, Vanessa, told me, "In every camp, including MST camps, there has been at least one death." While I could not verify this, it is entirely plausible. I had heard many stories of violence, and I had met at least three men who were widely known to have murdered others. One day after her garden was looted, Mona said, "I don't want to see what is going to happen when the camp turns into a settlement. Many will die, for *real*, many will die." If camp life beyond the MST might be even more dangerous for *lack* of organization, as Vanessa and Mona also claimed, the very presence of law in this camp had helped undermine *companheirismo*, caused divisions and enmities to proliferate, and turned friendship into something to both seek and be wary of. When, after seven months, these tensions inspired over a hundred camp residents, many from the coordination committee, to occupy the PA-150, it in turn led Anton and some of his allies to try and promote a new "friendship."

ANTON'S PROPOSAL

Under a low gray sky, I went looking for Anton's *barraco*. Once I got there, I could tell it belonged to an enthusiastic coordinator. Anton had built a meeting area, a square set of benches, to better host his nucleus. He was sitting on one of the benches, his foot resting on a stool, fixing a large fishing net. He motioned for me to sit. I took out my tape recorder, and Anton explained the thinking behind the declaration he had shown me at the coordinators' meeting earlier that day. "First, it was Eltenor who wrote," Anton said.

> My writing isn't very good. We wrote the text to form an association of groups in order to resolve the problems. . . . It was cooled off here. The MST has to be alive, many people left because of the coolness. We didn't know about anything, the *direção* (direction) did not come, only Timoteo. He was here, alone, and no one came to visit. No one came to visit people's houses to see how they were. The improvement (*melhoria*) of the camp would be to make it alive, for the *direção* to give attention to the residents, to come to the houses and speak, visit those people who had been thrown in the garbage. We are not finding what we need from the movement. I [give] a zero for the direction of the camp. I know that

the MST is only a form of support. But what is missing is to work more on the *direção*. Ten to twenty percent of people have negative thoughts. They don't think it will work out. You have to convince people by being a friend. We have the obligation to show [people] that when you join a group it is then that we really get respect, that we become people (*gente*), and can become free. Similar to what we read in the Bible, people need to seek unity with each other, and God will guide us to the promised land.

Shortly after he finished explaining this to me, three coordinators arrived for Anton's meeting. One sat on the bench facing Anton. The other two chose to sit closer, on low log benches. I had already had a long conversation with one of them on another occasion. He had recounted how he had been taken hostage for three days by an Indigenous community near the Xingú river and made to carry massive mahogany trunks across the rapids with his gold-miner companions. They hadn't known if they would survive. We smiled at each other. Anton welcomed everybody and then praised them for trying to think about ways to make camp life better:

> There needs to be order. Information needs to be given to the *compo-nentes*, and people need to stop committing infractions. I want it to stop in my group. The *componente* who doesn't comply, I don't want him in my group, not "my" group, but a group of friends who are contributing to organicity and conviviality. . . . We have to help the others, help work toward improving education, getting basic identification documents. . . . Here we are going to conquer land, and everything has to be you, with help from God, it isn't the MST . . . [although] we should never under-value the *companheiro* who extends his hand and helps to lead the way. I don't want to be better than any other coordinator; I just want to contrib-ute. I am inviting you to come aboard to socialize (*socializar*), discuss, to resolve these problems.

Then Darcilo read out the declaration on Anton's invitation. When he fin-ished, he passed around the clipboard with the declaration, and those coor-dinators present signed, representing their nuclei.

Anton expressed his reasons for dissatisfaction with the MST clearly. The current leadership was unable to maintain order in the camp, to enforce the "norms of the MST," to stop infractions being committed, to provide information, help other camp members, and keep people committed to the struggle for land. Simply put, the leadership was neither able to enforce and communicate the "law," nor to enact the social ethic of *companheirismo* that could fully consolidate a collective to continue the struggle. To solve the problem, rather than propose a stricter enforcement of the rules or a more active pursuit of news from the outside, Anton suggested more proximity and more friendship. "You have to convince people by being a friend," he said. In other words, Anton affirmed that actively cultivating friendship through attention, conversation, and visiting would help establish a common law to which everyone would willingly submit.

But there is more. Anton's invocation of God, the bible, and the need for unity throws into relief how his proposal for an association of friends drew its moral force from common Catholic understandings. And this allows us to directly address the relation between the mystic of friendship and law's enmity. Read with Christianity in mind, Anton's assertion that "when you join a group . . . we really get respect . . . we become people (*gente*) and can become free" takes on deeper significance than DaMatta might give it. To a certain extent, as DaMatta would predict, joining the MST transformed individuals into persons. But that is not all. Anton was implying that while the MST promised the excluded poor a new, more secular, set of inclusive and redeeming relationships (a *mística*-inspired *companheirismo*), it had actually unwittingly achieved the opposite. The MST had dehumanized camp residents by turning them into enemies expected to enforce the law by punishing each other. Let us remember that persons are always *divining*, in the sense of both interpreting the world and becoming divine. It follows that people forced to pay a *pena* were haunted by the specter of evil.

On the one hand, those who were punished clearly saw themselves being treated as internal enemies, excluded from the good society of Christians, *Cristãos*, which locally just means "people." On the other hand, it was clear to those excluded that the people applying the laws (or not) did not have the political authority to do so, because they did not have the *moral* authority. They were just humans like everyone else, always potentially animated by evil.

Thus Anton's proposal to form an association of friends catalyzed my central insights into the relation between the mystic of friendship and law's enmity. Still, it was Anton's own expulsion from the camp two days later and the conversations that followed that consolidated my understanding that the will to friendship corresponds to the longing for egalitarian law, just as friendship's instability due to the immanence of evil affects the authority, the perceived good, of terrestrial laws.

ANYONE CAN BE THE DEVIL . . .

Anton's expulsion was nervewracking, even for me. After all, I had been at Anton's meeting, so it felt perilous to have participated in what the militants perceived to be a major threat to their leadership and the camp's affiliation with the MST. A long conversation during the morning coordinators' meeting revealed that, while the militancy was worried about Anton's proposal and its implicit critique of the MST's leadership, what finally led to the decision to expel him was the fear that some of his moves could have been preparations to take over the camp from the MST. Specifically, Anton had used registration forms of the kind that the MST uses when people first join camps, sometimes accompanied by a small voluntary payment of a dollar or so. This was particularly threatening because, had more people joined him, Anton could have used the registration forms to prove to INCRA that he, rather than the MST, was the true leader of the camp. In other words, the threat was what Anton was setting himself up to achieve, not what he had actually accomplished.

If it is surprising that this might be a cause for expulsion, remember first that land occupation camps are delicate operations, pushing the borders of legality by occupying land that is already claimed or even titled. A camp's breakup could easily undermine its long-term success at forcing the appropriation of a large estate. And, as Bernardo pointed out in the assembly prior to the occupation, a camp's enemies could find ways to infiltrate and undermine its unity from within.

Second, like other democracies, the MST is not perfectly democratic. Although the MST is organized to make it seem like decisions are made by collectives—from the most powerful National *Direção* and National Coordinating Committees, to the state-level *Direções* and Coordinating Committees, on down—the collectives don't always or necessarily have the last word.[29] As we will see in the next chapter, some militants think that there is too much top-down decision-making. This was displayed in Anton's case. After going through the evidence of Anton's potential to undermine the camp leadership, the militant collective called for a decision. "All for him going?" Timoteo asked, and the militants all quickly raised their hands. This influenced everyone else's vote, effectively rendering anyone voting against the majority perhaps an enemy. After the majority voted in favor of expelling Anton, there was no need to ask who was against it.

After the expulsion, we all left the coordinators' *barraco* mostly speech-less. A bit later, under a forgiving rainy-season sky, people started gathering to relax and chat, letting the tensions of earlier in the day fade away. As I sat with a number of women outside Mona's *barraco*, I worked up the courage to ask what they thought. "Well, they felt that it had to be done," responded an older woman, Valenice. But then everyone fell silent. Clearly no one really wanted to talk about it. They appeared shaken too. Just then, a stray dog trotted past with its ear dangling precariously from its head. "*Olha o cão!*" I said, taken aback by the painful sight. All the women burst out laughing. I didn't understand why saying "Look at the dog!" could be funny. I looked to Mona for enlightenment. "We don't use the word *cão* for dogs, only *cães*, which we use to talk about *many* dogs. We only use *cão* to describe people, and *cão* is, well. . . ." I then realized my mistake. "The devil?" I asked. She cackled and slapped her knee, laughing to see me swear with this semi-dangerous word, which some, including her, claim attracts evil. But then Valenice clarified, pointing to the coordinators' hut and referring to the morning's expulsion: "And you should know that any one of us can be the devil at any time."

With this, the intersection between the mystic of friendship and law's enmity finally snapped fully into view. Valenice was not only talking about Anton. She was referring to all humans, especially those involved in applying the rules, even as she was also implicitly supporting Anton's criticism of the MST. In short, Valenice was suggesting that all of those involved in the application of law were exposed to or animated by evil or diabolical elements. Moreover, with her wave toward the coordinators' hut, Valenice also attributed these diabolical qualities to those entities who *make* the law. And in the camp, it isn't *quite* the coordinators who make the law; it is actually the MST.

But of course, law's enmity is widely distributed. One can keep moving up the hierarchy of powers, finding evil divisions and exclusions at each level. A case in point is Sebastião Curió, who most likely ordered the murder of Mona's son O Grandão for speaking to police in 2002 about the murder of the gold-miners' syndicate leader Antônio Clênio Lemos—an assassination that Curió also likely ordered.

Curió loomed large for many residents of the camp because of his power in the region, established since his original intervention at the Serra Pelada mine. In 1981 he was called in to break the miners' control of the gold mine and turn control over to the state, which had been unable to collect any money from the site since the gold rush began in 1980. The miners were armed and dangerous, and Curió did not want to take the mine by force with military police, so he tried alternative means to start. As the story goes, he told the gold-miners a clever lie: he wanted to give them licenses for their weapons and then return them. This meant that, with their unwitting consent, Curió managed to simply disarm the gold-miners and transfer control of the mine to the state, which gave de facto control to him and his group. Former gold-miners saw this as a huge betrayal.

In addition, Curió had since gone unpunished for his own misrule(s) of law, which had buttressed his power across more than two decades. For many people I knew, Curió stood for the inhuman evil infecting the laws of the land. The murders of O Grandão and the syndicate leader were just two of many deaths on Curió's hands, and they exemplified the betrayals and exploitation he perpetrated in the Amazonian region. As one camp resident put it as we took shelter from the rain under the front awning of his *barraco* one day, "I know Curió better than his own wife. . . . I was there when he betrayed the *garimpeiros*. . . . He is an evil [*mal*] man, almost not a human being." And Mona called him a *desgraça*, a more obviously Christian expression in Portuguese than in its English translation: a disgrace.

But though Curió was a local figure, he was not a merely local evil. He had begun his career as a face of Brazil's military government in the Amazon. As the *Folha de São Paulo* put it, "Curió is a controversial person in the region. An ex-agent of the National Intelligence Service (the SNI) in the decades of the '70s and '80s, he also commanded federal troops against Guerrilla fighters in the Araguaia, at the beginning of the '70s. In 1980, he was called to intervene in Serra Pelada, and afterward began his political career, as federal deputy and then as mayor" (Agência Folha 2002). One thing missing from this account is that Curió had also been called in to break up the MST's very first land occupation in Rio Grande do Sul, at Encruzilhada Natalino (the Natalino crossroads), tying his history indelibly to the national MST.

Curió's story hopefully makes it easier to grasp why it is important to contemplate both Christianity and secularity when trying to understand the experience of law's enmity in different political instances. Law's enmity is not just a political-economic product (as Holston might have it) and not just the result of the social person made to feel like a lone individual, as DaMatta has asserted. For whether we are talking about the laws of the land or rules created and imposed by *companheiros*, laws are always controlled by human beings, divining persons who can be the devil—the enemy—at any time.

CONCLUSION

Anton's proposal to form an association of friends, coming on the heels of the protest on the highway, illustrates how the mystic of friendship intersects with and helps produce both the longing for justice and the sense of law's enmity. In other words, in Brazil, and especially among Northeasterners, one should not assume that contemporary insurgencies against the misrule of law are merely secular. They might have an overtly secular valence, but to stop there would tell us only part of the story, particularly along the PA-150.

This doesn't mean that there is no "secular" in this context. On the contrary, if not everyone in the camp "believes" in a purely secular world because God is everywhere, the MST is actively creating a space for it in discursive practice, making a secular world *thinkable*. That is, the MST is the source of the discourse and practice where religious explanations of worldly processes do not predominate, with the result that some people separate from or even abandon their Christian understandings. This distinction of religion and nonreligion, this *secularizing*, coexists with common Catholicism rather than erasing it, and camp residents negotiated between these two forms of understanding alongside other emergent religions, too. This is why the MST contributes to the intensification of secularity along the PA-150, and also why the MST is shaped by both the mystic of friendship, the yearning for unity, and by the sense that law is for enemies.

As I noted above, this is a Brazilian story. Indeed, one can account for it purely through Brazilian ethnography, including its Christian elements. I have attempted to do that here first by describing the cultivation of *mística* and *companheirismo*—unity—leading up to the land occupation and then by showing how the application of camp law generated enmities which in turn produced a renewed longing for friendship. Here, we might also recall my discussion of the Canudos *cordel* in chapter 3, where it is clear that the Canudenses resisted not only the secular political, but also the application of secular law, especially the requirement for civil rather than religious marriage. I noted that Antônio Conselheiro saw this requirement as cutting humans off from God's love, disconnecting them from kin, and withering their souls and hearts. It was the *lei cão* (the devil's law), as the Canudos poet wrote. Though contemporary Southeast Pará is rather different from late nineteenth-century Canudos, the echoes of the Canudos war across the backlands must not be ignored. As Velho documented, anxieties about the captivity of terrestrial slavery in general, and being captive to the beast's law in particular, are both at the heart of Christianity (1995 [1991]). And these anxieties were both alive and well in early twenty-first century settler Amazonia.

But it is also important to note that such attitudes to the law are not only Brazilian and certainly not a unique product of Brazilian common Catholicism. I noted earlier that the phrase "For my friends everything, for my enemies the law" has been claimed as a Latin American catchphrase. Yet this new Latin American sense of what I am calling "law's enmity" has been given a purely secular political valence and explanation, like its earlier Brazilian counterparts.

That said, I cannot assert that beyond settler Amazonia law's enmity is an iteration of the mystic of friendship. Still, we can infer that the reason law's enmity resonates across Latin America is that it came to the New World with Catholic colonizers. We already saw a hint of this in the Fifth Visitation, an excerpt about the ills of worldly law from Brazil's first allegorical novel, written by the Portuguese Jesuit Alexandre de Gusmão. Yet even the critique of human terrestrial law is not a Brazilian invention. Instead, it has a recognized theological pedigree. John Bossy, for example, notes that St. Augustine deemed "that lawsuits were a form of enmity which Christians should avoid." Bossy argues that this Augustinian principle underlies "the general consensus in early modern Europe that disputes between neighbors should be settled by arbitration, not taken to court" (1985, 60).

While the stance against going to court was certainly Augustinian, Augustine acknowledged that it was St. Paul's argument first (Kaufman 2003). That position can be found in Paul's first letter to the Corinthians, which suggested that Christians should not allow non-Christians to adjudicate their disputes using pagan law. Instead, Christians should prefer to not seek redress for their grievances. They should absorb them, even if their complaints are justified. But if necessary, Paul does suggest that Christians should arbitrate their conflicts within the community of the church (R. Taylor 1986). While the injunctions of Paul, Augustine, and other exegetes to absorb injury rather than fight can be seen as a version of Christ's maxim to "turn the other cheek," the call to resolve disputes internally is motivated by more than an aversion to secular or pagan courts. Of course, early Christian leaders had a sense that non-Christians were less Godly and therefore less capable of proper judgment. But they had other concerns too: they felt that using pagan tribunals might expose Christian hypocrisy. While Christians affirmed unity and forgiveness, disputation in public tribunals might reflect badly on their message and render the gospel "unpersuasive" (R. Taylor 1986, 113).

Second, and more importantly, avoiding litigation could protect Christian piety, for litigation undermined necessary Christian dispositions. Indeed, entering a forum designed to place blame on one party effectively rendered litigants, and even judges, opponents and enemies. Augustine is known to have "liked to reflect upon the saying . . . that it was better to hear the cases of strangers than of friends, for as a result of his verdict in the first case he would gain a friend, in the second, he would lose one" (Lamoreaux 1995, 144). John Calvin—an Augustinian Catholic turned Protestant—put this another way. He thought Paul meant that litigation injured the fundamental Christian emotions of universal love, friendship, and charity. In other words, Calvin believed that litigation and judgments created exclusions and generated the will to seek redress for them. While I cannot speak for the presence of this thinking across Latin America, I certainly found similar sentiments recurring in this MST camp. And we will find them in other forms in the next chapter too, among the survivors of the Eldorado Massacre.

Nothing holds more promise for human nature or is more in accord with its greatest appetite or stands above all in this capacity than news of future times and events; and this is what is being offered here to Portugal, Europe, and the World by this news and never before seen history.[1] Other histories tell of past events; this one promises to tell of those yet to come. Others bring back to mind public events that the World has seen; this one intends to show the world those hidden and darkest secrets that have not been penetrated by our understanding. This material soars above the whole sphere of human capacity because God, who is the fountainhead of all wisdom, although He shared his treasures so liberally with mankind (and much more so with the first man), has always kept the knowledge of future things to himself as is the proper prerogative of divinity. . . . Man . . . knows little of the present, less of the past, and nothing of the future. . . .

So in order to satisfy the greatest craving of this appetite and bring up the curtain on the greatest and most occult secret of this mystery, today we present this *History* of ours in the theater of the World, and for that reason called *of the Future*. We are not writing with Berosus the ancient histories of the Assyrians, nor with Xenophon those of the Persians, nor with Herodotus those of the Egyptians, nor with Josephus those of the Hebrews . . . nor with Portuguese writers those of our own. We are writing without an author what none of them wrote or could have written. They wrote histories of the past for future times, we are writing a history of the future for present times. It would seem impossible to paint a copy before there is an original, but this is what the brush of our *History* will do. . . .

Oh Portugal (to whom I am only speaking now) . . . as a subtitle . . . I call this same writing the *Hopes of Portugal*, and this is a brief summation of all the *History of the Future*. . . .

The *History of the Future* is divided into seven parts or books: in the first it will be shown that there is to be a new Empire in the World; in the second what Empire this is to be; in the third its great deeds and good fortunes; in the fourth the means by which it is to be brought about; in the fifth in what land; in the sixth at what time; in the seventh in what person. The seven things are the ones that the new History we are writing about the Fifth Empire of the World will examine, resolve, and prove. . . .

The wondrous future events of the World and of Portugal, with which our *History* is to deal, were dreamed many years ago like those of Pharaoh and written down like those of Belshazzar, but up till now there has been no Joseph to interpret the dreams nor any Daniel to construe the writings. And this is what I am setting out to do, with the grace of that Lord who is always served by small instruments for great matters, so that the World and Portugal should know, with their eyes always upon Heaven and upon God, that all of it is the result of his power and the counsel of his Providence. And so that there be no ignorance so blind nor ambition so haughty that it takes away from God what is of God to give to Caesar what is not of Caesar, attributing to luck or human industry what must only be from divine disposition. . . .

I do not promise nor do I expect misfortunes for Portugal. But if they be for Portugal, or for Christianity, or for the World, as might be caused by necessity or the adversity of the times, for all of them I offer this cure. . . .

Let not Portugal trust in itself so as not to offend God. Let it trust in God himself and in his promises, and it will fight with assurance. Oh! How well-armed will our soldiers be awaiting the Lion in the field if they have weapons in their hands and the prophecies in their heart! *Leo rugiet, quis non prophetabit?* [The lion will roar, who will not prophesy? (Amos 3:8)] . . .

Divine Providence is accustomed to begin its miracles with opposite effects, either to test our faith or to raise its omnipotence even higher. It can do more than all human powers and there is only one thing it cannot do, which is to go back on what it has promised. . . . Christ left the disciples to fight the storm on the first vigil, on the second he did not come to them, nor on the third; and when, on the fourth, after frightening them with phantoms, he succored them with his presence, even then he reprimanded them for their little faith. Let the night grow dark, let the sea roar, let the sky break forth, let the winds be furious, because God must come by his word.

06

ELDORADO DO CARAJÁS

Divining the Event

Delegates had just returned from the annual meeting of the Landless Rural Workers' Movement–Pará, an Amazonian chapter of Brazil's largest agrarian movement, the MST. Osias and I had participated in the four-day event, where MST activists were instructed on the movement's current and future challenges as it sought to bring about agrarian reform in Brazil. Yet my visit to Osias's house that day did not concern the meeting. Rather, I wanted to talk about his life before and after the Massacre of Eldorado do Carajás. On April 17, 1996, police opened fire on more than 1,500 peaceful MST protestors blocking the PA-150 highway in Southeast Pará, killing nineteen instantly and wounding seventy-nine, with two dying some time later from their wounds, raising the numbers of deaths to twenty-one. Osias was one of the wounded survivors. After feeling bullets pierce his leg and hand, he had crawled off the highway and escaped with others through the brush. The wounded survivors would later be referred to as the "mutilated," "Os Mutilados de Eldorado do Carajás."

As during previous visits, we sat on plastic-string chairs in the front room of Osias's small clay-brick house in the 17th of April settlement, named in honor of the Massacre. The front door was shut to keep out the heat and dust from the road, though the high, paneless window was open onto the yard to the side of the house. Osias occasionally looked up to the sky as he told me about how *o Massacre*, as everyone called it, had changed his life and the movement—and that there had been many difficulties. At one point he paused. He wanted to show me something he had written. But first he explained:

It was two years after the Massacre. Shortly before twenty of us were opening our cases [to receive compensation from the government]. One night, I was alone. I decided to sit and think and write. I was conscious then. It had been some time that I had been asking God to give me a revelation—about how to continue my life. I didn't know what my future held, or what the past meant either. But then I put my head on my arms, and I guess I fell asleep. When I woke up I said: Oh, I have to finish writing, and there were these pages.

He passed the pages to me. They were lined, yellowed, and shakily written:

NEGATIVE THOUGHTS

The story of a king that doesn't know where or when he received his crown as king. Sometimes I stay up until late at night thinking where do I live where do I stay and who am I every day that I have spent in my life I thank God for having given me good thoughts and good happiness. I also thank my friends and *companheiros* who gave me so much courage so that I never felt sad. . . .

Sometimes I ask myself why I never had the opportunity to prove to the world that I am a king and I was never able to receive my majestic crown so someone could say that this is the true king of the earth. The true king lives in heaven and I am the king here on earth. As I was born in a poor family no one until today wanted to understand what I am, but one day everyone will understand. It won't be me who will show who will show is the king of heaven only he has power and no one on earth will go against your wish.

Me, here on earth, but god revealed to me that perhaps I will come to reach this date because due to god's grace and permission when my great grandchildren are born in 50 years and when they are 100 years old, I will still live 859 years / Whoever buys this book will know

How to add and how many years will this sentury bee. I don't need to put a date, it is enough that all have the memory to discover the time that the world will burst into flames to burn all of the sins on the face of the earth.

The sum is made by counting from 1998.

When you finish adding will come the year in which all matter on the face of the earth be burned so that everything will be cleen of sin after everything is cleen god will reconstruct his new garden free of sin so that we will live like angels without evil.[1]

Once I finished reading, Osias asked me, "Can you figure out the dates?"

"Yes . . . it's 3007," I said.

"That's right," he said, beaming.

"What have you done with this since writing it?"

"Well actually I felt that I had to spread the word. You know, to churches. But I showed it to some people, and they didn't think much of it, so I have left it. Ach. Now I don't know. . . ." Osias looked away. When I asked him if I could copy the text, he said no. Days later, he consented.

As I copied the text into my notebook, it hit me again how extraordinary and confounding it was. I had in my hands a prophecy of the destruction of the world and the creation of a divine afterworld—what both secular and theological scholarship refers to as "millenarian"—composed by a survivor of the Eldorado Massacre. Osias said he was unconscious when he wrote it, perhaps animated by a holy spirit? The text opens with optimism as Osias thanks his "friends and *companheiros*" for giving him courage in life. Yet proceeding in a mystic mode, the text quickly switches tone. Osias begins to lament those around him and then describes how the world will end in flames. He names no specific sins, only implying one: how no one has recognized the author of the text as King of the Earth, the Messiah, who will accompany the world through its final transition.

Osias's behavior around the text was also remarkable. He had shown it to many people over the years, and was met with complete disinterest. On this second visit, I asked him more about why he wanted to share it:

As if in a dream, I wrote this *historia* (history) of a king . . . about human-ity. It was not written only to be a story, though, it was produced with reference to a collective, [a] group. [It] had to be announced [to] the people. So I showed it to some churches, showed it on my travels, but no one seemed to be very interested. But there is a lot of reality in it (*tem muita realidade*). So I have to tell the story to people one by one. I can't just give you this paper; if I do not tell the story it has no foundation. Is it about 3007? Yes. But there is also the human side. [It tells us] that the world [and] the people (*o povo*) must be more human, more solidary, more honest. They have to give more value to their neighbor. And they shouldn't think that wealth leads us anywhere, [especially not to] God's

> Kingdom. In heaven, there are no rich, there are no poor, there is no Black
> or white. We are all of the same class. For God, difference does not exist.

Reiterating that the text was written while he was in an unconscious dream
state to imply that he was a vessel of prophecy, or perhaps the Messiah himself, Osias added new information. He explained that what he had written
had to be announced to the collective, the group, the "people." Significantly,
he also emphasized that there was "a lot of reality in there," before going on
to draw a connection between the evidently prophetic content of the text
and its allegorical-moral call for people to be more human(e), more solidary, more neighborly, and less covetous. While suggestive, Osias's answers
remained minimal. He clearly wanted me, the reader, both to do the work of
interpretation and, potentially, to help publicize the text further. Certainly,
as he wrote, he already saw his text as destined for publication—"everyone
who will read this book will know." I was already a certain public, but I
was also a researcher intending to publish my work one day. The potential for further publicity was real. The core group of fifteen *mutilados* who
had remained in the settlement had asked me to create a digital archive of
interviews with them and to bring selections of these interviews to Brasília
during the MST's 2005 National March, where they would be presented as
a gift to Brazil on the steps of the Supreme Court. (I did the interviews, but
the gift event did not occur as originally planned.)

───────────────────────────────

Over the years, I have returned repeatedly to Osias's text because it sheds
light on the most mediatized and publicly known event of the PA-150's history. Osias's hope that his prophecy might reach and galvanize the public
was never realized. But that he wanted to use his message to provoke public
reflection on reality presents an intriguing ethnographic question. What
relations animated Osias's will to share this text? That is, what conditioned
his expectation that reality could become the object of public deliberation?
While the initial answers to this question are ethnographically grounded,
they also speak to a broad set of scholarly concerns about politics, colonization, and publicity.

Certainly, Osias's experience as a wounded survivor is key to understanding why he shared his text, and I will discuss this below. But two further conditions we have already explored in this book were also determining. First,

there are common Catholic relations, including their latent millenarian features and allegorical-cum-mystic dimensions. Second, there is the MST's challenge to Christianity. Specifically, the MST's Marxist pedagogy works against allegorical thinking, training militants instead to grasp the "real," "material," and "historical" conditions of the landless working class without reference to the divine. In other words, it works to expand the secular domain. And it does so by promoting a new relationship: *companheirismo*, or comradeship. In fact, the creation of *companheirismo* is a key element of a wider secularizing program, perhaps especially because facilitating solidarity beyond friendship is perceived as vital to the institutional, political, and socio-structural transformations that the MST seeks to create. And yet, as we will see, MST participants continue to see and think allegorically; they can apprehend this new set of relations as embodying an illegitimate, even evil, secular political quest to exert power over others, instituting a new hierarchy.

These three conditioning processes—common Catholicism and Christianity more generally, being a *mutilado*, and the MST's secularizing—will animate my first ethnographic argument: that Osias sensed that his text might resonate with Christian and MST publics, whose interests in reality can be most fully understood by attending to an intensifying secularity. By an intensifying secularity I mean the shifting friends and kin who variously mobilize, evaluate, negotiate, and feel the effects of possible distinctions between religion and politics. In chapter 2, I explored how this intensifying secularity simultaneously produces both new hopes for political transformation and the rejection of such possibilities—especially of the form of politics that bears an exclusively human, secular valence. These concerns reappear with Osias and the *mutilados*, bringing back an issue that figured prominently in chapter 4: how common Catholics, and Christians more generally, value the divinity of unity and equality under God and how they can easily decry the evils of secular hierarchy and difference. This has effects on their political alliances, for while the state certainly embodies the evils of hierarchy, other secular forms might, too. For some people, including Osias, the MST too sometimes embodies such evils.

This close ethnographic analysis will produce more general insights on colonization, politics, and publicity in Brazil, both reinforcing and extending the arguments I have made so far in this book. In my introduction, I noted that the anthropology and sociology of politics, especially in Brazil and the Americas, have been conceived mostly at a remove from questions of both colonization and religion, and with even less regard for questions of secularity—especially as I conceive of it, with the flow of relations built in. In

chapters 1 and 5 I offered DaMatta as an early example of these scholarly tendencies, which have inspired the work of later studies of Brazil. Here I would
like to add that DaMatta's work arguably influenced the central argument
of Alfredo Bosi's *Brazil and the Dialectics of Colonization*, a classic work on
the culture of Brazilian colonialism read through colonial literature (2015
[1992]). While he does not cite DaMatta, Bosi clearly echoes him when he
argues that colonization is characterized by a dialectic between the search to
apply hierarchical versus universal, or egalitarian versus individual, values.
Bosi's book caused something of a scandal when it was published in 1992, in
part because he made space for Christian literature and a perceived Catholic
stance at a time when Marxist, secular criticism still dominated in many
fields (Schwarz 1998 [1993]).

Scholars who studied the seventeenth century were not really concerned
with his interest in Catholicism, but they had their own criticisms. Alcir
Pécora, for example, saw Bosi's discussions of the "contradictions" faced by
early modern missionary writers as "anachronistic"; Bosi had produced a
"revisionist" text from a Marxist and liberal Catholic perspective. Specifically, Pécora noted that the *topos* animating the Old and New Worlds during
the seventeenth century was not "contradiction" but rather "conciliation,"
the aim being to bring all "gentiles into the mystical body of Christ" (Pécora
1992, esp. n. 80; Luz 2007, 2013). Significantly, Bosi never mentions the mystical body, though it was a central allegorical image, as we have seen. Instead,
Bosi quarantines the allegorical from the mystical, attributing a radicalism
to the latter while labeling the former a "legitimist" form of power. I return
to this questionable distinction in the conclusion of this chapter, where I
show how Osias's radical interrogation of worldly power is an iteration of
baroque allegorical thinking, which in Brazil was inevitably shaped by the
legacy of Jesuit priest Antônio Vieira (Sixth Visitation, and see below).

For now, we can draw a more general lesson from Pécora's concern with
anachronism. While Bosi's (and DaMatta's) interest in dialectics, egalitarianism, and hierarchy may not be completely strange to contemporary
settlers, when we apply these descriptors to ethnography without attention
to relations and their religious referents we can misread real dynamics on
the ground. Certainly, along the PA-150, the application of their analytics
would occlude how the mystic of friendship and an intensifying secularity
animate sociality, politics, and the contemporary dynamics of settlement.

If the preceding chapters opened these arguments, this ethnography
around Osias consolidates them. In addition, Osias's efforts to share his
prophecy speaks to one final scholarly interest: the question of religions

"going public." Students of religion have been occupied with this theme for some time and have already successfully questioned the secularist nature of early studies of publicity inspired by Habermas.[2] Still, like the scholarship on mediation discussed in chapter 3, predominant analyses of publicity rarely question their premises. An underlying assumption of much of the debate around religious publicity is that it is a form of resistance to the state privatization of religion under secularism. Most also seem unwilling to address secularization.[3] I have already argued that the experience of secularity is not determined by secularism, but that it is constituted by "living with" secularization or secularizing, any distinction and expansion of a secular domain. That is, secularity entails interpersonally and conceptually negotiating emergent (even if never permanent or complete) distinctions between religion and its others, perhaps especially politics. Thus, the question of why a "will to publicity" arises under conditions of secularity now needs to be addressed. Osias's prophecy, moving between Christian and secularizing relations in both text and practice, will ultimately help answer this question. That is, it will help show how publicity is inextricably linked to secularity because reality, grasped ethnographically rather than analytically as ontology, is both made, and made to be contested, by secularization (see Lebner 2017b).

But first we must turn to the publics that Osias's text calls upon—Christian, *mutilado*, and MST—to understand why Christian exposure to the MST's secularizing shaped Osias's hope and expectation that his text could spark public reflection on reality. I begin by showing how the latent millenarianism of the common Catholic public allegorically interrogates the "good" of secular political hierarchies while at the same time fostering the mystic of friendship.

BRAZIL'S COMMON CATHOLIC—CHRISTIAN—PUBLIC

Osias kept his text with a selection of articles, reports, and commentaries on the Massacre that he had written or gathered over the years. As I sorted through these documents, a photograph and two articles caught my eye. The photo was of MST members carrying nineteen crosses along the PA-150 to the site of the Massacre on April 24, 1996, in honor of the seventh-day Masses being held for the fallen at Eldorado. The two articles also commemorated the seventh day, though well beyond Pará state. The first described the Mass

FIGURE 44. Clipping from Osias's archive of a photo from the *O Liberal* newspaper. Photo: Ashley Lebner. The caption reads: "Members of the Landless Workers Movement carry 19 crosses that were fixed at the place where the farmers were massacred by [Brazilian] Military Police."

held in São Paulo by the National Council of Brazilian Bishops (CNBB), in which the names of those killed in the Massacre "were entered on the list of Church martyrs" (A Provincia do Pará 1996a). The second article, on the same page, noted that Cardinal Roger Etchegaray, president of the Pontifical Council of Justice and Peace, sent a letter in the name of Pope John Paul II to the CNBB to acknowledge and lament the Eldorado Massacre and to "reinforce, with the most vivid solidarity, what the CNBB asked of the whole country . . . : to pray for the assassinated peasants and for an extraordinary effort to achieve social justice" (A Provincia do Pará 1996b). These articles show that Brazilians were well aware that the Eldorado Massacre was not only an important political event, but also a major Christian event. It was to this same Christian public that Osias's own text was addressed in the first instance—a public that flourishes across Brazil and that has been shaped in many ways by secularity.

These rituals and proclamations took place in the register of Catholicism, which remains the predominant religious affiliation in Amazonia and Brazil. However, as we saw in chapter 2, the Catholic public regularly draws on practices increasingly associated with other religions such as Afro-Brazilian and Euro-Brazilian Spiritism and Evangelical Christianity. Hence, one can speak of common Catholicism or even a "Christian public."

Traces of Spiritism and Evangelicalism appear throughout Osias's text. In the first place, Osias's unconscious writing indicated possession by a holy spirit. But that a millenarian prophecy emerged from his pen reminds us that awareness of the apocalypse animates more than just the Catholic past. Instead, millenarian thinking still operates in the present, connected to a sense of pervasive evil that shapes relational concepts and practices like friendship, and that is thought especially to drive, and to taint, the search for political power. In other words, the people I worked with and other Brazilian Catholics readily recognized millenarian discourse as a way to reflect on reality and its various evils, especially on the ills of secular political authority, hierarchy, power. I will expand on this latter point, hoping to convey the most general reason Osias imagined that his text's proclamation— that flames would burn all sins from the face of the earth—might have a ready public.

Catholic millenarianism was not always at odds with authority in Brazil. It first came with the sixteenth-century Portuguese, who mobilized prophecies and promises of salvation to sanctify their colonial project. Antônio Vieira's prolific messianic writings and sermons shaped the Catholicism that eventually melded with Indigenous millenarianism, and this is said to have been "the decisive influence [for the] continuation of these [Christian] beliefs . . . for centuries to come" (Pessar 2004, 238n2; see also Cohen 1991; Myscofski 1988). As colonialism expanded, millenarianism became embedded in "ecclesiastical teachings and monarchical/patrimonial rituals of rule" (Pessar 2004, 17), and royal authority came to be imbued with the promise of salvation for the masses.

This view came under threat in a secularizing nineteenth-century Brazil, which an emperor ruled by divine right until 1889. Brazilian elites were adopting Enlightenment ideas, especially the writings of Auguste Comte, whose positivism maintained that both science and "man" shared a "continuous preoccupation with reality" (cited in Pickering 2011, 62, my translation). Comte developed an anti-Catholic and republican political program to accompany his philosophy. Such calls for science, order, and progress motivated Brazil's elites to agitate in favor of a republic against the dual claims to power and knowledge of the church and the crown.

Many Catholic clergy were outraged, and millenarianism was transformed as a result. Clergy launched counterattacks, buttressed by a new set of European texts, in particular the *Missão Abreviada*, a thousand-page work peppered with apocalyptic passages, which soon came to inspire

FIGURE 45. The Brazilian flag drew inspiration from a key saying of August Comte: *"L'amour pour principe et l'ordre pour base; le progrés pour but"* (Love as the beginning and order as the foundation; progress as the goal).

"popular hymns, chap books [including *cordel*], and everyday discourse" across Brazil (Pessar 2004, 29; on *cordel* see my chapter 3). Thus, during and after the establishment of the republic in 1889, millenarianism gained new significance. The faithful began using it to condemn the new secularizing authority as illegitimate and to call for a return to the monarchy and a reunification of church and state.[4]

The most famous rejection of this new secular order was the movement and war of Canudos (1893–97), discussed in chapter 3. This millenarian community of some thirty thousand people in Northeast Brazil, some of whom called for the return of the monarchy, was decimated by the new Brazilian state in four bloody campaigns in 1896 and 1897. Despite this widely publicized violence, Canudos inspired similar movements such as the Contestado (1912–16) in the south and the Caldeirão (1936–37) in the Northeast (Pessar 2004). Significantly, many have read Eldorado and the MST as heirs to those uprisings, as evinced in a poem I found in Osias's archive on the second page of a printed report on the Massacre:

> Eldorado do Carajás . . .
> A hundred years ago

Canudos,
Contestado
Caldeirão . . .

. . . If we stay quiet,
the stones will scream (Tierra, April 25th 1996, emphasis in original).

When I asked Osias if he could tell me anything about Canudos or its leader Antônio Conselheiro, he simply said, "No." I was surprised by his answer, but the truth is that Osias didn't have to be conscious of Canudos or its history to have had a millenarian vision, or to know that people in Brazil understand millenarian and allegorical talk.[5] Both millenarianism and allegory have been at the heart of Brazilian Catholicism for hundreds of years, and my interlocutors in Southeast Pará, who came mostly from Brazil's Northeast, could all describe a fiery vision of the end of the world if asked. Some, like Osias, and also Olina, whom I quoted in the introduction, brought millenarian visions up spontaneously. The resonance of Olina's dream with Osias's text is striking: the world is destroyed by fire because evil is everywhere, but the dreamer is the one worthy to be saved. This resonance is no coincidence. The Christian public of Pará, and arguably of Brazil, harbors a latent and even sometimes literally unconscious millenarianism, whose logical allegorical source is a sense of pervasive evil.

I have shown that evil was perceived everywhere because it was deemed immanent to the human person, entering via the unconscious channeling of spiritual agency. "We [humans] never act alone," my interlocutors would say. Another agent or force—and ultimately a larger narrative about good or evil—always accompanied human action. Certainly, this agency is most often thought of as divine, especially with regard to oneself. As Osias emphasized: "Without God we have nothing. Everything that comes to our minds comes from God." Although this thought was a reference to the MST, and I will come back to it later, the very openness of humanity to divine agency also opens it to evil elements. "Any one of us can be the devil at any time," as I quoted Valenice in chapter 5. In other words, it is the always possible usurpation of human agency and intention that leads Christians to know that evil pervades human activities (see also Velho 1995 [1991]).

This knowledge equally leads people to question the possibility of true human friendship, even as they value and seek unity with others and God above all else. Significantly, this understanding of worldly evil is also what inspires people to question secular authority, especially relations that posit new secular hierarchical differences.

As my discussion of DaMatta and Bosi suggests, hierarchy, especially in patronage or clientelism, has been a staple of Brazilianist scholarship, both because hierarchy has always marked Brazil's history and because there have been consistent efforts to undo traditional hierarchies since the First Republic. These efforts have intensified in the contemporary period, especially in left-wing movements, from the Workers' Party (PT)[6] to the MST, which take long-standing hierarchies to be impediments to the expansion of a democratic and egalitarian political culture. In fact, the left's intellectual influence might be one reason why discussions of hierarchy have been so persistent in the literature (Ansell 2014), even in studies of Christianity in Brazil.[7]

Still, there has been a growing sense that attention to hierarchy and patronage cannot fully explain what happens on the ground. Velho's (1995 [1991]) call for scholars to investigate how Christianity informs political and economic practice among peasantries can be read as a call to shift away from traditional approaches to hierarchy and politics, especially the secular approaches that still predominate. While Velho's work has been a great inspiration for this ethnography, I have found that the allegorical ways of seeing in common Catholicism, and its latent millenarianism, not only shape and reinforce political practices but also generate perennial ambivalence toward "politics." This ambivalence is clearly a response to the way politics always entails new forms of secular hierarchy.

The ambivalence toward new hierarchy is important. However, it is not due only to the loss of traditional favors, privileges, and personal relationships as patronage networks have declined and bureaucratic, impersonal, democratic forms have emerged, though this is surely one source (see also Rebhun 1999; Ansell 2014; Mitchell 2017).[8] Anton's hope (chapter 5) to create an association of friends that visits people who have been "thrown in the garbage" certainly reflects concerns with failed patronage, but I have shown that there is more to it than that. In addition to sidelining personalist forms of patronage, new forms of secular hierarchy often openly marginalize Christianity. And this is significant, for the eclipse of Christian values evokes the specter of the devil's return. After all, is it not evil that challenges God's power on earth? The sense that the human search for power can always be read as an affront to divine power is real, and it remains a motivation for some to question secular political hierarchies—especially new ones.

As we have seen, this is an orientation that settlers in Southeast Pará share with their pre- and post-republic forebears, especially those from Northeast

Brazil. While distrust of the fallen human world no doubt existed prior to the nineteenth century, such distrust became more acute during that period of secularization, as new realities took shape with the establishment of the autonomy of the political domain. Today, while my interlocutors did not often speak of the existential threat of a Brazil bereft of its monarch,[9] they were often concerned with widespread evil and deeply ambivalent about the promises of (always potentially secular, Godless) politics. A humorous quip with the bite of truth says it all: in Pará and elsewhere, the election flyers of politicians, popularly called *santinhos* (little saints), can also be called *diablinhos* (little devils).

Osias's text appealed to this Christian public, a public that knows that God might be animating human activity but is also wary of potential evil and new political hierarchies—even while recognizing that evil is a necessary condition of politics. But this does not explain which more specific publics inspired Osias to try to circulate his prophecy and why he thought he could inspire the public to reflect upon reality. Among these more select publics are the *mutilados*, those who were shot but survived the Massacre. It is to them we now turn.

POST-MASSACRE LIFE, THE *MUTILADOS*, AND THE MST

"It was two years after the Massacre . . . shortly before . . . [we opened] our cases." With these words, uttered right before he showed me his text, Osias evoked the tumultuous time before the *mutilados* sued the state for compensation in 1998, purportedly against the MST's wishes. Osias's sense that his prophecy had public appeal turns on Christian understandings of that time, which threw into relief the limits of the MST and its separation of relations and reality from the divine. Indeed, as hierarchical difference between the organization and its militants became more visible—especially its distance from the *mutilados*—the MST's capacity to offer a real unity became increasingly questionable.

Like most migrants to Pará, Eldorado survivors had generally migrated from the Northeast backlands in the late twentieth century, often searching for gold. Osias came in 1980 to work in the famous *garimpo*, or manual or artisanal mine, of Serra Pelada, said to be the largest open-faced *garimpo* in world history. Years later, pushed out of the muddy and dangerous Serra,

Osias went to smaller *garimpos* hidden in the rainforest, where the work remained hard, the returns meager, and the relations violent. When in 1994 he heard that the MST was setting up a mass land occupation to force the government to redistribute the Macaxeira estate to the landless, he decided to join in hopes of acquiring land.

Osias had lived in the camp for some months, energized by the solidarity of its residents. He was one of the camp's up-and-coming militant-organizers before the entire camp joined a protest march to the state capital, Belém, to demand land, food, and credit in April 1996. The march lasted six days before the protestors, tired and parched from the hot, dusty walk, decided to occupy the PA-150 highway's "S-curve" to press their demands.

Negotiations began for food and buses to continue their journey, but at the hour appointed to announce the government's response to those demands, the police opened fire without warning, perpetrating a massacre that would immediately claim nineteen lives, with two more following some time later due to complications from their wounds.

Recollections of the horrors of the day and its aftermath came up early during my fieldwork in the 17th of April settlement.[10] The Massacre's memory was built into both the settlement's name and its very plan, which consisted of nineteen streets laid in a grid around a central plaza, each street named after a martyr of Eldorado. Ruddy clay-brick houses lined the yellow dusty streets forming the "agri-village" at the center of the former Macaxeira farm. It was mostly quiet by day and night, though not without crime and violence, and only a few residents owned motorcycles or trucks. Two trucks served as regular charters that took passengers daily to the rickety town of Eldorado, fifteen kilometers away where the PA-276 highway met the PA-150. Thus signs and memories of the Massacre were always nearby and would often return unexpectedly. After dinner, in the house I called home in the settlement, Arnaldo sometimes mentioned the shock of realizing the bullets were live. Other times, as I sat at dusk in the yard with Arnaldo's wife, children, and neighbors, they recalled how people met in the brush, hours after escaping the police. *Mutilados* in particular spoke of feeling numb as adrenaline rushed through them for hours as they made their way to safety, and of the anger and fear that gripped them later.

While survivors bore emotional and physical scars, the Massacre catapulted the MST to the position of the prime national and international representative of Brazil's poor and landless, creating the tension to which Osias's text referred. Prior to the Massacre, the MST had already begun to conquer political and public opinion in Pará and Brazil more widely. Its successful mobilization of men, women, and children to occupy land in various parts of the country had forced the government to follow the provisions of the Land Statute and redistribute farmland "not fulfilling its social function." While the MST was thus polarizing (some supported their efforts and some saw them as thieves), its success at organizing forced the state to see it as an important interlocutor on agrarian policy. After the Massacre, the visibility of the movement grew exponentially thanks to national and international media attention. João Pedro Stédile, the MST's main spokesman, became a household name. World-renowned photographer Sebastião Salgado documented the funerals of the dead. The national outcry against the Massacre also helped inaugurate the "most important judgment in Brazilian history" and produced the largest political demonstrations across the country since the transition to democracy (Caros Amigos 1999; Chaves 2000). The international left took note, and April 17 became the International Day of Peasant Resistance. All the media attention not only galvanized the MST's public, it refigured the MST itself as the "voice of the voiceless," the authority on, and protector of, rural workers across the country.

While this positive image of the MST was deserved and respected, I eventually became aware of critiques. Survivors I grew to know in the settlement

FIGURE 46. Caskets of the dead being driven to the funeral services after the Eldorado Massacre. Photo: J. R. Ripper.

FIGURE 47. Burial of the dead after the Eldorado Massacre. Photo: J. R. Ripper.

and elsewhere, *mutilados* among them, began to open up, initially hinting at their bitterness toward the MST in the wake of the Massacre, later saying that the MST leadership had put them in harm's way. Indeed, even though they knew the state government and police were the main culprits, many also blamed the MST. One *mutilado* who died after my initial fieldwork defiantly proclaimed that MST leaders had tried to force people to stay on the road, calling on them not to break their resistance even as the police were opening fire. The MST, he said, sitting up from his hammock with eyes afire, had put politics before security.

Mutilados critiqued the MST more readily because resentment remained fresh. While the MST had benefited politically from the Massacre, *mutilados* felt abandoned and silenced. They recalled that the MST had taken few pains to accompany the wounded, provided no special care in regard to the physical and emotional repercussions of having been shot, and made no effort to convey to them the money raised for the wounded around Brazil. I remember Amarildo choking up as he told me all this. The MST leadership, Amarildo and other *mutilados* said, had discouraged them from seeking government compensation through the courts. Their lawyer concurred. The MST's apparent reason for this was to protect the solidarity of the collective against the bourgeois state. MST activists argued that money might create divisions within the movement in the Massacre's wake, making the *mutila-*

dos different from the other survivors. In the MST's eyes, all landless should benefit from the struggle for agrarian reform, not just a select few. As one veteran MST militant put it to me, the *mutilados*' lawyer was an "opportunist," subtly suggesting that the *mutilados* were opportunists as well. Perhaps ironically, it was this stance that made the *mutilados* feel most excluded from the MST, as though the collective was a mere secular hierarchy that had prioritized its power over their needs and rights.

These perspectives have rarely appeared in published accounts of the Massacre (Brelaz 2006; Nepomuceno 2007). This is understandable, because the focus has been on bringing the real perpetrators to justice. Yet from the perspective of the *mutilados*, the MST has deliberately controlled the narrative, engaging in a curation of the "reality" seen by the public.

Yet the reality of the *mutilados* was not only a "material" reality; it was also a Christian one. Osias was certainly not the only one who brought God and evil into the matter. This was evident one evening as I sat with three *mutilados*—Ambrosio, Mané, and Efrânio—in the warm half-light of Ambrosio's living room, discussing how the Massacre had occurred. The room went silent as Ambrosio looked into the distance, and whispered : "*Só o diabo*" (Only the devil [does that]"). I timidly asked him to elaborate, and Mané added quietly, but a little surprised I had to ask: "It was the devil who was there, opening fire. . . ." No one could say any more, though they looked pained and angry, even confused. While speaking of the Massacre is never neutral, in a place where people read their lives allegorically, any violent collective event poses special problems for interpretation.

As we have seen, violence is often understood in the region as a *besteira*— a "bestial" act—committed by one whose humanity is taken over by animalistic, diabolical forces. Yet this clashes with the sense that the divine animates and controls everything and, after all, everyone suffering violence might be in that position as a result of God's punishment. If so, who was being punished? Was it the police, the MST, the survivors, the dead? This was hard to grapple with, and it was perhaps why few of the *mutilados* elaborated further that night at Ambrosio's. But it became clear during my conversation with Efrânio on another day that *mutilados* were concerned about the devil not only in others but also in themselves. "I converted to *crença* (Evangelical Christianity) shortly after the Massacre," Efrânio said. "There was evil, evil everywhere. I had to protect myself and my family."

In short, as survivors and *mutilados* sought to understand the Massacre and its aftermath, the common conclusion—arrived at again and again— was that their lives had been literally shot through with evil. Although this was *already* the condition of everyday life, certain conditions and conduits heighten the power and presence of evil. Who exactly brought the evil on was difficult to say definitively, as there was a lot happening even after the Massacre, including fissures between residents and the MST over agricultural projects, as well as new forms of violence in the 17th of April settlement. Still, the MST, both its representatives and as a political entity, could not be entirely left out of conclusions in this regard. While disappointments experienced by survivors in the wake of the Massacre caused some to suspect that evil was working through the MST, such suspicions cannot be separated from the MST's claims to establish a unified collective of *companheiros* uniquely able to know and transform a reality that was not reliant on God. What ensued instead was division, hierarchy, and all-too-human politics.

"Look at what happened to Nazário," Osias said to me when I visited him in 2012. "After he received his compensation money from the government—many thousands of reais—he spent most of it on a campaign for *vereador* (city councillor) for Eldorado, which he lost. Where were his *companheiros* then?" Osias asked, implying that Nazário's loss meant that his *companheiros* had not voted for him.

I had first heard this story from Dora, Arnaldo's wife, who told me that after he put much of his compensation money into his campaign and spent the rest on a major renovation on his house, Nazário sold the house for almost nothing after losing the election. He left the settlement *"com as cuecas na mão"* (with his underwear in his hands) and moved to Eldorado. After hearing this, I went to what used to be Nazário's house, which I had fond memories of. A woman from outside the settlement answered the door. She had bought the house for very little, she said a bit sheepishly. I asked if I could look inside and was amazed by the renovation—it had indeed been major. Nearly everyone in the settlement lived in the standard clay-brick house with a clay tiled roof and no internal ceiling or painted walls, just brick separations between a sitting room, a kitchen, and two or three bedrooms, each with sizable paneless windows that could only be shut by a single wood-planked shutter. Nazário, however, had had his house *forrado* (lined). That is, he put in a ceiling and walls and painted them a light blue. He had also put in light fixtures—long fluorescent bulbs, unusual in the settlement where rooms were typically lit by single-bulb fixtures drilled into a wall or hanging from the ceiling, if they were lit at all. Sometimes two bedrooms shared one bulb, hung above the separating wall.

In any case, that Nazário practically gave away his house after his election loss meant that he was devastated; he had been humiliated by people who were supposed to be his friends and *companheiros*. Would-be politicians are always soliciting promises of votes from friends—and among MST allies, from *companheiros*—and these promises often give candidates a sense that they are going to win. In my experience with a 2004 campaign I followed, the problem is that people just don't tell the truth. "You can never really tell," the 2004 MST candidate, Waldomiro, said to me. "Everyone tells you they will support you, but of course not everyone will." Waldomiro didn't win, though unlike Nazário he didn't leave the settlement. He was much better positioned within the community: he was about to get remarried to a young beautiful girl from the settlement and was much closer to the MST leadership than Nazário was when he ran in 2012. Years later, Waldomiro did leave, for reasons I have yet to learn, though the last news I had of him was shocking: he had been murdered in the city of Parauapebas, sixty-odd kilometers away.

What Waldomiro taught me, long before I heard Nazário's story, was that in addition to being potentially evil, politics can hurt. People with whom you have warm conversations in their houses—house visits are a key component of the campaign work—"lie to your face," betraying their pledges of friendship and *companheirismo*. Imagine how Nazário felt when he discovered that he had only gotten two votes. "*Two votes*," Nazário underscored his amazement when I visited him in Eldorado after discovering that he had left the settlement. "Where were all my friends?" he asked quietly, still evidently pained. His pain was compounded when, shortly after his election loss, a partner in a clothing business venture swindled him out of nearly every cent he had left. "I gave her the money so she could go buy the materials," he said, "and after I hadn't heard from her by the agreed time, I called her cell phone number. At first, I thought it was just the normal 'out of area' message, but then I kept calling and calling. . . ."

One might think that in Southeast Pará, where people are always concerned about both the constancy of others and the possible evils of politics, Nazário should have known better. But the mystic relational mode means that one can oscillate between real hope in others and in politics, and profound disappointment, which returns one to a sense of impossibility. For Nazário, the pain was worse, because he knew he had made grave mistakes. He not only felt betrayed; he felt stupid. I worried about him. He was living in one of the poorest wood-plank houses I had yet seen. It had gaps and holes everywhere that let in light and air and also had an unusually bumpy and rocky dirt floor. The house was directly across a grassy and rocky "road" from an Assembly of God church. Sitting on Nazário's living room couch with the front door open, we could see the church's front door. "Ever go to church?" I asked, pointing out the door. "I go without wanting to (*vou sem querer*)," he said, and we chuckled. We both knew that he didn't have to leave the house to hear the services, which blared from the church's loudspeakers several times every day. "No, I don't like religion," he said, seeming to equate religion with Protestantism. "You know how we got it, right?" I shook my head. "Religion began because of a sin of Luther's. I don't know what the sin was, but all I know is that it is because of this sin that he had to leave the [Catholic] Church, and that's how we got religion."

Nazário's story, and his take on "religion," encapsulates in miniature the experience of the *mutilados'* disappointment with the friends and *companheiros* of the MST—a failure of unity that indicated the illegitimacy and potential evil of the MST's political ambitions. The *mutilados* had let Nazário down, as only two had voted for him, presumably because they had no faith either in his capacity to lead or in his good intentions. After all, Nazário was seeking power, a goal always of dubious good. (By Nazário's own logic, one might say "Look at Luther! He sinned by acting to distinguish himself from his fellows and was expelled, producing the religious divisions that bedevil social and political life in Brazil to this day.") Osias, one of Nazário's two voters, saw him as another example of how the MST's secularizing of relationships and politics had failed to produce any unity, instead creating division and hierarchy in which people were separated, minimized, and excluded from the collective. Osias knew that, beyond the *mutilados*, a host of others connected to the MST had similar doubts about the movement. This was another key reason that Osias decided to go public with his text.

SECULARIZING POLITICS, REALITY, RELATIONS

"The MST has helped us, certainly," Osias said, leaning back in his plastic-string chair the day he showed me his text. "The movement has been like a mother to us. . . . But the MST is not perfect—it is a human product, of this world. Though some people don't see it that way. They give the MST, themselves, too much power. They forget God a bit." He paused and peered at me. "Well, you know, many people in the MST don't believe in God, and they try to convince others not to believe in God. That is wrong." I asked Osias if he believed in God. He leaned forward suddenly, making a breeze that cut through the heat. "Without God we have *nothing. Everything that comes to our minds* comes from God. Whatever survives *does not exist* without God."

Osias believed that God had chosen him to survive, even though he practically never went to church. "I speak to God myself, I always have," he said. Yet he was also referring to his prophetic text, which thanked God for "giving him good thoughts." This was in direct contrast to the MST's secularizing pedagogy, which we had just experienced during the annual meeting. Indeed, the lessons we encountered there immediately came to mind as reasons that Osias was sharing his text with me. That is, the MST's secularizing practices, and some of his fellow militants' responses to them during the meeting, had clearly conditioned his hope to provoke a public reflection on reality.

One of the key texts that Osias and I had read at the annual meeting was "The Consciousness of the Masses and the Training of Militants." The text was grounded in a subtle secularizing of consciousness and reality. That is, as we will see, it placed both consciousness and reality in a domain distinct from the divine. Moreover, it took as given that this distinction, this secularizing, could be achieved through the creation and reinforcement of a conscious and solidary collective grounded in (secular) relations of *companheirismo*, which would create a militant collective that would transcend the whole.

This article, over eight single-spaced pages, was read out loud by some four hundred militants in twenty groups of twenty, in rooms and spaces all around the Rural University of Amazonia outside Belém where the annual meeting was held. My group, which did not include Osias, sat outside on the spiky grass in the shade and took turns reading the text aloud. Often read out haltingly, the text was clearly intended to train its readers to be better members of the MST and ideally to become full-time militants. Those present at the meeting were not necessarily even militants proper, let alone full time, but they were all were *companheiros*, sharing in the struggle. With this more "mass" public in mind, the text describes the formation of the ideal MST *companheiro*: one who fully joins the MST collective and the struggle for land. This *companheiro* goes from an "object" to a conscious agentive "subject" who is ready to see reality, or "the material base," in order to transform the culture of silence, shape reality, and take charge of her own role in history. Meanwhile, the divine remains quietly off the page:

The peasants . . . of the MST undergo a process that turns them into subjects of transformation in the struggle against *latifúndio*. Objects are easily manipulable . . . [b]ut subjects are active agents of change.

If in the process of the struggle the Landless affirm themselves before reality in transformation, their role in history also changes. . . . [What] occurs in the material base . . . influence[s] the consciousness of the Landless. . . . [This change is important because] . . . peasants have developed a way to think . . . which is strongly influenced by the ideologies of the dominant group. . . . This way of thinking is crystallized . . . [in] what Paulo Freire calls the **"culture of silence"** (Freire 2001 [1968], 37) . . . [T]he **task of education** is to depart from [the] . . . "culture of silence" . . . by means of an increasingly conscious insertion in the reality that transforms itself and transforms them.

For this reason, whether in plenaries, assemblies, or even in speeches, a *Sem Terra* should be stimulated to participate, standing up to speak, looking at their *companheiros/as*. It is necessary to recuperate self-esteem, the courage to speak with one's head held high whatever one has to say. Ideas and opinions, even if they come to be defeated, need to be heard by all. The militant who coordinates needs to consider these thoughts. . . . The function [of consciousness] is to reflect the reality that surrounds the body. It is through the effort of doing things, that consciousness . . . [and] the human being itself . . . develops. That is, a *Sem Terra*, in engaging in the struggle for land constructs her identity and, in her ever more conscious participation, constructs the organization that represents her. In developing political actions, a *Sem Terra* also makes Political Being (*Ser Político*), and is transformed into a subject (Pizetta 2004, 2–3, bold in original).

The MST's secularizing is subtly encoded here in the allusions to the reality that "surrounds the body" as well as in the references to Paulo Freire, who although he believed in "transcendentality" and greatly influenced liberationism, wrote openly against traditional Christianity—especially its "fatalism" (Collins 1998; Dullo 2014, Freire 1997; and see below).[11] These citations work alongside classic secular concepts like "subjective consciousness," "history," "[political] agency," and "Political Being" (Asad 2003; see discussion in Lebner 2015). Because this text employs these concepts to contextualize what it means to be a *companheiro*, it gives insight into the secularizing and the limits of *companheirismo* within the MST that shaped the conditions under which Osias attempted to circulate his text.

The MST's intentional distinction from the progressive Catholic Church in 1985 marked the formal beginning of its own secularizing trajectory, which deepened in dialogue with the writings of Marx, Lenin, Mao, and Paulo Freire. The MST modeled its pedagogy on Freire's Marxian *Pedagogy of the Oppressed* (1970; published in Spanish in 1968), which built on the wider developmentalist and "culturally secularizing" aims that had been sweeping Latin America since the mid-twentieth century (Williams 1973). Freire advocated "conscientization," the process by which the oppressed developed critical awareness of reality so they could speak out against inequality and break the culture of silence.

The reference to the "culture of silence" in this training text clearly makes it a call to secularize, since it is a euphemism for the effects of traditional Christianity. The text quotes Freire's 1968 *Cultural Action and Agrarian Reform*, which describes the culture of silence as the result of "fatalist" Christian beliefs. According to Freire, these beliefs cause peasants to explain their situation only allegorically, by referring fatalistically to destiny or divine punishment (2001 [1968], 39). While Freire doesn't use the concept of allegory, his words suggest that allegorical thinking must be shown to mystify reality or the peasants' oppression will continue.

The MST's invocation of "conscientization" indicates that it shares Freire's long-standing secularizing aims.[12] We should remember that secularization does not mean producing the absence of religion but rather creating new distinctions, negotiations, and *relations* among persons, religion, and politics—that is, new realities. What is interesting for me is how, through their collectively perceived relationships, different publics respond to, elaborate on, and intensify secularizing practices. The training text makes clear that the MST has grounded and developed its secularizing, especially its "Political Being," in a new kind of interpersonal relation, that of *companheirismo*, which serves as the general relational ground of the MST's public.

As we saw in the last chapter, for many MST participants *companheirismo* is a new form of relation, which is supposed to make possible a new secular set of solidary relations beyond the usual and more religiously infused understandings of kinship, friendship, and brotherhood. Still, like religion and politics, friendship and *companheirismo* remain connected even as they are often distinguished, something that I learned from Bernardo. In the previous chapter, I quoted Bernardo differentiating *companheirismo* and friendship. He qualified this in a later conversation. Under the fluorescent lights in his shared office in the *Secretaria*, the headquarters of the regional MST, he leaned back in his chair and explained how, despite the predominance of the language of *companheirismo*, "Friendship was still the basis for the unity of the MST. Because where people do not like each other, ideas lose their value. . . . All of the vacillations that we have had until now have been due to ideas losing their quality because people have not been able to make friends with their ideas and friendship out of their ideas." Bernardo shared this as something he had learned in his own life as a militant and then leader in the MST. He still turns to those *companheiros* who are also friends, he said, people with whom he consolidated deep connections during an nine-month-long *prolongado* (extended) MST course.[13]

Reflecting on Bernardo's comments together with Osias's text and my wider ethnography has helped me understand that a certain more traditional mystic relational dynamic has continued to echo within the term *companheirismo* both despite and because of the term's secular political connotations. Osias's text and analyses elucidate this powerfully, as I will continue to show. I first encountered this longing and sense of absence, this mystic, when I attended the MST annual meeting, even before I saw Osias's text. While there were hardly any direct mentions of God at that meeting, people there clearly connected mystic understandings of relations to their assessments of the MST's claim to be the best source of knowledge about reality and the best means to change it. In other words, they questioned the MST's claim to be a transcendent authority that forged a unity from its base of *companheiros*.

WHOSE AUTHORITY?

After we had finished reading "The Consciousness of the Masses and the Training of Militants," Timoteo, my *companheiro* from the camp (chapter 5), who was moderating the discussion, opened the floor. With the exception of Timoteo, who facilitated without intervening himself, none of the militants in our discussion group were from Southeast Pará; most were in their twenties and thirties.[14] After a few people shared the usual supportive platitudes, to my surprise, the conversation quickly turned blunt.

A WOMAN: The MST has a proposal but it is not working. First, we have to implement the new MST directives for organizing: accompany families, fifty per coordinator. But sometimes I can't even follow my own! [There are problems] with our practice of criticism-self-criticism. Nobody wants to get burned, and we know that persecution exists. We have to stop the fear.

A MAN: The training of the people is difficult. It hasn't succeeded in providing political training. The university courses are an embarrassment (*vergonha*). We are going to end up training people who are not committed to the working class.

A WOMAN: We know that our organization is in crisis, but we don't know what needs to be fixed. There is a lack of transparency, no debate. There are meetings of the *direção* (leaders), but the militants aren't allowed in. It is not participative, only representative. This is not an advance, it is regression. I propose greater participation.

A MAN: Probably in many states there are two or three people who decide on what happens for the movement. We must go and discuss this because, you are right, it doesn't work that way, and we are losing the confidence of the people. And losing people to the Pastoral Land Commission, because our militants are kids . . . and are not people with responsibility who understand the necessities of a father and his family.

A WOMAN, OLDER THAN THE REST: We militants aren't old enough to advance the MST. We must start with practice. We must create a love for the movement. If we do not practice, we do not become passionate about the movement. We must learn to love the struggle. But there are few good people and many dangerous ones. There's always a Big Man (*grandão*) in the middle.

A MAN: If the base keeps being coordinated [from above] they aren't going to become *Sem Terra*.

I was impressed with the militants' openness. These were serious critiques given the rhetoric and aims of a movement advocating complete and disciplined devotion. The militants' comments were rife with mystic disquiet regarding the effects of division within a collective that was otherwise supposedly unified. On the one hand, some expressed worries about unworthy hierarchies, such as unnecessary distinctions among leaders, Big Men, militants, and the base. On the other hand, some expressed concerns with distinctions between good people and dangerous or bad people and between those who have real love for the movement and the struggle and those whose real love, or real *companheirismo*, had yet to develop.

While no one mentioned God, the references to love and family commitment were especially telling. As we have persistently seen, love, sacrifice, and friendship are not purely secular concepts in rural Brazil, even if they are conditioned by secularity. As they are used in Pará, even when mobilized within secular contexts, these are Christian or sometimes generically religious concepts that refer to the divine origins of the social and provide the grounds on which sociality is broadly problematized (Lebner 2012; Mayblin 2012). Our discussion group's comments showed that for some militants the MST's sense of itself as the agent capable of transforming Brazilian reality—that is, its offer of secular political redemption—was not as real, as in true or good, as it professed to be. The comments reflected the way Christian forms remained relevant to the militants, helping them make sense of the world and engage it ethically. Finally, and most importantly, the comments allow us to see that Osias was not alone in his concerns about the forms of reality the MST presented.

Having seen me participate in this discussion at the annual meeting, Osias knew that *I* knew that there was a public for a text that called for renewed Christian reflections on reality. He came up to me shortly after our discussion of the pedagogical text and said, "I heard that the militants in your session said a lot of things (*falaram muito*). You are starting to know us [the MST] well, but the *mutilados* and I have much to teach you." In a way, he was preparing me for what was to come—our interview and his message. Given what I knew by then of the movement's consistent secularizing, the tensions between the *mutilados* and the MST, and the common Catholic ambivalence toward politics and new secular hierarchies, when I saw Osias's prophecy I easily recognized the message it encoded. That message was that the MST is not alone in its capacity to know, write, or transform the relations that form reality, and moreover that the MST was not where people necessarily find the unity, the good, or the powerful protection they seek.

As I went through Osias's archive, I came across other texts that he had written since the Massacre. A few recounted the Massacre's specific details from his perspective. But one text offered additional context. It began, "The story on Eldorado / at every years being / less explained / We want this story to return to/ Being investigated again. . . . Take a team of lawyars to / Intterview the *mutilados* / So we can have/the real story / of the Eldorado Massacre." This undated text puts the *mutilados*' request that I interview them in perspective. That is, the *mutilados* clearly agreed that more interviews would keep their story alive. Yet the text also highlights a choice Osias made to try to publicize his millenarian text, rather than, say, this one. This might mean many things. One is that Osias thought his millenarian prophecy offered a more important and more widely resonant message, which could better express the real story of Eldorado and its survivors to and beyond the MST. After all, as I showed in the first section, millenarian Christianity has long served as the idiom in which the poor and oppressed have articulated and legitimized their critique of secular authority and the reality it authorizes. And clearly, even after the birth of the republic, this critique has not received the public attention and redress it deserves.

CONCLUSION

While Osias's text never reached any public, this chapter shows that its potential publics included Brazilian Christians in general and those struggling with the MST's claims about reality in particular. I spoke especially to the *mutilados*, who retained more allegorical views of reality than a secularizing Marxist pedagogy prescribes. In other words, I have demonstrated that Osias's awareness of people's questions about the MST's claims to construct a new reality, including questions about whether the MST offered the appropriate forms of political authority and relations (*companheirismo*), conditioned his expectation that his text could publicly resonate.

While offering new ethnographic insights into the Eldorado Massacre and its aftermath, this chapter has reminded us of the core message of this book: that ethnographic attention to religion, especially to allegorical ways of seeing and relating, can shed light on the settlement of Brazil's colonial frontiers. Taking us beyond the usual secular analytical frames of hierarchy, political economy, and history, such attention shows us that along the PA-150 longings for unity and friendship with God and other humans recur and animate actions within, and evaluations of, overtly secular political life.

Let me emphasize that I am not arguing that "there is no secular" in Brazil or in the Americas. Instead, I have used Osias's case to show that distinctions between religion and secular politics exist and are negotiated by persons in relation, whether in dialogue with friends, *companheiros*, or kin, or with other kinds of publics. Even if some reject these distinctions between religion and secular politics, like Osias claiming that secular politics is not

the "real reality," others in the MST and outside it disagree. This is what living with secularization is like. Such ongoing and increasing evaluations of
religion and politics among persons in both private and public relation are
what I have called an intensifying secularity. And this understanding helps
answer the question of why publicity might be inextricable from secularity: namely because living with secularization entails encounters with other
publics, with other views of reality, making reality publicly contestable.

All this suggests that Catholicism, secularity, and interpersonal, conceptual, and public relationships merit serious attention from both scholars
and activists, whether within or outside the MST, whether in Brazil or other
parts of Latin America, and whether they are concerned with colonization
or with other kinds of institutions or politics. As I noted in the introduction,
politically minded scholars and activists have given relatively little attention
to Catholic relations and the secularity they animate. As this chapter and
this book have shown, however, such relations are crucial for understanding
the embrace of politics and critical rejections of politics in settler Amazonia.

Allegory is particularly key, since it shapes settlers' relations, reflections,
and actions along the highway. With Osias, we see once again allegory's link
to the millenarian tradition, and we have also seen that allegorical thinking
is radical, able to interrogate any potential site of hierarchy or power, from
the state to leftist movements. Which brings us back to Bosi. In the second
chapter of his *Dialectic of Colonization*, Bosi acknowledges that allegory was
part of the colonial process, though only as a "cipher for a legitimist vision
of power" (2015 [1992], 63). Bosi's chapter is an analysis of the lyric poetry
and catechistic plays of José Anchieta (1534–97), Brazil's "first militant intellectual," a Jesuit who was canonized in 2014 as the "Apostle of Brazil." Bosi
contrasts Anchieta's lyric poetry to the "allegoric didacticism" of his plays,
often written in Indigenous-language Tupi-Guarani rhymes for missionary purposes. It is only in the poetry, however, that Bosi finds "mysticism,"
because the poetry communicates Anchieta's "spiritual tensions": a hope for
mystical union coupled with a sense of "moral distance" that acknowledges
the "ineffability of its [divine] object" (64, 69, 72).

Bosi's denigration of allegory builds on an established tradition. Citing
"modern aesthetic theory" from Goethe to the young Lukács, he argues
that "the use of allegory is the residual trace of an older subordination of
art to other ends, whether religious, political, or moral. . . . [Allegory is] the
rule of the abstract over the subject's concrete, free expression" (63). Significantly, Bosi acknowledges Walter Benjamin's critique of this view, especially
Benjamin's attempts to reclaim the specificity of baroque allegory as entail-

ing "a radical judgment of Power" that echoes into modernity. Admittedly, Bosi is only interested in showing that Benjamin's reading does not apply to Anchieta's work. However, Bosi's seemingly strict opposition between allegory and mysticism can obscure mystic modes of allegory, through which it simultaneously promotes unity between humans and the divine and separates them. "Considered in allegorical terms," as Benjamin puts it, the profane world is both elevated and devalued" (W. Benjamin 2003, 175).

The simultaneous divination and devaluation of the profane world, which I consider the heart of the mystic approach to relations, is precisely where Benjamin sees the radical potential of allegory. Allegory perennially throws terrestrial powers into question, pointing to the possibility of their evil, a point that one of Benjamin's most astute readers, Samuel Weber (2008), underscores. And while Bosi rejects this mystic dynamic of allegory for the Brazilian context, I found it tucked elsewhere in his discussion of baroque literature, despite his disavowals. I discovered allegory's mystic dynamic especially in Bosi's discussion of another famed Jesuit whom we have already met, Antônio Vieira.

Vieira was a missionary for nearly a decade in earliest colonial Maranhão and Pará, the region I have been describing in this book. He exemplified a mystic allegorical mode, as I noted above and in the Sixth Visitation. But he was also a millenarian thinker whose prolific writings have shaped Brazilian Catholicism and Christianity into the present. Bosi does not focus on Vieira's millenarianism, but he does inadvertently show how motile and potentially radical baroque allegories can be, emphasizing the ways Vieira both promoted and critiqued conventional power structures by demonstrating that they were both potentially of divine origin and of uncertain good.

This simultaneous divinization and devaluation is uniquely visible in two of Vieira's sermons on African slavery that Bosi quotes, originally published in a compendium of thirty sermons dedicated to "Mary Mystical Rose." For example, in his Sermon XIV on the rosary, delivered to a Black Catholic brotherhood on a Bahian plantation in 1633, Vieira allegorically equates the slaves to Jesus:

> You are the imitators of Christ on the plantation, because your sufferings are quite similar to those suffered by the Lord Himself on his cross, and during the entirety of his passion. His cross was made of two beams, and yours on the plantation is made of three. There was no lack of cane there either, for cane entered twice into the story of the Passion, first as the scepter for Christ's ridicule, and second to collect his vital fluids.

> Christ's passion occurred over a sleepless night, and a day without rest,
> just like your nights and your days. Christ naked, and you naked: Christ
> without food, and you starving: Christ mistreated in every way, and you
> mistreated in everything (cited in Bosi 2015 [1992], 119).

The equivalence Vieira draws between Christ's passion and the lives of
slaves, from their physical mistreatment to the torments of "cane" (in the
slaves' case, sugar cane), unmistakably condemns the slaves' masters, even
as it affirms slaves' destiny to suffer until they are redeemed. This allegorical divinization and devaluation of the lives of both masters and slaves is
similarly present in Vieira's Sermon XXVII. This sermon explicitly communicates that the slaves' situation is part of God's plan: "It is God's specific
design that for the present you live as slaves and captives so that through
your temporal captivity you can achieve freedom . . . eternal manumission"
(cited in Bosi 2015 [1992], 121). However, Vieira's comparison of the slaves'
present and future to the Roman feast of Saturnalia has a telling conviction
built in:

> Among the gods of the pagans there was one called Saturn, who was
> the god of the slaves, and during the feast . . . [of] Saturnalia, one of the
> rituals . . . was that the slaves would be seated and their masters would
> stand, and would serve them. But once the feast came to an end, so would
> that comedy, and each one would return to how he was before. And in
> Heaven, what will the slaves' feasts be like? They will be much better than
> Saturnalia, because each slave who in this world has served his master
> as if he were a God Incarnate, will be served by him in Heaven. Who
> would dare to say or imagine such a thing, if Christ Himself had not said
> it? . . . (Luke 12:37): "Blessed are those servants, whom the Lord when he
> cometh shall find vigilant in their duty" (Bosi 2015 [1992], 121–22).

Vieira here asks slaves to dutifully await their reward by submitting to their
passion. However, he also likens the slaves' situation to pagan times—almost
equating their world to the evil that led to Christ's crucifixion. Or perhaps he
is suggesting that the evil is even greater under slavery and thus the slaves'
heavenly reward will be even better? My point is that Vieira's allegories allow
for multiple interpretive possibilities, including the condemnation of colonial masters, even as he sometimes admits to not understanding the ways of
the world and God. It is this allegorical motility, I argue, that is the hallmark
of the mystic allegorical mode, which was already present in the early mod-

ern world but has arguably continued to intensify as it recurs in the present with new unknowns and im/possibilities.

Osias offers a particularly dramatic example of this allegorical recurrence, as his text echoes but does not quite repeat Vieira's more millenarian and prophetic writings, such as the one in the Sixth Visitation. But Osias and so many of my interlocutors made more "mundane" calls as well, pressing, for example, for more friendship and unity. "Die, die enmities, die hatred, die disunities," Vieira says in his 1662 sermon on the "Saintliest Sacrament." "May only peace, friendship, and concord live, along with that much desired unity that Christ intended for us, when he ennobled us with his blood" (2001 [1662], 168). In short, reading Osias through Viera, exposing the ways they both *divine*, interpret, events, call for friendship and unity, and speak to and through various publics, brings me back to the points with which I began this book. A merely secular history of the present is not sufficient to tell the story of the settlement of the PA-150 highway. And in the same way, a merely secular history of the present is not sufficient to aid activists, within the MST and without, to effect transformations on Brazil's southeast Amazonian frontier.

EPILOGUE

I distinctly remember one conversation I had before the MST's 2005 National March. Spirits were high on the *mística* of it all: some twelve thousand MST militants and supporters from all over the country had come together to walk in two single files for 230 kilometers from Goiânia to Brasília, the nation's capital, over a period of two weeks (May 2–17). Once gathered in Goiânia, the militants had training activities for two days leading up to the beginning of the march. One of these activities was a speech by the renowned Chilean Marxist Marta Harnecker, who had studied with Louis Althusser in Paris, later moved to Cuba, and had recently published a book on the MST (Harnecker 2003). Her speech, given to around a hundred people arranged in chairs to one side of an airy gymnasium, had been fiery. She clearly meant to inspire militants in the struggle, like she had done in her breakout first book *The Elemental Concepts of Historical Materialism*, which was written for workers (Harnecker 1969). As the audience dispersed after she finished, I saw Geraldo, a veteran activist of the MST-Pará, walking toward me. He was moving slowly, even somewhat dejectedly, though I knew that he was also often lost in thought like that. I waved and moved toward him, noticing the MST shirt with corduroys, rather than jeans, that he was wearing. "What did you think of the talk?" Geraldo asked before I could say anything. I gave a rather banal answer—that I had liked it, that it had been powerful and encouraging—and then returned the question to him, not expecting much more than I had offered. But to my surprise he hesitated, looked down, and swayed a bit on his feet before pulling himself back up and looking directly at me through his small, thick-lashed brown eyes. "She should have been speaking about the *crisis* of the left," he said with some defiance, "which is what we really need to address. On one side are the global forces that constrain us and on the other there's the problem that the people (*povo*) just do not rise up—despite knowing about their oppression. And when they do, they often don't stay committed to the cause. We need better ways to address both issues."

Even though I was surprised by Geraldo's admission, it wasn't the first time I had heard such concerns. Others had spoken even more directly— like Elio, when he asked me quietly one evening during the MST's 2004 annual meeting, "Why doesn't the MST form quite work?" His question had really taken me by surprise, even more so than Geraldo's comment would later. Still, I also knew that Elio's question was coming on the heels of what I described in chapter 5, the attempt to undermine the new MST camp leadership by residents hoping to found an "association of friends." It had shaken many of the young militants, and even Geraldo. All were made newly aware that although the MST was a national organization that had successfully secured land for millions of landless workers across the country since the 1980s, its future was always uncertain. The MST had enemies, and more importantly, not everyone stayed the course—militants demobilized, despite the value of the cause.

The Mystic of Friendship has not been a study of the MST or its activists, but it has been written in part with Geraldo and Elio, and other activists like them, in mind. Of course, I set out wanting to contribute to the ethnographic record and intervene in scholarly debates. Most generally, I wanted to describe the mystic of friendship and help recenter relations in the study of colonization, religion, politics, and secularity. And to this end I have shown that to fully understand the dynamics of settlement along the PA-150, we needed less a "history of the present" than a "divining of the present."

This divining of the present, an approach distilled in dialogue with my interlocutors, goes beyond conventional understandings of historical (material, political, linear) causation. I began outlining this divining in the introduction, connecting it to past and present allegorical practice, which is never identical or linearly conceived. That is, I underscored the recurring-while-transforming attempts of my interlocutors to decipher the divine meanings of worldly images that comprise constellations of relations, to help make themselves more divine through unity—friendship—with God and others. Crucially, this approach has brought to light the vital transformative force of relations, which are animated by instability. In particular, as I worked through different images of my interlocutors' lives along the PA-150, this divining helped uncover the mystic of friendship and its effects on religion, politics and settlement. Recall that in Goianésia (chapter 1), where I explored a pilgrimage native to the frontier, we saw how allegorical ways of seeing are connected to the divining person, the mystic of friendship, and the genesis of new religious practice. Then in Marabá (chapter 2), through an account of the Solanha family and their migrant father's prayers, we learned how the mystic of friendship has been driving a major religious transformation—both the pluralization of religions and the possibility of exclusive humanism—which I have called the intensification of secularity. In Cleusa's settlement (chapter 3) we caught a glimpse of life in the region before the construction of the PA-150 and saw how both the past and the present resonated with the allegorically minded *cordel* poetry that has reflected and shaped Northeastern relations since the late nineteenth century, including during the war at Canudos. Next, in Jacundá (chapter 4), we examined how liberationists of the 1980s deployed allegorical images of unity to inspire poor settlers to "see-judge-act" against wealthy would-be landowners who wanted to clear them from the land. Finally, through the occupation of Fazenda Peruano and the memories of the Eldorado massacre (chapters 5 and 6), we saw how the mystic of friendship inspired people to first join the MST and the struggle for land, only to later lament the limits of a secular *companheirismo* that cannot live up to friendship's promise. Both the hopes and disappointments were thus implicated in reshaping settlement, as people shifted their commitments to communities along the highway.

Still, this research has also taught me something else, which has been implicit in the foregoing chapters: that traditional political-economic critique is not enough to spark and maintain mobilization over time, at least not on the PA-150. This does not mean that political critique is not valuable and tactically effective, but it does suggest that other kinds of analyses and strategies are necessary, too. This is why I hope these pages will also be read by activists along the PA-150 and elsewhere and inspire them to draw not only on political theory but also on ethnography to help them devise and hone new ways of mobilizing on the ground.

Of course, the political conjuncture at the level of state politics has changed substantially since I began my research in the mid-2000s. Most obviously, Brazil has seen the dramatic rise of the far right. The election of Jair Bolsonaro to Brazil's presidency in 2018 made it suddenly visible, and now, even though Bolsonaro lost the 2022 election to Lula, the far right retains significant power as "Bolsominions" continue to oppose the new government inside and outside of Congress.[1] Still, my ethnography remains relevant for thinking about mobilization in the present because, despite all the worries about a dramatically changed Brazil, there remain fundamental continuities. Indeed, though I had no inkling of what was to come during my research, this ethnography ultimately sheds light on the rise of Bolsonaro, and can therefore continue to speak to activism in this changed political context. I will speak first about the 2018 election and its effects before I return to what this ethnography teaches us about rallying political communities in the present.

It is common knowledge that Bolsonaro's election to the presidency shocked much of the country, especially after his divisive underdog campaign. As one commentator noted at the time, Brazil had seemed poised to return to the left, rejecting the factions that had impeached President Dilma only a few months before the election. Was it possible, he asked, "that Brazilians had become fascist in a few weeks?" (Lambert 2018, 4). He and others concluded that, no, Brazilians were not fascists—they were simply tired of economic crisis and untrustworthy politicians. While this was partly correct, Bolsonaro's general anti-political and authoritarian rhetoric profoundly resonated with Brazil's Christian public: some 70 percent of Evangelicals and 51 percent of Catholics voted for him (see Melo 2018). In a postscript written and published in December 2018 for an earlier version of chapter 6, I suggested that my ethnography offered insight into how Bolsonaro convinced this Christian public to elect him (Lebner 2019 [2018]). Indeed, I noted that my account added to what political scientist Reginaldo Moraes argued in the weeks after the election: that Bolsonaro succeeded due to a "well-thought-out movement among the media and other organizations that shape ideas and sentiments (like churches), to depict a decomposing world, under attack by the forces of evil, that requires an almost divine intervention, the intervention of myth, of he that comes" (Moraes 2018, 9). Moraes here not only referred to one of Bolsonaro's monikers (*mito*, myth); he also clearly evoked a messiah. ("Messias" also happens to be Bolsonaro's middle name.) The intervention of "he that comes," Moraes said, is what inspired people to vote. Yet Moraes ultimately made little direct mention of this messiah—or of Christianity. I reflected at the time that, for many Brazilian intellectuals, attention to Christianity was likely just too obvious; after all, Bolsonaro's campaign (neither specifically Catholic nor Protestant) marshaled the slogan "Brazil before everything, God above all."[2] Still, I concluded that by ignoring Christianity, commentators failed to offer a fundamental insight, that in Brazil "the rhetoric of moral crisis, especially around the fundamental corruption of politics, is very old indeed; it has repeatedly mobilized masses against various political powers, especially after the foundation of the secular Republic, when politics became autonomous from the Catholic Church" (Lebner 2019 [2018], 144).

Here, I was not referring to the new Protestant and charismatic Catholic forms that helped bring Bolsonaro to power, as many journalists and scholars have since discussed (see Abreu 2021; Barrocal 2019; Bonfim 2020; Lacerdo 2022). Rather, I was speaking about common Catholicism and especially its vital concern with evil, which is entwined with a millenarian tradition that preceded and continues to serve as the ground of conversions and deconversions across Brazil (see also Hatzikidi and Dullo 2021). What I didn't have space to discuss in that article and postscript, and what I have expanded on in this book, is how these common Catholic senses of evil were connected to the mystic of friendship and mystic relational dynamics more generally. And so let me add here that it was not only ambivalence toward politics that positioned Bolsonaro, a perceived political outsider, as a promising choice. Rather, common Catholic ambivalence toward politics exists in the first place because the search to create new distributions of human (political) power intensifies divisions—strains the possibility of friendship—among humans and among humans and God, whose true sovereignty is affronted by the struggle for earthly authority. Thus, although Bolsonaro clearly stoked interpersonal, class, and racial divisions during his campaign, his simultaneous Christian offer of near-divine unity became an energizing (if well-worn) option for counteracting those same divisions.

The question remains, how should people mobilize in this context—for example, against authoritarianism, for the democratization of rights and resources? I am not the only one who argues that despite some differences in the present, insights from the past continue to be relevant. Lilia Moritz Schwarcz (2022), for example, reminds readers that contemporary ("Bolsonarista") authoritarianism is merely an iteration of authoritarianism's past, suggesting that knowing these histories can help combat it in the present. It is certainly important to be reminded, as Schwarcz reminds us, of the continuities in racism, bossism, intolerance, gender inequality, and corruption. However, as I have suggested in this book, "histories of the present" like Schwarcz's (2022, 213), with their secular and often linear bent, still impart only some of what activists need to know to mobilize their publics, whether for decolonization and opposing authoritarianism or to support other political causes, including agrarian reform.

In short, when reflecting on strategies for mobilization, especially on the PA-150, I think it might help to keep in mind my concluding message:

while centuries of Catholic colonization may be a source of the enduring authoritarianisms and injustices faced in Amazonia and beyond, common Catholicism and especially the mystic of friendship will be part of how these injustices are confronted and transformed going forward, at least on the PA-150.

To explain how the mystic of friendship might be a useful image to help with mobilization on the PA-150, let us recall the Schmitt-Benjamin debate I explored early in this book. In contrast to Schmitt's aim to legitimate modern authoritarianism by drawing analogies between secular and (baroque) Catholic forms, for Benjamin baroque allegory had a subversive power that Schmitt ignored. Namely, allegorical ways of seeing, including in the baroque period, always contained the potential to delegitimize current sources of power, even while longings for authority, sovereignty, and the status quo might also recur.[3] I have been inspired by Benjamin's insights, though not only because he diagnosed allegory's past. Benjamin has also been helpful because his later work continued to explore how allegory—and especially allegorical images—could shape action in the present.[4] In essence, Benjamin helped me perceive allegory's resonance in my interlocutors' seeing and acting in response to good, evil, and divine justice on earth. And by interlocutors, I of course mean both those who came to settle on the margins of the PA-150 and the organizations that have helped these settlers in their struggle for land, namely the liberationist church and the MST. For example, both have brought modified images from the past into the present to catalyze action, whether from the bible in the case of liberationism or images of past peasant struggles in the case of the MST.

Still, this book has shown that their reflections on relations were limited. Specifically, both liberationists and the MST could have developed more complex, and more locally informed, approaches to relationships, and especially to unity and disunity. That said, in the MST there is recognition of the need to address relations more directly. As in the conversation with Bernardo I quoted in chapter 6, despite the preference for the language of *companheirismo*, "Friendship was still the basis for the unity of the MST. Because where people do not like each other, ideas lose their value. . . . All of the vacillations that we have had until now have been due to ideas losing their quality because people have not been able to make friends *with* their ideas and friendship *out of* their ideas."

Bernardo's insight reflects a sentiment that I have charted in this book: that a certain lack of friendship is felt to be pervasive and considered a challenge for long-term mobilization. Nevertheless, my ethnography has taught me that the answer is not more friendship, not more unity, on their own. I have come to the conclusion that rather than merely assert *more friendship* as the solution to political failures, the mystic of friendship should be added to the repertoire of images that can help sustain mobilization over time.

In fact, emphasizing the mystic of friendship in practice can deepen Benjamin's antiauthoritarian critique of Schmitt and work it into the political present. Recall that a decade after *Political Theology* (1985 [1922]), Schmitt wrote *On the Concept of the Political* (1996 [1932]), yet another manifesto for authoritarian political systems despite Schmitt's claims to objectivity (Ananiadis 1999). In the latter book, Schmitt identified the friend-enemy distinction as the essence of the political. What he meant to achieve by this definition was to disqualify liberal democracy, to depict it as depoliticizing. Indeed, Schmitt felt that the debate and compromise promoted in liberal democracies diluted the political, so his definition showed that the "true political" obtains when groups of (homogeneous, political) friends, essentially under a sovereign, radically oppose themselves to (political) enemies—who they should also be ready to kill.[5] Benjamin never really wrote about friendship, but in his spirit, the mystic of friendship radically complicates Schmitt's model of the political. While the mystic of friendship entails longings for unity (political, social, religious, and otherwise), it also interrogates this unity. More specifically, the mystic of friendship teaches us that the enemy is never only external, it can also potentially be internal, be *us*.[6] At first this might sound like a bad thing, but it isn't necessarily. Rather, the mystic of friendship conveys an important lesson: that unity in practice does not and cannot entail perennial sameness (friendship) in opposition to a perennial otherness (enmity). This does not mean that there are no adversaries, or that communities shouldn't organize around a common cause to fight specific opponents. Instead, it means that any struggle must always work across difference—both within and without. It means that clear friend-enemy distinctions are an authoritarian fiction that can never actually be sustained. Even if such hardened distinctions appear to promote unity against others, they can actually undermine solidarity from within. Instead, true awareness of perennial internal differences is a radical democratic disposition; it implies that achieving unity and solidarity is real work, and even sometimes a struggle. And this is why the mystic of friendship should be cultivated: to remind those struggling for rights that learning how to relate well means being open to divergences. This openness is part of the struggle to create more radically democratic movements, spaces, worlds.

Of course local activists will have to adapt this message to particular local circumstances. Still, they can highlight the positive side of what the *povo* already knows: that differences will always proliferate. At the same time, they might emphasize how difference, or even agonism, *within* a community does not point to that community's fundamental evil or corruption. Instead, these are essential parts of relating—the nature of both the human *and* the divine. In other words, rather than seeking to harden friend-enemy distinctions, activists can draw on the *povo*'s own tradition to contemplate and manage the challenge of difference(s) *inside* communities. To put it in MST/liberationist terms, the mystic of friendship should be seen as a necessary part of *mística*: the practices that build unity for the struggle. Put otherwise still, more emphasis on the possibilities of disunity within solidarity can help communities, movements, and democratic spaces be more flexible and durable over time.

Let me emphasize that, unlike the early twenty-first century politico-philosophical turn to Christianity—especially to St. Paul[7]—I am not arguing that the mystic of friendship will be a mobilizing image for every place and time. My aim has not been to identify a "Christian universalism" to help craft an equally universal secular politics (as in the case of Alain Badiou [2003], for example). I have not even been concerned to assert an essential aspect of "Global Christianity," though admittedly, something like a mystic search for unity and friendship recurs widely, especially in the history of Catholicism globally (Boyarin 2009). Still, it is worth listening to Simon Coleman, who has pointed out that both approaches have their limits, whether the definitional calls of the anthropology of Christianity, or the universalizing impetus of philosophers marshaling Paul (Coleman 2010). My approach has been different. I have developed my arguments over long-term ethnographic research along the PA-150 to reflect and ultimately speak to the concerns of the settlers and their descendants who live there. Still, because these settlers came from elsewhere, and because they also brought various pasts, presents, theologies, and spirits with them to their Amazonian lives, my conclusions can have broader relevance—even beyond Brazil.

In the most general and pragmatic sense, what I have offered is another way to consider and address political conundrums. I have shown that political action in colonized spaces cannot be understood, or sustainably catalyzed, merely by sharing secular histories of the present, whether via accounts of domination and political exclusion, or by diagnoses of the power/knowledge(s) that have formed how people think and live. While some might simply conclude that I have restaged Certeau's critique of Foucault's often totalizing accounts of disciplinary governmental power, my aims, I think, have been more ambitious (Certeau 1984, 1986, 1992).[8] Of course Certeau has been an influence; I have leaned on his historical accounts of *mystics* to support my ethnography, which brings into view that Catholicism has continued to recur while transforming, profoundly shaping the *saudade* for unity among humans and God along the PA-150 (Certeau 1992, 2015). Still, I have parted ways with Certeau's psychoanalytically derived sense that desire is the ground of the human, what some call ontological (Sheldrake 2001; Westerink 2021). Readers may have even noticed that I avoid the term ontology—even in its more recent anthropological incarnations—to avoid its tendency to obscure or minimize the vitality of relations (see Lebner 2017b; Strathern 2012).[9] In other words, while it might be ultimately impossible to achieve, I have tried to avoid any term that I think can inhibit the ethnographic apprehension of the interpersonal and conceptual connections and distinctions that transform lives, especially on the PA-150.

Which brings me to what I *have* been making a case for: that ethnography has real social and political value, especially ethnography that is unafraid to challenge conceptual conventions and divine the present alongside its interlocutors. While I admit that this is partly a response to Foucault's relatively successful bid to assert the primacy of philosophy as a discipline,[10] I also truly think that to craft better ways of living together we cannot rely solely on critiques of governmental or secular political forms, via genealogies, archaeologies, or otherwise. Rather, it is important to remember that attending to the ways that our interlocutors cultivate their relations—in all of their divine and transtemporal uncertainties—can help inspire communities in the present as they mobilize for more radical democratic alternatives, whether they reside far from, or near to, centers of Euro-American knowledge and power.

NOTES

INTRODUCTION

1. To protect privacy, I have changed names and identifying characteristics of all people mentioned in this text, unless they are public figures.
2. Unless otherwise indicated, all translations from Portuguese are mine.
3. There was no "PA-150" proper until 1977, when a 186-kilometer stretch of highway from Marabá to Goianésia was inaugurated. However, the name PA-150 was eventually given to the highway opened around 1971 south of Marabá, which extended in stages 353 kilometers south to Redençao.
4. I spent over two years in Southeast Pará. I first went for six weeks in 2002 to see if research was viable there. I returned to live there in late November 2003, beginning full-time research in 2004 and remaining until July 2005 (19.5 months). I then returned for a series of visits of six to eight weeks each in 2006, 2010, 2012, 2013, and 2015.
5. Today, the Gavião Akrãtikatêjê, Gavião Kykatejê, Gavião Parkatêjê, Guarani, and Guarani Mbya live the closest to the stretch of PA-150 discussed in this book. According to the Instituto Socioambiental, these groups' Indigenous Territory, Mãe Maria, although already "Reserved" (*reservada*) in 1943, was formally approved (*homologada*) in 1986. This Indigenous Territory contains sixty-three thousand hectares, and its largest residential area is some forty kilometers from the city of Marabá, the main population center of the PA-150. As of 2022, the Indigenous Territory had 1302 residents. In 1996, it had 333 residents.
6. For example, Canãa do Carajás, which can only be reached by traveling the PA-150, was the fastest-growing city in Brazil according to the last census—with 189 percent growth (Poder360 2023). Also, the south and southeast of Pará were among the first places singled out for a visit by the new Arns Commission on Human Rights (Agência Brasil 2023). The Arns Commission, founded in 2019, documents and denounces violence and illegal actions taken with impunity in the countryside, which has long been a concern in the region, but worsened during the Bolsonaro years.
7. I want my use of "longing" to include the wide-ranging significance of Portuguese/Brazilian *saudade*, which is why I sometimes leave the word untranslated. *Saudade* has long been deemed unique to Portuguese, and recently made its way into the *Dictionary*

of Untranslatables (Santoro 2014, original French 2004; see also Antunes 1983 on Fernando Pessoa's celebration of the term; and DaMatta 1993 for a Brazilian discussion of its fundamental cultural importance in Brazil). Fernando Santoro (2014, 929) says that *saudade* "proceeds from a memory that wants to renew the present by means of the past in a loving soul that is restrained by the limits of its condition, whatever that might be." Although it is often colloquially said to describe missing relatives and friends, the word isn't always attached to a wish to see a particular human person again, but rather "everything, from literature to religion and politics, is capable of an interpretation modulated by *saudade*" (931). *Saudade* is also not only a mental or emotional state, but can be a physical sensation too: a "tender malaise of a body drawn out by the mind, corporal ecstasy itself" (929). What is especially interesting for our purposes is that the sentiment is traceable to the first texts in Portuguese literature, the *cantigas d'amigo*, "songs or poems of the friend," and that *saudade* as a concept began to spread in the sixteenth century following the loss of King Sebastian in battle. Sebastian's disappearance (rather than sure death) lead to a period of Portuguese subjection to Spanish rule (1580–1640), which saw the development of millenarian hopes that the king would return to save them. In chapter 3, we see that this yearning for the lost king comes to Brazil, mixes with Indigenous and African forms, and profoundly marks common Brazilian Catholicism. According to Santoro, Antônio Vieira's *History of the Future*, which we will encounter in the sixth Visitation, "is the best example" of this kind of redemptive *saudade* (930). It expresses a longing for a Portuguese glory that would also prove God's love. And this brings us to perhaps most important aspect of *saudade* for the purposes of this ethnography: one can also have *saudade* of God, of the transtemporal infinite, even if no living being can truly be said to have completely known this infinite being. This is not just a metaphor for "desire for God," Alfredo Antunes affirms: "In effect, saudade of God can sometimes be characterized as a 'yearning' sentiment . . . but in other [cases, it should be characterized] as saudade-expectation." And the Portuguese poet Teixeira de Pascoaes, Antunes notes, goes even further, by identifying *saudade* of God as the very essence of *saudade*: "Saudade, in the highest sense," he says, "signifies the divine Portuguese tendency for God" (cited in Antunes 1983, 384). I encountered a similar *saudade* along the PA-150, shaded by a sense that other humans, more than God, were a challenge for true unity. For more on why desire isn't quite the appropriate term to use to describe the mystic of friendship, see note 8.

8. In earlier iterations of this ethnography I defined the "mystic of friendship" as a "desire and hope . . . for support and unity within and beyond the family" (Lebner 2021, 477). I have since realized that *desire* is not the right term to describe my interlocutors' dispositions toward friendship or unity. As I have reflected on my time on the PA-150, I have realized that I never actually heard anyone using the term desire (*desejo*). And in fact, one time when I used it with Ina (who we meet in chapter 2), she had clearly never heard or used the word. In response to my use of the word *desejo*, she used *desvejo*, which seemed to mean something closer to envy. Colleagues who work among Northeasterners have also confirmed this: *desejo* is rarely used colloquially in these regions. In addition, desire is a relatively weighty Euro-American term that can smuggle in heavy theoretical (psychoanalytic, post-structuralist) frameworks that might distract

from and misrepresent my ethnography and my interlocutors. (For scholarship on Catholicism that has fruitfully drawn on psychoanalytic and poststructuralist theories of desire, including in Brazil, see Certeau 1986, 1992; Mayblin 2024; Napolitano 2015. Scholars who have studied hope and will in social theory and in Latin America include Ahmed 2014; Bloch 1986 [1959]; Miyazaki 2004; Murphy and Throop 2010; Nuijten 2013; O'Neill 2010). I have thus chosen instead to use the terms *will, hope, want,* and *longing* because they are more straightforward translations of regularly used terms: *vontade, esperança, querer,* and *saudade.* (I sometimes leave the latter term untranslated; see note 7 for discussion of its unique meaning). I am investing in the concept of *mystic,* which requires all these terms, shaded by a sense of their incompletion.

9. In a conversation with Ana Claudia Marques about a version of this argument (probably in 2018), she reminded me that settlement and colonization are driven by many other things besides issues of friendship. She has created fascinating accounts of the roles of families, ancestors, enemies, and friends in the foundation of towns in Pernambuco and Mato Grosso (Marques 2013a, 2013b). I have benefitted greatly from our years of discussion, and drawn much inspiration from her work, including from *Intrigas e Questões,* a book whose descriptions of brittle kinship and friendship resonate with what I encountered along the PA-150 (see also Comerford 2003; and below, note 42). The present book includes religious concerns and what I now call the mystic of friendship, however, because they emerged as an overwhelming concern among the people I worked with in Pará. The disposition that the mystic of friendship captures might also be easily overlooked by scholars, despite interlocutors referring to it, as Claudia Barcellos Rezende suggested when I met her in 2010 (for an example, see Rezende 1999, 82; 2002).

10. I have offered "common Catholicism" to help open up ethnographic understanding. I see it as another way to push against the focus on religious ascetics (joining Mayblin 2017), and to more generally move on from predominant framings of Catholicism. Descriptions of Catholicism as "lived," or "vernacular," have been popular since the 1990s. These terms were meant to 1) cancel the distinction between "popular" and "official religion," 2) relegitimize the use of anthropological/cultural approaches in religious studies, and 3) increase attention to religion in the lives of "individuals" (on the latter point see especially McGuire 2008, 3; Primiano 2022 [1995], 4; see also D. Hall 1997). How scholars have applied the first and the last of these concerns has unwittingly restricted the ethnographic and historical record.

    Regarding the first aim, while I agree that scholars should avoid rendering everyday religion less authentic or worthy of study, the fear of "official religion" expressed by studies of lived religion has often led to the occlusion of orthodoxies and how they can persist within broader shifts. On the third and last point, since a main aim of this book is to recenter relations in the study of religion, I want to avoid the prescribed focus on the individual that I find in the label of "lived religion."

    In essence, my use of "common Catholicism," rather than being the opposite of "official," contains a range of both present and past "official" theologies and practices— including those that have since been discouraged (like pilgrimage) or even relatively repressed (like millenarianism and liberationism). Common Catholicism helps me underscore how faithful people draw on all of these theologies and practices, not only to choose their forms of devotion, but also, through allegory, to understand life situations and relationships. Moreover, avoiding the more individualized assumptions of conventional "lived religion," common Catholicism more closely reflects everyday Catholicism itself. Specifically, it highlights how it is a tradition in which community and relationships are a core value—and a core challenge.

This brings me to another more recent framing that scholars have used to emphasize Catholicism's internal variety: Carl Schmitt's definition of Catholicism as a "complex of opposites" (*complexio oppositorum*) (Abreu 2021; Norget et al. 2017; see also Schmitt 1996 [1923]; Muehlebach 2009). While this does capture some of the complexity at play in Catholicism, it also leaves uncriticized the political aims supported by Schmitt's description: to highlight so as to emulate Catholicism's *political oppositionality*, its creation of (especially external) enemies (Weber 2005). The rubric of *complexio oppositorum* tends to obscure, in other words, the true importance of "unity" in historical Catholicism. Of course, Catholicism has always recognized its internal tensions— including the various "opposed" natures of God. However, what has been most commonly emphasized is their *coming together*. Some, since Nicholas of Cusa, have called this *coincidentia oppositorum* (Webb 2010). I don't wholly embrace this moniker either, but I do want to restore a certain balance for ethnography's sake. Indeed, I want to remind readers of Catholicism's relentless search for the common, for unity, which as I show later in this book has its own, sometimes problematic, implications.

11. Moacir Palmeira and Beatriz Heredia (2009 [1997], 167) were among the first to note an ambivalence toward politics in Northeast Brazil, including due to a sense that it is a "painful" and "unpredictable thing" (*coisa melindrosa*). However, they elaborate little on evil or other Catholic sources of this popular critique of politics, or on what it might mean for ethnographic research and writing more broadly. More recently, Laurie Denyer Willis (2023) has usefully documented that Evangelical *Maranhenses* in Rio de Janeiro are tired of politics and want to avoid it, though she does not address Catholicism. Beyond Brazil, Marisol de la Cadena (2010) and Matei Candea (2011) have pushed on the category of the political to contemplate new ways to write ethnographically in their fields. I write in that spirit, trying to push further by contemplating politics alongside religion and, most importantly, relations.

12. A number of anthropological works discussing aporia, doubt, and (ontological) mistrust resonate with my ethnography (see especially Bubandt 2014; Velho 1995 [1991]). However, my focus on the mystic of friendship begins from the impetus to stay conceptually close to the ethnography, past and present—especially the relational challenges of friendship, kinship, and their divine entailments as my interlocutors put it to me. Much of this introduction is devoted to explaining my conceptual choices. Still, I should note here that before any concerns with "being/ontology" (a problem that arguably even Derrida's aporia keeps in play), my interlocutors grapple with the never-only-social problem of impossibility residing at the heart of relations, which begins with their simultaneous nature as both connection and distinction. On a fuller relational critique of ontology, see Lebner 2016b, 2017a, 2017b. In the acknowledgments I also discuss some reasons why I do not use the language of trust, though here I will add that the

Christianity of my interlocutors reinforced my decision to avoid it. It is true that trust played an important role in the development of Christian belief (see Coleman 2021b; also Lebner 2016b, 246). However, the intimate relation between debates about "trust" and predominant (and secularizing) reflections on "society" meant that trust presented a number of descriptive perils. I am not seeking to affirm that mistrust can serve as the foundation of "society" too (cf. Carey 2017). On important but secular approaches to unity, friendship, and agonism in Brazil, see Comerford 2003; Marques 2002; and note 42 below.

13. See also Webb Keane (2007, 31) on why it is helpful to speak about "Christianity" generally: its common elements, including that faithful recognize a shared tradition despite denominational diversity.

14. An efflorescence of scholarship coincided with the 1970s–1980s (re-)opening of the Amazonian frontier in Brazil. After early discussions of colonization (Hébette and Marin 1977; Ianni 1979; Velho 1972, 1976), colonization as such has been of relatively marginal concern among Brazilianist social scientists. Existing studies of Amazonia, for example, focus largely on the environment, labor, land, and the economy, especially capitalism and its effects (Campbell 2015; Cleary 1990; Esterci 1984, 1987; Geffray 1995; A. Hall 1989; Harris 2000; Hecht and Cockburn 1989; Nugent 1993; Raffles 2003; Schmink and Wood 1992; Velho 1972, 1976).

Among these works, Velho's (1995 [1991]) pathbreaking essay has been inspiring for the present work. Velho explored aspects of Christianity—especially the Beast and questions of evil. Although Velho didn't explore this in relation to colonization per se, he did note that his earlier work on the frontier had ignored religious issues, and he urged students of peasants in Amazonia and across Brazil to pay more attention to the "biblical culture" of peasantries. Scholars have been rather slow to take up this call, especially in southeast Amazonia. One notable study on religion in the region is Rolemberg (2023), which focuses on the regional Pastoral Land Commission activists. For a thorough account of Catholicism in northern Pará (with a very different ethnic composition), see Maués (1995).

15. Jorge Klor de Alva (1992, 1994) presents the most radical and, in my opinion, most problematic of these views. He narrowly sees colonialism as being about European domination; further, he only sees Indigenous peoples of the Americas as being colonized. (He does include African slaves, in a different way, though he doesn't discuss them much). He argues that because mestizos who fought wars of independence identified with Europe, they were not postcolonial. He mentions Brazil, which had a less radical process of independence than other Latin American countries (see above), only in passing. I agree with Coronil's (2008, 405) comprehensive critique, especially with his call to "pluralize" colonialism. That is, we should not assume colonialism has only one narrow definition. I discuss an allied approach articulated by Stoler (2016) below.

16. "Coloniality" is a concept introduced by Aníbal Quijano in the 1980s and early 1990s and later developed by Walter Mignolo and others to name "the underlying logic of the foundation and unfolding of Western civilization from the Renaissance to today of which historical colonialisms have been a constitutive, although downplayed, dimension" (Mignolo 2000; 2011, 2). Although it is necessary to contemplate the role of colo-

nialism, and especially the place of the Americas, in the production of modernity, I concur with Frederick Cooper (2005) that the concept of coloniality can drive us further away from the study of particular colonialisms on the ground. My position is somewhat different, however. I think we should be allowed to remove the assumed scale(s) of colonial governance from our analysis, to see what other relations, practices, and legacies we can find animating colonizations—settlements—on the ground.

17. The call for agrarian reform long predates the MST, a movement which was founded in the Southern Region of Brazil in the mid-1980s. Reasons for calling for agrarian reform in Brazil have changed over time. For example, in the 1950s there were more worries regarding industrialization as compared to today. Still, the demand for reform retains a concern with the inherited structure of land redistribution, which has remained highly unequal since colonial times. The PA-150 is of course recently (re-)colonized, but the point remains: agrarian reform is arguably a call to change the form of land distribution in a country marked by its colonial heritage (Guimarães 1964; Silva 1980).

18. My concern with relations is indebted to the work of Marilyn Strathern, whose scholarship I have written about elsewhere (Lebner 2016a, 2017a, 2017b). I summarize some of the key themes of her complex work in chapter 2 and especially chapter 3.

19. Paul Carter (1987) is an important exception. Carter also wanted to write a history of colonization from the ground up. He aimed to get away specifically from what he called "imperial history": histories that focus on successions of events that narrate how order was established, how places known in the present "came to be." Carter instead sought to write a "spatial history" of Australia, showing how colonial spaces were shaped and experienced through the practices of settlers on the ground. Like other scholars of colonialism, however, Carter ignored religion.

20. Dipesh Chakrabarty's *Provincializing Europe* (2000) was an important early critique of (post)colonial studies' lack of attention to religion, although it didn't transform the field in this regard as much as expected. Of course, Chakrabarty wasn't the first or only scholar to pay attention to religious or spiritual forces (beyond missionization) that animated (post)colonial forms (see especially Chidester 1996; Meyer 1999; Taussig 1987; Worsley 1957; also Mueggler 2001; Van der Veer 2001; Viswanathan 1998). However, Chakrabarty can be credited with specifically *calling out* this lack of attention to religion in (post)colonial studies as well as its cause: how secular universalist thought, specifically Marxism, had epistemologically taken over (post)colonial historical scholarship. Chakrabarty therefore called for "provincializing Europe" because European intellectual traditions are "both indispensable and inadequate in helping us to think through the various life practices that constitute the political and the historical in India" (6). The book had a tremendous impact in anglophone academia and elsewhere, yet neither religion nor its conceptual cognates gained a new and more serious place in the field of (post)colonial studies. While this isn't the place for a full assessment of why that is, I'll suggest two reasons.

First, Chakrabarty's critique was not complete because it still held on to "politics/the political" as a necessary analytical domain. To be sure, his stated aim was to displace developmental and secular understandings of history, which he calls "historicism," and to pluralize understandings of history, time, and the political by making space for gods and spirits to animate them. However, we should recall that perhaps even more than history, "politics" is a major pillar of modern, secular European thought. Therefore, keeping it *necessarily* in place as an analytic, rather than seeing how it appears "ethnographically" among peoples of the present or past, left little chance for truly "provincializing Europe." This is not to say that I think gods and spirits can't be political—of course they can. But holding the political in place *does not allow us to see that it might not always be politics driving contemporary processes.* Without loosening the epistemological grip of the political, the force of other things remain hard to see. Certainly, politics' perennial companion, religion, is eclipsed, and perhaps more crucially, relations are obscured, which interpersonally and conceptually animate the overlaps and distinctions among religion, politics, and their others.

Note that I reject the concept of the "prepolitical," a Marxist-inspired evolutionist term used by Eric Hobsbawm and critiqued by Chakrabarty following Ranajit Guha. However, it should be recognized that only people who are ideologically committed to the traditionally Euro-American idea that politics is the most important force would consider it anathema to explore the analytical implications of *how our interlocutors might reject the label of the political.* What I argue in this book is that our task is also not to merely reverse the terms, and see religion as uniquely causal, but rather to make space for seeing how interpersonal and conceptual relations, which are never only human, produce and are shaped by religious and political discourses. *I underscore that recentering relations is not the same as deeming "the social" causal.*

A second reason that religion has not gained more space within (post)colonial studies is because the anthropology of Christianity, the scholarly initiative that was perhaps best placed to study colonialism and religion within and beyond the mission encounter, has mostly avoided discussion of colonialism. There were reasons for this. Most overtly and understandably, it would seem that they did not want to turn the study of Christianity into a discussion about colonialism. They wanted to focus on what constitutes Christianity. However, the founder of this subfield, Joel Robbins, was also keen to distance the anthropology of Christianity from earlier anthropologists and anthropological historians who had produced major works addressing colonialism and Christianity, especially Jean and John Comaroff (1991; see discussion in Robbins 2007) and Talal Asad (1993). The distancing from Asad is less explicit than the critique of the Comaroffs, but key authors of the subfield do not ascribe to Asad's critique of the category of religion and his translational approach more generally. For other members of the subfield, Asad, despite having written a series of influential essays on Christianity, is not considered an anthropologist of Christianity. But things are changing, if slowly: there are now other anthropologists of Christianity who have begun thinking seriously about how secularity might be lived (though as an effect of secularism); see Cannell 2013; King 2023; Oliphant 2021. Similarly, anthropologists of Christianity have begun turning to the study of (post)colonialism; see Hovland (2013) and Handman (2018).

21. Preliminary results on religion from the 2022 census were released only shortly before I received the proofs for this book. I have updated the figures, but my comments are restricted; see next note.

22. In 1970, 91.8 percent of Brazilians identified as Catholic and 5.2 percent identified as

Evangelical. The 2000 and 2010 censuses documented the astonishing rise of Evangelicalism in Brazil, but the 2022 census shows that Evangelicalism's growth has slowed.
Evangelicals now represent 26.85 percent of the population, and the majority remains
Catholic (at 56.75 percent). As of July 2025, the 2022 data on religion in Southeast Pará
had not been released (Alves 2022; IBGE 2022; Madeiro 2022; O Liberal 2025).

23. Eamon Duffy (2016) sums up Bossy's argument's well:

> The central contention of Bossy's short but scintillating *Christianity in the West* was
> that medieval Christianity had been fundamentally concerned with the creation and
> maintenance of peace in a violent world. "Christianity" in medieval Europe denoted
> neither an ideology nor an institution, but a community of believers whose religious
> ideal—constantly aspired to if seldom attained—was peace and mutual love. The
> sacraments and sacramentals of the medieval Church were not half-pagan magic,
> but instruments of the "social miracle," rituals designed to defuse hostility and create
> extended networks of fraternity, spiritual "kith and kin," by reconciling enemies and
> consolidating the community in charity.

24. Things might have been very different had Foucault's *Confessions of the Flesh* been
published earlier. Indeed, *Confessions*, volume 4 in Foucault's *History of Sexuality* series,
is a sustained attempt to address the role of early Christianity in the eventual modern
emergence of (desiring) Man. Had Foucault's executors decided to publish it immediately despite Foucault's ban on posthumous publications—apparently it was completed
shortly before his death—one can imagine that it would have inspired more interest in
Christianity as an important part of the genealogy of modern governance, sexuality,
and the individual. As it stands, *Confessions*' intellectual impact has yet to be absorbed.

25. Asad (1993, 2003) argued that religion was not always and everywhere an autonomous
domain distinct from politics. Rather, he showed that this notion emerged from Christian history, was produced by forces of power/knowledge, and was then enshrined and
enforced in predominant forms of secularism.

26. Strathern has perhaps only cited Benjamin once—in *Property, Substance, and Effect*
(1999). While there she quotes directly only from Benjamin's "Storyteller" essay, she
cites all of *Illuminations* (W. Benjamin 1969) in the bibliography, implying an engagement with the whole work, which contains some of Benjamin's most important later
thinking on images, including *On the Concept of History*. Recall that Benjamin's reflections on images entail an interrogation of conventional historical writing, an aim
that Strathern shares in her own discussion of images. While I cannot compare their
approaches here at length, note that I have borrowed from Strathern a focus on the relations that compose images. Centering the relations animating images helps elucidate
the practice of allegory, including its implications for what I have called the divining
person.

27. In this book, I use *baroque* and *early modern* interchangeably—baroque is not just a
term for an artistic movement, but can be used to characterize a sensibility, a form of
worldmaking that dominated the early modern period in Europe and shaped the representatives leading its global extensions. Still, I also acknowledge that baroque sensibili-

ties are not wholly of the past. It is widely known that Benjamin's unfinished Arcades Project (1999) was going to explore questions of allegory, especially through the works of Charles Baudelaire and the culture of nineteenth-century capitalism in Paris. Thus Benjamin was going to develop a connection between the Arcades and his early work on allegorical baroque drama (W. Benjamin 1994, 2006, 2019). Such a connection is arguably visible even in with his more famous late works as well (W. Benjamin 2003a, which I discuss below). Since Benjamin, many other scholars have explored the possibility of baroque dispositions in the modern period both in Brazil and elsewhere, though rarely with explicit discussions of Christianity (Corsín-Jiménez 2013; Deleuze 1993; Law and Ruppert 2016; see especially Port 2011; and note 30 below).

28. Among scholars of (post)colonial literature in the 1980s, there was a spate of interest in allegory as a literary form, rather than a religious practice (Slemon 1988). The historian Thomas Scanlan drew on this interest in his history of British colonization of North America (1999). Although this book *does* contemplate religion, in this case Protestantism, he writes about it as an identity rather than as a theology or practice. He sees descriptions of British Protestant colonization as distinct from Spanish Catholic colonization and largely as an allegory for an emerging British national identity.

29. *The Origin of German Tragic Drama* (W. Benjamin 2003b) was recently retranslated as *Origin of the German Trauerspiel* (W. Benjamin 2019). I quote from both translations in this introduction.

30. Mathijs van de Port (2011) made a significant contribution to discussions of allegory and baroque sensibilities in the study of contemporary Brazil. I build especially on his claims that Afro-Brazilian religions (he studied Candomblé in Bahia) rely on allegory. However, he mostly sidelines Catholicism, which is vital for understanding allegory in general and arguably for grasping Afro-Brazilian religions as well. Renata Menezes (2022), also a scholar of Brazil, mentions the open-ended allegorical narratives entailed by objects used in carnival, which sometimes have a religious origin.

31. Notable of course is Talal Asad's (1983, 1993) early critique of Geertz's symbolic anthropology, which he showed to be unwittingly entwined with a modern Christian definition of religion. Religion in this approach was assumed to be inherently and symbolically meaningful, generative of belief, and autonomous from power and politics (Asad 1983, 1993, 2003). The critique of the symbolic made space for a series of other approaches: from studies of practice, the body, and mediation, to politics, ethics, secularism and the focus on materiality.

32. Romantics deemed allegory to have dominated medieval literature and art; specifically, they thought it was "mere convention, inauthentic, not grounded in experience, cut off from being and concerned only with manipulating its repertoire of signs" (Cowan 1981, 111). Romantics then conceived of symbols as autonomous totalities that could offer direct access to truth, beauty, and the transcendent. Benjamin maintained, however, that the symbol was a product of a desire for clarity that emerged from the more anxious post-Reformation condition that had transformed allegory and made it vital to modernity (see below).

33. A healthy number of scholars have either sought to work creatively with Benjamin's concept of image or tried to imagine what a completed Arcades Project might have

looked like (to cite just a handful: Buck-Morss 1990; Jennings 1987; Stevenson 2014; Taussig 1987; Weigel 2013). With few exceptions, however, these scholars have rarely engaged much with *Origin*. Most notably, few have absorbed how *Origin* informed the allegorical-theological aspects of his interventions (W. Benjamin 1994).

34. Given that Germany was the epicenter of the Reformation, German *Trauerspiel* and allegorical sensibilities were more fretful there than in other places, for example in the Iberian peninsula, where Catholic kingdoms remained more stable. Nevertheless, as Howard Eiland notes in his introduction to his new translation (W. Benjamin 2019, xi–xxvi), Benjamin affirmed that the theater of Pedro Calderón de la Barca in Spain could also be considered *Trauerspiel*, in part because it was also responding to the Reformation. However, Benjamin also noted that Spanish allegorical plays were less "responsible" because they "dissimulated [regarding] the desolation of [their] historical moment" (Camps 2023, 687).

35. Benjamin called emblem books "the authentic documents of the modern allegorical mode of perception" (2019, 169), writing that these books pointed to how allegory "established itself in every field of spiritual activity . . . from theology, the study of nature, and morality, down to heraldry, occasional poetry, and the language of love" (W. Benjamin 2003b, 172–3; see also McCole 1993, 134).

36. More has actually been written on how the shift in meaning of the *corpus mysticum* in the twelfth century created the ruptures between the Eucharist and the Church that led to the Reformation and other modern crises. There are classic analyses by Henri de Lubac (2006 [1944]), Ernst Kantorowicz (2016 [1957]), and Michel de Certeau (1992) (and see a brilliant discussion by Rust 2014). Yet Jennifer Garrison (2017) has been unique among commentators for noting that, as a result of changes in the meaning of the mystical body, *allegorical thinking had already begun to intensify before the Reformation*. This statement qualifies Benjamin's description of a rupture between distinct medieval and baroque periods, but it also reinforces it, implying that the more serious rupture of the Reformation may have had even more radical allegorical and social effects.

37. To acknowledge the enslaved isn't a contradiction: in the mystical body of Christ, every member had their place in the hierarchy.

38. Cardim (1999) does not mention the mystical body, and one can read his piece as an example of how early modern scholarship has, until recently, tended to cordon off religion from the social, economic, and political spheres.

39. We should also remember that the Jesuits were at the center of this. Jesuits were among the most prolific producers of emblems, rituals, and performative practices promoting unity not only in Europe, but in colonies like Portuguese America, where they led evangelizing missions until their expulsion in 1759 (Daly and Dimler 2016).

40. Although from the eighteenth century the church became more formally juridical than mystical (Ratzinger 1972), as noted earlier, the Brazilian church was influenced relatively little by reforming trends originating in Europe until after the 1889 proclamation of the Brazilian Republic. The Brazilian church's isolation until the Republic is generally regarded as an effect of the *Padroado* regime. The *Padroado* was awarded by the Vatican to the Portuguese and Spanish crowns in the mid-fifteenth century, giving them the

extraordinary right to control the church in their overseas dominions. In practice this meant that the disciplinary powers of the church were subordinated to the needs of the crown, and generally kept "weak" (Azzi 1978).

41. See William Cavanaugh (1998, 209). Overtly, these two theological moments seemed very different. To start, following Cavanaugh it can be argued that early modern mystical body theologies were invoked by churches with "no intention of abandoning temporal space" (220). This was the opposite to what was happening in the early twentieth century, when temporal space had been definitively lost by the church, and the idea of a "New Christendom" was being embraced in Europe and Latin America. New Christendom focused precisely on securing the spiritual plane, leaving the temporal/political planes to the state. There were resonances, however, across the centuries. As Cavanaugh has affirmed, "the doctrine of the mystical body is, in both cases, a plea for trans-political unity under the Pope's guidance in a world where a certain political and social unity fostered by the church was being torn asunder by nationalism and statism" (220).

42. My account resonates with important works on kinship, friendship, and agonistic sociality in rural Brazil. Many focus on their political and secular elements (Comerford 1999; Comerford et al. 2015; Marques 2002, 2013a; Marques and Leal 2018; Rebhun 1999; Villela 2004, 2009). And while John Comerford (2003) usefully explores languages of agonism and unity in Syndicates and Ecclesial Base Communities, he focuses little on theology and religiosity. Fennella Cannell (2005) has noted that this more secular perspective is a fixture of anthropological approaches to kinship, especially in Christian contexts. Yet Maya Mayblin's (2010, 2012) and Renata Menezes's (2004) respective works on conjugality in Brazil's Northeast and Catholic "sociability" in a Rio convent have offered special stimulus. And Mayblin's evocation of the "doleful abyss" between human and divine (Sahlins 1996) reflects a growing acknowledgment of oppositions animating Catholicism (Norget et al. 2017). Otávio Velho (1995), João Pina-Cabral (2007), and Aaron Ansell (2014) have proved especially inspiring with their discussions of evil, often elided in academic discussions. My focus on the flows and problems of relations (kinship/friendship) and their entwining with divine and evil forces within an intensifying secularity (see below) hopefully adds to our perspectives on current transformations in Brazil. More recent work on Christianity and spiritual kinship and friendship has also been inspiring (Kaell 2020; Moore 2021; Thomas et al. 2017; Thomas 2021).

43. Certeau wanted to distinguish his history from the theological "return to the sources" of Lubac. For this reason, despite its obvious relevance, Certeau used the term *corpus mysticum* only a handful of times and then as essentially a synonym for "the *missing* body"—certainly not as Lubac intended. Although Certeau was, like Lubac, a Jesuit, by the time *The Mystic Fable* was published he had become an overtly secular scholar. Lubac, in contrast, was a theologian and had returned to early medieval discussions precisely to *recapture* for twentieth-century Catholics the spirit of *corpus mysticum*—the sense of dynamic unity between the community of faithful and the Eucharist (Grumett 2011; Rust 2014). Lubac claims that this unity between community and Eucharist had progressively waned after the Eucharist was designated the *corpus verum*, the "real

body," in the twelfth century, banishing the church to a more mystical and less real connection to Christ. Certeau didn't disagree with this part of Lubac's argument, but he did bury the importance of *corpus mysticum* after the Reformation. That Certeau's work was felt to be critical of Lubac is confirmed by Certeau's biographer, who notes that Lubac considered Certeau's work to have been set against his own life's project (Dosse 2002).

44. Igor Rolemberg has also noted that *mística*, as a certain form of spirituality, operates as an animating force among church activists employed in the Pastoral Land Commission (CPT). However, it should be underscored that the CPT does not only employ clergy or strict Catholics—and it also produces the secular (Rolemberg 2020). The shared MST and CPT term comes from the shared history of the progressive church and the MST. Still, the meanings of *mística* are different. See chapter 5, especially note 12.

45. Mysticism, Smith writes, is "far too generic . . . a term to convey the historical specificity [of Certeau's study]" (Certeau 1992, ix–x).

46. What I mean when I say that Certeau's *mystics* is analogous to settlers' relational concerns is this: *mystics* seemed to describe the precarious desire for friendship in southeast Pará even when I bracketed its historic conditions and content. Indeed, what resonates between them in the abstract is that, like Certeau's *mystics*-as-practice, my interlocutors in Pará also express a paradoxical and ineffable "intuition of the absolute" that takes place at a non-place—or at least at a place of union that is inaccessible, endlessly sought rather than definitively found (Certeau 2015, 20). Most importantly, they share a "strange 'historicity'" because "*mystics* does not have its own content: it is an exercise of the other in relation to a given site" (21, 22). Thus, Certeau emphasizes that even the disappearance of *mystics* as a distinct science by the eighteenth century does not consign it to failure or to the past. Instead, Certeau notes that the desire for the other "continues to reappear" (20).

47. It is well known that Certeau's study of *mystics* saw desire as a driving force—especially desire for the absent body (Sheldrake 2001). However, given his more psychoanalytic leanings, Certeau tended to see desire as a universal-ontological energy grounded in lack, not necessarily something uniquely bound up with Catholicism (Westerink 2021). As I mention briefly in note 8, above, anthropologists of Catholicism have begun exploring questions of desire, extending Valentina Napolitano's (2015) part-psychoanalytic and part-Deleuzian notion of institutional Catholicism as a "passionate machine" that seeks to both produce and govern the passions/affects through governmental and material forms (Mayblin 2024; Oliphant 2019).

48. The description of secularization preceding secularism put José Csanova's (1994) argument in check (see Lebner 2019 [2018]).

49. Of course many have focused on religions going public (Meyer 2009; Hirschkind 2006). Yet the attention to secularism seems to eclipse many relations beyond religion that have been consigned to the private sphere.

50. I adopt the "flow of relations" from Marilyn Strathern (2017a, 2020), who suggests seeing kinship and friendship as being "cut out" from this flow. In contrast, scholars have often tried to establish friendship as a distinct area of study, in much the same way as kinship has been made into a distinct realm (Bell and Coleman 1999; Desai and Killick

2010; Simoni and Throop 2014). One result has been that, like kinship, friendship is rarely described in light of religion or cosmology, especially outside Indigenous worlds. While this has recently begun to change, I maintain that it is fruitful to take the less restricted approach suggested by Strathern: one might explore modern kinship and friendship as they emerge out of the flows of relations—as they are practiced alongside one another—making cosmologies and analogies newly visible, transforming what we know of each. Also note that Strathern distinguishes medieval kinship-friendship from the epistemologically transformed kinship and friendship of the seventeenth century. She is careful not to call for a continuous "history of friendship."

51. If Taylor's secularity refers to conditions of belief, my own is grounded, first, *in persons in relation who are living with secularization.* For me, secularization entails the emergent possibility of motile distinctions from, including multiplications of, religion. In an earlier article I focus on the secularizing distinction of politics from religion (Lebner 2019). Here I expand further on this to show how a more autonomous politics emerged with the diversification of religions out of a thoroughly relational Catholicism.

52. While Lambek (2013) helpfully identifies secularism's struggle to contain the excess of kinship, only Cannell's essay "The Re-enchantment of Kinship" (McKinnon and Cannell 2013) uses ethnography to address the secular, with an argument about kinship's religious character in the United States.

53. I necessarily highlight friendship, conventionally understood as a voluntary and sentimental connection between persons, though not because it is the modern relationship par excellence. Certainly this predominant history of friendship is important to keep in mind—friendship's very distinctiveness was made possible by the emergence of contract (Silver 1990). Yet the rise of friendship in modernity is not the only story to tell. Some argue that it has declined, or not yet even arrived (see Bray 2004 and Foucault 1997). Here I focus on the fact that, although kinship can often be distinguished from friendship, their respective roles also continue to overlap: kin can be friends, friends can become kin, and most importantly, the mystic of friendship, its oft-cited instability, also operates in kinship.

54. I join the recent calls of Constance Furey (2012, 2017) and Brenna Moore (2015, 2021) to focus on relations in the study of religion (also Bush 2020; Dağtaş 2025). In chapter 3, I discuss how my contribution builds specifically on the work of Marilyn Strathern.

55. Perhaps the easiest way to exemplify this is to note that 55.91 percent of the (heavily African descended) electorate in Marabá, the largest city on the PA-150, voted for the racist Christian populism of Jair Bolsonaro in 2018 (Eleições 2018). As friends in Pará told me when we spoke on the phone, people voted in part because they didn't see themselves as targets of the anti-Black statements of Bolsonaro and his ilk. If racism was considered at all, it tended to be thought of as a problem for people whom voters saw as ("truly") Black.

56. Simon Coleman has been an exception, consistently studying pilgrimage to understand social phenomena beyond it (Coleman and Eade 2004; Coleman 2021a).

FIRST VISITATION

1. These are excerpts from a "Testament" written in 1985 and held in the São João Batista Parish Archives (Jacundá, Pará). See the image of the first page, above. The signature in the church daybook, the *Livro Tombo*, is illegible, though the person who wrote the testament is likely Padre Paulo Joanil da Silva, who was a major force in the region until 1986, when he was moved to another diocese.
2. This is a reference to Dorothy Stang, an American-born nun who arrived in Brazil in 1966 and who stayed and supported land and environmental struggles in the region from the 1970s until her murder in the town of Anapú on February 12, 2005 (393 kilometers east of Jacundá), which fell during the main period of this research. Her murder was widely mourned and condemned across the region.

CHAPTER ONE

1. In August and September, Weather Spark (2024) suggests averages of highs in the mid-90s for Marabá, though while I lived there, I never felt that weather was particularly well-recorded.
2. I concur with Cécile Fromont and Michael Iyanaga (2021, 4–5) when they say that that views of Christianity "as a thin veneer over deeper, non-Christian [African and African-American] allegiances are inaccurate or at least lack nuance."
3. Beatriz Santos's book is specifically about the Corpus Christi procession; however, it is crucial to note that it served as a "model" for all other public processions in Brazil (Santos 2005, 33). This meant that while Corpus Christi was supposed to be the grandest festival of all, all official public forms of Catholic devotion had similar form and significance, whether they paraded the Eucharist or not.
4. Anthropologists have rightly criticized DaMatta for generalizing about "Brazil." In fact, some no longer engage with his work at all because of its flaws in this regard. Still, DaMatta's work has had broad resonance and influence, and my aim here is to show how Catholicism, including baroque forms, profoundly elucidates and transforms his perspective, even while I write about a particular place and time. I will hopefully invite more attention to Catholicism in specific and located social studies across the country.
5. While DaMatta does mention Catholicism occasionally, it is subordinated to a secular reading of personhood and processions, which tend to be over-generalized to "Brazil." That is, DaMatta neither pays attention to Catholicism on its own terms, nor studies how it resonates in and shapes relationships and politics—an approach I am pursuing here.
6. For an account of my meeting with Velho, see the acknowledgments, where I also mention some reasons why I do not use the analytic of "mistrust." See also introduction, note 12. It is interesting that Velho qualifies this mistrust as "ontological" (significantly predating the recent popularity it has acquired in anglophone and francophone anthro-

pologies). On my own wariness of the concept of ontology, see epilogue, note 9; and Lebner (2017b).

7. Instead, DaMatta draws on literary scholar Antônio Cândido's "Dialectic of the Rogue" (1970), which made a silent, unmarked concession to baroque influence after he famously excluded the baroque from his monumental study *The Formation of Brazilian Literature* (see Cândido 1959; Campos 2007 [1989]).

8. Despite critiques of DaMatta's overgeneralizing (see also introduction, note 4) his cast of characters still ring true in many corners of Brazil—especially the rogue, the martyr, and the ruling hierarchical superior imposing his authority and privilege.

9. What was called the Burgo de Itacayunas was settled by some one hundred families in 1895, close to today's Marabá. The settlement was originally dedicated to agriculture and livestock, but within about two years rubber trees had been discovered in the region and the "Burgo" began to dissolve (Mattos 1996). Marabá became a city in 1913 and its settlement concentrated near the confluence of the Tocantins and Itacayunas rivers. "New Marabá" and "New City" were conceived in the wake of a massive flood of Old Marabá in the mid-1970s that left 80 percent of its buildings underwater. As of the early 1980s, however, with slow building of these nuclei, people started spontaneously organizing to occupy land to build neighborhoods (Cardoso 2010).

10. Marabá had a campus of the Federal University of Pará that was transformed into a campus of the Federal University of South and Southeast Pará, UNIFESSPA, in 2013.

11. The ambivalence of the church might be one reason why the term *romaria* was used, as opposed to the traditional Portuguese word for pilgrimage, *peregrinação*. In fact, *romaria*, which does not have a direct translation into English, evokes (a more orderly) procession, even though it can mean pilgrimage, too.

12. Still, pilgrimage has been a worry—even processions have been worries. The early modern Portuguese church and its iteration in the Americas placed increasing attention on processions, though as with pilgrimage, they sought to exert increasing control over them, precisely in order to monitor their religious content (Sanchis 1983).

13. Various shrines are sometimes visited by pilgrims as part of a larger cycle of journeys (Steil 1996, 201), like the Bom Jesus da Lapa shrine (Good Jesus of Lapa) in Bahia, the Divino Pai-Eterno shrine (Eternal Divine Father) in Goiás, or Marian shrines like the Círio de Nazaré in northern Pará, whose feast has begun to be celebrated in Marabá, and Nossa Senhora da Conceição Aparecida (Our Lady of the Immaculate Conception, Aparecida, the national patron saint, in São Paulo state).

14. These letters are of the liberationist period, but neither quite reflect it in conventional form—and are in fact closer to the language I found today among my interlocutors. Indeed, liberationists discussed evil relatively rarely (see chapter 4)—in part because of those same modernizing tendencies mentioned above. Moreover, rather than friendship, liberationism tended to promote unity alongside relations of *companheirismo*, brotherhood, and especially the powerful allegorical image of the "people of God." Yet in these two letters, we see invocations of Lucifer and of friendship.

15. Goianésia has only 28,853 residents, compared with Marabá's 287,664.

16. And most Catholics still knew about how a Protestant pastor, named Sérgio Von Helder, kicked the national patron saint on live television back in 1995. Helder's attempt

to prove that Aparecida was nothing more than plaster was not enough to displace the faith of all Catholics; most saw no reason to abandon the religion of their parents and ancestors.

17. On conflict versus communitas, see Eade and Sallnow (1991). See also the earlier Durkheimian-Marxist approach in Gross (1971; echoed by Greenfield 1990 and Lanna 1995). See my discussion in Lebner (2012).

18. Although dust can be found on every unpaved path throughout the year in both rural and urban areas in the region, it rises more freely in the summer months (June to October), when it might not rain for a week at a time or more.

19. *Brega* is a relatively new genre of music popular in Amazonia. It combines romantic themes (hence the name, which means, literally, "cheesy" or "bad taste") and electronic music. *Forró* is both the name of a dance and its musical accompaniment, which became popular in Brazil's northeast. It is often played during the June saints' festivals, especially during São João (St. John's Day), which is on June 24 each year. *Música sertaneja*, the Brazilian equivalent of country music, employs rural/cowboy references and romantic crooning.

20. Alan Kardec was the nom de plume of Hippolyte Léon Denizard Rivail (1804–1969), the founder of Spiritism in France. Spiritism was a practice that focused on communications with spirits and is now a religion in Brazil (Hess 1991). This European Spiritism has influenced other practices as well, including Afro-Brazilian practices, and adepts of the latter in southeast Pará often called what they did "Spiritism." "Afro-Brazilian religions" is what scholars often call them.

21. The elision of the concept of sin in everyday talk may be due to the liberationist Catholicism that predominated in the region until the 1980s; see chapter 4.

22. By the 2006 pilgrimage the shrine had been painted yellow. The photograph of the blue shrine was taken in 2004.

23. Goianésia is part of the diocese of Marabá (Diocese Marabá 2024), as are all the towns that appear in this book.

24. Aragão's residence was only discovered after it was learned that he had hired two hitmen to murder the notary of the State Ministry of Security, Carlos Alberto Alves da Rocha. The captured hitmen, angered by not having been informed that they were hired to kill an official, revealed Aragão's location. Since he had escaped from prison, Aragão had vowed that he would never be taken prisoner again, and if the police wanted him they would have to kill him. When the police arrived at the Tinigu farm outside of Santarém where he was living incognito and announced his prison order, he began shooting. The police shot back, and the "supergunman" Aragão was "liquidated with 40 shots" (O Liberal 1990).

25. Martel (2009) and Thiem (2013), for example, both focus on Benjamin's "eschatology."

26. Benjamin was developing the concept of dialectical images in the late 1930s, when he wrote *On the Concept of History*. It was never completed, but still, as part of his Arcades Project, which looped back to his work in *Origin*, the concept was very much connected to Benjamin's thinking on allegory and images (W. Benjamin 1985; see also W. Benjamin 1994).

SECOND VISITATION

1. From an interview with Lilia Solanha, fifty-four years old, Marabá, 2006.

CHAPTER TWO

1. I discuss common Catholicism more in the introduction and chapter 1.
2. Brazilianists have produced important work on religious pluralism (Burdick 1993; Giumbelli 2002; Montero 2006; Selka 2010; Shapiro 2016). I add here a focus on how persons in relation negotiate Catholicism, politics and the possibility of unbelief, all of which are vital for understanding Brazilian secularity.
3. On "Black invisibility, see Sullivan (2017, 131) and the introduction. The self-conscious search for "Africanity" and Blackness is a relatively recent phenomenon, including its relationship to religion. Brazilianists who study Bahia, one of the most "African" regions of Brazil, have even made this point (Port 2005; see also Palmié 2012 on Cuba). That said, the fact that "Afro-Brazilian" religion was not a key concern among my Paraense interlocutors (even as they might embrace practices that scholars categorize in this way), does not mean they will not *become* concerned with race or Africanity.
4. See Strathern (2017a, 2020) and the introduction, note 50.
5. In the wake of David Schneider's critique of "kinship" at least two things happened: there was an initial decline of interest in kinship, followed by attempts to rehabilitate interest by relabeling the field—the discussion of "relatedness" being one example (Carsten 2000). However, following Strathern, I acknowledge that we can never entirely get away from our own languages of description, so the issue is not with avoiding "kinship" or "friendship" per se (Strathern 2017; Lebner 2016a, 2017a). Rather, ethnographically the task is to remain aware and describe how specific relationships are classified and negotiated. In the context described here, "friendship"—a relationship of help—is sought and lamented both inside and outside the family. In the conclusion I discuss how a focus on relations, both conceptual and interpersonal, is as much a political as it is an ethnographic task. Moreover, it should become clear that there is no "politics" without interpersonal and conceptual relations to sustain it.
6. Many Euro-American languages make it difficult to describe how relationships might be *constituted* by what we call religion, rather than separate from it (see Bakker Kellogg 2019).
7. I bring up unbelief carefully: like belief, unbelief is difficult to ascertain, perhaps even impossible. João's story helps us see that secularity in Pará entails negotiations with the *possibility* of unbelief, which is a byproduct of the distinction between religion and other domains, such as politics.
8. Little attention has been given to brotherhood in the anthropology of Christianity and Catholicism, despite its importance across mainline denominations (see especially

Ratzinger 1993 [1960/66], which helped establish him as an important theologian). Valuable discussions of spiritual kinship appear in Thomas, Malik, and Wellman (2017), focusing on Abrahamic religions (see also Thomas 2021), though they focus little on Catholicism or secularity as such.

9. As mentioned in the introduction, there was relative continuity in Brazilian Catholicism until the late twentieth century. For this reason, the Catholicism of the masses, especially in the interior, retained much of its pre-Republican, "unreformed" character, historically mixed with African and Indigenous traditions. Moreover, even in the atmosphere of increased religious freedom that the Republic allowed, the only way to seek legitimacy for any practice continued to be to translate it into the "universal language" of Catholicism (i.e. not "secularism"; Montero 2006, 61). See more discussion in the conclusion.

10. See Bell and Coleman (1999); Desai and Killick (2010); Simoni and Throop (2014); and discussion in Strathern (2017a).

11. See Konstan (1996); Lebner (2012). This historic issue is visible in the Easter Fraternity Campaign liturgies, where Jesus is identified with "fraternity" and Caesar is identified with "friendship" (Campanha da Fraternidade 1986, 59). Still, of course, there is a slippage in everyday life, where brotherhood should contain friendship.

12. See also Lebner (2020).

13. It is interesting to note that Lévi-Strauss primed anthropologists long ago on the impossibility at the heart of knowledge and life—even of history—when he said that less socially interested historians tend to model "a confused outline of Gödel's theorem in the clay of 'becoming'" (1966, 262). Here, Lévi-Strauss was not *opposed* to history as such; he was critiquing history in its ideological forms, questioning the history of those like Sartre (whom he was debating) who assume that history has an end, a linear logic, that is embodied in the Western understanding of progress. By recalling Gödel's theorem of incompleteness, which holds that even in complete systems some things will remain impossible to prove, Lévi-Strauss was reminding us that while it is impossible to *know* everything, the very existence of impossibility means that things can change. An encounter with impossibility—an event at the limit of classification—provokes a necessary response: the production of further classifications; the proliferation of differences, resulting in transformation. Before poststructuralism proper, then, impossibilities, perennial encounters with difference, were at the heart of Lévi-Strauss's thinking on history (Keck 2009; Johnson 2013).

THIRD VISITATION

1. From an interview with Antônio Comarinho, forty years old, Marabá, 2015.

CHAPTER THREE

---

1. Cleusa's account comes from the period before the 1970 Plan for National Integration (the Programa de Integração Nacional, "PIN") started building highways to better connect the Amazon to the rest of Brazil. From the 1920s to the 1970s, Brazil-nut harvesting ran the local economy. It is decidedly true that some Brazil-nut groves were appropriated by powerful families, including from Indigenous peoples, once the Brazil-nut trade got underway following the decline of rubber in the 1910s. In addition to outright appropriation, groves were also purchased and leased (*arrendado*) from the state and municipality. In fact, sometimes appropriation was supported by the state so that businessman could take on a lease, as in the case when Nagib Mutran appropriated groves held by the Gavião Indigenous people in 1936 (Emmi 1999, 91). The Mutran family remain a powerful force in the southeast of Pará, having survived the new capitalist interests and political economic transformations that came with the building of the highways.

2. Slater's own classic monograph mentions religion sparingly (1982). Besides literary concerns, studies of *cordel* often focus on politico-historical issues (Arantes 1982; Curran 1998).

3. Grusin aims to "substitute mediation for [William] James' relation . . . to insis[t] upon an immediacy [of mediation] that . . . disrupts experienced relations" (2015, 128).

4. Although Latour is credited with challenging the modern distinction between subjects and objects, he can also be seen as multiplying individuals: subjects as much as objects are given agency and, though their networks are important, relations are more like intermediaries between mediators. A mediator, for Latour, "is an original event; and creates what it translates as well as the entities between which it plays the mediating role" (1993, 77–78). Compare this to the relation or intermediary for Latour, which "simply transports, transfers . . . is void in itself" (Latour 1993, 77–78). See Strathern (2020, 173).

5. Beyond Orsi, monographs on Catholicism in religious studies that have attended to interpersonal relations as a way to help speak to their main theoretical concerns include Nabhan-Warren (2005) and Castañeda-Liles (2018). See also J. Scheper-Hughes (2010) and Peña (2011) for discussions of intimacy, materiality, affect, and space.

6. The anthropologist Maya Mayblin's (2010) ethnography of marriage and the constitution of family among Catholics in Northeast Brazil, which rethinks gender, personhood, and morality, deserves a wide readership among scholars interested in developing more relationally minded descriptions in religious studies. Mayblin speaks little of the devil, however, because her interlocutors either rarely mentioned him, or were loath to do so. On shifting attitudes to the devil in Catholicism, see also the conclusion to this chapter.

7. In a debate with Charles Hirschkind (2011), who critiqued some Protestant aspects of the media turn, Matthew Engelke (2011a) responded that a focus on mediation as religion, stemming from the work of Hent de Vries, was actually more "Catholic." However, note that this does not escape the reification of another Protestant assumption, that Catholicism is defined by material mediation. Maria José de Abreu's (2021)

ethnography of Charismatic Brazilian Catholics extended Hirschkind's critique in
another way. Without referring explicitly to Engelke's response, Abreu also expressed
reservations about the analytic of mediation. She ultimately displaces mediation in her
own ethnographic context because "it is not Christological enough" (12).

8. Science studies scholars and allied researchers have regularly drawn on Strathern,
although they have generally assimilated her to a Latourian-like approach, whether in
discussions of ontology or otherwise (Lebner 2017b).

9. Some studies of religion and media explicitly state their interest in politics (Hirschkind
and Larkin 2008; Stolow 2005), but it is implicit in many others, as religion and media
research is deemed relevant in part *because* of its perceived political effects.

10. And the push against mediation has continued. See also Bruno Reinhardt (2020); Maria
José de Abreu (2021); note 7, this chapter, above.

11. For example, Birgit Meyer (2011) has usefully called on scholars of mediation to attend
to when the medium appears and disappears, but such an approach still presumes and
begins from "a" medium. Instead, I am suggesting we take seriously what it means to
be unable to know *what* or *who* the medium is.

12. *Cordel* were also printed with arresting covers to attract even illiterate patrons.

13. The casa Rui Barbosa, which hosts a digital archive of *cordel*, including of Barros's
cordel, classes "The Migrant" with Atayde's name under the section "Poemas inéditos e
não inéditos de Leandro Gomes de Barros" (Unpublished and not unpublished poems
by Leandro Gomes de Barros), https://app.docvirt.com/ruicordel/pageid/1958.

14. The conditions of Barros's death are debated. According to some sources, his death
certificate records "aneurysm" as the cause of death. Another account, by Permínio
Ásfora in the *Diário da Noite* of Recife in December of 1949, said that a poem of Barros's
landed him in jail, where he died of "humiliation." This poem purportedly celebrated
the revenge of a worker on the owner of a plantation. Ruth Terra (1983) contests various aspects of these accounts and claims to have spoken to his family, who published
an obituary that notes that he died in his home. Other accounts also conjecture that
his death was due to Spanish flu or a long-term illness (see discussion in Acorda 2017;
Terra 1983).

15. Popular from the sixteenth century in Portugal, chapbooks probably arrived in Brazil
with the first Portuguese settlers, but there is only evidence of them in Brazil in the
mid-nineteenth century (Slater 1982).

16. The lack of study means the actual number of works Barros published is still up for
debate, with the *Brazilian Academy of Cordel Literature* estimating that he published
around a thousand pamphlets, alongside more common estimates of around 240 *cordel*
(R. Benjamin 2020).

17. This *cordel* was printed without capitalizations of the first words of each line, unlike the
other two.

18. "Where the devil lost his spur" (*onde o diabo perdeu a espora*) is part of a network of
popular sayings that include "where Judas (/or the devil) lost his boots." This saying
is generally employed to mean far-off, rarely visited places (somewhat like "the boon-
docks" or "the back of beyond" in English).

19. The translations of stanzas 2, 3, 5, and 7 are quoted from a recently translated version

of "The Backlands" (Cunha [1902] 2010. I offered my own translations of stanzas 1, 4, and 6 to foreground the poets' and Euclides's actual word choices rather than privilege the rhyme (Cunha 1984 [1902], 120).

20. See especially Madden (1993) for more historiographic discussion of the "modernizing" trend within Canudos scholarship, especially regarding Levine (1992).

21. The field notebook version is an "ABC" poem, which means that each verse begins with a letter of the alphabet in order. Euclides does not mention this in his book.

22. The Bragança family, from which both Pedros descended, still ruled in Portugal, though Pedro II died in France in 1891.

23. References to sacraments in general appear in another poem in Euclides's field notebook, although without any comment from Euclides (Cunha 2009 [1897], 177). The editor of the notebooks hints at a reason for Euclides's relative lack of interest in these verses: "In the collection undertaken by the writer without books [sic] there was no lack of verses like these, deriving from a sentimental, commonplace, poor Catholicism, [which were] visibly copied from a manual. Euclides did not even refer to them" (O. Andrade 2009, 344).

24. Strathern's interrogation of the individual is part of an elaborate epistemological critique (see especially Strathern 1988, 2004; and Lebner 2017a, 2020). Nevertheless, this is a vital intersection with current debates in religious studies.

25. Hirschkind and Larkin (2008, 8), despite their useful critique of the marginalization of religion, still reinstall the need to study politics.

FOURTH VISITATION

1. These are excerpts from the *cordel* "ABC of the Constitutional Assembly" by João do Jegue (The Cry 1982, 7).

CHAPTER FOUR

1. "OP" means *Ordinis Praedicatorum*, "Order of Preachers," a name for the Dominican Order (Bohan 2018).

2. In the first year of *The Cry*, which started in May 1980, the Evangelizing Committee managed to produce one issue per month until April 1981 (although the Pastoral Land Commission archives in Marabá, where I photographed the newsletter, was missing the July 1980 issue, #3). The second calendar year of *The Cry*'s production, May 1981–April 1982, output began to fall—they skipped the December 1981 issue, only producing the January 1982 issue, #20 (the archive also did not have a copy of the August 1981 issue, #16). The third year is when output dropped more dramatically: there was no May 1982 issue, there was a June 1982 issue (#24), and then #25 was only published six months later, in December 1982. The year 1983 as a whole saw only four issues published until

December (#26, 27, 28, 29). The years 1984 and 1985 only had two issues each (the archive was missing #33). Finally there was only one issue, #34, in 1986.

3. In Portuguese, *irmãos* means "brothers," but conventionally it can refer to a sibling cohort with sisters as well. Indeed, in general the masculine term prevails when a plural contains masculine and feminine. However, as in Spanish, the predominance of the masculine is becoming less and less accepted today, leading to variations such as "todes" instead of "todos" for "all, everyone"

4. Many settlers in the region were active participants in liberationism in its heyday. After years of talking to people along the highway, however, I realized that the best way to understand liberationism as it happened was through archival research. People's memories were relatively muddy about specific liberationist language and method, and what they said was always shaded by the effects liberationism's decline (whether they supported this decline or not).

5. The less frequently mentioned reasons for the shift to "the people of God" are also important to absorb. Indeed, while "the people of God" is more of an Old Testament notion, its invocations of Israel were seen as an advantage. On the one hand, this idea worked against the antisemitism that had marked the horrors of the Holocaust. On the other hand, it drew more deeply on the image of the biblical exodus from Egypt, including pilgrimage through the desert and entry into the promised land. Of course, Christians had been using that image since the earliest times. Nevertheless, emphasizing the church as a vulnerable people in process "united by its memories (of Jesus, of the exodus) and pressing on as pilgrims in hope towards a future (the Canaan of the eschaton)" was a way to address secular modern concerns with history and change while infusing them with an eschatological hope (Walden 1975, 88).

6. Avery Dulles, in his classic work *Models of the Church* (2002 [1974]), notes that while the Catholic church chose new images to capture its work at different moments of its history, the insights offered by older images have not been entirely dispensed with; their influences can return at subsequent moments. Such is the case for the mystical body. See discussion in the introduction.

7. The acronym CELAM derives from the Portuguese "Conselho Episcopal Latino-Americano e Caribenho."

8. See-judge-act was devised in the early twentieth century (1913–25) by Joseph Cardijn, a Belgian priest who also spearheaded the Young Catholic Workers Movement and eventually became a cardinal (Kelly 2017). He was a member of what Gerd-Rainer Horn (2008) called the first wave of Western liberation theology (1924–59).

9. Since at least the Reformation there have been anxieties about allegorical readings of the bible on Catholic and Protestant sides (Sandberg 2020). In the twentieth century, the tension has been especially around the problem of history (Morgan 2015).

10. The first issue called for a vote on the title of the newsletter. Readers were asked to choose between the titles of *Exodus, The Cry of the PA-150, The Current,* or *The Peasant* (*Cry* 1980d).

11. The reason why "crickets" (*grilos*) is in the title of this article is that the word *grilagem* comes from the use of crickets in falsifying titles to land. The procedure goes like this: a fake title is produced and then put in a drawer with crickets, who nibble the paper

and yellow the document with their feces. This gives the title the appearance of age and it is then used to illegally claim ownership of public lands (Luciano Lima 2022).

12. There were four requirements that had to be observed simultaneously for a property to fulfill its social function: a) productivity; b) observation of labor legislation; c) environmental preservation; and d) the guarantee of the health of those who work the land (Dickel 2019).

13. INCRA stands for "Instituto Nacional de Colonização e Reforma Agrária."

14. A critique of the mystical compared to the historical appears at various junctures of Ellacuría's text. Indeed, it marks liberationists' move away from the "mystical body theology" that inspired Catholic Action, the pre–Vatican II initiative to inspire the laity (Horn 2008). Still, not all liberationists jettisoned talk of mystery and mysticism; see for example L. Boff (1978). Nevertheless, Boff is otherwise very similar to Ellacuría. He certainly shares Ellacuría's implicit critique of Catholic Action and its apolitical commitments. For Boff, as for Ellacuría, the cross is both the result of evil and an inspiration for the contemporary struggle against it.

15. As Nelson puts it, "while Boff does not directly ascribe agency to inanimate structures and arrangement of persons, he identifies *so closely* the orientation of a person with the orientation of the culture that it becomes hard to see how sin could be anything but hypostatized in inhabitants of a sinful society" (2009, 104, emphasis in original).

16. The original title in Portuguese was *Igreja: Charisma e Poder*.

17. Boff (1994 [1981]) refers to Satan only five times, and evil only eight times.

18. Boff proposed "a new model of Church in which power should be conceived without theological privileges, as a pure service for articulating the necessities of the people, the community" (see Ratzinger 1994 [1984], 274).

19. The October issue has seven pages of content in total, including the three pages of the report.

20. It is unclear if all or part of the next five pages are reprinted from materials used elsewhere, but the formatting suggests this is the case. Prior to the five and a half more pages on politics is inserted the following: "REFERENCE TO THE MEETING OF THE ECCLESIAL BASE COMMUNITIES IN ITAICI, SAO PAULO ON THE 21, 22, and 23 of April 1981" (*Cry* 1981c, 3). This suggests that much of these five-odd pages are copied from the 1981 meeting in Itaici.

21. Jesus says to his disciples, preparing them for the challenges ahead "Behold, I send you out as sheep in the midst of wolves; so be wise as serpents and innocent as doves" (Matthew 10:16).

22. John Burdick (2004) subsequently published on institutional liberationist legacies, in the form of the Pastoral Land Commission, the Landless Workers' Movement, and various progressive pastoral ministries operating in Brazil today. I am interested in the noninstitutional, relational legacies.

23. The bumper message of the truck driver quoted by Tepe (1966), which implicitly likened the world to a farm, resonates profoundly with the dream that opens this book, except that the dreamer, Olina, found herself alone on the last farmstead, after divine fire had consumed the evil of all other farms and people.

FIFTH VISITATION

1. These are excerpts from what some have called "the first Brazilian novel," *História do Predestinado Peregrino e seu Irmão Precito* (The story of the predestined pilgrim and his brother reprobate) (2016 [1682]) by the Jesuit Alexandre de Gusmão (1629–1724). Scholars have debated this designation of Gusmão's work, noting that he did not himself call his *Story of the Predestined Pilgrim* a novel, and that the tale is not tied to the idea of the individual. Indeed, the account itself is an allegory, in which the "Predestined" is not an individual but "all of the good Christians who are saved," while the Reprobate represents all the "sinners who distance themselves from Catholic precepts" (Martini and Silva 2021, 144). It is more of a parable than a novel proper, Martini and Silva say, and it was certainly used by Gusmão to teach the young, teaching being one of his most abiding concerns. Gusmão occupied a number of important positions in his long life, including as rector of a number of prestigious Jesuit schools, for example, the College of Santos, the College of Espírito Santo, and the College of Bahia. He was also responsible for the 1686 foundation of the first residential school in Portuguese America, the Seminary of Belém da Cachoeira. From this excerpt we can see that Gusmão, and therefore Jesuit education and catechism, was not only interested in discussing strictly spiritual issues: he was also keen on reinforcing the superiority of divine law over the law of the world, ecclesiastical law over civil law (see also Santos 2004).

CHAPTER FIVE

1. According to local residents today, climate change has scrambled any stable "rainy season."
2. The acronym in Portuguese stands for Movimento dos Trabalhadores Rurais Sem Terra.
3. I did not actually encounter this phrase in everyday life in Pará. However, I certainly found a sense, especially among my interlocutors in the camp, that "law was for enemies." Note that DaMatta takes friendship for granted in a way that I do not.
4. President Lopez Obrador apparently uses the sentence "For my friends, justice and grace; for my enemies the law alone" (*A los amigos, justicia y gracia; a los enemigos, la ley a secas*). I have found little to explain this, but have discovered newspaper articles that cite President Juárez as a potential source (Núñez 2020; Sandoval 2021; Sodi 2022). One blog mentions a Peruvian president, Oscar Benavides (1933–39), as a source (*Having My Say* 2020). The United Nations Development Program titled an article with the phrase, but attributed it to no one (López-Calva 2019). Meanwhile, an American-based Paraguayan professor, Alan Redick (2020), writing in the Paraguayan newspaper *El Nacional*, admits that the genealogy of the sentence is fuzzy: "It is difficult to know who it was who introduced this phrase. Some maintain that it was Benito Juárez, others say that it was Juscelino Kubitschek, others even swear that it was a Peruvian. Even Perón

had his own version, 'For the friend, everything, for the enemy, not even justice.' But the sentence is just too familiar to Latin Americans; so much so, that now it doesn't even matter who said it first, because it seems to have been in our collective consciousness now for many years."

5. See also Luís Cardoso de Oliveira (2002), who explores moral injury and the law in Brazil, the United States, and Québec.

6. Alex Ungprateeb Flynn makes it clear that even a spiritual understanding of *mística* does not negate the MST's secularizing bent: "It was clear that *mística* for Thiago had the potential to go beyond the mundane or the 'produced'. Rather, it was the spiritual plane of the movement, its conscience, the manner in which to express transcendent objectives to keep people honest. Of course, Thiago believed that it had helped to construct community and had helped to keep people strong in times of repression, but Thiago seemed to indicate that the secular direction of the movement had required a nascent spiritualism, one based in praxis" (Flynn 2013, 186). Even a "spiritual" *mística*, in other words, retains more terrestrial objectives: to shore up solidarity, to keep people honest, to stay focused on the higher objectives of agrarian reform.

7. *Companheiro* became popular in Latin America after the Cuban Revolution (1959) and was in a sense an Indigenous replacement of the more traditional *comrade* to recognize revolutionary commitments. As Antônio de Moraes (2007) pointed out, *companheiro* derives from the popular Latin words *companio/commensal*, meaning the one with whom you divide bread/with whom you share a table, which are both synonyms of sorts with the Latin *conviva*, meaning the one with whom you live). However, during *companheiro*'s revived political use in 1960s Latin America, there was a specific political logic to it. On the one hand, masculine and feminine versions of *companheiro/a* could be used, denoting a "logic of difference . . . [aimed at] 'revalorizing the role of women in history,'" while on the other, it carried with it an "anti-Stalininst" subtext (Moraes 2007). According to Moraes, the term *comrade* had acquired hierarchical connotations due to its use among civil and military bureaucrats in the USSR (Moraes 2007). However, he notes that it was originally adopted by the Bolsheviks as a means to abolish the use of hierarchical status markers (like *sir*) while paying homage to the Paris Commune, where it was first used to indicate the equality of members. One might also note that *companheiro* is purposely not the concept of brotherhood, indicating a certain distance from traditional Catholic forms of forging solidarity via traditional kinship/friendship links. This is one reason we need to be careful of simply asserting kinship as a rubric for political anthropology, especially in Latin America.

8. Some people had brought large pieces of furniture to the camp, and the residents had to arrange for the transport of numerous very large items.

9. Regarding the politically retrograde resonance of "friend" in Russia, see Lenin's extended attack on the reactionary group "friends of the people" (2001 [1894]).

10. *Coronel* is a late-nineteenth and early twentieth-century term for a local landowning boss or politician, who is not always connected to the army.

11. In practice the term *companheiro* is often extended to those who support working class struggles and the left more generally.

12. Frei Betto's article, "Of *Mística* and Politics," published in the first journal issue of the

Faith and Politics Movement (*Cadernos de Fé e Política*, 1989), sheds unique light on the significance of *mística* for the progressive church and its possible connection to the MST. There, Betto made a plea for Christians to navigate the "de-ecclesiasticalization" of politics in post-dictatorship Brazil through the cultivation of *mística*. Activists originally trained by the liberationist church were leaving to work in decidedly nonreligious political organizations after the transition to civilian rule in 1985. Betto suggested that *mística*, which he defined as an "amorous energy, impregnated with the ineffable presence of God turned towards the constant affirmation of the sovereignty of life," was a way to bridge increasingly separate political and religious lives, especially outside the church. The style or mode by which one lived faith and *mística*, he said, was spirituality, though he didn't offer more clarifications. But for our purposes, the article suggests how the MST "got" *mística* from the church: by initially sharing militants (Stédile himself was trained in the church). Nevertheless, by the late 1990s at the latest, MST *mística* was no longer about keeping ties to the church and Christian spirituality but was about uniting for the struggle for land. Chaves (2021) and Rolemberg (2020, 2023) don't describe this particular turning point. But Rolemberg makes it clear that for Pastoral Land Commission militants in Pará *mística* has remained an animating force into the twenty-first century, even if it has a slightly more secular meaning than what Betto once described.

13. Stédile and Fernandes describe Ademar Bogo as "A Leader of the MST who acts in the Sector of Education *(Formação)*. He is distinguished as a poet and author of music used by the movement. He is the author of the MST's hymn" (1999, 131).

14. Bogo then quotes Stédile to conclude the point: "Our base uses its religious faith to nourish their struggle, which is a struggle against the state and against capital" (Stédile and Fernandes 1999, 131, cited in Bogo 2002, 125).

15. While these *mística*-geared activities did bring camp members together at various points, others felt excluded. As Paula confided to me, she felt nearly barred from participating in the preparation of the *mística*. "They have their ideas and that's it. They say they want us to participate and then they don't let us. I have experience and interest to work in theatre, I offered my help and they rejected it," she said, staring into a corner, stopping herself from speaking further. I had met this reflective and soft-spoken woman and her husband Samuel on my first visit to the camp. To my surprise, I discovered that he was Head of the Department of Leisure for the municipality of Eldorado. Although this situation was somewhat unusual, it opened my eyes to how varied the Landless could be. They claimed that Samuel had decided to join the MST because he wanted to change his life and live off the land. I believe that he was sincere, although perhaps he was thinking of his future political career, which can be launched through involvement in grassroots politics. Seemingly gentle people, they could not withstand the arduous physical, social, and political life of the camp and left one month after the occupation.

16. Two of the militants were soon to commence an MST university course: one in history, the other in literature. Bernardo himself, while he had not yet had time to do a university course, had learned to read in the MST at the age of fifteen, and had dedicated himself to writing poetry and reading widely.

17. "Sickle" is the literal translation of the Portuguese word *foice*, but the version used in

the region looks more like a billhook on a long, as opposed to a short, stick. It is used to cut away underbrush.

18. It was not mere chance that the encamped were afraid of being left in a dangerous position. Many were kin to, children of, or friends of residents from the 17th of April settlement, and everyone knew the story of the Massacre that had tragically preceded that settlement's formation—we were on its lands, after all. Moreover, many knew that survivors of the Massacre did not feel entirely comfortable with official MST accounts. I describe this at greater length in the next chapter.

19. My digital camera had been employed for various forms of recording at previous events—this was years before anyone in the local MST sphere had a digital camera, let alone a smartphone. Indeed, in 2004 few people had regular mobile phones. Although I was participating in this important process and thus becoming a *companheira* of sorts, I was still definitively an outsider, so I was not given any proper responsibilities.

20. Burned Brazil-nut trees, *castanheiras*, are a common feature of the landscape in Pará. When pastures are created by farmers, nearly all trees are cut, although a few Brazil-nut trees are left standing. Then a fire is set, and while the rest turns to ash, the *castanheiras* remain standing, blackened by the flames.

21. Dan Baron Cohen is a British-Canadian popular educator who now resides in Brazil. He facilitated the collective decision-making process that resulted in the monument. Sacha Baron Cohen is his cousin.

22. Over time many residents would properly move in to their *barracos*. Some, in fact, sold much of what they had wherever they were living before and moved all of their remaining possessions to the camp. In addition to beds, tables, and chairs, I saw a number of people who had brought their buffets, filled with plates and knicknacks, and even stoves and fridges, which could not work in the camp.

23. *Picuinha* is the appropriate spelling, but people pronounced it *picunha*.

24. This event generated much hope and excitement, particularly together with recent discoveries that CPT lawyers had made about the *fazenda*: that much of it was likely on public lands. The land's public status still had to be verified, however, which was no simple task, given that land tenure throughout Brazil, and particularly in the Amazon, is notoriously problematic (Campbell 2015; Holston 1991).

25. As the *latifúndio* is considered the enemy, to work for large landowners is considered undesirable. Likewise, landowners did not like employing *sem terra*. Residents sometimes did keep their affiliations to themselves, however. They needed the money, and some saw no contradiction in working for the *latifúndio*. For example, it was discovered after a year of living in the camp that the husband of a close interlocutor of mine had just been convicted in Maranhão for working as a hitman for a local landowner. This was the kind of contradiction that, of course, the MST was trying to avoid.

26. The security sector, for example, organized groups to sit at the guard posts at the camp's three entrances. The production sector was put in charge of overseeing gardens, so camp residents could start producing staples like beans, manioc, squash, and corn after three and a half months. Farming became part of an otherwise minimal daily routine for those who chose to participate. Food preparation and carrying water occupied much time for women, and firewood cutting was delegated to men. People occasion-

ally hunted or fished in the nearby forests, lakes, and lagoons. On one of these fishing trips a group of us had to scramble out of the water after a piranha tried to bite off one woman's nipple, leaving the water bloody after; thankfully, it only managed to open a gash on her finger.

27. As I mention in the introduction (see especially note 42), ethnographers of Brazil have recently begun studying similar social agonism and concerns with friendship, without attention to Christianity.

28. Bolsonaro's 2018 campaign slogan was *"Brasil acima de tudo, Deus acima de todos"* ("Brazil above all, God above everyone").

29. The MST is organized in an ascending set of collectives that make decisions and action plans. This collective leadership is in part meant to promote collective thought, but it also protects leaders from being identified and targeted and potentially killed by enemies. Outside of camp coordinators (and sectors, see above), there are more powerful collectives. For example, there is the State Coordinating Committee and the State *Direção*. The *Direção* makes decisions at the state level, and the Coordinating Committees help implement them. But then there is the National Coordinating Committee and the National *Direção*. The latter makes the most important decisions for the MST at the national level. And while this is a collective, within it there are very powerful figures who have more de facto decision-making power than others do. João Pedro Stédile is a member of the National *Direção*, but he has been a key MST leader and spokesman since the MST's inception and certainly has more influence than others. The next chapter shows that there are militants in the MST who feel that decisions have been made in a very top-down fashion, and who want more collective decision making at the grassroots.

SIXTH VISITATION

1. These are excerpts from *Historia do Futuro: Esperanças de Portugal e o Quinto Império do Mundo* (History of the future: The hopes of Portugal and the fifth empire of the world), written c. 1649–55 by Jesuit Antônio Vieira (1608–97). It is a prophetic text that was published posthumously in 1718 (2009; see pages 77, 80, 84, 88, 94, 104, 105–6), though Vieira had disseminated such prophecies throughout his lifetime. Vieira's *History of the Future* has drawn much interest, as have many of his writings. Vieira was a major figure over his long lifetime, having fulfilled important roles in Portugal and Brazil, where he lived on and off from the age of six. Vieira was trained in Brazil by Jesuits and ordained a priest in 1635, and when a Portuguese king (João IV) ended sixty years of Spanish rule, Vieira was sent to Portugal to help celebrate the new monarch. Vieira then spent years in Portugal as a royal tutor, counselor, preacher, and diplomat, until he returned to Brazil to work as a missionary in Maranhão-Grão Pará (an area that includes present-day Pará) in 1653. There he actively campaigned against most forms of enslavement of Indians—even negotiating a royal decree for Jesuit control of missions in 1654—until local Jesuits were expelled from the region in 1661 for their

interference. Vieira was sent back to Portugal, where the political context had changed, and he was denounced to the Inquisition and eventually imprisoned in 1665, although he was released in 1667, and his name was eventually cleared. Vieira was investigated precisely for some of the prophetic assertions that appear in the *History of the Future*, including those about the "Fifth Empire," which are peppered across his voluminous letters, sermons, and other works.

Vieira drew on other prophecies to craft his own, from nationalist and Sebastianist-millenarian to Jewish. For example, he was inspired by the interpretation of Nebuchad-nezzar's dream in the Book of Daniel, and also the four beasts of the sea, which he cor-related to four preceding empires. He also promoted a series of prophetic poems (called "*Trovas*") credited to a poor and supposedly illiterate shoemaker, Antônio Gonçalves de Bandarra, whose capacity to foresee the resurrection of the Portuguese kingdom by João IV greatly impressed Vieira and many others. For Vieira, the Fifth Empire would begin after the world's population had all converted to Catholicism, including the peoples of the New World and Jews, who would then return to their promised land. Finally, with all heresies eliminated, a simultaneously worldly and heavenly empire would begin, characterized by universal peace, justice, and sobriety.

CHAPTER SIX

1. The spelling errors here are meant to evoke and mimic those in the original Portuguese.
2. As a field, the anthropology of religious publicity began by usefully contesting the Habermasian exclusion of religion from reflections on the public sphere. Anthropologists showed instead that religious actors do "go public" by variously using media to contest privatization by the modern state, which separates and excludes religion from (public) politics (Hirschkind 2006; Meyer and Moors 2006). More recently, Engelke (2013, xxiii) extended the point slightly by affirming that there exists an "inextricable link" between (religious) publicity and secularity. Nevertheless, Engelke drew back from further discussion: "Had this [book] been written in more fully sociological mode," he writes, "the approach to the secular might have been more consistently explicit, engaged with the 'secularization thesis' and its afterlife." Consequently, although he flags (an undefined) secularity more than earlier scholarship, his conclusions implicitly echo it: for Engelke too, religious publicity is a byproduct of, a resistance to, the state privatization of religion under secularism. See below.
3. Certainly, scholars of publicity agree that publics are "concatenations of texts [amply defined] through time" (Warner 2005, 90). Nevertheless, they have generally not attended to secularizing publics, nor have they explored how these secularizing publics define their reality through written and spoken text and practice, molding even religious publics.
4. There were also profound social, political, economic, religious, and even environmental changes that happened at that time, which also contributed to millenarianism being used against authority.

5. I remain somewhat surprised that Osias did not know about Canudos or Conselheiro, not only because there was an MST settlement founded near to the 17th of April called Canudos, or because the MST occasionally makes reference to it (for example, it has a popular chant that cites Conselheiro by name; see chapter 5). But I am also surprised because 1997 was the centenary of Canudos's defeat, and it was amply discussed in the Brazilian press. There was even a television miniseries on the rebellion launched that same year.

6. The Workers' Party is currently leading the government, with Luiz Inácio "Lula" da Silva as president.

7. Hierarchy and patron clientelism continue to be staples in the Brazilianist literature, though Christianity has rarely figured in more politically focused analyses, and has been of little general interest until recently. When Christianity did become a focus of social scientific attention, questions of hierarchy and clientelism often recurred (Gross 1971; Greenfield 1990; Greenfield and Cavalcante 2006; Lanna 1995).

8. Laura Rebhun (1999) has argued that the sense of "love's" decline in the Pernambucan backlands has precisely to do with the waning of patronage and the persistence of the idea that the rich should take care of the poor.

9. It is not insignificant that in 1991 there was a national referendum on the preferred governmental form for a new Brazil. To many people's surprise, monarchy was a popular choice. Otávio Velho (2007) elsewhere attributes this to popular Christianity. This may have something to do with the "King" in Osias's text.

10. The Macaxeira estate had been appropriated by the government and was redistributed to survivors in 1997.

11. The fact that Freire greatly inspired liberationists should not obscure his "happily radical impatience with traditional Christianity" (Collins 1998, 120). To say that Freire was secularizing, although he may not have used the term himself, is a legitimate way to describe what he thought he was doing—in fact, "secularizing" was even a way that liberationists described what they were doing (at least before the Vatican's 1980s attacks had serious effects). If this comes as a surprise, it has simply long been ignored in the scholarship that when Freire and liberationists were writing, "secularizing" was not seen as a bad thing (today, and unfortunately, scholars can often see the label "secularizing" as a criticism rather than just as description). For example, prominent Brazilian liberationists Leonardo and Clodovis Boff saw themselves as pursuing an "authentic secularization" to turn Catholic attention to the world and to the human to help minimize inequality (Boff and Boff 1986, 95). Gustavo Gutierrez (1988 [1971], 42), for his part, was more celebratory, noting that "it has been recalled often lately" that secularization, understood as a transformation of human understanding, "is a process which not only coincides perfectly with a Christian vision of human nature, of history, and of the cosmos; it also favors a more complete fulfillment of the Christian life insofar as it offers human beings the possibility of being more fully human." Note that I am using the concept of secularizing in the descriptive sense I have defined it in this book: as the creation/emergence of distinctions among the domain of religion (the divine etc.) and its others. Freire, as I discuss below, was secularizing in this sense, trying to cultivate an understanding of reality—of the cause of poverty, say—that was separable

from the divine. Specifically, he wanted people to be able to see their poor life conditions as caused by material relations among persons and things on the ground, not by a punishing God. This would make it possible for people to change their situation. Of course, this doesn't mean that Freirean ideas couldn't be Christian, too (and they were similar to those of liberationists, after all). To elaborate on Eduardo Dullo (2016), who has helpfully noted that Freire's ideas could be both "Christian" and "secular," I would say that Freire can be used in both Christianizing and secularizing programs (and some Christianizing programs can be simultaneously secularizing in the sense I am using it, though for another sense see Casanova 2011). Dullo (2014), engaging with Casanova (2011), prefers to call the process *mundanização* ("mundanization") because Dullo defines secularization in the classical sense as the decline of religion. This is a fair approach, though I think it is important to recuperate secularization and secularizing as useful social scientific terms, hence the description I pursue here.

12. On liberationism's related secularizing, see note 11, above.

13. The *prolongado* is a course that must be completed for one to be officially considered a militant in the MST. By the early 2000s it had been reduced to three months.

14. By some accounts, the MST presence in the Belém was fraught in a way which the MST in the southeast of the state was not. One person in the group mentioned that two camps had disassociated themselves from the MST there in the recent past—a pretty direct statement of dissatisfaction, although not unique to Belém, as we have seen.

EPILOGUE

1. In fact, the term *Bolsominions* was coined using the English word *minions* to denote the avid supporters of Bolsonaro, indicating, as the term suggests, a certain obedient following.

2. Bolsonaro is Catholic, and his wife Michelle is Evangelical, a member of a Baptist church. However, his supporters continued to be confused about his religious affiliation well after the election, thinking he was also Evangelical (UOL 2022).

3. Here I have built on a combination of the excellent readings of Benjamin's *Origins* by Weber (1992, 2008); Thiem (2013); Martel (2009); and de Camps (2023). However, I have added greater attention to allegory; see especially discussion in chapter 1.

4. On dialectical images as heirs, if not the same as allegorical images, see chapter 1, note 26.

5. Although Schmitt claimed to define politics at a remove from the state or sovereignty, as Grigoris Ananiadis cogently shows, "the crux of the matter lies in this metonymic sliding from 'grouping' through 'political entity' or unity to sovereignty. . . . The friend-enemy dichotomy that defines the political, in his schema, acquires its political necessity only on the assumption of a purified instance of absolute decision and command" (1999, 134).

6. Jacques Derrida (1996) showed Schmitt's friend-enemy distinction to be untenable, but he made no mention of Christianity, which distinguishes the present work on many counts.

7. In the early 2000s, in part inspired by the posthumous publication of Jacob Taubes's 1987 seminar *The Political Theology of St. Paul* (1993 in German, 1999 in French, 2004 in English), a series of philosophers turned to Christianity as a "new" way to think about transformative, revolutionary politics (Badiou 2003; Agamben 2005; Žižek 2003). This had a broad impact on both philosophy and the social sciences.

8. Recall that Foucault's *Confessions of the Flesh* was not released until 2022 in English, 2018 in French; see also introduction, note 24.

9. From the early 2000s, the concept of ontology began to gain popularity outside of its traditional field of philosophy. However, as I have argued briefly above and at more length elsewhere following Strathern, cultivating this concept presents a series of problems for anthropologists. Among the more serious problems, ontology holds the ideas of "being" and "the foundational" in place in ways that can obscure the vitality of relations (Lebner 2017b; Strathern 2012).

10. This point has been rarely underscored, but it is quite clear that early in Foucault's career the weakening power of philosophy compared to the social sciences was of concern to many, including to him (see opening question and answer of Fellous and Foucault 1994 [1967]). Of course these worries in France have been going on since Durkheim (Fabiani 2020). Yet Foucault's oeuvre shows his particular work in favor of philosophy: his interest in the death of man, for example, shows his interest in the demise of anthropology broadly—but not always so broadly—conceived. Then, as he moved into his genealogical phase, Foucault usurped some social scientific, including anthropological, ways of thinking to replace them. And Foucault was largely successful: anthropology and many social sciences were remade at least in part in his image. Yet as this book shows, there are ready new relations to explore.

BIBLIOGRAPHY

A Província do Pará. 1996a. "Trabalhadores sao Mártires da Igreja." 25 April.

A Província do Pará. 1996b. "Cardeal Lamenta em Nome do Papa." 25 April.

Abreu, Maria José de. 2021. *The Charismatic Gymnasium: Breath, Media, and Religious Revivalism in Contemporary Brazil.* Duke University Press.

Acorda, Cordel. 2017. "A Morte de Leandro." March. http://acordacordel.blogspot.com/2017/03/a-morte-de-leandro.html.

Adorno, Rolena. 1993. "Reconsidering Colonial Discourse for Sixteenth- and Seventeenth-Century Spanish America." *Latin American Research Review* 28 (3): 135–45.

Agamben, Giorgio. 2005. *The Time That Remains: A Commentary on the Letter to the Romans.* Translated by Patricia Dailey. Stanford University Press.

Agência Brasil. 2023. "Comissão Arns Denuncia Violência e Impunidade No Sul e Sudeste Do Pará." *UOL.* June 1. https://noticias.uol.com.br/ultimas-noticias/agencia-brasil/2023/06/01/comissao-arns-denuncia-violencia-e-impunidade-no-sul-e-sudeste-do-para.htm.

Agência Folha. 2002. "Prefeito de Curionópolis (PA) Diz Que Acusação é 'Armação Política.'" *Folha de São Paulo.* March 12. https://www1.folha.uol.com.br/folha/brasil/ult96u43117.shtml.

Agrama, Hussein. 2012. *Questioning Secularism: Islam, Sovereignty and the Rule of Law in Modern Egypt.* University of Chicago Press.

Agrama, Hussein. 2015. "Religious Freedom and the Bind of Suspicion in Contemporary Secularity." In *Politics of Religious Freedom,* edited by Winnifred Sullivan, Elizabeth Hurd, Saba Mahmood, and Peter Danchin, 301–12. University of Chicago Press.

Ahmed, Sara. 2014. *Willful Subjects.* Duke University Press.

Alva, Jorge Klor de. 1992. "Colonialism and Postcolonialism as (Latin) American Mirages." *Colonial Latin American Review* 1 (1–2): 3–23.

Alva, Jorge Klor de. 1994. "The Postcolonization of the (Latin) American Experience: A Reconsideration of 'Colonialism,' 'Postcolonialism,' and 'Mestizaje.'" In *After Colonialism: Imperial Histories and Postcolonial Displacements,* edited by Gyan Prakash, 241–75. Princeton University Press.

Alves, José Diniz. 2022. "A Aceleração da Transição Religiosa no Brasil: 1872–2032." *EcoDebate: Plataforma de Informação, Artigos e Notícias Sobre Temas Socioambientais.* https://www.ecodebate.com.br/2022/10/12/a-aceleracao-da-transicao-religiosa-no -brasil-1872-2032-artigo-de-jose-eustaquio-diniz-alves.

Amory, Frederic. 1999. "Euclides da Cunha and Brazilian Positivism." *Luso-Brazilian Review* 36 (1): 87–94.

Ananiadis, Grigoris. 1999. "Carl Schmitt and Max Adler: The Irreconcilability of Politics and Democracy." In *The Challenge of Carl Schmitt*, edited by Chantal Mouffe, 118–37. Verso.

Andrade, Carlos Drummond de. 1976. "Leandro, o Poeta." *Jornal do Brasil.* September 9. Cited in "Ariano Suassuna Recita 'Quem Foi Temperar o Choro. E Acabou Salgando o Pranto?,' do Poeta Leandro Gomes de Barros." *Revista Prosa Verso Arte.* https:// www.revistaprosaversoearte.com/ariano-suassuna-recita-quem-foi-temperar-o-choro -e-acabou-salgando-o-pranto-do-poeta-leandro-gomes-de-barros.

Andrade, Olímpio de Souza. 2009. "Comentários." In *Caderneta de Campo*, by Euclides da Cunha, edited by Olímplio de Souza Andrade, 307–31. Fundação Biblioteca Nacional.

Ansell, Aaron. 2014. *Zero Hunger: Political Culture and Antipoverty Policy in Northeast Brazil.* University of North Carolina Press.

Antunes, Alfredo. 1983. *Saudade e Profetismo em Fernando Pessoa: Elementos para uma Antropologia Filosófica.* Publicações da Faculdade de Filosofia—Braga.

Arantes, Antonio. 1982. *O Trabalho e a Fala: Estudo Antropológico Sobre os Folhetos de Cordel.* Editora Kairós/FUNCAMP.

Apter, Emily. 2013. *Against World Literature: On the Politics of Untranslatability.* Verso.

Asad, Talal. 1983. "Anthropological Conceptions of Religion: Reflections on Geertz." *Man* 18(2): 237–59.

Asad, Talal. 1993. *Genealogies of Religion: Discipline and the Reasons of Power in Christianity and Islam.* Johns Hopkins University Press.

Asad, Talal. 2003. *Formations of the Secular: Christianity, Islam, Modernity.* Stanford University Press.

Azzi, Riolando. 1978. *O Catolicismo Popular no Brasil: Aspectos Históricos.* Vozes.

Badiou, Alain. 2003. *Saint Paul: The Foundation of Universalism.* Stanford University Press.

Bakker Kellogg, Sarah. 2019. "Perforating Kinship: Syriac Christianity, Ethnicity, and Secular Legibility." *Current Anthropology* 60 (4): 475–97.

Baron, Dan. 2004. *Alfabetização Cultural: A Luta Íntima por uma Nova Humanidade.* São Paulo: Alfarrabio.

Barreiros, Rogger, Danilo Fernandes, Renata Amaral, and Graciele Sbizero. 2017. "A Transição Histórica das Oligarquias da Castanha na Região de Marabá: Redes Sociais, Hegemonia e Transformações no Bloco de Poder das Elites Locais Entre os Anos de 1920 e 1980." *Congresso Brasileiro de História Econômica* 12:1–35.

Barrocal, André. 2019. "Direita Cristã é o Novo Ator e Líder do Neoconservadorismo no País." *Carta Capital.* July 22. https://www.cartacapital.com.br/politica/direita-crista-e -o-novo-ator-e-lider-do-neoconservadorismo-no-pais.

Barros, Leandro Gomes de. 1908. *Peleja de Manoel Riachão com o Diabo*. Pedro Baptista. http://rubi.casaruibarbosa.gov.br/handle/123456789/1732.

Barros, Leandro Gomes de. 1910. *A Força Do Amor*. http://rubi.casaruibarbosa.gov.br /handle/123456789/1732.

Barros, Leandro Gomes de, and João Martins de Atayde. 1946. *O Retirante*. Cruzeiro. http://rubi.casaruibarbosa.gov.br/handle/123456789/1889.

Baum, Gregory. 1989. "Structures of Sin." In *The Logic of Solidarity: Commentaries on Pope John Paul II's Encyclical on Social Concerns*, edited by Gregory Baum and Robert Ellsberg, 110–26. Orbis.

Bell, Sandra, and Simon Coleman. 1999. "The Anthropology of Friendship: Enduring Themes and Future Possibilities." In *The Anthropology of Friendship*, edited by Sandra Bell and Simon Coleman, 1–19. Berg.

Beliso-De Jesús, Aisha. 2015. *Electric Santería: Racial and Sexual Assemblages of Transnational Religion*. Columbia University Press.

Benjamin, Roberto. 2020. "Biografia: João Martins de Ataíde." http://antigo .casaruibarbosa.gov.br/cordel/JoaoMartins/joaoMartinsdeAtaide_biografia.html.

Benjamin, Walter. 1969. *Illuminations*. Translated by Harry Zohn. Schocken Books.

Benjamin, Walter. 1985. "Central Park." Translated by Lloyd Spencer and Mark Harrington. *New German Critique* 34:32–58.

Benjamin, Walter. 1994. "Exchange with Theodor W. Adorno on the Essay 'Paris, the Capital of the Nineteenth Century.'" Translated by Edmund Jephcott and Howard Eiland. In *Selected Writings Volume 3: 1935–1938*, edited by Howard Eiland and Michael Jennings, 50–67. Belknap Press.

Benjamin, Walter. 1999. *The Arcades Project*. Translated by Howard Eiland and Kevin McLaughlin. Belknap Press.

Benjamin, Walter. 2003a. "On the Concept of History." Translated by Harry Zohn. In *Walter Benjamin: Selected Writings, Volume 4: 1938–1940*, edited by Howard Eiland and Michael Jennings, 389–400. Harvard University Press.

Benjamin, Walter. 2003b. *The Origin of German Tragic Drama*. Translated by John Osbourne. Verso.

Benjamin, Walter. 2006. *The Writer of Modern Life: Essays on Charles Baudelaire*. Edited by Michael Jennings. Harvard University Press.

Benjamin, Walter. 2019. *Origin of the German Trauerspiel*. Translated by Howard Eiland. Harvard University Press.

Bialecki, Jon. 2017. *A Diagram for Fire: Miracles and Variation in an American Charismatic Movement*. University of California Press.

Bingemer, María. 1998. *A Identidade Crística: Sobre a Identidade, a Vocação e a Missão dos Leigos*. Edições Loyola.

Bloch, Ernst. 1986 [1959]. *The Principle of Hope*. Translated by Neville Plaice, Stephen Plaice, and Paul Knight. Blackwell.

Boff, Clodovis. 1987. "Os Cristãos e a Questão Partidária." In *Cristãos: Como Fazer a Política*, edited by Clodovis Boff, Frei Betto, Pedro Ribeiro de Oliveira, Rogério de Almeida Cunha, Luiz Eduardo Wanderley, Luiz Alberto Gómez de Souza, Herbert de Souza, Leonardo Boff, and Domingos Barbé, 9–46. Vozes.

Boff, Leonardo. 1978. *Passion of Christ, Passion of the World*. Translated by Robert R. Bar. Orbis Books.

Boff, Leonardo. 1994 [1981]. *Igreja: Carisma e Poder: Ensaios De Eclesiologia Militante*. Editora Atica.

Boff, Leonardo, and Clodovis Boff. 1986. *Como Fazer Teologia da Libertação*. Vozes.

Bogo, Ademar. 2000. *O MST e a Cultura: Caderno de Formação 34*. MST.

Bogo, Ademar. 2002. *O Vigor da Mística*. Associação Nacional de Cooperação Agrícola.

Bohan, Maria. 2018. "What Does O.P. Stand For?" *Passion for the Possible: Sisters of St. Dominic*. https://www.opblauvelt.org/post/__o-p.

Bonfim, Evandro De Sousa. 2020. "O Espírito Santo e o 'Rei do Fim do Mundo.'" *Ciencias Sociales y Religión / Ciências Sociais e Religião* 22: 1–18.

Bosi, Alfredo. 2015 [1992]. *Brazil and the Dialectic of Colonization*. Translated by Robert Newcomb. University of Illinois Press.

Bossy, John. 1985. *Christianity in the West, 1400–1700*. Oxford University Press.

Boyarin, Jonathan. 2009. *The Unconverted Self: Jews, Indians, and the Identity of Christian Europe*. University of Chicago Press.

Bray, Alan. 2004. *The Friend*. University of Chicago Press.

Brelaz, Walmir. 2006. *Os Sobreviventes do Massacre de Eldorado do Carajás: Um Caso de Violação da Dignidade da Pessoa Humana*. Belém.

Bubandt, Nils. 2014. *The Empty Seashell: Witchcraft and Doubt on an Indonesian Island*. Cornell University Press.

Buck-Morss, Susan. 1990. *The Dialectics of Seeing: Walter Benjamin and the Arcades Project*. MIT Press.

Burdick, John. 1993. *Looking for God in Brazil: The Progressive Catholic Church in Urban Brazil's Religious Arena*. University of California Press.

Burdick, John. 2004. *Legacies of Liberation: The Progressive Catholic Church in Brazil at the Start of a New Millennium*. Ashgate.

Bush, J. Andrew. 2020. *Between Muslims: Religious Difference in Iraqi Kurdistan*. Stanford University Press.

Cadena, Marisol de la. 2010. "Indigenous Cosmopolitics in the Andes: Conceptual Reflections Beyond 'Politics.'" *Cultural Anthropology* 25 (2): 334–70.

Cadena, Marisol de la. 2015. *Earth Beings: Ecologies of Practice Across Andean Worlds*. Duke University Press.

Callahan, Richard, Kathryn Lofton, and Chad Seales. 2010. "Allegories of Progress: Industrial Religion in the United States." *Journal of the American Academy of Religion* 78 (1): 1–39.

Campanha da Fraternidade. 1986. *Terra de Deus, Terra de Irmãos*. CNBB.

Campbell, Jeremy M. 2015. *Conjuring Property Speculation and Environmental Futures in the Brazilian Amazon*. University of Washington Press.

Campos, Haroldo de. 2007. "Disappearance of the Baroque in Brazilian Literature: The Case of Gregório De Matos." In *Novas: Selected Writings*, edited by Antonio Bessa and Odile Cisneros, 178–93. Northwestern University Press.

Camps, Jacobo de. 2023. "Calderón y el Drama Barroco Según Walter Benjamin en el Origen del Trauerspiel Alemán (1928)." *Bulletin of Hispanic Studies* 100 (7): 675–90.

Candea, Matei. 2011. "'Our Division of the Universe': Making a Space for the Non-Political in the Anthropology of Politics." *Current Anthropology* 52 (3): 309–34.

Candea, Matei. 2019. *Comparison in Anthropology: The Impossible Method.* University of Cambridge Press.

Cândido, Antônio. 1959. *Formação da Literatura Brasileiro: Momentos decisivos.* Martins.

Cândido, Antônio. 1970. "Dialética da Malandragem." *Revista do Instituto de Estudos Brasileiros* 8:67–89.

Cândido, Antônio. 2002 [1957]. "O Homem dos Avessos." In *Tese e Antítese*, 121–39. T.A. Queiroz.

Cannell, Fenella. 2005. "The Christianity of Anthropology." *Journal of the Royal Anthropological Institute* 11 (2): 335–56.

Cannell, Fennella. 2013. "The Re-Enchantment of Kinship." In *Vital Relations: Modernity and the Persistent Life of Kinship*, edited by Susan McKinnon and Fennella Cannell, 228–51. School for Advanced Research (SAR) Press.

Cardim, Pedro. 1999. "Amor e Amizade na Cultura Política dos Séculos XVI e XVII." *Lusitania Sacra (2a Série)* 11:21–57.

Cardoso, Ana Claudia. 2010. "Urban Design in Western Amazonian Cities—the Case of Marabá." *Urban Design International* 15 (2): 90–104.

Carey, Matthew. 2017. *Mistrust: An Ethnographic Theory.* HAU Books.

Caros Amigos. 1999. "Massacre de Eldorado dos Carajás em Discussão: O Maior Julgamento da História do Brasil." *Caros Amigos*, front page.

Carsten, Janet, ed. 2000. *Cultures of Relatedness: New Approaches to the Study of Kinship.* University of Cambridge Press.

Carter, Paul. 1987. *The Road to Botany Bay: An Essay in Spatial History.* Faber and Faber.

Casanova, J. 1994. *Public Religions in the Modern World.* University of Chicago Press.

Casanova, José. 2011. "The Secular, Secularizations, Secularisms." In *Rethinking Secularism*, edited by Craig Calhoun, Mark Juergensmeyer and Jonathan VanAntwerpen, 54–73. Oxford University Press.

Castañeda-Liles, Maria. 2018. *Our Lady of Everyday Life: Contextualizing Narratives on Everyday Faith, Devotion, and Existence Across Generations of U.S. Mexican Women.* Oxford University Press.

Cava, Ralph Della. 1968. "Brazilian Messianism and National Institutions: A Reappraisal of Canudos and Joaseiro." *The Hispanic American Historical Review* 48 (3): 402–20.

Cavanaugh, William. 1998. *Torture and Eucharist: Theology, Politics, and the Body of Christ.* Wiley-Blackwell.

Certeau, Michel de. 1984. *The Practice of Everyday Life.* Translated by Steven Rendall. University of California Press.

Certeau, Michel de. 1986. *Heterologies: Discourse on the Other.* Translated by Brian Massumi. University of Minnesota Press.

Certeau, Michel de. 1992. *The Mystic Fable: the Sixteenth and Seventeenth Centuries.* Vol. 1. Translated by Michael B. Smith. University of Chicago Press.

Certeau, Michel de. 2015. *The Mystic Fable: the Sixteenth and Seventeenth Centuries.* Vol. 2. Edited by Luce Giard. Translated by Michael B. Smith. University of Chicago Press.

Chakrabarty, Dipesh. 2000. *Provincializing Europe: Postcolonial Thought and Historical Difference*. Princeton University Press.

Chaves, Cristine. 2000. *A Marcha dos Sem Terra*. Relume Dumará.

Chestnut, Andrew. 1997. *Born Again in Brazil: The Pentecostal Boom and the Pathogens of Poverty*. Rutgers University Press.

Chidester, David. 1996. *Savage Systems: Colonialism and Comparative Religion in Southern Africa*. University Press of Virginia.

Cleary, David. 1990. *Anatomy of the Amazonian Gold Rush*. Macmillan.

Cohen, Thomas. 1991. "Millenarian Themes in the Writings of Antonio Vieira." *Luso-Brazilian Review* 28 (1): 23–46

Coleman, Simon. 2010. "An Anthropological Apologetics." *The South Atlantic Quarterly* 109 (4): 791–810.

Coleman, Simon. 2021a. *Powers of Pilgrimage: Religion in a World of Movement*. New York University Press.

Coleman, Simon. 2021b. "Comment on Ashley Lebner's *The Work of Impossibility in Brazil: Friendship, Kinship, Secularity*." *Current Anthropology* 62 (4): 452–83.

Coleman, Simon, and John Eade, eds. 2004. *Reframing Pilgrimage: Cultures in Motion*. Routledge.

Collins, Denis. 1998. "Review Essay: From Oppression to Hope: Freire's Journey toward Utopia." *Anthropology & Education Quarterly* 29 (1): 115–24.

Collins, John. 2015. *Revolt of the Saints: Memory and Redemption in the Twilight of Brazilian Racial Democracy*. Duke University Press.

Comaroff, Jean, and John Comaroff. 1991. *Of Revelation and Revolution: Christianity, Colonialism, and Consciousness in South Africa (Volume I)*. University of Chicago Press.

Comerford, John. 1999. "Brincando: Estudo Sobre uma Forma de Construção Social da Amizade e suas Reapropriações." In *Fazendo a Luta: Sociabilidade, Falas e Rituais na Construção de Organizações Camponesas*, 81–93. Relume Dumará.

Comerford, John Cunha. 2003. *Como uma Família: Sociabilidade, Territórios de Parentesco e Sindicalismo Rural*. Relume Dumará.

Comerford, John, Ana Carneiro, and Graziele Dainese, eds. 2015. *Giros Etnográficos em Minas Gerais. Casa, Comida, Prosa, Festa, Política, Briga e o Diabo*. 7 Letras/Faperj.

Conselheiro, Antônio. 1978. "Sobre a República." In *Antônio Conselheiro e Canudos: Revisão Histórica*, edited by Ataliba Nogueira, 175–80. Editora Nacional.

Cooper, Frederick. 2005. *Colonialism in Question: Theory, Knowledge, History*. University of California Press.

Coroníl, Fernando. 2008. "Elephants in the Americas? Latin American Postcolonial Studies and Global Decolonization." In *Coloniality at Large: Latin America and the Postcolonial Debate*, edited by Mabel Moraña, Enriqué Dussel and Carlos Jáuregui, 396–416. Duke University Press.

Corsín-Jiménez, Alberto. 2013. *An Anthropological Trompe L'Oeil for a Common World: An Essay on the Economy of Knowledge*. Berghahn Books.

Costa, Dilvanir. 2006. "A Família nas Constituições." *Revista de Informação Legislativa* 43 (169): 13–19. http://www2.senado.leg.br/bdsf/handle/id/92305.

Costa, Luciana Miranda. 1999. *Discurso e Conflito: Dez Anos de Disputa Pela Terra em Eldorado do Carajás*. Prêmio Núcleo de Altos Estudos Amazônicos (NAEA), Dissertação de Mestrado. NAEA/UFPA, Universidade Federal do Pará.

Coutinho, Raquel Zanatta, and André Braz Golgher. 2014. "The Changing Landscape of Religious Affiliation in Brazil between 1980 and 2010." *Revista Brasileira de Estudos de População* 31:73–98.

Cowan, Bainard. 1981. "Walter Benjamin's Theory of Allegory." *New German Critique* 22:109–22.

Cox, Harvey. 1988. *The Silencing of Leonardo Boff: The Vatican and the Future of World Christianity*. Meyer-Stone Books.

Crosson, J. Brent. 2020. *Experiments with Power: Obeah and the Remaking of Religion in Trinidad*. University of Chicago Press.

The Cry. 1980a. "Apresentação." *Informativo do PA-150*. Issue 1, 1.

The Cry. 1980b. "Carta do Bispo ao General." *Informativo do PA-150*. Issue 1, 6.

The Cry. 1980c. "Chamados a Ser Povo, Homem Novo, e Assembléia." *O Grito do PA-150*. Issue 6, 2-4.

The Cry. 1980d. "Este Informativo Precisa um Nome." *O Grito do PA-150*. Issue 1, 4.

The Cry. 1980e. "Fala o Bispo." *O Grito do PA-150*. Issue 2, 5.

The Cry. 1980f. "Grilos e Grilagens." *O Grito do PA-150*. Issue 1, 4.

The Cry. 1980g. "Nascendo a Esperança." *O Grito do PA-150*. Issue 8, 2.

The Cry. 1980h. "O Caso Lourival." *O Grito do PA-150*. Issue 1, 2.

The Cry. 1980i. "Povo de Deus, Comunidade de Fé de Luta." *O Grito do PA-150*. Issue 6, 1.

The Cry. 1980j. "Como Todos Já Sabem . . . Nosso Assembléia." *O Grito do PA-150*. Issue 2, 5.

The Cry. 1980k. "Você Entende o Significado de Este Desenho?" *O Grito do PA-150*. Issue 4, 9.

The Cry. 1980l. "A Luta é Necessária para Reforma Agrária." *O Grito do PA-150*. Issue 6, 7.

The Cry. 1980m. "Política da Terra." *O Grito do PA-150*. Issue 5, 2.

The Cry. 1981a. "5a Assembléia do Povo de Deus." *O Grito do PA-150*. Issue 18, 2.

The Cry. 1981b. "A Força Da União." *O Grito do PA-150*. Issue 10, 9.

The Cry. 1981c. "Igreja—Povo Oprimido que se Organiza para a Libertação." *O Grito do PA-150*. Issue 18, 3–7.

The Cry. 1981d. "Little Fish Against Big Fish: Stronger United." *O Grito do PA-150*. Issue 14, 1.

The Cry. 1981e. "Unity Trounces the *Grileiro*." *O Grito do PA-150*. Issue 14, 2.

The Cry. 1981f. "Um Povo Unido Vai Longe!!!" *O Grito do PA-150*. Issue 12, 7.

The Cry. 1981g. "União é a Mãe Da Liberdade." *O Grito do PA-150*. Issue 12, 3.

The Cry. 1981h. "The Politicking of the Oppressor." *O Grito do PA-150*. Issue 18, 7.

The Cry. 1982. "The People's Struggle." *O Grito do PA-150*. Issue 22, 8.

The Cry. 1986. "Terra e Justiça na PA-150." *O Grito do PA-150*. Issue 34, 3.

Cunha, Euclides da. 1984 [1902]. *Os Sertões*. Três. http://www.dominiopublico.gov.br/download/texto/bv000091.pdf.

Cunha, Euclides da. 2003 [1902]. *Os Sertões*. Editora Record.

Cunha, Euclides da. 2009 [1897]. *Caderneta de Campo*. Fundação Biblioteca Nacional.

Cunha, Euclides da. 2010 [1902]. *Backlands: the Canudos Campaign*. Translated by Elizabeth Lowe. Penguin Books.

Curran, Mark. 1998. *História do Brasil em Cordel*. EDUSP.

Dağtaş, Seçil. 2025. *Under the Same Sky: Everyday Politics of Religious Difference in Southern Turkey*. University of Pennsylvania Press.

Daly, Peter, and G. Richard Dimler. 2016. *The Jesuit Emblem in the European Context*. Saint Joseph's University Press.

DaMatta, Roberto. 1991 [1979]. *Carnivals, Rogues, and Heroes: An Interpretation of the Brazilian Dilemma*. University of Notre Dame Press.

DaMatta, Roberto. 1993. "Antropologia da Saudade." In *Conta de Mentiroso: Sete Ensaios de Antropologia Brasileira*. Rocco.

Davis, Kathleen. 2008. *Periodization and Sovereignty: How Ideas of Feudalism and Secularization Govern the Politics of Time*. University of Pennsylvania Press.

Deleuze, Gilles. 1993. *The Fold: Leibniz and the Baroque*. Translated by Tom Conley. University of Minnesota Press.

Denyer Willis, Laurie. 2023. *Go with God: Political Exhaustion and Evangelical Possibility in Suburban Brazil*. University of California Press.

Derrida, Jacques. 1996. *The Politics of Friendship*. Translated by George Collins. Verso.

Desai, Amit, and Evan Killick, eds. 2010. *The Ways of Friendship: Anthropological Perspectives*. Berghahn.

Dezemone, Marcus. 2016. "A Questão Agrária, o Governo Goulart e o Golpe de 1964 Meio Século Depois." *Revista Brasileira de História* 36:1–24.

Dickel, Simone Lopes. 2019. "O Princípio da Função Social no Estatuto da Terra e o Processo de Desapropriação da Fazenda Annoni, no Norte Sul Rio-Grandense." *Manduarisawa* 3 (2): 18–32.

Diocese Marabá. 2024. https://diocesedemaraba.com.br/institucional/nossa-historia.

Dosse, François. 2002. *Michel de Certeau: Le Marcheur Blessé*. Découverte.

Duffy, Eamon. 2016. "The End of Christendom." *First Things*. November. https://www
.firstthings.com/article/2016/11/the-end-of-christendom.

Dulles, Avery. 2002 [1974]. *Models of the Church*. Expanded ed. Doubleday.

Dullo, Eduardo. 2014. "Paulo Freire, o Testemunho e a Pedagogia Católica: A Ação Histórica Contra o Fatalismo." *Revista Brasileira de Ciências Sociais*. 29 (85): 49–61.

Dullo, Eduardo. 2016. "Testemunho: Cristão e Secular." *Religião & Sociedade* 36 (2): 85–106.

Dunn, Mary, and Brenna Moore, eds. 2020. *Religious Intimacies: Intersubjectivity in the Modern Christian West*. Indiana University Press.

Eade, John, and Michael J. Sallnow, eds. 1991. *Contesting the Sacred: The Anthropology of Pilgrimage*. Routledge.

Eleições. 2018. "Resultados para Presidente no Pará em Marabá (PA)." *Eleições 2018: Resultados por Município*. https://especiais.gazetadopovo.com.br/eleicoes/2018
/resultados/municipios-para/maraba-pa/presidente.

Ellacuría, Ignacio. 1978. "El Pueblo Crucificado: Un Ensayo en Soteriología Histórica." In *Cruz y Resurrección: Presencia y Anuncio de una Iglesia Nueva*, edited by Hugo Assmann, 49–82. Centro de Reflexión Teológica.

Emmi, Marília. 1999. *A Oligarquia do Tocantins e o Domínio dos Castanhais*. Núcleo de Altos Estudos Amazônicos, Universidade Federal do Pará.

Engelke, Matthew. 2011a. "Response to Charles Hirschkind: Religion and Transduction." *Social Anthropology* 19 (1): 97–102.

Engelke, Matthew. 2011b. "Material Religion." In *The Cambridge Companion to Religious Studies*, edited by Robert Orsi, 209–29. Cambridge University Press.

Engelke, Matthew. 2013. *God's Agents: Biblical Publicity in Contemporary England*. University of California Press.

Esterci, Neide, ed. 1984. *Cooperativismo and Colectivização no Campo: Questões Sobre a Prática da Igreja Popular no Brasil*, edited by Cadernos do ISER: 11. ISER.

Esterci, Neide. 1987. *Conflito no Araguaia: Peões e Posseiros Contra a Grande Empresa*. Vozes.

Esterci, Neide. 1994. *Escravos da Desigualdade: Um Estudo Sobre o Uso Repressivo da Força do Trabalho Hoje*. CEDI.

Fabiani, Jean-Louis. 2020. "Durkheim and the Philosophy of His Time." In *The Oxford Handbook of Émile Durkheim*, edited by Hans Joas and Andreas Pettenkofer, 129–44. Oxford University Press.

Faulhaber, Priscilla. 1999. "Prefácio (do livro da Luciana Miranda Costa)." In *Discurso e Conflito: Dez Anos de Disputa Pela Terra em Eldorado do Carajás*, by Luciana Miranda Costa. Prêmio Núcleo de Altos Estudos Amazônicos (NAEA), Dissertação de Mestrado. NAEA/UFPA, Universidade Federal do Pará.

Fellous, Gérard, and Michel Foucault. 1994 [1967]. "La Philosophie Structuraliste Permet de Diagnostiquer ce qu'est «Aujourd'hui»." In *Dits et Écrits: Tome I 1955–1969*, edited by Daniel Defert and François Ewald with Jacques Lagrange, 580–84. Gallimard.

Fernandes, Rubem César. 1982. *Os Cavaleiros do Bom Jesus: Uma Introdução às Religiões Populares*. Brasiliense.

Fernandes, Rubém. 1984. "Religiões Populares: Uma Visão Parcial da Literatura Recente." *BIB* 18 (2): 3–26.

Fernando, Mayanthi. 2014. *The Republic Unsettled: Muslim French and the Contradictions of Secularism*. Duke University Press.

Ferraz, Iara. 2000. "Gavião Parkatêjê: Povos Timbira, Povos Indígenas no Pará." Instituto Socioambiental. https://pib.socioambiental.org/pt/Povo:Gavi%C3%A3o_Parkat%C3%A3%AAj%C3%AA.

Filho, Carlos. 2005. "Religião na Literatura de Cordel: Análise da Religiosidade Popular do Nordeste Brasileiro." *Revista de Cultura Teológica* 13 (52): 65–77.

Flynn, Alex. 2013. "*Mística*, Myself, and I: Beyond Cultural Politics in Brazil's Landless Workers' Movement." *Critique of Anthropology* 33 (2): 168–92.

Foucault, Michel. 1997. "Friendship as a Way of Life." In *Ethics: Subjectivity and Truth*, edited by Paul Rabinow, 135–40. The New Press.

Foucault, Michel. 2021. *Confessions of the Flesh*. Translated by Robert Hurley. Edited by Frédéric Gros. Pantheon Books.

Freire, Paulo. 1970. *Pedagogy of the Oppressed*. Translated by Myra Ramos. Herder & Herder.

Freire, Paulo. 1997. "Última Entrevista de Paulo Freire." April 17, 1997, com Luciana Burlamaqui. http://www.youtube.com/watch?v=Ul90heSRYfE.

Freire, Paulo. 2001 [1968]. "Ação Cultural e Reforma Agrária." In *Ação Cultural para a Liberdade e Outros Escritos*, 35–41. Paz-e-Terra.

Freston, Paul. 1995. "Pentecostalism in Brazil: A Brief History." *Religion* 25 (2): 119–33.

Fromont, Cécile, and Michael Iyanaga. 2021. "Introduction: Kongo Christianity, Festive Performances, and the Making of Black Atlantic Tradition." In *Afro-Catholic Festivals in the Americas: Performance, Representation, and the Making of Black Atlantic Tradition*, edited by Cécile Fromont, 1–22. Penn State University Press.

Furey, Constance. 2012. "Body, Society, and Subjectivity in Religious Studies." *Journal of the American Academy of Religion* 80 (1): 7–33.

Furey, Constance. 2017. *Poetic Relations: Faith and Intimacy in the English Reformation*. University of Chicago Press.

Garrison, Jennifer. 2017. *Challenging Communion: The Eucharist and Middle English Literature*. Ohio State University Press.

Gaspar, Lúcia. 2009. "Leandro Gomes de Barros." *Pesquisa Escolar Online*. http://basilio .fundaj.gov.br/undefined/pesquisaescolar.

Geffray, Christian. 1995. *Chroniques de la Servitude en Amazonie Brésilienne*. Karthala.

Giumbelli, Emerson. 2002. *O Fim da Religião: Dilemas da Liberdade Religiosa no Brasil e na França*. Attar/PRONEX.

Giumbelli, Emerson. 2013. "The Problem of Secularism and Religious Regulation: Anthropological Perspectives." *Religion and Society* 4:93–108.

Glissant, Édouard. 1997. *Poetics of Relation*. Translated by Betsy Wing. University of Michigan Press.

Greenfield, Sidney. 1990. "Turner and Anti-Turner in the Image of Christian Pilgrimage in Brazil." *Anthropology of Consciousness* 1 (3–4): 1–8.

Greenfield, Sidney, and Antonio Mourão Cavalcante. 2006. "Pilgrimage and Patronage in Brazil: A Paradigm for Social Relations and Religious Diversity." *Luso-Brazilian Review* 43 (2): 63–89.

Gross, Daniel. 1971. "Ritual and Conformity: A Religious Pilgrimage to Northeastern Brazil." *Ethnology* 10:129–48.

Grumett, David. 2011. "Henri de Lubac: Looking for Books to Read the World." In *Ressourcement: A Movement for Renewal in Twentieth-Century Catholic Theology*, 236–49. Oxford University Press.

Grusin, Richard. 2015. "Radical Mediation." *Critical Inquiry* 42 (1): 124–48.

Guilhaumou, Jacques. 2005. "La Langue Politique et La Révolution Française." *Langage et Société* 113:63–92.

Guilhaumou, Jacques. 2008. "Les Signes du Politique: Language and Sociability in France from the Fourteenth to the Nineteenth Century." *Contributions to the History of Concepts* 4 (2): 137–59.

Guimarães, Alberto dos Passos. 1964. *Quatro Séculos de Latifúndio*. São Paulo: Fulgor.

Gusmão, Alexandre de. 2016 [1682]. *The Story of the Predestined Pilgrim and His Brother Reprobate: In Which, through a Mysterious Parable, Is Told the Felicitous Success of the One Saved and the Unfortunate Lot of the One Condemned*. Translated by Christopher Lund. Arizona Center for Medieval and Renaissance Studies.

Gutiérrez, Gustavo. 1988 [1971]. *A Theology of Liberation*. Translated by John Eagleson, Sister Caridad Inda, and Matthew J. O'Connell. Orbis.

Hall, Anthony. 1989. *Developing Amazonia: Deforestation and Social Conflict in Brazil's Carajás Programme*. Manchester University Press.

Hall, David. 1997. *Lived Religion in America: Toward a History of Practice*. Princeton University Press.

Handman, Courtney. 2018. "The Language of Evangelism: Christian Cultures of Circulation beyond the Missionary Prologue." *Annual Review of Anthropology* 47:149–65.

Harnecker, Marta. 1969. *Los Conceptos Elementales del Materialismo Histórico*. Siglo Veintiuno Editores.

Harnecker, Marta. 2003. *Landless People: Building a Social Movement*. Editora Expressão Popular.

Harris, Mark. 2000. *Life on the Amazon: An Anthropology of a Brazilian Peasant Village*. Oxford University Press.

Hatzikidi, Katerina, and Eduardo Dullo. 2021. "Introduction." In *A Horizon of (Im)Possibilities: A Chronicle of Brazil's Conservative Turn*, edited by Katerina Hatzikidi and Eduardo Dullo, 1–36. Centre for Latin American Studies.

Having My Say. 2020. ""For My Friends Anything, for My Enemies the Law!"" *Having My Say*. April 26. https://www.havingmysay.net/blog/2020/4/26/for-my-friends -anything-for-my-enemies-the-law.

Hayes, Kelly. 2011. *Holy Harlots: Femininity, Sexuality, and Black Magic in Brazil*. University of California Press.

Hébette, Jean, and Rosa Acevedo Marin. 1977. *Colonização Espontânea, Política Agrária e Grupos Sociais*. MEC.

Hecht, Susanna, and Alexander Cockburn. 1989. *The Fate of the Forest: Developers, Destroyers and Defenders of the Amazon*. Verso.

Hess, David. 1991. *Spirits and Scientists: Ideology, Spiritism, and Brazilian Culture*. Pennsylvania State University Press.

Hirschkind, Charles. 2006. *The Ethical Soundscape: Cassette Sermons and Islamic Counterpublics*. Columbia University Press.

Hirschkind, Charles. 2011. "Media, Mediation, Religion." *Social Anthropology* 19 (1): 90–97.

Hirschkind, Charles, and Brian Larkin. 2008. "Introduction: Media and the Political Forms of Religion." *Social Text* 26 (3): 1–9.

Hollywood, Amy M. 2012. "Love Speaks Here: Michel de Certeau's Mystic Fable." *Spiritus* 12 (2): 198–206.

Holston, James. 1991. "The Misrule of Law: Land and Usurpation in Brazil." *Comparative Studies in Society and History* 33 (4): 695–725.

Holston, James. 2008. *Insurgent Citizenship: Disjunctions of Democracy and Modernity in Brazil*. Princeton University Press.

Hoornaert, Eduardo. 1992. "The Church in Brazil." In *The Church in Latin America, 1492–1992*, edited by Enrique Dussel, 185–201. Orbis.

Hoornaert, Eduardo. 1997. *Os Anjos de Canudos: Uma Revisão Histórica*. Vozes.

Horn, Gerd-Rainer. 2008. *Western European Liberation Theology: The First Wave (1924–1959)*. Oxford University Press.

Hovland, Ingie. 2013. *Mission Station Christianity: Norwegian Missionaries in Colonial Natal and Zululand, Southern Africa 1850–1890*. Brill.

Hovland, Ingie. 2017. "Beyond Mediation: An Anthropological Understanding of the Relationship between Humans, Materiality, and Transcendence in Protestant Christianity." *Journal of the American Academy of Religion* 86 (2): 425–53.

Ianni, Octavio. 1979. *Colonização e Contra Reforma Agrária na Amazônia*. Vozes.

IBGE. 2010. "Censo 2010, Instituto Brasileiro de Geografia e Estatística." https://censo2010.ibge.gov.br.

IBGE. 2022. "Censo 2022, Instituto Brasileiro de Geografia e Estatística." https://censo2022.ibge.gov.br/.

Jegue, João do. 1982. "ABC do Constitutunte." *The Cry* (March), 7.

Jennings, Michael. 1987. *Dialectical Images: Walter Benjamin's Theory of Literary Criticism.* Cornell University Press.

Johnson, Christopher. 2013. "All Played Out? Lévi-Strauss's Philosophy of History." *New Left Review* 79 (Jan–Feb): 55–69.

Johnson, Paul, Pamela Klassen, and Winnifred Sullivan, eds. 2018. *Ekklesia: Three Inquiries in Church and State*. University of Chicago Press.

Kaell, Hillary. 2020. *Christian Globalism at Home: Child Sponsorship in the United States*. Princeton University Press.

Kantorowicz, Ernst. 2016 [1957]. *The King's Two Bodies: A Study in Medieval Political Theology*. Princeton University Press.

Kaufman, Peter. 2003. "Augustine, Macedonius, and the Courts." *Augustinian Studies* 34 (1): 67–82.

Keane, Webb. 2007. *Christian Moderns: Freedom and Fetish in the Mission Encounter.* University of California Press.

Keck, Frédéric. 2009. "The Limits of Classification: Claude Lévi-Strauss and Mary Douglas." In *The Cambridge Companion to Lévi-Strauss*, edited by Boris Wiseman, 139–55. Cambridge University Press.

Keenan, James. 2016. "Raising Expectations on Sin." *Theological Studies* 77 (1): 165–80.

Kelly, Patricia. 2017. "See, Judge, Act: The Foundation of the Citizens Project?" In *Everyday Social Justice and Citizenship: Perspectives for the 21st Century*, edited by Ann Marie Mealey, Pam Jarvis, Jonathan Doherty, and Jan Fook, 24–32. Routledge.

Kendi, Ibram. 2019. *How to Be an Antiracist*. Random House.

Klooster, Wim. 2013. *The Iberian Empires*. Vol. 3 of *The Cambridge History of the Age of Atlantic Revolutions*. Cambridge University Press.

King, Rebekka. 2023. *The New Heretics: Skepticism, Secularism, and Progressive Christianity*. New York University Press.

Konstan, David. 1996. "Problems in the History of Christian Friendship." *Journal of Early Christian Studies* 4 (1): 87–113.

Lacerda, Erasmo Peixoto. 2014. "Representações do Diabo na Literatura de Cordel: a Demonização do Negro em Leandro Gomes de Barros (1893–1918)." *Fato and Versões-Revista de História* 6 (11): 1–16.

Lacerda, Marina. 2022. "Contra o Comunismo Demoníaco: O Apoio Evangélico ao Regime Militar Brasileiro e seu Paralelo com o Endosso da Direita Cristã ao Governo Bolsonaro." *Religião & Sociedade* 42 (1): 153–76.

Lambek, Michael. 2013. "Kinship, Modernity, and the Immodern." In *Vital Relations:*

Modernity and the Persistent Life of Kinship, edited by Susan McKinnon and Fennella Cannell, 252–71. School for Advanced Research (SAR) Press.

Lambert, Renaud. 2018. "Os Brasileiros São Tudos Fascistas?" *Le Monde Diplomatique Brasil*, November, 4–5.

Lamoreaux, John. 1995. "Episcopal Courts in Late Antiquity." *Journal of Early Christian Studies* 3 (2): 143–67.

Lancaster, Roger N. 1988. *Thanks to God and the Revolution: Popular Religion and Class Consciousness in the New Nicaragua*. Columbia University Press.

Lanna, Marcos. 1995. *A Dívida Divina: Troca e Patronagem no Nordeste Brasileiro*. Editora UNICAMP.

Laraia, Roque, and Roberto DaMatta. 1967. *Índios e Castanheiros: A Empresa Extrativa e os Índios No Médio Tocantins*. Difusão Europeia do Livro.

Latour, Bruno. 1993. *We Have Never Been Modern*. Translated by Catherine Porter. Harvard University Press.

Law, John, and Evelyn Ruppert, eds. 2016. *Modes of Knowing: Resources from the Baroque*. Mattering Press.

Lebner, Ashley. 2012. "A Christian Politics of Friendship on a Brazilian Frontier." *Ethnos* 77 (4): 496–517.

Lebner, Ashley. 2015. "The Anthropology of Secularity Beyond Secularism." *Religion and Society* 6: 62–74.

Lebner, Ashley. 2016a. "La Redescription de l'Anthropologie Selon Marilyn Strathern." Translated by Arianne Dorval. *L'Homme* 218 (2): 117–50.

Lebner, Ashley. 2016b. "The Anthropology of Religion: Historical and Contemporary Trends." In *Macmillan Interdisciplinary Handbook: Social Religion*, edited by William B. Parsons, 235–52. Macmillan Reference.

Lebner, Ashley. 2017a. "Introduction: Strathern's Redescription of Anthropology." In *Redescribing Relations: Strathernian Conversations on Ethnography, Knowledge and Politics*, edited by Ashley Lebner, 1–37. Berghahn Books.

Lebner, Ashley. 2017b. "Interpreting Strathern's Unconscious Critique of Ontology." *Social Anthropology* 25 (2): 221–33.

Lebner, Ashley. 2019 [2018]. "On Secularity: Marxism, Reality and the Messiah in Brazil." *Journal of the Royal Anthropological Institute* 25 (1): 123–47.

Lebner, Ashley. 2020. "No Such Thing as a Concept: a Radical Tradition from Malinowski to Asad and Strathern." *Anthropological Theory* 20 (1): 3–28.

Leite, Fábio. 2011. "Laicismo e Outros Exageros Sobre a Primeira República no Brasil." *Religião e Sociedade* 31 (1): 32–60.

Lemons, Katherine. 2019. *Divorcing Traditions: Islamic Marriage Law and the Making of Indian Secularism*. Cornell University Press.

Lenin, Vladimir Illich. 2001 [1894]. *What the "Friends of the People" Are and How They Fight the Social-Democrats*. https://www.marxists.org/archive/lenin/works/1894/friends/index.htm.

Lévi-Strauss, Claude. 1966. *The Savage Mind*. University of Chicago Press.

Levine, Robert. 1992. *Vale of Tears: Revisiting the Canudos Massacre in Northeastern Brazil, 1893–1897*. University of California Press.

O Liberal. 1990. "Mais de 40 Tiros Liquidam Aragão." *O Liberal,* April 30, 1, 12.

O Liberal. 2025. "Pará tem Maior Percentual de Católicos do Norte e 6° Maior de Evangélicos no País, diz IBGE." *O Liberal,* June 6. https://www.oliberal.com/para/para
-tem-maior-percentual-de-catolicos-do-norte-e-6-maior-de-evangelicos-no-pais
-diz-ibge-1.973907.

Lima, Luciano. 2022. "Termo 'Grilagem' Tem Origem Realmente na Ação de Grilos; Entenda." *G1.* December 12. https://g1.globo.com/sp/campinas-regiao/terra-da-gente
/noticia/2022/12/14/termo-grilagem-tem-origem-realmente-na-acao-de-grilos
-entenda.ghtml.

Lima, Luís Silvério. 2010. *O Império dos Sonhos: Narrativas Proféticas, Sebastianismo e Messianismo Brigantino.* São Paulo: Alameda.

Lomnitz, Claudio. 1999. "Modes of Citizenship in Mexico." *Public Culture* 11 (1): 269–93.

Lomnitz, Claudio. 2001. *Deep Mexico, Silent Mexico: An Anthropology of Nationalism.* University of Minnesota Press.

López-Calva, Luis Felipe. 2019. "To My Friends, Anything; to My Enemies, the Law." *United Nations Development Program: Latin America and the Caribbean.* February 21. https://www.undp.org/latin-america/blog/graph-for-thought/%E2%80%9C-my
-friends-anything-my-enemies-law%E2%80%9D.

Lubac, Henri de. 2006 [1944]. *Corpus Mysticum: The Eucharist and the Church in the Middle Ages: Historical Survey.* Translated by Gemma Simmonds with Richard Price and Christopher Stephens. Edited by Laurence Hemming and Susan Parsons. SCM.

Luz, Guilherme. 2013. *Flores do Desengano: Poética do Poder na América Portuguesa (Séculos XVI–XVIII).* Editora Fap-Unifesp.

Luz, Guilherme. 2007. "Produção da Concórdia: A Poética do Poder na América Portuguesa (Sécs. XVI-XVIII)." *Varia História* 23(38): 543–60.

Madden, Lori. 1993. "The Canudos War in History." *Luso-Brazilian Review* 30 (2): 5–22.

Madeiro, Carlos. 2022. "Era Lula: País Ganhou 16 Milhões de Evangélicos na 1a Década dos Anos 2000." *UOL.* October 8. https://noticias.uol.com.br/colunas/carlos-madeiro
/2022/10/08/era-lula-pais-ganhou-16-milhoes-de-evangelicos-na-1-decada-dos-anos
-2000.htm?cmpid=copiaecola.

Mahmood, Saba. 2015. *Religious Difference in a Secular Age: A Minority Report.* Princeton University Press.

Mariz, Cecília. 1994. *Coping with Poverty: Pentecostals and Christian Base Communities in Brazil.* Temple University Press.

Marques, Ana Claudia. 2002. *Intrigas e Questões: Vingança de Família e Tramas Sociais no Sertão de Pernambuco.* Relume Dumará.

Marques, Ana Claudia. 2013a. "Founders, Ancestors, and Enemies: Memory, Family, Time, and Space in the Pernambuco *Sertão.*" *Journal of the Royal Anthropological Institute* 19: 716–33.

Marques, Ana Claudia. 2013b. "Pioneiros de Mato Grosso e Pernambuco: Novos e Velhos Capítulos da Colonização No Brasil." *Revista Brasileira de Ciências Sociais* 28 (83): 85–103.

Marques, Ana Claudia, and Natacha Leal, eds. 2018. *Alquimias do Parentesco: Casas, Gentes, Papéis, Territórios.* Gramma.

Martel, James. 2009. "Walter Benjamin, Sovereignty and the Eschatology of Power." In *After Sovereignty: On the Question of Political Beginnings*, edited by Charles Barbour and George Pavlich, 180–92. Routledge.

Martini, Marcus de, and Isabel Scremin da Silva. 2021. "A Caminho do Céu e do Inferno: Configurações do Peregrino e do Réprobo da História do Predestinado Peregrino e Seu Irmão Precito." *Revista Cerrados* 30(56): 140-158.

Mattos, María Virginia Bastos de. 1996. *História de Marabá*. Grafil.

Maués, Raymundo Heraldo. 1995. *Padres, Pajés, Santos e Festas: Catolicismo Popular e Controle Eclestiástico*. CEJUP.

Mayblin, Maya. 2010. *Gender, Catholicism, and Morality in Brazil: Virtuous Husbands, Powerful Wives*. New York.

Mayblin, Maya. 2012. "The Madness of Mothers: Agape Love and the Maternal Myth in Northeast Brazil." *American Anthropologist* 114: 240–52.

Mayblin, Maya. 2014. "The Untold Sacrifice: The Monotony and Incompleteness of Self-Sacrifice in Northeast Brazil." *Ethnos* 79 (3): 342–64.

Mayblin, Maya. 2017. "The Lapsed and the Laity: Discipline and Lenience in the Study of Religion." *Journal of the Royal Anthropological Institute* 23 (3): 503–22.

Mayblin, Maya. 2024. *Vote of Faith: Democracy, Desire, and the Turbulent Lives of Priest Politicians*. Fordham University Press.

McCole, John. 1993. *Walter Benjamin and the Antinomies of Tradition*. Cornell University Press.

McGuire, Meredith. 2008. *Lived Religion: Faith and Practice in Everyday Life*. Oxford University Press.

McKinnon, Susan, and Fenella Cannell, eds. 2013. *Vital Relations: Modernity and the Persistent Life of Kinship*. School for Advanced Research (SAR) Press.

Melo, D. 2018. "Bolsonaro, Religião e Estado Laico: O que Esperar do Futuro Governo." *Huffpost Brasil*, November 12. https://www.huffpostbrasil.com/2018/11/12/bolsonaro-religiao-e-estado-laicoo-que-esperar-do-futuro-governo_a_23586593. Accessed December 4, 2018.

Mello, Thiago de. 2024 [1965]. "Madrugada Camponesa." In *Encyclopédia Itaú Cultural de Arte e Cultura Brasileira*. http://enciclopedia.itaucultural.org.br/obra64903/madrugada-camponesa

Menezes, Renata. 2004. *A Dinâmica do Sagrado: Rituais, Sociabilidade e Santidade num Convento de Rio de Janeiro*. Relume Dumará.

Menezes, Renata. 2022. "Allegorical Inspirations of a Hat-Altar." *Etnográfica* December: 133-138.

Meyer, Birgit. 1999. *Translating the Devil: Religion and Modernity among the Ewe in Ghana* Edinburgh University Press.

Meyer, Birgit, ed. 2009. *Aesthetic Formations: Media, Religion and the Senses*. Palgrave Macmillan.

Meyer, Birgit. 2011. "Mediation and Immediacy: Sensational Forms, Semiotic Ideologies and the Question of the Medium." *Social Anthropology* 19:23–39.

Meyer, Birgit, and Annelies Moors. 2006. *Religion, Media, and the Public Sphere*. Indiana University Press.

Mignolo, Walter. 1993. "Colonial and Postcolonial Discourse: Cultural Critique or Academic Colonialism?" *Latin American Research Review* 28 (3): 146–52.

Mignolo, Walter. 2000. *Local Histories/Global Designs: Coloniality, Subaltern Knowledges, and Border Thinking.* Princeton University Press.

Mignolo, Walter. 2011. *The Darker Side of Western Modernity: Global Futures, Decolonial Options.* Duke University Press.

Mitchell, Sean. 2017. *Constellations of Inequality: Space, Race, and Utopia in Brazil.* University of Chicago Press.

Miyazaki, Hirokazu. 2004. *The Method of Hope: Anthropology, Philosophy and Fijian Knowledge.* Stanford University Press.

Modern, John. 2011. *Secularism in Antebellum America.* University of Chicago Press.

Moltmann, Jürgen. 1993 [1974]. *The Crucified God: The Cross of Christ as the Foundation and Criticism of Christian Theology.* Translated by R. A. Wilson and John Bowden. Fortress Press.

Montero, Paula. 1999. "Religiões e Dilemas da Sociedade Brasileira." In *O Que Ler na Ciência Social Brasileira (1970–1995)*, edited by Sergio Miceli, 327–67. CAPES.

Montero, Paula. 2006. "Religião, Pluralismo e Esfera Pública no Brasil." *Novos Estudos* 74:47–65.

Montero, Paula. 2013. "Religião, Laicidade e Secularismo: Um Debate Contemporâneo à Luz do Caso Brasileiro." *Cultura y Religión* 2:132–50.

Moore, Brenna. 2012. "How to Awaken the Dead: Michel de Certeau, Henri de Lubac, and the Instabilities Between the Past and the Present." *Spiritus* 12 (2): 172–79.

Moore, Brenna. 2015. "Friendship and the Cultivation of Religious Sensibilities." *Journal of the American Academy of Religion* 83 (2): 437–63.

Moore, Brenna. 2021. *Kindred Spirits: Friendship and Resistance at the Edges of Modern Catholicism.* The University of Chicago Press.

Moraes, Antonio de. 2007. "Em Busca das Origens da Palavra Camarada." *Partido dos Trabalhadores Socialista Unificado: Teoria*, January 1. https://www.pstu.org.br/em -busca-das-origens-da-palavra-camarada.

Moran, Emilio. 1990. "Private and Public Colonisation Schemes in Amazonia." In *The Future of Amazonia: Destruction or Sustainable Development?*, edited by David Goodman and Anthony Hall, 70–89. Palgrave Macmillan.

Morgan, Brandon. 2015. "The Efficacy of Salvation in the Allegorical Reading of Scripture: Learning from Origen." *Logos: A Journal of Catholic Thought and Culture* 18 (3): 151–71.

Mueggler, Erik. 2001. *The Age of Wild Ghosts: Memory, Violence, and Place in Southwest China.* University of California Press.

Muehlebach, Andrea. 2009. "Complexio Oppositorum: Notes on the Left in Neoliberal Italy." *Public Culture* 21 (3): 495–515.

Mueller, Charles C. 2018. "Traditional Agriculture and Land Distribution in Brazil." In *The Oxford Handbook of the Brazilian Economy*, edited by Edmund Amann, Carlos R. Azzoni and Werner Baer, 288–308. Oxford University Press.

Murphy, Keith, and Jason Throop, eds. 2010. *Toward an Anthropology of the Will.* Stanford University Press.

Myscofski, Carole. 1988. *When Men Walk Dry: Portuguese Messianism in Brazil.* Scholars Press.

Nabhan-Warren, Kristy. 2005. *The Virgin of El Barrio: Marian Apparitions, Catholic Evangelizing, and Mexican American Activism.* New York University Press.

Napolitano, Valentina. 2015. *Migrant Hearts and the Atlantic Return: Transnationalism and the Roman Catholic Church.* Fordham University Press.

Nuijten, Monique. 2003. *Power, Community and the State: The Political Anthropology of Organisation in Mexico.* Pluto Press.

Nelson, Derek R. 2009. *What's Wrong with Sin? Sin in Individual and Social Perspective from Schleiermacher to Theologies of Liberation.* T & T Clark.

Nepomuceno, E. 2007. *O Massacre Eldorado do Carajás: Uma Historia de Impunidade.* Planeta.

Neto, Thiago Oliveira. 2019. "As Rodovias na Amazônia: Uma Discussão Geopolítica." *Confins: Revue Franco-Brésilienne de Géographie* 501:1–15.

Norget, Kristin, Valentina Napolitano, and Maya Mayblin, eds. 2017. *The Anthropology of Catholicism: A Reader.* University of California Press.

Nugent, Stephen. 1993. *Amazonian Caboclo Society: An Essay on Invisibility and Peasant Economy.* Berg.

Núñez, Leonardo. 2020. "Para los Amigos, Justicia y Gracia; Para los Enemigos, la Ley a Secas." *Mexicanos Contra la Corrupción y la Impunidad.* September 1. https://contralacorrupcion.mx/para-los-amigos-justicia-y-gracia-para-los-enemigos-la-ley-a-secas.

Nys, Erwin de, Nathan Engle, and Antonio Magalhães. 2016. *Secas no Brasil Política e Gestão Proativas.* CGEE-World Bank. https://www.cgee.org.br/documents/10195/734063/seca_brasil-web.pdf. Accessed November 1, 2021.

Oliphant, Elayne. 2019. "Christ in the Banlieues: The Passionate Infrastructure of the French Catholic Church." *Exchange* 48 (3): 236–50.

Oliphant, Elayne. 2021. *The Privilege of Being Banal: Art, Secularism, and Catholicism in Paris.* University of Chicago Press.

Oliveira, Luís Cardoso de. 2002. *Direito Legal e Insulto Moral: Dilemas da Cidadania no Brasil, Quebec e EUA.* Relume Dumará.

O'Neill, Kevin Lewis. 2010. "The Reckless Will: Prison Chaplaincy and the Problem of Mara Salvatrucha." *Public Culture* 22 (1): 67–88.

Orsi, Robert. 2005. *Between Heaven and Earth: The Religious Worlds People Make and the Scholars Who Study Them.* Princeton University Press.

Orsi, Robert. 2011. "What Are Our Academic Assumptions About Religion?" In *Proceedings: Second Biennial Conference on Religion and American Culture*, 9–11. Purdue: Indiana University.

PAJU. n.d. "Jovem, Fé, Política, Participação." *Cadernos Populares Paz e Justiça (PAJU)* 3:1.

Palmeira, Moacir, and Beatriz de Heredia. 2009 [1997]. "Política Ambígua." In *Política Ambígua*, 167–86. Relume Dumara.

Palmié, Stephan. 2012. *The Cooking of History: How Not to Study Afro-Cuban Religion.* University of Chicago Press.

Palmié, Stephan. 2014. "Historicist Knowledge and its Conditions of Impossibility." In *The Social Life of Spirits*, edited by Diana Espirito Santo and Ruy Blanes, 225–46. University of Chicago Press.

Palmié, Stephan. 2023. *Thinking with Ngangas: What Afro-Cuban Ritual Can Tell Us About Scientific Practice and Vice Versa*. University of Chicago Press.

Peloso, Ranulfo. 1994. *A Força que Anima os Militantes*. Movimento Sem Terra.

Pécora, Alcir. 1992. "Vieira, o Índio e o Corpo Místico." *Artepensamento*. https://artepensamento.ims.com.br/item/vieira-o-indio-e-o-corpo-mistico/#_edn80.

Peña, Elaine. 2011. *Performing Piety: Making Space Sacred with the Virgin of Guadalupe*. University of California Press.

Penna, Camila, and Marcelo Rosa. 2015. "Estado, Movimentos e Reforma Agrária no Brasil: Reflexões a Partir do INCRA." *Lua Nova* 95:57–86.

Pessar, Patricia R. 2004. *From Fanatics to Folk: Brazilian Millenarianism and Popular Culture*. Duke University Press.

Petit, Pere. 2003. *Chão de Promessas: Elites Políticas e Transformações Econômicas no Estado do Pará Pos-1964*. Paka-Tatu.

Pickering, Mary. 2011. "Le Positivisme Philosophique: Auguste Comte." *Revue Interdisciplinaire d'Études Juridiques* 67 (2): 49–67.

Pina-Cabral, João de. 2007. "A Pessoa e o Dilema Brasileiro: uma Perspectiva Anticesurista." *Novos Estudos CEBRAP* 78:95–112.

Pizetta, Adelar. 2004. *A Consciência das Massas e a Formação de Militantes*. MST.

Poder360. 2023. "Saiba Quais São as 10 Cidades Que Mais Cresceram No Brasil Em 12 Anos." *Poder360*. https://www.poder360.com.br/brasil/saiba-quais-sao-as-10-cidades-que-mais-cresceram-no-brasil-em-12-anos.

Port, Mathijs van de. 2005. "Candomblé in Pink, Green and Black: Re-scripting Afro-Brazilian Religious Heritage in the Public Sphere of Salvador, Bahia." *Social Anthropology* 13 (1): 3–26.

Port, Mathijs van de. 2011. *Ecstatic Encounters: Bahian Candomblé and the Quest for the Really Real*. Amsterdam University Press.

Primiano, Leonard. 2022 [1995]. "Introduction: Vernacular Religion and the Search for Method in Religious Folklife." In *Vernacular Religion: Collected Essays of Leonard Norman Primiano*, edited by Deborah Dash Moore, 1–13. New York University Press.

Queiroz, Maria Isaura Pereira de. 1965. *O Messianismo, no Brasil e no Mundo*. Dominus Editora.

Raffles, Hugh. 2003. *In Amazonia: A Natural History*. Princeton University Press.

Ramberg, Lucinda. 2014. *Given to the Goddess: South Indian Devadasis and the Sexuality of Religion*. Duke University Press.

Ratzinger, Joseph. 1972. "El Concepto de la Iglesia y el Problema de Pertencimento de la Misma." In *El Nuevo Pueblo de Dios: Esquemas Para una Eclesiologia*, 103–18. Editorial Herder.

Ratzinger, Joseph. 1984. *Instruction on Certain Aspects of "Theology of Liberation."* Vatican City: Sacred Congregation for the Doctrine of the Faith.

Ratzinger, Joseph. 1986. *Instruction on Christian Freedom and Liberation*. Vatican City: Sacred Congregation for the Doctrine of the Faith.

Ratzinger, Joseph. 1993 [1960/1966]. *The Meaning of Christian Brotherhood*. Ignatius.

Ratzinger, Joseph. 1994 [1984]. "Documento: Carta, do Cardeal Joseph Ratzinger." In *Igreja: Carisma e Poder: Ensaios de Eclesiologia Militante*, edited by Leonardo Boff, 269–76. Editora Atica.

Ratzinger, Joseph, and Vittorio Missori. 1985. *The Ratzinger Report*. Translated by Salvator Attanasio and Graham Harrison. San Francisco: Ignatius Press.

Rebhun, Laura-Ann. 1999. *The Heart is Unknown Country: Love in the Changing Economy of Northeast Brazil*. Stanford University Press.

Redick, Alan. 2020. ""Para Mis Amigos Todo; Para Mis Enemigos la Ley."" *El Nacional*. September 23. https://elnacional.com.py/politica/2020/09/23/justicia-paraguaya/.

Reinhardt, Bruno. 2020. "Atmospheric Presence: Reflections on 'Mediation' in the Anthropology of Religion and Technology." *Anthropological Quarterly* 93 (1): 1523–53.

Reinhardt, Bruno, and Letícia Cesarino. 2017. "Antropologia e Crítica Pós-Colonial." *Ilha Revista de Antropologia* 19 (2): 9–35.

Rezende, Claudia Barcellos. 1999. "Building Affinity through Friendship." In *The Anthropology of Friendship*, edited by Sandra Bell and Simon Coleman, 79–97. Berg.

Rezende, Claudia Barcellos. 2002. *Os Significados da Amizade*. Editora FGV.

Rezende, Ricardo. 2004. *Pisando Fora da Própria Sombra: A Escravidão por Dívida no Brasil Contemporâneo*. Civilização Brasileira.

Robbins, Joel. 2007. "Continuity Thinking and the Problem of Christian Culture: Belief, Time and the Anthropology of Christianity." *Current Anthropology* 48 (1): 5–38.

Rolemberg, Igor. 2020. "Onde está o Religioso? Mística e Espiritualidade no Político, no Público e no Secular." *Religião e Sociedade* 40 (3): 49–72.

Rolemberg, Igor. 2023. "Mobilizar, Acompanhar, Denunciar: Uma Etnografia da Comissão Pastoral da Terra na Amazônia Oriental." PhD diss., Museu Nacional, Brazil, and École des Hautes Études en Sciences Sociales, France. http://www.theses.fr/2023EHES0022/document.

Romaria da Libertação. 1983. *Jornal da Segunda Romaria da Libertação: Povo Unido Jamais Será Vencido 12 À 17 De Setembro*. Goianésia do Pará: MS.

Rust, Jennifer. 2014. *The Body in Mystery: The Political Theology of the Corpus Mysticum in the Literature of Reformation England*. Northwestern University Press.

Sahlins, Marshall. 1996. "The Sadness of Sweetness: The Native Anthropology of Western Cosmology." *Current Anthropology* 37 (3): 395–415.

Sallnow, Michael. 1987. *Pilgrims of the Andes: Regional Cults in Cusco*. Smithsonian Institution Press.

Sanchis, Pierre. 1983. "A Caminhada Ritual." *Religião e Sociedade* 9:15–26.

Sandberg, Julianne. 2020. "Utopian Literality: Thomas More and the Faith of Catholic Reading." *Studies in Philology* 117 (2): 261–84.

Sandoval, Jonathan. 2021. "Para Mis Amigos Todo; Para Mis Enemigos la Ley." *Confidencial Colombia*. May 30. https://confidencialnoticias.com/opinion/para-mis-amigos-todo-para-mis-enemigos-la-ley/2021/05/30.

Santoro, Fernando. 2014. "Saudade." In *Dictionary of Untranslatables: A Philosophical Lexicon*, edited by Barbara Cassin, translated by Steven Rendall, Christian Hubert,

Jeffrey Mehlman, Nathanael Stein, and Michael Syrotinski, translation edited by Emily Apter, Jacques Lezra, and Michael Wood, 929–31. Princeton University Press.

Santos, Beatriz Catão Cruz. 2005. *O Corpo de Deus na América: A Festa de Corpus Christi nas Cidades da América Portuguesa—Século XVIII*. Annablume.

Scanlan, Thomas. 1999. *Colonial Writing and the New World, 1583–1671: Allegories of Desire*. Cambridge University Press.

Scheper-Hughes, Jennifer. 2010. *Biography of a Mexican Crucifix: Lived Religion and Local Faith from the Conquest to the Present*. Oxford University Press.

Scheper-Hughes, Jennifer. 2021. *The Church of the Dead: The Epidemic of 1576 and the Birth of Christianity in the Americas*. New York University Press.

Scheper-Hughes, Nancy. 1992. *Death without Weeping: The Violence of Everyday Life in Brazil*. University of California Press.

Schmink, Marianne, and Charles H. Wood. 1992. *Contested Frontiers in Amazonia*. Columbia University Press.

Schmitt, Carl. 1985 [1922]. *Political Theology: Four Chapters on the Concept of Sovereignty*. Translated by George Schwab. University of Chicago Press.

Schmitt, Carl. 1996 [1932]. *The Concept of the Political*. Translated by George Schwab. University of Chicago Press.

Schmitt, Carl. 1996 [1923]. *Roman Catholicism and Political Form*. Translated by G. L. Ulmen. Greenwood Press.

Schwarcz, Lilia Moritz. 2022. *Brazilian Authoritarianism: Past and Present*. Princeton University Press.

Schwarz, Roberto. 1998 [1993]. "Discutindo com Alfredo Bosi." *Veredas: Revista da Associação Internacional de Lusitanistas* 1: 87–111.

Schwartz, Regina Mara. 2008. *Sacramental Poetics at the Dawn of Secularism: When God Left the World*. Stanford University Press.

Scott, Joan. 2017. *Sex and Secularism*. Princeton University Press.

Segato, Rita. 2022 [2013]. *The Critique of Coloniality: Eight Essays*. Translated by Ramsey McGlazer. Routledge.

Selby, Jennifer. 2012. *Questioning French Secularism: Gender Politics and Islam in a Parisian Suburb*. Palgrave Macmillan Press.

Selka, Stephen. 2010. "Morality in the Religious Marketplace: Evangelical Christianity, Candomblé, and the Struggle for Moral Distinction in Brazil." *American Ethnologist* 37 (2): 291–307.

Shapiro, Matan. 2016. "Curving the Social, or, Why Antagonistic Rituals in Brazil Are Variations on a Theme." *Journal of the Royal Anthropological Institute* 22 (1): 47–66.

Sheldrake, Peter. 2001. "Unending Desire: de Certeau's 'Mystics.'" *The Way*, Supplement 102, 38–48.

Sigaud, Lygia. 2000. "A Forma Acampamento: Notas a Partir da Versão Pernambucana." *Novos Estudos* 58:73–92.

Silva, José Graziano da. 1980. *O Que é a Questão Agrária*. São Paulo: Editora Brasiliense.

Silver, Allan. 1990. "Friendship in Commercial Society: Eighteenth-Century Social Theory and Modern Sociology." *The American Journal of Sociology* 95 (6): 1474–504.

Simoni, Valerio, and Jason Throop. 2014. "Introduction: Friendship, Morality, and Experience." *Suomen Antropologi: Journal of the Finnish Anthropological Society* 39 (1): 4–18.

Slater, Candace. 1982. *Stories on a String: The Brazilian "Literatura de Cordel."* University of California Press.

Slemon, Stephen. 1988. "Post-Colonial Allegory and the Transformation of History." *Journal of Commonwealth Literature* 23 (1): 157–68.

Sobrino, Jon. 1978. *Christology at the Crossroads: A Latin American Approach.* Orbis Books.

Sodi, Demetrio. 2022. "A Los Amigos Justicia y Gracia." *El Economista.* March 11. https://www.eleconomista.com.mx/opinion/A-los-amigos-justicia-y-gracia-20220311-0001.html.

Souza, Matilde de. 2020. "Transamazônica: Integrar Para Não Entregar." *Nova Revista Amazônica* 8 (1): 133–52.

Stédile, João Pedro. 2002. "Landless Battalions: The Sem Terra Movement of Brazil." *New Left Review,* no. 15, 77–104.

Stédile, João Pedro, and Bernardo Mançano Fernandes. 1999. *Brava Gente: A Trajetória do MST e a Luta Pela Terra no Brasil.* Fundação Perseu Abramo.

Steil, Carlos Alberto. 1996. *O Sertão das Romarias: Um Estudo Antropológico Sobre o Santuário Bom Jesús da Lapa.* Vozes.

Stevenson, Lisa. 2014. *Life Beside Itself: Imagining Care in the Canadian Arctic.* University of California Press.

Stoler, Ann. 1995. *Race and the Education of Desire: Foucault's "History of Sexuality" and the Colonial Order of Things.* Duke University Press.

Stoler, Ann. 2010 [2002]. *Carnal Knowledge and Imperial Power: Race and the Intimate in Colonial Rule.* 2nd ed. University of California Press.

Stoler, Ann. 2016. *Duress: Imperial Durabilities in Our Times.* Duke University Press.

Stolow, Jeremy. 2005. "Religion and/as Media." *Theory, Culture and Society* 22:119–45.

Strathern, Marilyn. 1988. *Gender of the Gift.* University of California Press.

Strathern, Marilyn. 1999. *Property, Substance and Effect. Anthropological Essays on Persons and Things.* Athlone Press.

Strathern, Marilyn. 2004. *Partial Connections.* Altamira Press.

Strathern, Marilyn. 2012. "Response: A Comment on 'The Ontological Turn' in Japanese Anthropology." *Hau: Journal of Ethnographic Theory* 2 (2): 402–5.

Strathern, Marilyn. 2017a. "Connections, Friends, and their Relations: An Issue in Knowledge-Making." In *Comparative Metaphysics: Ontology after Anthropology,* edited by Gildas Salmon, Pierre Charbonnier, and Peter Skafish, 74–99. Rowman and Littlefield.

Strathern, Marilyn. 2017b. "Naturalism and the Invention of Identity." *Social Analysis* 61 (2): 15–30.

Strathern, Marilyn. 2020. *Relations: An Anthropological Account.* Duke University Press.

Sullivan, LaShandra. 2017. "Black Invisibility on a Brazilian 'Frontier': Land and Identity in Mato Grosso do Sul, Brazil." *African and Black Diaspora* 10 (2): 131–42.

Tambling, Jeremy. 2018. "Bunyan, Emblem, and Allegory." In *The Oxford Handbook of John Bunyan,* edited by Michael Davies and W. R. Owens. Oxford University Press.

Taubes, Jacob. 2004. *The Political Theology of Paul*. Translated by Dana Hollander. Edited by Aleida and Jan Assmann, et al. Stanford University Press.

Taussig, Michael. 1987. *Shamanism, Colonialism and the Wild Man: A Study in Terror and Healing*. University of Chicago Press.

Taylor, Charles. 2007. *A Secular Age*. Belknap Press.

Taylor, Robert. 1986. "Toward a Biblical Theology of Litigation: A Law Professor Looks at 1 Cor 6:1–11." *Ex Auditu* 2:105–16.

Tepe, Valfredo. 1966. "The Problem of Evil and its Contemporary Pastoral Relevance." *Revista Ecclesiastica Brasileira* 26 (4): 851–71.

Terra, Ruth Brito Lêmos. 1983. *Memória de Lutas: Literatura de Folhetos do Nordeste, 1893–1930*. Global Editora.

Thiem, Annika. 2013. "Theological-Political Ruins: Walter Benjamin, Sovereignty, and the Politics of Skeletal Eschatology." *Law and Critique* 24:295–315.

Thomas, Todne, Asiya Malik, and Rose Wellman, eds. 2017. *New Directions in Spiritual Kinship: Sacred Ties Across the Abrahamic Religions*. Palgrave Macmillan.

Thomas, Todne. 2021. *Kincraft: the Making of Black Evangelical Sociality*. Duke University Press.

UOL. 2022. "Católico ou Evangélico? Qual a Religião de Bolsonaro?" *UOL*, October 6. https://noticias.uol.com.br/politica/ultimas-noticias/2022/10/06/catolico-ou -evangelico-qual-a-religiao-de-bolsonaro.htm.

Van der Veer, Peter. 2001. *Imperial Encounters: Religion and Modernity in India and Britain*. Princeton University Press.

Vásquez, Manuel. 1998. *The Brazilian Popular Church and the Crisis of Modernity*. Cambridge University Press.

Velho, Otávio. 1972. *Frentes da Expansão e Estructura Agrária*. Zahar Editores.

Velho, Otávio. 1976. *Capitalismo Autoritário e Campesinato*. DIEFL.

Velho, Otávio. 1991. "The Peasant and the Beast." *European Review of Latin American and Caribbean Studies* 51:7–25.

Velho, Otávio. 1995 [1991]. "O Cativeiro da Besta-Fera." In *Besta-fera: Recriação do Mundo*, edited by Otávio Velho, 13–44. Relume Dumará.

Velho, Otávio. 2007. "Mais Realistas do Que o Rei." In *Mais Realistas do Que o Rei: Ocidentalismo, Religião e Modernidades Alternativas*, 135–57. Topbooks.

Vieira, Antônio. 2001. "Santíssimo Sacramento (1662)." In *Antônio Vieira: Sermões*, edited by Alcir Pécora, Tomo 2, 153–76. Hedra.

Vieira, Antônio. 2009. "History of the Future: The Hopes of Portugal and the Fifth Empire of the World." In *The Sermon of Saint Anthony to the Fish and Other Texts*, translated by Gregory Rabassa, 77–106. University of Massachusetts Dartmouth.

Villela, Jorge. 2004. *O Povo em Armas: Violência e Política no Sertão de Pernambuco*. Relume Dumará.

Villela, Jorge. 2009. "Família como Grupo? Política como Agrupamento? O Sertão de Pernambuco no Mundo Sem Solidez." *Revista de Antropologia* 52 (1): 201–45.

Viswanathan, Gauri. 1998. *Outside the Fold: Conversion, Modernity, and Belief*. Princeton University Press.

Walden, Ron William. 1975. "The Concept of the Church in Recent Roman Catholic Theology." PhD diss., Yale University.

Warner, Michael. 2005. *Publics and Counterpublics.* Verso.

Weather Spark. 2024. "Average Temperature in Marabá." *Weatherspark.com.* https://weatherspark.com/y/29998/Average-Weather-in-Marabá-Brazil-Year-Round #Sections-Temperature.

Webb, Hillary S. 2010. "Coincidentia Oppositorum." In *Encyclopedia of Psychology and Religion,* edited by David A. Leeming, Kathryn Madden, and Stanton Marlan, 157–59. Springer US.

Weber, Samuel. 1992. "Taking Exception to Decision: Walter Benjamin and Carl Schmitt." *Diacritics* 22 (3): 5–18.

Weber, Samuel. 2005. "'The Principle of Representation': Carl Schmitt's Roman Catholicism and Political Form." In *Targets of Opportunity: On the Militarization of Thinking,* 22–41. Fordham University Press.

Weber, Samuel. 2008. *Benjamin's -abilities.* Harvard University Press.

Weigel, Sigrid. 2013. *Walter Benjamin: Images, the Creaturely, and the Holy.* Stanford University Press.

Westerink, Herman. 2021. "The Subversive Practices of the Desiring Subject: Michel De Certeau between Lacan's Psychoanalysis and Foucault's Genealogy." *Studies in Spirituality* 31:229–46.

Williams, Edward. 1973. "Secularization, Integration and Rationalization: Some Perspectives from Latin American Thought." *Journal of Latin American Studies* 5 (2): 199–216.

Worsley, Peter. 1957. *The Trumpet Shall Sound: A Study of "Cargo" Cults in Melanesia.* MacGibbon & Kee.

Žižek, Slavoj. 2003. *The Puppet and the Dwarf: The Perverse Core of Christianity.* MIT Press.

Zylberstajn, Joana. 2012. "O Princípio da Laicidade na Constituição Federal de 1988." PhD diss., Universidade de São Paulo.

INDEX

Page locators in italics indicate figures.

www.ingramcontent.com/pod-product-compliance
Lightning Source LLC
Chambersburg PA
CBHW022135020426
42334CB00015B/908